W9-DJC-271

Great African-American Women

Great
African-American
Women

Darryl Lyman

3 1489 00439 6592

JD | JONATHAN DAVID PUBLISHERS, INC.
Middle Village, New York 11379

GREAT AFRICAN-AMERICAN WOMEN

Copyright © 1999
by
Darryl Lyman

No part of this book may be reproduced
in any form without the prior written consent
of the publisher. Address all inquiries to:

Jonathan David Publishers, Inc.
68-22 Eliot Ave.
Middle Village, New York 11379

www.JonathanDavidOnline.com

2   4   6   8   10   9   7   5   3   1

Library of Congress in Publication Data

Lyman, Darryl
    Great African American Women/ Darryl Lyman.
        p. cm.
    Includes index
    ISBN 0-8246-0412-1
    1. Afro-American women — Biography.   I. Title.
E185.96. L95 1999
920.71'089'96073—dc21

[B] 98-51973
CIP

Book design and composition by John Reinhardt Book Design

Printed in the United States of America

*To the new generation of
African-American young women
whose accomplishments
will brighten the world.*

Acknowledgments

T HANKS ARE DUE to the following for supplying information and/or photographs for this book: The Alvin Ailey Dance Theater Foundation; Dr. Johnnetta B. Cole; Ruby Dee; Rita Dove; Marian Wright Edelman; Phoebe Frosch, executive secretary, University of Virginia; Nikki Giovanni; Carra Greenberg, director of marketing, Elite International Sports Marketing; Jan Harris-Temple, assistant to the chairman, NAACP National Board of Directors; The King Center; Ambra Leonard, assistant, Owensby & Co. Communications; Movie Star News; Jerry Ohlinger's Movie Material Store; the Schomburg Center for Research in Black Culture; Monica Smith; Jean Weisinger. A special thank you goes to Fiorella deLima of Jonathan David Publishers for finding photographs and guiding the production of *Great African-American Women*.

Contents

CONTENTS

Introduction

MOST WOMEN struggle against discrimination to participate fully in their chosen fields. African-American women face even greater barriers than other women, having to overcome prejudice against both their sex and their race. Therefore, when African-American women achieve great success, their accomplishments are all the more remarkable.

This book is a compendium of one hundred biographies that illustrate the outstanding contributions of African-American women to our society. The stories of these one hundred women, through their struggle, courage, and achievement, can inspire all readers and provide role models for today's young people.

The one hundred women in these biographies were selected to encompass a wide range of fields of endeavor, such as sports, politics, education, literature, performing arts, and civil rights activism. Individuals were chosen because of their impact within their own fields, so that the "greatness" of an actress, for example, was not compared with that of a politician. Among the one hundred women in *Great African-American Women* are those who broke world records in track and field (Jackie Joyner-Kersee), hosted the highest-rated television talk show in history (Oprah Winfrey), and won the Nobel Prize in literature (Toni Morrison).

Nearly all of the women had to overcome formidable obstacles and endure painful experiences. Marian Anderson was denied entrance to a music school that told her, "We don't take colored," but she studied elsewhere and rose to win critical acclaim. In 1939 she was refused permission, because of her race, to sing at Constitution Hall; but she persevered with her career, and when she set out on her farewell tour in 1964, she was given a tumultuous welcome at her first stop—Constitution Hall. Althea Gibson, despite her proven tennis prowess, suffered many years of humiliation by remaining uninvited to the most prestigious event in American tennis—Forest Hills. After having to depend on the lobbying of others to be finally invited, she showed the world what African-Americans could do in the supposedly unfamiliar world of tennis by winning two consecutive Forest Hills titles (1957–58). Harriet Tubman was born into slavery and was nearly killed when, while protecting another slave, she was struck in the head by a heavy object. With her indomitable spirit she not only escaped slavery but also returned into slave territory again and again to lead other slaves to freedom. The people she rescued called her Moses. *Great African-American Women* is filled with similar stories.

While the one hundred biographies fairly represent the breadth of great achievements by African-American women, other significant careers also deserve to be mentioned. Consequently, brief sketches of over three hundred other women follow the principal biographies.

An asterisk (*) after the name of a woman mentioned in the text means that she is the subject of a biography elsewhere in the volume.

Darryl Lyman

Marian Anderson

CLASSICAL MUSIC PIONEER

(1897-1993)

A CONTRALTO KNOWN FOR HER wide-ranging repertory of art songs, opera arias, and spirituals, Marian Anderson was one of the most celebrated singers of the twentieth century. In the 1930s she anticipated the civil rights movement through her efforts to break down discrimination against blacks in the American arts.

Marian Anderson was born in Philadelphia on February 27, 1897, the eldest of three daughters. Her father, John Berkeley Anderson, was an ice and coal dealer. Her mother, Anna Anderson, had taught school in Virginia before moving to Philadelphia, where she worked as a laundress and cleaning woman.

Baby Contralto

"Singing in the presence of other people seemed to me a normal activity all through the years of growing up," Marian Anderson later recalled. "I loved to sing. I liked to have other people listen and was likewise glad to hear others perform."[1]

She first developed her musical ability at the local Union Baptist Church, where she joined the junior choir when she was six years old and the senior choir at thirteen. In her first public appearance, she sang a solo in the hymn "Dear to the Heart of the Shepherd." By her early teens she was a natural contralto, but her range was so wide that she often substituted for absent choir members by singing soprano, tenor, or even bass up an octave from the written part. At an early age she began singing at functions outside her church, and admirers soon called her the "baby contralto."

While she was in high school, she attracted the attention of the distinguished black actor John Thomas Butler, who sent her to Mary Saunders Patterson for serious vocal training. Anderson later studied with Agnes Reifsnyder and the well-known Philadelphia teacher Giuseppe Boghetti, who taught her for many years and gave her musical advice for the rest of his life.

Throughout her high school years Anderson sang at local churches and schools, often earning small fees. G. Grant Williams, editor of the *Philadelphia Tribune*, was her first manager.

After graduating from South Philadelphia High School for Girls, she continued concertizing. In her early days as a concert artist Anderson accompanied herself on the piano (on which she was self-taught), but later she was accompanied by William ("Billy") King, who became her new manager, accompanying her by train to her performances in southern schools and churches. She gave her earnings to her parents, who used the money to buy their own home.

During the summer of 1925 Anderson won first prize over several hundred other contestants in a competition to sing with the New York Philharmonic Orchestra. In August of that year she appeared as soloist with the orchestra at Lewisohn Stadium in New York City, singing the aria "O mio Fernando" from Donizetti's opera *La favorite* (The favorite).

Despite scoring a triumph at the concert, Anderson made little immediate progress in her career. Other than an engagement with the Philadelphia Orchestra, she found major opportunities for either concert or opera performances difficult to obtain. The obvious reason was discrimination against her because of her race. When she attempted to enroll in a school of music in Philadelphia, she was told, "We don't take colored."[2]

After the New York Philharmonic Orchestra con-

MARIAN ANDERSON

Critical Acclaim

In October 1930 Anderson gave a concert in the Bach Saal in Berlin. The critical acclaim she received from that concert led to many European tours in the early 1930s, with occasional returns to the United States. During one twelve-month period, she gave over one hundred concerts in the Scandinavian countries, where she learned songs in Swedish, Norwegian, and Finnish and sang for the great Finnish composer Jean Sibelius, who dedicated his song "Solitude" to her.

While engaged in this heavy schedule of concertizing, Anderson continued to study in Europe. She absorbed French music under Germaine de Castro and Mahler songs under Madame Charles Cahier (Sara Jane Layton-Walker).

Anderson's new accompanist, Kosti Vehanen, helped her to extend her personal repertory. Eventually she commanded a body of several hundred songs, including opera arias, patriotic anthems, and works by Bach, Brahms, Handel, Rachmaninoff, Saint-Saëns, Richard Strauss, and other master composers. Audiences always implored her to sing or perform an encore of Schubert's "Ave Maria."

One of her mainstays was spirituals. "I love them because they are truly spiritual in quality," she explained; "they give forth the aura of faith, simplicity, humility and hope."[3] Among the spirituals with which she became especially associated were "Crucifixion" and "My Lord, What a Morning."

In Salzburg, Austria, in 1935, the legendary conductor Arturo Toscanini praised Anderson's vocal art as something heard only once in a hundred years. Later that year the great impresario Sol Hurok, equally impressed, became Anderson's manager.

Her career under Hurok began with a highly successful concert at Town Hall in New York City on December 31, 1935. In 1936 she appeared at Carnegie Hall in New York City and the White House in Washington, D.C. For the next thirty years she undertook extensive concert tours in the United States and other

cert, the well-known Arthur Judson Company of New York City took over Anderson's management, but it produced little advancement in her concertizing.

Feeling the need to make a change, she shifted her studies for a time to Frank LaForge before returning to Boghetti. In the late 1920s she went to England, where she studied for about a year with Raimund von Zur Mühlen, Mark Raphael, and Amanda Ira Aldridge. In September 1930 Anderson made her English debut, performing at Wigmore Hall, London. Soon thereafter she returned to the United States and resumed concertizing under Judson's management, with King as her accompanist.

Receiving a fellowship from the Julius Rosenwald Fund, she traveled to Berlin so that she could master the German language, a key factor in performing lieder by Schubert, Schumann, and other composers. She studied there with Sverre Joran and Michael Raucheisen.

countries, giving sixty or more recitals and concerts a year in her prime. When Vehanen retired as her accompanist, in 1941, he was replaced by Franz Rupp, who stayed with her for the rest of her career.

DAR Controversy

Early in 1939 Anderson became the subject of national attention when, because of her race, the Daughters of the American Revolution (DAR) refused to allow her to sing at Constitution Hall (which they controlled) in Washington, D.C. First Lady Eleanor Roosevelt resigned from the DAR in protest and encouraged Harold Ickes, secretary of the interior, to arrange for Anderson instead to give a free concert at the Lincoln Memorial on April 9, 1939. The concert drew about seventy-five thousand people, including members of Congress and Supreme Court justices, as well as ordinary citizens. That July, Eleanor Roosevelt presented Anderson with the prestigious Spingarn Medal of the National Association for the Advancement of Colored People.

During World War II Anderson gave many concerts to support the war effort, one of which was held at Constitution Hall, where the DAR, on patriotic grounds, finally allowed her to perform. However, when she requested that the audience not be separated into the usual racial categories, the DAR refused. She decided to sing anyway because the concert was for the benefit of the Army Emergency Relief Fund.

In July 1943 Anderson married Orpheus Hodge ("King") Fisher, a New York architect she had known since they were both in their teens. They settled on a farm in Danbury, Connecticut, where she prepared for her tours and enjoyed her hobbies of sewing, upholstery, photography, playing jazz piano, and listening to jazz recordings. After World War II she resumed her international concertizing.

Opera Debut

In September 1954 Rudolph Bing, general manager of the Metropolitan Opera in New York City, invited Anderson to sing the role of the sorceress and fortune teller Ulrica in Verdi's *Un ballo in maschera* (A masked ball) at the Met. She agreed, and on January 7, 1955, at the age of nearly fifty-eight, she finally made her opera debut. As the first African-American to play a principal role for the company, she paved the way for others. Her breakthrough was so important in the history of American race relations that the story made the front page of the next day's *New York Times*. She sang the role seven more times for the company until she left the Met in 1956, the same year she published *My Lord, What a Morning: An Autobiography*.

"The chance to be a member of the Metropolitan has been a highlight of my life," she wrote in her autobiography. "It has meant much to me and to my people. If I have been privileged to serve as a symbol, to be the first Negro to sing as a regular member of the company, I take greater pride from knowing that it has encouraged other singers of my group to realize that the doors everywhere may open increasingly to those who have prepared themselves well."[4]

Anderson resumed her concert tours. In 1957 the United Nations sponsored her on a singing tour of the Far East, which was so successful that in 1958 President Eisenhower named her delegate to the United Nations. In 1961 she sang the national anthem as an official guest at the inauguration of President John F. Kennedy. During 1964-65 she gave her farewell tour, beginning at Constitution Hall in October 1964 and ending at Carnegie Hall in April 1965.

After her retirement Anderson spent much of her time at her farm in Danbury, but she still performed on special occasions. In 1966 she sang for the initial World Festival of Negro Arts, held in Dakar, Senegal. Several times she narrated, accompanied by various orchestras, Aaron Copland's *A Lincoln Portrait*.

Presidential Medal of Freedom

Anderson received many important awards. In 1963 she and Ralph Bunche became the first African-American recipients of the Presidential Medal of Freedom. She also received the Kennedy Center Honor for her lifetime achievement (1978), the first Eleanor Roosevelt Human Rights Award from New York City (1984), and a Grammy Award for her lifetime achievement (1991).

Anderson died at the home of the conductor James DePreist, her nephew, in Portland, Oregon, on April 8, 1993. She was ninety-six years old.

Anderson had a big, striking voice and an exceptionally wide range. She was especially known for her artistic integrity, always emphasizing the true inner meaning of the music itself, whether it be lieder, opera arias, or spirituals. Never known as a militant, she nevertheless became a pioneering civil rights activist when she sought to convince the American cultural establishment that blacks should be given a fair chance to succeed in classical music at the highest levels.

Selected recordings:

ALBUMS

Schubert: Lieder (1950, RCA)

Brahms: Alto Rhapsody / Mahler: Kindertotenlieder (Songs on the death of children) (1951, RCA)

Handel: Three Arias / Schubert: Lieder (1951, RCA)

Schubert: Beloved Schubert Songs (1951, RCA)

Bach: Bach Arias and Great Songs of Faith (1953, RCA)

Spirituals (1953, RCA)

Verdi: Un ballo in maschera (A masked ball) (1955, RCA)

Spirituals (1956, RCA)

Lady from Philadelphia (1958, RCA)

Christmas Carols (1962, RCA)

"He's Got the Whole World in His Hands" and Eighteen Other Spirituals (1962, RCA)

Robert Russell Bennett: Songs at Eventide (1964, RCA)

Songs by Schubert, Schumann, Brahms, Strauss, and Haydn (1964, RCA)

Farewell Recital (1964, 1965, RCA)

Just Keep On Singing (1965, RCA)

Brahms: Alto Rhapsody (1969, RCA)

"The Lord's Prayer" and Other Songs of Faith and Inspiration (1971, RCA)

Sibelius: Tapiola (1971, Scandia)

Sibelius: Symphony no. 6 (Come Away, Death) (1972, Scandia)

Spirituals (1976, RCA)

When I Have Sung My Songs: The American Art Song, 1900-1940 (1976, New World Records)

Maya Angelou
CAGED BIRD SINGING

(1928—   )

WRITER, POET, EDUCATOR, singer, dancer, actress, producer, director, and civil rights activist, Maya Angelou has successfully followed many creative paths on her "journey to selfhood, the gradual appreciation of herself as a unique individual."[1] She is especially celebrated for her writings, "which attest to her gift for survival in the face of hardship and injustice, demonstrate her inexhaustible capacity for renewed hope, determination, and love."[2] Her famed series of autobiographical books began in 1969 with *I Know Why the Caged Bird Sings*.

Born Marguerite Annie Johnson in Saint Louis, Missouri, on April 4, 1928, she was originally called Rita in public, but her family soon nicknamed her Maya because her older brother babytalked that name while trying to call her "My" or "Mine." Her father, Bailey Johnson, was a doorman and naval dietitian, while her mother, Vivian (Baxter) Johnson worked as a card dealer, boardinghouse proprietor, and registered nurse.

Soon after Maya's birth, the family moved to Long Beach, California, but after the Johnsons' marriage broke up a few years later, Maya and her brother, Bailey Johnson, Jr., were sent to live with their paternal grandmother, Annie Henderson, in Stamps, Arkansas.

The Power of Language

When Maya was seven, she and her brother returned to Saint Louis to join their mother. A few months later, however, Maya was raped by her mother's boyfriend. She testified at his trial, at which he was convicted and sentenced to one year and one day in prison. Temporarily released from custody that same day, he was beaten to death, apparently by some of Maya's uncles. Believing that her words at the trial had led to the man's death, she decided to stop talking in public.

She and her brother were sent back to their grandmother in Stamps. There, for the next five years, Maya maintained her public silence, all the while absorbing further lessons in the power of language by reading great literature, including the Bible and works by Langston Hughes, James Weldon Johnson, Edgar Allan Poe, and William Shakespeare. By the time she graduated from eighth grade in 1940, she was speaking in public again, but during her mute phase she developed an exceptional ability to listen intently to the subtle inflections and nuances of spoken words.

Dancer and Singer

In 1940 Maya and her brother moved to San Francisco to live with their mother, who had remarried and was again operating a boardinghouse. A few years later, while still attending George Washington High School and studying dance and drama at the California Labor School, Maya, at the age of sixteen, became the first black and the first female streetcar conductor in San Francisco. In August 1945 she graduated from high school, and a few months later she gave birth to her son, Clyde ("Guy") Johnson.

During the next several years she held a number of low-level jobs to make ends meet—she was a restaurant cook in San Francisco and a nightclub waitress in San Diego. Then, after a brief stay in Stamps, she returned to San Francisco.

The Schomburg Center / NYPL

MAYA ANGELOU

Early Writings

In 1960 Angelou raised money for the Reverend Martin Luther King, Jr.'s, Southern Christian Leadership Conference (SCLC) by writing and, with Godfrey Cambridge, producing, directing, and starring in the revue *Freedom Cabaret*. Soon she became the SCLC's northern coordinator, a position she held for about a year. In May 1961 she appeared in an all-black, Obie Award-winning production of Jean Genet's *The Blacks*.

Later that year Angelou moved to the Egyptian capital, Cairo, with her second husband, Vusumzi Make, a South African lawyer. From 1961 to 1962 she worked there as an associate editor of the *Arab Observer*, an English-language newspaper. When her marriage ended in 1963, she moved to Accra, Ghana, to join her son, now a student at the University of Ghana. While there, she served as a teacher and assistant administrator at the university's School of Music and Drama (1963-66), worked as features editor of the *African Review* (1964-66), and wrote for the *Ghanaian Times*.

Shortly after Angelou returned to California in 1966, she performed in a production of Jean Anouilh's modern version of Euripides' tragedy *Medea*. At this time Angelou's own writing career began to blossom. She wrote *The Least of These*, a two-act drama staged in Los Angeles in 1966, and *Black, Blues, Black*, a ten-part National Educational Television series broadcast in 1968. The latter work focused on the prominent role of African culture in American life.

Maya was married for three years in the early 1950s to a former sailor, Tosh Angelos. When the marriage ended, she got a job as a dancer and singer at the Purple Onion, a San Francisco cabaret where she performed in the West Indian calypso style. It was at this time that she took the stage name Maya Angelou, the second name being a variation on her ex-husband's surname. She then toured Europe and Africa in a State Department-sponsored production of George Gershwin's opera *Porgy and Bess*.

Returning to the United States in 1955, Angelou settled in California and developed a cabaret act. In 1957 she sang in the film *Calypso Heat Wave* and recorded an album entitled *Miss Calypso*. In the late 1950s she moved to New York City, where she sang at the Apollo Theater in Harlem, performed at other venues, and attended meetings of the Harlem Writers Guild.

Autobiographer and Poet

Encouraged by friends to tell the story of her life, Angelou then wrote *I Know Why the Caged Bird Sings* (1969), the story of her childhood up to the age of seventeen and the birth of her son. The book, which received wide critical acclaim and was nominated for the National Book Award, was followed by four more autobiographical volumes, including *Gather Together in My Name* (1974) and *All God's Children Need Traveling Shoes* (1986).

During those years she also published volumes of poetry, including *Just Give Me a Cool Drink of Water 'fore I Diiie* (1971), for which she was nominated for a Pulitzer Prize; *And Still I Rise* (1978); and *I Shall Not Be Moved* (1990). Her poetry centers on such subjects as love, African-American history, and her pride as a black woman. Among her most popular poems are "Phenomenal Woman," "Still I Rise," and "Weekend Glory."

Versatile and Creative Artist

While writing her autobiographies and poetry, Angelou continued to engage in a wide range of other creative endeavors. For example, in 1972 she became the first black woman to have a screenplay (*Georgia, Georgia*) produced, and in 1974 she wrote and directed the film *All Day Long*. She won a Tony Award nomination for her performance in the 1973 Broadway production *Look Away* and an Emmy Award nomination for her portrayal of Kunta Kinte's grandmother in the 1977 television miniseries *Roots*.

In 1979 she prepared the script and music score for a national television production of *I Know Why the Caged Bird Sings*. Later she wrote the teleplay for the film *Sister, Sister* (1982); directed Errol John's play *Moon on a Rainbow Shawl* (1988); wrote the poetry for the film *Poetic Justice* (1993), in which she also briefly appeared; and played a leading role in the film *How to Make an American Quilt* (1995).

Angelou's books in the 1990s reflected her ever-expanding versatility. She published *Lessons in Life* (1993) and *Wouldn't Take Nothing for My Journey Now* (1993), both collections of essays; *Life Doesn't Frighten Me* (1993), a children's book combining her 1978 poem of the same name and paintings by Jean-Michel Basquiat; *My Painted House, My Friendly Chicken, and Me* (1994), a children's storybook about a Ndebele girl in South Africa; and *The Complete Collected Poems of Maya Angelou* (1994).

Awards and Honors

Angelou has been widely recognized for her creative writing achievements. Among her academic honors are a Yale University fellowship in 1970, a Rockefeller Foundation scholarship in 1975, a position as writer in residence at the University of Kansas at Lawrence in the mid-1970s, a lifetime chair as the Reynolds Professor of American Studies at Wake Forest University in 1981, visiting professorships at many universities throughout the United States, and about fifty honorary degrees. She also received the Horatio Alger Award in 1992, and in January 1993 she wrote and delivered the poem, "On the Pulse of Morning" at the inauguration of President Bill Clinton. She was the first poet so honored since Robert Frost appeared at John F. Kennedy's inauguration in 1961. Her recording of the poem won her a Grammy Award in 1994.

During the 1990s Angelou continued her long commitment to social and political causes. In October 1995 she spoke at the Million Man March rally in Washington, D.C., and in August 1996 she attended a New York City fund-raiser celebrating President Clinton's fiftieth birthday.

Despite the abundance of her autobiographical writings, Angelou generally declines to discuss her private life. She has been married several times since her divorce from Tosh Angelos, and she has, besides her son, one grandson.

About her artistic achievements, however, Angelou has provided many revealing comments. "All my work, my life, everything is about survival," she has observed. "All my work is meant to say, 'You may encounter many defeats, but you must not be defeated.' In fact, the encountering may be the very experience which creates the vitality and the power to endure."[3] She has recorded one African-American woman's life in such a way as to give it universal interest and relevance.

Maya Angelou brings people together. "Perhaps travel cannot prevent bigotry," she wrote in one essay aimed at uniting people, "but it can introduce the idea that if we try to understand each other, we may even become friends."[4]

Selected performances:

STAGE

Porgy and Bess (1954-55)
Freedom Cabaret (1960)
The Blacks (1961)
Medea (1966)
Look Away (1973)

FILMS

Calypso Heat Wave (1957)
Poetic Justice (1993)
How to Make an American Quilt (1995)

TELEVISION MINISERIES

Roots (1977)

Selected writings:

FICTION

Freedom Cabaret (play, 1960)

The Least of These (play, 1966)

Black, Blues, Black (television documentary script, 1968)

Georgia, Georgia (film script, 1972)

All Day Long (film script, 1974)

I Know Why the Caged Bird Sings (made-for-television movie script, 1979)

Sister, Sister (made-for-television movie script, 1982)

NONFICTION
(autobiographical unless otherwise indicated)

I Know Why the Caged Bird Sings (1969)

Gather Together in My Name (1974)

Singin' and Swingin' and Gettin' Merry like Christmas (1976)

The Heart of a Woman (1981)

All God's Children Need Traveling Shoes (1986)

Lessons in Life (essays, 1993)

Wouldn't Take Nothing for My Journey Now (essays, 1993)

POETRY

Just Give Me a Cool Drink of Water 'fore I Diiie (1971)

Oh Pray My Wings Are Gonna Fit Me Well (1975)

And Still I Rise (1978)

Shaker, Why Don't You Sing? (1983)

Now Sheba Sings the Song (1987)

I Shall Not Be Moved (1990)

Poetic Justice (poetry in film script, 1993)

The Complete Collected Poems of Maya Angelou (1994)

JUVENILE FICTION

Life Doesn't Frighten Me (based on 1978 poem, 1993)

My Painted House, My Friendly Chicken, and Me (1994)

Evelyn Ashford

FIVE-TIME OLYMPIC SPRINTER

(1957–   )

A MEMBER OF FIVE United States Olympic track and field teams, Evelyn Ashford broke Olympic and world sprint records and tied an American record by winning four career Olympic gold medals. She achieved all this despite suffering a chronic hamstring problem and missing the 1980 Olympic games because of the American boycott. Ashford "epitomized speed, power, endurance, and dedication, becoming one of America's best track athletes in the 1980s."[1]

Born in Shreveport, Louisiana, on April 15, 1957, Evelyn Ashford was the daughter of Samuel and Vietta Ashford. Her father's job as a sergeant in the United States air force kept the family on the move during much of her childhood. They finally settled in Roseville, near Sacramento, California, when she was a teenager.

While attending Roseville High School, Ashford showed such remarkable ability as a runner that the track coach invited her to join the boys' track team. She competed against boys from her school and other schools in track meets, winning most of her races. As a senior she served as cocaptain of the team.

In 1975 the University of California at Los Angeles (UCLA) offered Ashford one of its first women's athletic scholarships. By the end of her freshman year she had qualified for the 1976 Olympic Games in Montreal. Few people had heard of the nineteen-year-old phenomenon when she ran the 100-meter dash in 11.24 seconds to finish fifth at these Olympics.

Over the next few years, however, she built a significant international reputation. While running for UCLA, she became an All-American in 1977 and 1978, but she then left college to train full-time to achieve her great athletic goal: Olympic gold.

The extra training soon paid off. In 1979 Ashford ran the 200 meters in 21.83 seconds, an American record. In 1980, a few months before the next Olympics, she won the World Cup 100 meters and 200 meters. Most experts favored her to win gold medals in both events at the upcoming Olympics.

Overcoming Boycott and Injury

When President Jimmy Carter ordered the U.S. boycott of the 1980 Moscow Olympic Games because of the Soviet Union's invasion of Afghanistan, many American athletes lost the opportunity of a lifetime. No one was more affected than Evelyn Ashford, now reaching her athletic prime.

Disappointed at missing the Olympics, she nevertheless continued to train and compete. Soon, however, she had to face yet another setback. After she tore her right hamstring muscle at a Los Angeles meet late in 1980, she had to take the rest of the year off to let her injury heal and to make a decision about her future.

During that time Ashford realized that the competitive fire still burned within her, and it would do so till she won her Olympic gold medal. She now set her sights on the 1984 Games.

In 1981 Ashford returned to the track and successfully defended her two World Cup titles. During the 1983 season she recorded twenty of the twenty-three fastest times for the 100 meters in United States track and field history.[2] That summer, at the National Sports Festival in Colorado, she set a new world record of 10.79 seconds.

Later in 1983 she traveled to Helsinki for the World

Track and Field Championships, eager to face the previous world record holder, Marlies Göhr of East Germany, who had defeated her in a meet earlier that season. However, after easily winning her quarterfinal and semifinal heats, Ashford injured her hamstring again during the finals and fell to the ground, unable to complete the race.

She thus not only lost the race to Göhr but also faced the possibility of missing yet another Olympics, this time from injury. Once again she carefully nursed her leg back to competitive condition and continued to train. In 1984 she qualified for the United States Olympic team for the third straight time. She dropped one of her events, the 200 meters, to protect her leg.

Olympic Gold

At the 1984 Los Angeles Olympic Games, after waiting eight years and suffering two serious hamstring injuries, Ashford finally got her coveted Olympic gold medal by easily winning the 100 meters in 10.97 seconds, a new Olympic record. And she earned a second gold medal by anchoring the American 4 x 100-meter relay team to victory.

However, she still had some unfinished business. The Soviet bloc, including East Germany, had boycotted the Los Angeles Games in retaliation for the American boycott of the 1980 Moscow Olympics. Ashford, therefore, did not have an opportunity to race against her greatest rival, Göhr. They finally met in a competition on August 22 in Zurich, Switzerland. "Göhr jumped out of the blocks quickly, but Ashford surged past her in the final 40 meters of the race, winning with a new world record of 10.76 seconds."[3]

Because of her Olympic victories and her new world record, Ashford was named the Track and Field Athlete of the Year for 1984. After taking the next year and a half off to spend time with her husband, Ray Washington, and to give birth and take care of their baby daughter, Raina, Ashford returned to competition in 1986 and placed third in the 100 meters in the United States Championships. At the Good-

will Games in Moscow that year she won the 100 meters and ran on the winning 4 x 100-meter relay team, and in January 1987 her successful comeback was confirmed when she received the Vitalis Award for excellence in track and field.

Soon, however, Ashford's right hamstring problems began to recur. Unable to compete again for most of 1987, she had to withdraw from that year's United States Sports Festival and the World Track and Field Championships. Once again, though, Ashford fought back. In 1988 she qualified for her fourth Olympic team and was given the honor of carrying her country's flag at the Olympic opening ceremonies in Seoul, South Korea. Though now thirty-one years old, she managed to win a silver medal in the 100 meters, finishing just .29 second behind teammate Florence Griffith Joyner.* Running the anchor leg of the American women's 4 x 100 relay team, she overcame a large lead by the East German team to clinch the race for the United States, winning her third Olympic gold medal.

At this point she had already had a wonderful career. In 1989 the Women's Sports Foundation awarded her the prestigious Flo Hyman Trophy for her commitment to excellence in women's sports.

But Ashford saw yet another Olympics in her future. Over the next four years she continued to train and compete. In 1991, for example, she took third place in the 100 meters at the United States Championships.

In 1992, at the age of thirty-five, she qualified for the United States Olympic team for the fifth time. In Barcelona in August 1992, her maturity and stability played a key role in leading the American women to Olympic victory yet again in the 4 x 100-meter relay. Her fourth Olympic gold medal tied the career record for American women, previously held by the diver Patricia McCormick and also equaled in 1992 by the swimmer Janet Evans.

Evelyn Ashford's stature as a five-time Olympian, despite suffering recurring hamstring injuries and being denied participation in the 1980 Games, puts her in a class of her own. She remains an outstanding model of tenacity and endurance for all track athletes who follow her.

Pearl Bailey

AMBASSADOR OF LOVE

(1918—1990)

SINGER, ACTRESS, COMEDIENNE, and author—Pearl Bailey was one of the most popular entertainers of her time. But her big, people-loving personality and her concerns and actions for the benefit of humanity transcended show business. She also spent many years as a representative at the United Nations after President Nixon appointed her the United States Ambassador of Love in 1970.

Pearl Mae Bailey was born in Newport News, Virginia, on March 29, 1918. In later years fans and friends affectionately called her Pearlie Mae, but as a child she was known to her family as Dick, a name that her father gave her because he was hoping for a son.

She was the youngest of four children (three girls and one boy) of Joseph James Bailey, a revivalist minister, and Ella Mae Bailey, both descendants of Creek Indians. They divorced when Pearl was a child.

By the age of three she was already singing in her father's church, grounding her early technique in the congregation's Holy Roller style. She never received formal music training.

When she was four years old, Pearl Bailey moved with her family to Washington, D.C. Later she went with her mother and stepfather, Walter Robinson, to Philadelphia, where she attended elementary and high school until she dropped out at the age of fifteen to become an entertainer.

Early Years as a Singer and Dancer

Bailey began her show business career in 1933 when she won an amateur contest as a singer and dancer in Philadelphia at a theater where her brother, Willie ("Bill"), was appearing (he became a well-known tap dancer and, later, a minister). She also won a prize for her buck-and-wing dance performance at an inn in Washington, D.C., where she was visiting one of her older sisters.

Soon Bailey was singing and dancing with vaudeville troupes in small towns throughout Pennsylvania. She also performed at small nightclubs in Washington, D.C. After winning an amateur contest at the famed Apollo Theater in the Harlem district of New York City, she had a brief engagement as a dancer with Noble Sissle's band. Despite the difficulties of building a career in entertainment during the Great Depression of the 1930s, she endured the hard times and gradually developed a reputation as a singer.

In the early 1940s Bailey began to appear with major groups of the big band era, such as those led by Charles ("Cootie") Williams and William ("Count") Basie, and she sang in nightclubs in New York City, Baltimore, and Washington, D.C. Her solo debut, in New York City at the Village Vanguard (1944), was followed by an eight-month engagement at Manhattan's exclusive Blue Angel (1944-45). During that time she also worked with Cab Calloway at the Strand Theater, later appearing with him again at Broadway's Zanzibar Nightclub.

Acting Debut

Bailey made her acting debut when she appeared on Broadway in the all-black musical drama *St. Louis Woman* (1946). Critics compared her favorably with the great singing actress Ethel Waters* and praised her renditions of "Legalize My Name" and "A Woman's Prerogative" (also known as "It's a Woman's Prerogative"). Her performance won her the Donaldson\Award as the best newcomer on Broadway in 1946.

She returned to Broadway for other important performances. In the Theater Guild operetta *Arms and the Girl* (1950) she played a runaway slave. In 1954 she became a Broadway solo star in *House of Flowers*, a musical in which she played a madam at a West Indian bordello. One of the high points of Bailey's career was her starring role in the all-black Broadway production of the musical comedy *Hello, Dolly!* (1967, originally produced with a white cast in 1964). Her performance won her a special Tony Award.

Hollywood, too, beckoned. She began her film career in *Variety Girl* (1947), in which she sang her popular song "Tired." In *Carmen Jones* (1954), based on Georges Bizet's opera *Carmen*, she played the earthy Frankie, one of Carmen's friends. Bailey appeared as Gussie, the narrator and matchmaker, in *That Certain Feeling* (1956) and as Aunt Hagar, a relative of W. C. Handy, father of the blues, in *St. Louis Blues* (1958). The following year she played Maria, the cookshop woman, in the screen version of George Gershwin's folk opera *Porgy and Bess*, which at her insistence was made without the exaggerated black dialect called for by the original script.

Bailey appeared many times as a guest on television programs, including *The Mike Douglas Show*, *What's My Line?*, *The Love Boat*, and Bob Hope specials. In 1971 she hosted her own variety series, and a decade later she acted in the made-for-television movies *The Member of the Wedding* (1982) and *Peter Gunn* (1989).

Her Unique Style

While she enjoyed her activities as an actress, comedienne, and hostess, Bailey always regarded herself first and foremost as a singer. Songs with which she was closely associated include "Bill Bailey, Won't You Please Come Home?," "Row, Row, Row," "St. Louis Blues," "Takes Two to Tango," "That's Good Enough for Me," and "Tired." In the 1940s and 1950s she recorded many singles of these songs and others. In the 1950s and 1960s she issued a large number of albums, including *Pearl Bailey* (1953), *The One and Only Pearl Bailey Sings* (1956), *For Women Only*

(1965), and *Hello, Dolly!* (1968).

Bailey developed a unique performance style that combined skillful jazz interpretations, characteristic vocal qualities, and a humorous presentation. Her musical technique was based on evoking delicate nuances. She "relied on subtle variation of phrasing and intonation rather than indulging in bravura scat singing."[1] Yet the timbre of her voice—heavy, throaty, and brassy—was anything but subtle. She delivered her lyrics in a manner that she herself likened to preaching (perhaps a reflection of her early years of listening to her father, the minister). Bailey developed a comical, offhand way of performing songs by ad-libbing musical embellishments and incorporating a steady stream of droll asides. She added to the light-hearted effect by wearing striking costumes, often including rhinestones and a feather boa.

A Pearl of a Person

A woman of remarkable intelligence and wide-ranging interests, Bailey read voraciously, and in her later years she wrote humorous and inspirational books, such as her autobiography *The Raw Pearl* (1968) and *Duey's Tale* (1975), a juvenile storybook that won the Coretta Scott King Book Award from the American Library Association. *Hurry Up, America, and Spit* (1976) is a collection of essays and poems. *Between You and Me* (1989) presents many of her mature gems of wit and wisdom. One topic in this book is the decline of the family in the United States. "I believe the nation starts in the home," she affirmed; "that the family is the 'feeder' our nation is seeking. The process begins with communication."[2]

Family was important in her own life. Bailey was married briefly to a musician in the 1930s, and from 1948 to 1952 she was married to John Randolph Pinkett, Jr. She finally found happiness with her third husband, the white jazz drummer Louis Bellson, Jr., to whom she was married from 1952 till her death. Often working and recording together, the couple also adopted a son, Tony, and a daughter, Dee Dee. When a reporter asked her about her interracial marriage, she answered, "There is only one race, the human race."[3]

Bailey became known at home and abroad for being an ambassador of goodwill. She was named Woman of the Year by the March of Dimes (1968) and the United Service Organizations (1969). In 1975 she accepted a presidential appointment as a member of the American delegation to the United Nations. She served in that capacity for the rest of her life, becoming a United Nations senior public delegate, but continued her concert and television appearances, as well as making a number of international tours.

Bailey's last years were marked by two special events. In 1985, at the age of sixty-seven, she graduated from Georgetown University in Washington, D.C., having earned a degree in theology. In 1988 President Reagan presented her with the Presidential Medal of Freedom, the nation's highest civilian honor.

She had begun suffering from heart disease as early as the 1960s, but she continued to perform, achieving many of her greatest successes while battling her illness. Finally, however, she succumbed in Philadelphia on August 17, 1990. At her funeral, attended by more than two thousand people, her old friend Cab Calloway, who had costarred with her in *Hello, Dolly!*, spoke for millions of her admirers when he said farewell to her in words from the musical: "You'll always be here in our hearts where you belong."[4]

PEARL BAILEY

Selected recordings:

SINGLES

"Tired" (1946, Columbia)

"Legalize My Name" / "It's a Woman's Prerogative" (1946, Columbia)

"That's Good Enough for Me" / "Row, Row, Row" (1946, Columbia)

"Takes Two to Tango" (1952, Coral)

ALBUMS

Pearl Bailey Entertains (1950, Columbia)

Pearl Bailey (1953, Coral)

St. Louis Woman (1955, Capitol)

The One and Only Pearl Bailey Sings (1956, Mercury)

Gems by Pearl Bailey (1958, Vocalion)

Porgy and Bess (1959, Columbia)

St. Louis Blues (1959, Roulette)

The Best of Pearl Bailey (1961, Roulette)

Happy Sounds (1962, Roulette)

For Women Only (1965, Roulette)

Hello, Dolly! (1968, RCA Victor)

Selected performances:

STAGE

St. Louis Woman (1946)
Arms and the Girl (1950)
Bless You All (1950)
House of Flowers (1954)
Call Me Madam (1966)
Hello, Dolly! (1967)
Festival at Ford's (1970)
The Pearl Bailey Show (1973)
Hello, Dolly! (1975)
Night of One Hundred Stars (1982)

FILMS

Variety Girl (1947)
Isn't It Romantic? (1948)
Carmen Jones (1954)
That Certain Feeling (1956)
St. Louis Blues (1958)
Porgy and Bess (1959)
All the Fine Young Cannibals (1960)
The Landlord (1970)
The Last Generation (1971)
Norman . . . Is That You? (1976)
The Fox and the Hound (animated, voice only, 1981)

TELEVISION MOVIES

The Member of the Wedding (1982)
Peter Gunn (1989)

TELEVISION SERIES

The Pearl Bailey Show (1971)

Selected writings:

NONFICTION

The Raw Pearl (1968)
Talking to Myself (1971)
Pearl's Kitchen: An Extraordinary Cookbook (1973)
Hurry Up, America, and Spit (1976)
Between You and Me: A Heartfelt Memoir on Learning, Loving, and Living (1989)

Juvenile Fiction

Duey's Tale (1975)

Maria Louise Baldwin

FIRST BLACK WOMAN PRINCIPAL IN MASSACHUSETTS

(1856—1922)

FOR FORTY YEARS Maria ("Mollie") Louise Baldwin served as principal of the well-known, predominantly white Agassiz Grammar School in Cambridge, Massachusetts. She was one of the very few African-Americans to head such a northern school at the time, and she was the first black woman school principal in the state. Conscious of her position as a pioneer representative of her race, she once said, "I dare not fail."[1]

Maria Louise Baldwin was born in Cambridge on September 13, 1856, the eldest of two daughters and a son of Peter L. Baldwin and Mary E. Baldwin. Her father was for many years a postal worker in Boston, while her mother hailed from Baltimore. Baldwin attended Cambridge primary, grammar, and high schools, and in 1875 she graduated from the Cambridge training school for teachers.

Career at Agassiz

She began her teaching career in Chestertown, Maryland, where she remained for two years. In 1881 Baldwin became a primary grade teacher at the Agassiz Grammar School, named for the scientist Louis Agassiz and located near the campus of Harvard University. After teaching all grades from the first to the seventh, she became principal of the school in 1889.

In 1916 the school building was torn down and replaced by one that Baldwin helped to plan. Higher grades were added, her title changed from principal to master, and she took charge of twelve teachers and five hundred students. In her later years she also taught summer classes for teachers at Hampton Institute in Virginia and at the Institute for Colored Youth in Cheyney, Pennsylvania.

Baldwin treated her students and teachers with gentleness and courtesy, maintaining order not by using discipline but by earning love and respect. According to a 1922 biography published in the *AME Church Review*, she was noted for being "harmonious in every detail of her personality and her work; in the frictionless running of her perfect school machine."[2]

Community Activist

Baldwin participated in the community works of various organizations, including the Boston Ethical Society, the League of Women for Community Service, the Teachers' Association, and the Twentieth Century Club. Through her activities she met and corresponded with many of the most respected people of her time, such as Charles W. Eliot, Edward Everett Hale, Julia Ward Howe, and Alice Freeman Palmer.

Baldwin also associated with prominent African-Americans and performed functions specifically aimed at the black community. She met black Bostonians through her work with the Banneker Club, the Woman's Era Club (which she had helped to found), and the Omar Club, where she became acquainted with William Monroe Trotter. A dedicated reader and book collector, she invited black Harvard students to her home for weekly reading classes.

Baldwin lectured in many areas of the United States and developed a reputation for her skill with English and the art of public speaking. She lectured on the lives and works of such figures as Thomas Jefferson, Abraham Lincoln, and George Washington and on such topics as history, poetry, and woman suffrage. In 1897 she gave the Washington Birthday Memorial Address at the Brooklyn Institute of Arts and Sciences, speaking on the life and works of Harriet Beecher Stowe, the first black woman to be so honored by the institute.

Despite her acceptance by much of Boston society, Baldwin knew that some Bostonians harbored prejudice against blacks. When the film *The Birth of a Nation* (1915), which presents an insulting picture of her race, was screened in Boston, she was asked to read some poems at the showing and then to join in singing "My Country, 'Tis of Thee." "Please do not sing that then," she requested, "for it would break my heart when I know of the feeling of so many in Boston and throughout the country, who do not recognize truly the fact that this is our country. I might sing it another time, but not now."[3]

Baldwin collapsed and died of heart disease on January 9, 1922, while addressing the Council of the Robert Gould Shaw House Association at a hotel in Boston. The entire nation mourned her loss.

Honors

Many more honors were bestowed on Baldwin after her death. The Agassiz class of 1922 presented the school with a tablet in her memory. The school also established a scholarship in her honor and renamed its auditorium Baldwin Hall. Howard University in Washington, D.C., named a women's dormitory Maria Baldwin Hall, and the League of Women for Community Service created the Maria L. Baldwin Memorial Library.

At her death many tributes poured in from admiring colleagues, students, and friends. One, printed in a Cambridge newspaper, spoke for many: "Children and adults have learned from contact with Miss Baldwin a new respect and appreciation for the Negro race, whose noble possibilities her whole life exemplified. She has left to all whose lives touched hers the memory of a rare and radiant nature, the keynote of whose character was service."[4]

Janie Porter Barrett

SOCIAL REFORMER

(1865—1948)

THOUGH SHE SPENT her childhood in great material comfort, during her adult years Janie Porter Barrett eschewed an easy life and devoted herself to working for social reform. She established the Virginia Industrial School for Colored Girls, which was a pioneering rehabilitation center for black female delinquents, and helped to organize the Virginia State Federation of Colored Women's Clubs.

Janie Porter was born in Athens, Georgia, on August 9, 1865. Her mother, Julia, worked as a live-in housekeeper and seamstress for the Skinners, a white family who pampered and educated Janie along with their own children. Janie's unknown father may have been white, for she had fair skin and glossy, curly hair.

After Julia married a railway worker and set up house with her husband, she commuted to work at the Skinners' house, but her daughter continued to live there. Eventually Mrs. Skinner wanted to become Janie's legal guardian and to send her to a northern school so that the young woman could live there as a white person. Julia, however, vetoed the plan and decided to send her daughter to Hampton Institute in Hampton, Virginia, where Janie would live as a black person in a black environment.

A New Life at Hampton Institute

In truth, Janie had never lived among blacks or been required to do manual labor. The privileged, genteel life she had enjoyed with the Skinners had in no way prepared her for Hampton, where she encountered both these elements for the first time. Hampton emphasized vocational education, with young women receiving training in morality and housekeeping in preparation for careers as wives or domestics.

Barrett gradually adapted to the Hampton system, being especially influenced by a novel about a cultured, advantaged young woman just like herself devoting her life to social service. Even while still at Hampton, she began to volunteer for community projects aimed at helping others.

Founding a Social Settlement

After graduating from Hampton, Janie taught school for a time in Dawson and Augusta, Georgia, before returning to Hampton to teach night school classes. In 1889 she married Harris Barrett, the institute's cashier and bookkeeper. The couple had four children.

To help neighborhood girls, Janie Porter Barrett established a sewing class for them in her own home. The class later grew into a club organized to improve home and community life. She even built a special house on her property where the girls could practice their homemaking skills.

Within three years the club outgrew the family home, so Barrett organized the Locust Street Social Settlement. By 1909 the settlement had clubs for girls, boys, women, and senior citizens. While committees supervised the activities, Barrett herself concentrated her efforts on large-scale annual events.

Establishing a Rehabilitation Center

In 1908 Barrett helped to organize the Virginia State Federation of Colored Women's Clubs, which engaged in a wide range of social service activities. One particular concern was the problem of black female juvenile delinquents, for whom Barrett initiated a plan to create a rehabilitation center. The federation provided funds to open the Industrial Home for Wayward Girls in Hanover County, north of Richmond. In 1915 and 1916 the Virginia Assembly appropriated more money for the home. A matron was hired to oversee the first group of fifteen girls, and a farmer began to cultivate the land surrounding the rehabilitation home. Barrett was named secretary of the board of trustees. After several name changes, the center came to be known as the Virginia Industrial School for Colored Girls.

After Barrett's husband died at about this time, she turned down a job offer as dean of women at Tuskegee Institute to become the resident superintendent at the rehabilitation center. Barrett functioned superbly in this role, one reason being that her aristocratic background equipped her to deal with the socially prominent white women who either controlled the trustee board or were able to influence state legislators into appropriating state funds for the school. Because of the high regard in which Barrett was held, she could demand—and be assured—that future white employers of her girls would treat the parolees humanely. "You know," she once said, "we cannot do the best social welfare work unless, as in this school, the two races undertake it together."[1]

In the 1920s, under Barrett's supervision, the Virginia Industrial School for Colored Girls came to be ranked as one of the five best such schools in the country, known especially for its cultivation of character and moral development. The school operated on the honor system, with no corporal punishment and no bars on the school windows. Because of Barrett's success in obtaining state funding, the Virginia State Federation of Colored Women's Clubs eventually turned over the property to the state, which completely financed the school. The institution became a model of its type, exemplifying the true meaning of successful rehabilitation through its countless cases of young women being released, finding jobs, getting married, and setting up happy homes.

Barrett's Achievements Recognized

In 1929 Barrett received the William E. Harmon Award for Distinguished Achievement among Negroes. The following year she took part in the White House Conference on Child Health and Protection. For twenty-five years she served as president of the Virginia State Federation of Colored Women's Clubs, and for four years she chaired the executive board of the National Association of Colored Women.

Barrett retired in 1940 and died in Hampton on August 27, 1948. Two years later, her training school was renamed the Janie Porter Barrett School for Girls. She would surely have been pleased to learn that after her death the school became racially integrated and began to house boys as well as girls. Janie Porter Barrett possessed the rare gift "of true, unselfish love which seeks no reward for itself."[2]

Kathleen Battle

SPECIAL SOPRANO

(1948–   )

ONE OF THE MOST highly regarded lyric sopranos of her time, Kathleen Battle has been praised for her "special quality of communicating with the public."[1] She has conquered opera with major companies in the United States and Europe and is one of the most sought-after concert and recital artists.

Kathleen Deanna Battle was born in Portsmouth, Ohio, on August 13, 1948, the youngest of seven children of Grady Battle, a steelworker, and Ollie (Layne) Battle. She began piano lessons at the age of thirteen and voice study during her high school years.

After graduating from Portsmouth High School in 1966 she enrolled in the College-Conservatory of Music at the University of Cincinnati, Ohio, where she majored in music education, not performance. She received her bachelor's degree in 1970 and her master's degree in 1971.

Battle then began teaching fourth, fifth, and sixth graders at the Garfield School in Cincinnati's inner city. In the evenings she took German classes and studied voice with Franklin Bens.

Debut

In 1972 Battle auditioned for Thomas Schippers, director of the Cincinnati Symphony Orchestra. He hired her to sing the soprano solo part in Brahms's *Ein deutsches Requiem* (A German requiem), as well as several Handel arias, at the 1972 Spoleto (Italy) Festival of Two Worlds, which Schippers had cofounded. Her Spoleto performance was her formal debut and the turning point in her career. "That night was very magical and significant for me," she later said. "After that experience I knew I wanted to be a singer."[2]

Battle continued to teach elementary school for a while but spent her spare time intensively studying opera interpretation, song literature, and acting. In 1973 Schippers introduced her to the pianist-conductor James Levine, who became her coach and adviser. Levine engaged her to perform with him at the Cincinnati and Ravinia (Illinois) festivals that year.

Battle's career now progressed quickly. In March 1974 she won the WGN-Illinois Opera Guild's Auditions of the Air, and a year later she placed first in the Young Artists Awards, a national operatic competition held at the Kennedy Center for the Performing Arts in Washington, D.C. Later in 1975 she received the Martha Baird Rockefeller Fund for Music Award, and that fall she accepted an offer to understudy, and eventually succeed, Carmen Balthrop in the title role of Scott Joplin's folk opera *Treemonisha* on Broadway. One year later she made her New York City Opera debut, playing Susanna in Mozart's *Le nozze di Figaro* (The marriage of Figaro).

Singing for the Metropolitan Opera

In 1977 Battle joined the Metropolitan Opera, where James Levine was now the principal conductor and music director. She soon became one of the most successful of the company's younger artists, specializing in the light lyric coloratura repertory. In her debut at the Met on December 22, 1977, she sang the part of the Shepherd in Wagner's *Tannhäuser*, and over the next several seasons her roles included Sophie in

Naxos), Zdenka in Strauss's *Arabella*, Sophie in Strauss's *Der Rosenkavalier* (The knight of the rose), and Zerlina in Mozart's *Don Giovanni*.

Recital and Concert Artist

During Battle's years with the Met she also gave recitals and concerts featuring a wide variety of music, including art songs and arias by Bach, Fauré, Mozart, Purcell, and Schubert; popular songs by Duke Ellington and George Gershwin; and spirituals. Her concert appearances as the two queens in Handel's oratorio *Solomon* won her great critical acclaim. She performed as a soloist with many of the world's great orchestras, such as the New York Philharmonic, the Boston Symphony, the Philadelphia Orchestra, the Chicago Symphony, and the Berlin Philharmonic. Battle made her Salzburg Festival debut in 1982, and in 1987 she was selected as the soloist for the worldwide telecast of the New Year's Day Concert by the Vienna Philharmonic.

When Battle left the Metropolitan Opera in Februrary 1994 because of personality conflicts with other members of the company, she began to concentrate on her already well-established career as a recital and concert artist, with

KATHLEEN BATTLE

Massenet's *Werther*, Blonde in Mozart's *Die Entführung aus dem Serail* (The abduction from the seraglio), and Pamina in Mozart's *Die Zauberflöte* (The magic flute).

While performing at the Met from the late 1970s to the early 1990s, Battle made guest appearances with other important opera companies, among them the San Francisco Opera, the Chicago Opera, the Vienna Staatsoper, the Paris Opéra, and the Royal Opera at Covent Garden in London. During those years her roles, in addition to those already mentioned, included Nannetta in Verdi's *Falstaff,* Oscar in Verdi's *Un ballo in maschera* (A masked ball), Despina in Mozart's *Così fan tutte* (Thus do all women), Rosina in Rossini's *Il barbiere di Siviglia* (The barber of Seville), Zerbinetta in Richard Strauss's *Ariadne auf Naxos* (Ariadne on

the New York Philharmonic and at Carnegie Hall in New York City. In October 1997 she was a featured performer at the gala opening program of the New Jersey Performing Arts Center in Newark.

Battle has recorded regularly for many years. Among her distinguished recordings are *Kathleen Battle Sings Mozart* (1986), *Kathleen Battle: Salzburg Recital* (1987), and *Kathleen Battle: Bel Canto* (1994).

"Battle is gifted with a high, sweet soprano of considerable intrinsic charm," wrote one critic, "which she governs with technical finesse."[3] Her special ability to communicate with audiences results especially from a combination of her sensuous tone, her wide range of expressiveness, and her projection of a multidimensional personality.

Selected recordings:

ALBUMS

Brahms: Songs of Brahms (1984, RCA)

Pleasures of Their Company (Bach, Gounod, Villa Lobos) (1986, Angel)

Kathleen Battle Sings Mozart (1986, Angel)

R. Strauss: Ariadne auf Naxos (1987, Deutsche Grammophon)

Kathleen Battle: Salzburg Recital (1987, Deutsche Grammophon)

Kathleen Battle and Placido Domingo: Live in Tokyo, 1988 (1988, Deutsche Grammophon)

Schubert: Lieder (1989, Deutsche Grammophon)

Kathleen Battle: At Carnegie Hall (recorded live 1991, released 1992, Deutsche Grammophon)

The Bach Album (1992, Deutsche Grammophon)

Kathleen Battle and Wynton Marsalis: Baroque Duet (1992, Sony)

Rossini: Il barbiere di Seviglia (The barber of Seville) (1993, Deutsche Grammophon)

Handel: Semele (1993, Deutsche Grammophon)

Kathleen Battle: Bel Canto (1994, Deutsche Grammophon)

So Many Stars (1995, Sony)

Grace (1997, Sony)

Mary McLeod Bethune

MOST INFLUENTIAL AFRICAN-AMERICAN WOMAN

(1875—1955)

EDUCATOR, CIVIL AND WOMEN'S rights leader, adviser to United States presidents, government official, humanitarian—Mary McLeod Bethune probably ranks as the most influential African-American woman in her country's history. It was she who helped to initiate the black pride movement in America. "Look at me," she often said. "I am black. I am beautiful."[1]

Mary Jane McLeod was born near Mayesville, South Carolina, on July 10, 1875. She was the fifteenth of the seventeen children of Samuel McLeod, of African and Indian descent, and Patsy (McIntosh) McLeod, of African heritage. Her parents and most of her brothers and sisters were former slaves, freed by the Union victory in the Civil War. By the early 1870s the family owned a small farm.

Through her parents' help and encouragement, Mary acquired a good education. She attended the local Trinity Presbyterian Mission School; Scotia Seminary (later Barber-Scotia College) in Concord, North Carolina; and, in preparation to become an African missionary, the Bible Institute for Home and Foreign Missions (later Moody Bible Institute) in Chicago, Illinois. However, after graduating from the institute in 1895, she was extremely disappointed to learn that the Presbyterian Mission Board would not assign an African-American to Africa.

Education Pioneer

With her first career choice closed to her, Mary turned to teaching, beginning her career at the Presbyterian-sponsored Haines Institute in Augusta, Georgia, where she observed the work of the school's founder and principal, Lucy Laney. She soon came to see the education of black students as the most important factor in improving the lives of African-Americans.

While teaching at the Presbyterian Kendall Institute in Sumter, South Carolina, the young educator met and married Albertus Bethune. They had one child, Albert. The marriage was not a happy one, and they were together for only about eight years, though they remained legally married till Albertus's death in 1918.

In 1900 Mary McLeod Bethune established a Presbyterian parochial school in Palatka, Florida. From 1902 to 1904 she operated an independent school and offered social services in the same city. Then in October 1904 Bethune founded the Daytona Educational and Industrial Institute, a school for black girls, in Daytona (later incorporated with other towns as Daytona Beach), Florida. Over the next two decades her efforts to build the school brought her to national attention.

Bethune based her institute on the traditional mind-hands-heart program. Academic instruction was initially offered only up to the eighth grade, but in 1911 a nurse training course was added, and after World War I the curriculum was extended to the high school level and included teacher training. Hands-on vocational education included sewing and the production and preparation of food. The heart was enriched through religious study as well as outreach programs, such as community holiday projects.

The girls also benefited from observing Bethune personally as a role model. She insisted on desegregated seating at all institute functions, organized local blacks to vote in 1920 despite threats by the Ku Klux Klan, and offered young black females the tools to make a better future for themselves.

Besides being assisted by local black leaders, she called on the white community to help the school. Socially prominent white women took part in the school's activities, and white males, notably James N. Gamble of the Proctor and Gamble Manufacturing Company, were her greatest financial benefactors. By 1922 the school's enrollment had grown from five children to three hundred girls and a faculty and staff of about twenty-five. Bethune also provided boys with adjunct classes and services.

In 1923 she merged her school, by then called the Daytona Normal and Industrial Institute, with the coeducational Cookman Institute of Jacksonville, Florida, which was sponsored by the Methodist Episcopal church. The purpose of the union was to develop the new insitution into a junior college. The school, renamed Bethune-Cookman College in 1929 earned its official junior college accreditation in 1935, and in 1943 it awarded its first bachelor of science degrees in education as a senior college.

By then, however, Bethune had turned the reins over to James A. Colson. From 1936 to 1943 she directed the Division of Minority Affairs at the National Youth Administration in Washington, D.C., and in 1942, after a serious illness, she resigned the presidency of the college. Later she briefly took the president's chair again till 1947, when she left permanently. She was the only woman of her time who had founded a school for disadvantaged youth and built it into a senior college. To honor her efforts, the National Association for the Advancement of Colored People (NAACP) awarded her its prestigious Spingarn Medal in 1935.

Leader of Black Women's Organizations

Bethune played a major role in developing the black women's club movement, using her school to host state and regional meetings of clubwomen. In 1917 she became president of the Florida Association of Colored Women, and in 1920 she established the Southeastern Association of Colored Women.

From 1924 to 1928 Bethune served as president of the National Association of Colored Women (NACW), the most important black women's secular organization in the United States. She tried to pull together the loose groups within the association, especially by raising the funds to establish a national headquarters in Washington, D.C. In 1928 the NACW became the first all-black organization permanently stationed in the nation's capital.

However, Bethune eventually became frustrated with the NACW's reluctance to centralize its efforts. Consequently, in December 1935 in New York City, she founded the National Council of Negro Women (NCNW), which she headed as president for the next fourteen years. By the time she left office in 1949, this new umbrella organization included twenty-two national professional and occupational groups. "The scattered work and independent programs of national organizations of Negro women," she wrote in the NCNW annual report of October 1941, "needed the strength that unity could bring."[2]

Under her leadership the NCNW lobbied federal leaders on such issues as lynching, public housing, job discrimination, and social welfare programs. The NCNW's greatest successes came when Bethune fought to gain equality for black women in the armed forces during World War II. In 1942 her intervention with army leaders helped to ensure that blacks would be accepted in the newly created Women's Army Auxiliary Corps (WAAC). She also induced army officials to allot almost 10 percent of the places in the WAAC's first officer candidate class to black Americans. In 1945 she was appointed a special assistant to the secretary of war to help select prospective female officers in the organization, by then renamed the Women's Army Corps (WAC).

Government Official

Bethune's service to the federal government had actually begun back in the 1920s. Beginning with the Coolidge administration, she served as an adviser on African-American issues, especially education, to five successive presidents, while also serving on the National Child Welfare Commission during the Coolidge and Hoover administrations.

Under President Franklin D. Roosevelt, Bethune's influence greatly expanded. In August 1935 she became one of the thirty-five members of the advisory committee of the National Youth Administration (NYA), a New Deal agency formed to help young people obtain vocational training and job placement. In June 1936 she was appointed the director of the NYA division that specialized in black youth, thus achieving the highest federal government position held by any African-American woman up to that time.

The Schomburg Center / NYPL

MARY MCLEOD BETHUNE

Soon Bethune's stature in Washington grew beyond her role with the NYA, as she became Roosevelt's unofficial overall race relations strategist. To get the best possible advice for this expanded position, in August 1936 she organized the Federal Council on Negro Affairs, popularly known as the Black Cabinet, consisting of more than one hundred black advisers from the National Urban League, the NAACP, the black press, and other groups. The Black Cabinet called two historic national black conferences in Washington in January 1937 and January 1939. Presided over by Bethune herself, these conferences presented African-American needs, recommended government policies, and spread the results throughout official Washington.

While working for the government, Bethune continued her independent activies. In 1941, for example, she endorsed black labor leader A. Philip Randolph's March on Washington Movement, which led to an executive order barring racial discrimination in employment in government and defense industries.

In August 1943 the NYA ceased to operate, but Bethune continued to have a voice in national affairs. In 1945, as a special representative of the State Department, she attended the San Francisco conference that established the United Nations, and throughout the late 1940s and early 1950s she continued to advise Presidents Truman and Eisenhower on matters affecting race relations.

In her later years she established the Mary McLeod Bethune Foundation and promoted Frank Buchman's Moral Re-Armament, an international movement aiming to unite people behind a set of absolute values. She also traveled widely and received recognition in other countries. In 1949 Haiti presented her with its Medal of Honor and Merit, and in 1952 Liberia gave her its Star of Africa award.

Mary McLeod Bethune died at her home in Daytona Beach on May 18, 1955 having become the nation's preeminent symbol of black dignity and achievement.

Her long-range goal was to open doors so that blacks could assume roles of leadership in American society. Therefore, besides overseeing the disbursement of funds for vocational training for young black Americans, she lobbied for the support of black college students, the community's future leaders. Furthermore, she pushed for the employment of qualified black assistants in the state and regional offices of the NYA itself.

Bethune developed a close personal association with President Roosevelt and especially with First Lady Eleanor Roosevelt. She met with them often to discuss race-related issues and vigorously backed the president in his campaigns for reelection. Her efforts helped to provide blacks with a strong political voice within the Democratic party.

Jane M. Bolin

AMERICA'S FIRST BLACK WOMAN JUDGE

(1908—)

T THE AGE OF ONLY thirty-one, Jane M. Bolin was appointed a judge in the Domestic Relations Court of the City of New York, thus becoming the first black woman judge in the history of the United States.

Jane Matilda (also recorded as Mathilda) Bolin was born in Poughkeepsie, New York, on April 11, 1908, one of four children of Gaius C. Bolin and Matilda (Emery) Bolin. Gaius, born in Poughkeepsie of a Native American mother and black American father, became the first black American graduate of Williams College (1889), practiced law in Poughkeepsie for more than fifty years, and served as president of the Dutchess County Bar Association. Matilda, born in England, immigrated to the United States with her parents and settled with them in Poughkeepsie.

In Her Father's Footsteps

After attending Poughkeepsie public schools, Jane M. Bolin entered Wellesley College in Massachusetts, from which she graduated with honors in 1928. Inspired by her father, she decided to enter law, and in 1931 she became the first black woman to graduate from Yale University Law School.

After clerking in her father's law office for six months, she passed the New York State Bar examination and practiced law in Poughkeepsie for a short time. In 1933 she moved to New York City and married fellow attorney Ralph E. Mizelle, with whom she worked as a law partner till 1937. In 1936, she ran unsuccessfully as the Republican candidate for the state assembly seat representing New York's seventeenth district.

In 1937 Bolin was appointed an assistant corporate counsel in New York City's law department. She used her position to encourage private employers to hire people according to their qualifications, without discrimination against African-Americans.

Career on the Bench

After Mayor Fiorello La Guardia appointed Bolin to a ten-year term as judge of the Domestic Relations Court of the City of New York in 1939, she used her position over the next decade to draw public attention to the racial discrimination widely practiced against children by New York City private schools and child care institutions. During her first ten years on the bench, she was never reversed by the higher courts.

Bolin was reappointed for successive ten-year terms by the mayors William O'Dwyer, John Lindsay, and Robert F. Wagner, Jr. She remained a justice when the court was reorganized in 1962 to become the Family Court of the State of New York. When retirement became mandatory, she left the bench after forty years on December 31, 1978.

Community Activist

In addition to joining many professional organizations—notably the Bar Association of the City of New York, the Harlem Lawyers Association, and the New York State Association of Family Court Judges—Bolin devoted much of her valuable time to community activities, serving on the boards of such groups as the

Child Welfare League of America, the local and national branches of the National Association for the Advancement of Colored People, and the Neighborhood Children's Center. Her other commitments included the Committee against Discrimination in Housing, the Committee on Children of New York City, the Scholarship and Service Fund for Negro Students, and the Urban League of Greater New York.

Bolin met several presidents of the United States and had an especially close association with Eleanor Roosevelt, wife of President Franklin D. Roosevelt. Bolin also traveled widely throughout the world and met many African heads of state. Her friends and associates included the famed educator Mary McLeod Bethune* and Judge J. Waties Waring of South Carolina, the judge in the first public school desegregation case.[1]

Bolin's first husband, Ralph E. Mizelle, with whom she had a son, Yorke Bolin Mizelle, died in 1943. In 1950 she married Walter P. Offutt, Jr., a minister, who died in 1974. Yorke Bolin's daughter, Natascha, is Bolin's only grandchild.

Retirement Years

After retiring, Bolin spent two years as a volunteer tutor in math and reading for children in the New York City public school system. Later she was appointed to the Regents Review Committee of the New York State Board of Regents, which oversees discipline in thirty-two professions licensed by the New York State Board of Regents.

Bolin has fought for racial justice all her life, but as a judge she always saw herself as a guardian for the

JANE BOLIN

The Schomburg Center / NYPL

whole city and for all children in trouble. "When asked why he had originally selected Bolin," according to Wendy Brown in *Black Women in America*, "Mayor La Guardia explained that she had common sense, patience, courtesy, and a broad sympathy for human suffering."[2] These qualities enabled Jane M. Bolin to become an outstanding role model as the nation's first African-American woman judge.

Gwendolyn Brooks

POET OF THE ORDINARY

(1917—)

GWENDOLYN BROOKS WAS the first African-American, male or female, to win a Pulitzer Prize. Throughout her career she has written about ordinary people and events, discovering early that, in her words, "what was common could also be a flower."[1] A "G. B. voice" is what Brooks herself calls this approach. "Although she believes in the power of the ordinary to be both significant and beautiful," according to the critic Jacquelyn McLendon, "her motivation is not to mythologize or to romanticize her characters. She simply writes about black people as people, not as curios."[2]

Gwendolyn Elizabeth Brooks was born in Topeka, Kansas, on June 7, 1917, the elder of two children of David Anderson Brooks and Keziah Corinne (Wims) Brooks. Though he worked as a janitor, her father was highly educated, having studied premedicine for a year and a half at Fisk University in Nashville, Tennessee. He read stories and sang songs to his children. But it was her mother, a former schoolteacher, who strongly encouraged Gwendolyn's early literary efforts. "I have notebooks dating from the time I was eleven," Gwendolyn Brooks later wrote, "when I started to keep my poems in composition books. My mother decided that I was to be the female Paul Laurence Dunbar."[3]

Brooks grew up in Chicago, where as a teenager she continued to write poetry. When she was sixteen,

GWENDOLYN BROOKS

The Schomburg Center / NYPL

she received encouragement from the poet Langston Hughes, who read some of her poems.

After graduating from Englewood High School, she attended Woodrow Wilson Junior College, graduating in 1936. During the next two years Brooks served as publicity director of the National Association for the Advancement of Colored People Youth Council in Chicago. She also wrote poetry with increasing artistry.

In 1939 she married Henry Lowington Blakely II, a writer who worked on the Woodrow Wilson Junior College student newspaper, the *Wilson Press*. The couple had two children; Henry Lowington and Nora.

Pulitzer Prize Winner

During the early 1940s Brooks devoted increasing effort to gaining recognition as a poet, and by 1945 she had not only written enough poems to complete a book, but also succeeded in having her first collection, *A Street in Bronzeville*, issued by the New York publishing company Harper and Brothers. Although she drew her poetic topics from the black community, Brooks' style at this early stage in her career strongly reflected the techniques of the white poets she had read and studied, from the classical writers Shakespeare, Milton, and Donne to such moderns as Eliot and Pound. She demonstrated a deep knowledge of the various sonnet forms, used alliteration with great wit, and produced subtle rhyme schemes.

In 1949 Harper published Brooks's collection *Annie Allen*, including the long piece "The Anniad." This volume, too, showed her impressive grasp of complex stylistic traditions, and it was for this work that Brooks received a Pulitzer Prize in 1950, becoming the first black person to win a Pulitzer Prize of any kind.

During the 1950s and 1960s she continued to publish highly praised books, including *Maud Martha* (1953), an autobiographical novel; *Bronzeville Boys and Girls* (1956), a book of children's poems; and the adult poetry collection *The Bean Eaters* (1960). In these works she further developed her art, not just honing her stylistic craft but also enriching her narrative gift through the use of a wide range of situations and characters, both white and black. In *The Bean Eaters*, for example, she wrote dramatically well-crafted poems about a murder, the bravura of young black boys, and the visit of a black reporter to Little Rock, Arkansas, in 1957.

A Change of Style

In 1967, as a result of attending the Second Black Writers' Conference at Fisk University, Brooks made a distinct change in her writing style. The conference, she explained a few years later, stimulated her through her exposure to "young people, full of a new spirit. They seemed stronger and taller, really ready to take on the challenges.... I was still saying 'Negro,' for instance."[4] She became determined to write poetry that came nearer to the hearts of her own people.

Her first important publication in that new spirit was *In the Mecca* (1968), a book of poems exploring the urban black experience. The title poem is a long, poignant narrative work detailing the search for a missing girl named Pepita, and thereby realistically revealing black life and thought in the Mecca, a building crowded with poverty-stricken people. The remainder of the collection consists of short poems, including ones dedicated to Medgar Evers and Malcolm X.

Beginning with *In the Mecca*, Brooks consciously strove to write not only *about* black subject matter but also *to* black readers. She streamlined her style and language to appeal directly to ordinary black readers; yet she did not sacrifice her characteristic use of words to convey music, pictures, and complex patterns of meaning.

Soon after Harper published *In the Mecca*, Brooks stopped issuing works through that or any other white publishing company and began to publish exclusively through black companies. Broadside Press, a Michigan-based company started by the black poet Dudley Randall, published her poetry collections *Riot* (1969), *Aloneness* (1971), *Beckonings* (1975), and other works, including *Report from Part One: An Autobiography* (1972). The Third World Press of Chicago issued *To Disembark* (1981) and *Winnie* (1988), and her own David Company published, among other books, *Children Coming Home* (1991).

Awards and Honors

Brooks has received many awards and honors, including honorary degrees from over fifty colleges and universities, and she has taught poetry at many insitutions of higher learning, including Columbia College, City College of the City University of New York, and Chicago State University. Besides her

Pulitzer Prize for *Annie Allen* in 1950, she received the *Mademoiselle* Merit Award for Distinguished Achievement (1945), the American Academy of Arts and Letters Award for creative writing (1946), the Eunice Tietjons Memorial Prize from *Poetry* magazine (1949), the Thormod Monsen Literature Award (1964), the Anisfield-Wolf Award (1968), the Black Academy of Arts and Letters Award (1971), the Shelley Memorial Award (1976), the Lifetime Achievement Award of the National Endowment for the Arts (1989), the Aiken-Taylor Award (1992), the National Book Foundation Medal for Distinguished Contribution to American Letters (1994), and the National Medal of Arts (1995).

Among her other honors were being named the poet laureate of Illinois (1968), being appointed poetry consultant to the Library of Congress (1985-86), being inducted into the National Women's Hall of Fame (1988) becoming the first person to hold the Gwendolyn Brooks Chair in Black Literature and Creative Writing at Chicago State University (1990), delivering the Jefferson Lecture in the Humanities for the National Endowment for Humanities (1994), and having the Gwendolyn Brooks Elementary School of Aurora, Illinois, named after her (1995).

Gwendolyn Brooks has reached extraordinary heights as the poet of the ordinary.

Selected writings:

FICTION

Maud Martha (novel, 1953)

NONFICTION

Report from Part One: An Autobiography (1972)
Young Poet's Primer (writing manual, 1981)
Very Young Poets (writing manual, 1983)
Report from Part Two (autobiography, 1995)

POETRY

A Street in Bronzeville (1945)
Annie Allen (1949)
The Bean Eaters (1960)
In the Mecca (1968)
Riot (1969)
Family Pictures (1970)
Aloneness (1971)
Aurora (1972)
Beckonings (1975)
Primer for Blacks (1980)
To Disembark (1981)
Black Love (1982)
The Near-Johannesburg Boy and Other Poems (1987)
Gottschalk and the Grande Tarantelle (1988)
Winnie (1988)
Children Coming Home (1991)

JUVENILE FICTION

The Tiger Who Wore White Gloves or, You Are What You Are (1974)

JUVENILE NONFICTION

Very Young Poets (writing manual, 1983)

JUVENILE POETRY

Bronzeville Boys and Girls (1956)

Hallie Q. Brown

INTERNATIONALLY RENOWNED SPEAKER

(c. 1845—1949)

O NE OF THE MOST IMPORTANT black leaders ever to emerge,"[1] Hallie Q. Brown was an educator, author, internationally renowned speaker, and activist in the fields of religion, women's rights, political issues, and civil rights for African-Americans.

Hallie Quinn Brown was born in Pittsburgh, Pennsylvania, on March 10, about 1845 (the exact year is uncertain, with estimates ranging from 1845 to 1855, but she was believed to be over one hundred years old when she died in 1949), the fifth of six children of Thomas Arthur Brown and Frances Jane (Scroggins) Brown. Thomas was the son of a Scottish woman who owned a Maryland plantation and the plantation's black overseer. Frances was born into slavery in Virginia. Thomas was allowed to purchase his freedom, while Frances was freed by one of her grandfathers, a white Revolutionary War officer and planter. After Thomas Brown and Frances Scroggins married in about 1840, they settled in Pittsburgh, where he became a steward and express agent on riverboats.

The family acquired real estate and lived comfortably, but when they allowed their home to become a station on the Underground Railroad, young Hallie Q. Brown saw the other side of life and recognized the need for African-Americans to fight for human rights.

After spending 1865 to 1870 in Ontario, Canada, where Thomas worked at farming and Hallie attended school, the family moved to Wilberforce, Ohio, so that she could study at the predominately black university there. Hallie Q. Brown earned a B.S. degree in science at Wilberforce University, graduating in 1873 and serving as class salutatorian.

Educator

Soon after graduating, Brown went to South Carolina, where she taught children and adults at a plantation school and in the public schools of Columbia. Moving to Mississippi, she taught at the Sonora Plantation and in the Yazoo City public schools.

From 1875 to 1887 Brown taught classes and served as dean at Allen University in Columbia, South Carolina. Returning to Ohio, she taught in the Dayton public schools for four years and established an adult night school for migrant workers from the South. During 1892-93 she served as lady principal (dean of women) at Tuskegee Institute in Alabama.

Lecturer and Elocutionist

Brown developed an interest in public speaking and enrolled in summer courses at the Chautauqua Lecture School, where she graduated in 1886. She was also influenced by Professor Robertson of the Boston School of Oratory, whom she met while she was teaching in Dayton.

In the 1880s, to help raise funds for Wilberforce University, Brown joined a group of people touring to benefit the school and served as its elocutionist (reader) for four years.

Brown then began to travel on her own as a lecturer and elocutionist, being well received wherever she went throughout the United States. Between 1894 and 1899 she toured Europe, especially England, where she appeared before Queen Victoria on two occasions. On a later visit to England, in 1910, a British newspaper called her "one of the finest female elocutionists in the world."[2]

Brown undertook many more trips to raise funds for Wilberforce University, including tours to obtain money for a library and a dormitory. Her principal speaking topic was life among blacks in the United States, with temperance being another favorite subject.

In 1906, however, Brown reduced her speaking tours so that she could concentrate on her new job as a full-time professor of elocution at Wilberforce University. She remained there for several years and also became a member of the school's board of trustees.

Social Activist

Besides teaching and speaking, Brown contributed to social progress through her activism in religion, women's rights, politics, and civil rights for her race. She was active in the African Methodist Episcopal (AME) church, with which Wilberforce University was associated, and for many years she taught a Sunday school class of college students.

In 1910 she attended the World Missionary Conference in Edinburgh, Scotland, as a representative of the Women's Parent Missionary Society of the AME church.

After Brown heard Susan B. Anthony speak, when she was still a student at Wilberforce University, she became a dedicated proponent of women's rights. She fought for the equal rights of women in the AME church, started the Neighborhood Club for black women in Wilberforce, and helped to stimulate national interest in black women's organizations. From 1905 to 1912 she served as president of the Ohio State Federation of Women's Clubs, and from 1920 to 1924 she was president of the National Association of Colored Women (NACW), of which she remained honorary president till her death. While leading the NACW, she created a scholarship fund for the higher education of black girls, and she began the renovation and preservation of the Frederick Douglass home in Washington, D.C. "Full citizenship must be given the colored woman," she once said, "because she needs the ballot for her protection and that of her children."[3]

An active supporter of the Republican party, in the 1920s Brown served as vice president of the Ohio Council of Republican Women and chaired of the executive committee of the Negro Women's National Republican League. In addition, she was a member of the Advisory Committee of the National League of Women Voters and a member of the Colored Women's Department of the Republican National Committee. She participated in the presidential campaigns of Warren G. Harding and Herbert Hoover, and in 1924 she spoke at the Republican National Convention in Cleveland.

Her powerful voice often rang out in support of civil rights for blacks. In 1922 she met with President Harding and several United States senators to call for a national antilynching bill. In 1925, when the Daughters of the American Revolution enforced segregated seating at an American music festival held in Washington, D.C., her strong protest led to a boycott of the festival by black performers and audience members. She joined forces with the National Association for the Advancement of Colored People to block bills designed to prohibit interracial marriages.

Author

Brown was a skilled writer of books and pamphlets. *Bits and Odds: A Choice Selection of Recitations* (1880) reflects her early interest in elocution, while *First Lessons in Public Speaking* (1920) is the first speech textbook written by a black American. In addition to compiling and editing *Homespun Heroines and Other Women of Distinction* (1926), a collection of about sixty biographies by over two dozen authors, Brown also wrote *The Beautiful: A Story of Slavery* (1924); *Tales My Father Told and Other Stories* (1925), a book of fiction; *Our Women: Past, Present, and Future* (1925); and *Pen Pictures of Pioneers of Wilberforce* (1937).

Brown never married. She lived in her family home, Homewood Cottage, in Wilberforce till she died on September 16, 1949. Her exact age was unknown, but she was thought to have been at least one hundred years old. The Hallie Quinn Brown Community House in Saint Paul, Minnesota, and the Hallie Q. Brown Memorial Library in Wilberforce stand as lasting tributes to this remarkable woman.

Nannie Helen Burroughs

LEADER OF THE WOMAN'S CONVENTION

(1879—1961)

A T THE AGE OF ONLY twenty-one, Nannie Helen Burroughs became a national leader when her powerful speech "How the Sisters Are Hindered from Helping" sparked the formation of the Woman's Convention Auxiliary to the National Baptist Convention in Richmond, Virginia, in 1900. As a leader of the Woman's Convention, the largest black women's organization in America, she championed women's rights and racial equality for over six decades.

Nannie Helen Burroughs was born in Orange, Virginia, on May 2, 1879, to John and Jennie (Poindexter) Burroughs. While her father worked as an itinerant preacher, her mother took Nannie and her sister (who died in childhood) to Washington, D.C.

Developing Her Talents

Nannie Helen Burroughs attended public schools in the District of Columbia and developed her budding oratorical talents in the literary society of her high school and in the church programs at the Nineteenth Street Baptist Church. When her high school domestic science teacher failed to keep her promise to arrange for Burroughs to become her assistant, Burroughs vowed to herself to do everything she could in the future to open doors of opportunity to other black women, especially those from humble backgrounds.

Moving to Philadelphia, she found a clerical job and also did part-time work for the Reverend Lewis G. Jordan, pastor of the Union Baptist Church. When Jordan moved to Louisville, Kentucky, Burroughs went with him. In Louisville she organized a women's industrial club, which offered evening classes in such

vocational skills as sewing, typing, cooking, and bookkeeping.

Woman's Convention

In 1900 Burroughs traveled from Louisville to Richmond, Virginia, where the National Baptist Convention was being held. There, voicing the long-standing discontent of black women at not having a larger role within the church, she gave her historic speech "How the Sisters Are Hindered from Helping," which soon led to the birth of the Woman's Convention (WC).

Burroughs was elected the WC's corresponding secretary, and in her first year in office she delivered 215 speeches and organized twelve societies for the WC. By 1903 she had built up the group's constituency base to nearly 1 million, and by 1907 it had reached 1.5 million. In 1908 she initiated the annual National Woman's Day, a fund-raising celebration in local churches.

Burroughs, who never married, devoted herself wholeheartedly to the WC. Every year she was reelected to her position as corresponding secretary till 1948, when she was voted president, a title she held for the rest of her life. In her leadership roles with the WC, she spoke out for the right of women to vote and to have equal economic opportunity. Her stand on racial equality included her denunciations of lynching, segregation, and employment discrimination. "Without stint I have given my entire life to the Woman's Convention," she wrote in the preamble to her will, "and have proudly built it and watched it grow from the humblest beginnings to world service and security."[1]

Active Republican

Loyal to the Republican party as the party of Abraham Lincoln, Burroughs helped to found the National League of Republican Colored Women in 1924 and was elected the league's president, in which capacity she campaigned for the Republican candidates during the presidential races of the 1920s. In 1928 President Hoover appointed her to chair a fact-finding commission on housing, which under her leadership published a study called *Negro Housing: Report of the Committee on Negro Housing* in 1932.

While the majority of black voters shifted to the Democratic party, especially under President Franklin D. Roosevelt in the 1930s, Burroughs continued to support the Republicans. Consequently, her political influence weakened, but her popularity in the black community remained intact because of her leadership roles in other organizations, such as Baptist groups, the National Association for the Advancement of Colored People (NAACP), and the Association for the Study of Negro Life and History.

National Training School

One of her most important achievements was the founding of the National Training School for Women and Girls in 1909, of which Burroughs was president. Associated with the WC, the school taught students at the high school and junior college levels and offered missionary training as well as vocational studies preparing women for a wide range of jobs. Although some students pursued traditional female domestic work as cooks, maids, nurses, housekeepers, dressmakers, and laundresses, others opted for business jobs as clerks, bookkeepers, and stenographers. The school even prepared black women to become printers, barbers, and shoe repairers.

Burroughs called her institution the "school of the three B's"[2] because of her emphasis on the Bible, bath, and broom (symbolic of all labor). The school's first motto was "Work, Support Thyself, to Thine Own Powers Appeal." It was later replaced by "We Specialize in the Wholly Impossible." In 1964 the school was renamed the Nannie Helen Burroughs School, which became an elementary school.

Cultivating Black Pride

Burroughs had a tremendous impact on her time because of her emphasis on black pride. "If in our homes," she proclaimed to her WC members in 1905, "there is implanted in the hearts of our children, of our young men and of our young women the thought they are what they are, not by environment, but of themselves, this effort to teach a lesson of inferiority will be futile."[3]

Burroughs did not hesitate to call for militant action in the pursuit of equal justice. In 1933 she told an audience of young black people that they should be willing to die for their rights. In 1934 she was quoted as saying that black Americans must use "ballots and dollars" to fight racism rather than "wasting time begging the white race for mercy."[4] She firmly supported the NAACP's advocacy of boycotts, petitions, and other forms of protest.

Nannie Helen Burroughs devoted her last years to her role as president of the WC (1948-61). She died in Washington, D.C., on May 20, 1961. "No other person in America has so large a hold on the loyalty and esteem of the colored masses as Nannie H. Burroughs," wrote William Pickens, a pioneer NAACP administrator, before her death. "She is regarded all over the broad land as a combination of brains, courage, and incorruptibleness."[5]

Eunice Hunton Carter

NEW YORK'S FIRST BLACK WOMAN DISTRICT ATTORNEY

(1899—1970)

EUNICE HUNTON CARTER was one of the most important black lawyers and community leaders of her time. She maintained a successful law practice for many years and held high leadership positions within the National Council of Negro Women and the Young Women's Christian Association. Carter is best remembered, however, for being the first female African-American district attorney in the state of New York.

She was born Eunice Hunton in Atlanta, Georgia, on July 16, 1899, the third of four children of William Alphaeus Hunton and Addie (Waites) Hunton. Only she and her younger brother, William, survived infancy. After the 1906 race riots in Atlanta, the family moved to Brooklyn, New York. Her father was a pioneer in establishing Young Men's Christian Association (YMCA) services for blacks, while her mother was a teacher and a leader of the Young Women's Christian Association (YWCA). During World War I Addie Hunton volunteered through the YMCA to help American soldiers in Europe. "Eunice Hunton," Jean Blackwell Hutson wrote in *Notable American Women*, "learned from her parents a commitment to public service that marked her career."[1]

In 1917 Eunice enrolled at Smith College in Northampton, Massachusetts, where she received both an A.B. degree and an A.M. degree in 1921. For the next eleven years she worked with various family service agencies.

In 1924 she married Lisle Carter, a New York City dentist. They had one child, a boy named after his father.

"Although her unusual talents had swiftly brought her recognition in the social work field," according to Jean Blackwell Hutson, "Eunice Carter's religious beliefs—she was a devout Episcopalian—and her commitment to the improvement of society led her to want a more active and public life."[2] She began taking night classes in law at Fordham University in 1927, she received her LL.B. degree in 1932, and two years later opened a private law practice in New York City.

Deputy Assistant District Attorney

Following the Harlem riots in the spring of 1935, New York City Mayor Fiorello La Guardia appointed Eunice Hunton Carter secretary of the Committee on Conditions in Harlem.

In August of that year Special Prosecutor Thomas E. Dewey named her as the only woman and the only black on his ten-person staff investigating organized crime in New York City. Dewey had a special interest in the rackets of Harlem, an area of the city that Carter knew especially well because of her earlier work on the Committee on Conditions in Harlem. "Carter's work on theories about organized crime," wrote Wendy Brown in *Black Women in America*, "triggered the biggest organized crime prosecution in the nation's history in New York City in the late 1930s."[3] It was Carter who developed the principal evidence in the case against Lucky Luciano.

After Dewey became district attorney for New York County in late 1935, he named Carter deputy assistant district attorney. The first black woman to hold a district attorney's position anywhere in the state of New York, she built a distinguished record as a trial prosecutor over the next ten years until she returned to private practice in 1945.

Carter played a prominent role in Republican politics for many years. She strongly supported the political campaigns of her old boss Thomas E. Dewey and of Nelson Rockefeller.

Women's Rights Activist

Besides engaging in politics to achieve her social goals, Carter became involved in women's organizations. A charter member of the National Council of Negro Women (NCNW), she served the organization as legal adviser, chairperson of the board of trustees, representative at the founding conference of the United Nations (UN) in 1945, and observer at the UN till 1952. In 1947 she acted as a consultant to the Economic and Social Council of the UN for the International Council of Women and chaired its Committee of Laws.

Following her parents' example, Carter also devoted much of her energy to the YWCA. She was active in the Upper Manhattan (Harlem) branch of the YWCA and served on the organization's national board as a member of the administrative committee for the foreign division and as cochair of the committee to develop leadership in other countries.

Carter retired from her law practice in 1952, but remained active with the NCNW and other organizations. In 1954 the German government invited her to serve as an adviser to women in public life. At a 1955 UN conference in Geneva, she chaired the International Conference of Non-Governmental Organizations.

After being widowed in 1963 she continued to live in New York City until her death on January 25, 1970. Eunice Hunton Carter contributed much to advancing the status of African-American women through her commitment to public service as a social worker, lawyer, political activist, and internationally renowned women's rights advocate. In her most memorable role, that of successful trial prosecutor in the toughest sections of New York City, she broke new ground for black women.

Mary Ann Shadd Cary
PIONEER JOURNALIST AND LECTURER

(1823—93)

As a racial activist, writer, editor, speaker, educator, and suffragette, Mary Ann Shadd Cary fought on many fronts to achieve equality for all black men and women. She became best known for her pathbreaking roles as the first black woman newspaper editor and one of the earliest black women lecturers in North American history.

Born Mary Ann Shadd in Wilmington, Delaware, on October 9, 1823, she was the eldest of thirteen children of the free blacks Abraham Doras Shadd and Harriet (Parnell) Shadd. Abraham, a prosperous shoemaker, was a prominent abolitionist who spoke out for racial equality, stressed education for blacks, and opened his home to runaway slaves. His views and activism strongly influenced Mary's later career.

Because Delaware was a slave state where education for blacks was forbidden, the Shadds enrolled Mary at the age of ten in a Quaker boarding school in West Chester, Pennsylvania, where she studied for six years. Returning to Wilmington and still resenting the lack of educational opportunity for African-Americans in Delaware, she organized a private school for black children and taught there from 1839 to 1850.

During those years she also began her writing career. One of her works was the pamphlet *Hints to the Colored People of North America* (1849), in which she extolled the virtues of self-reliance.

Advocate of Migration to Canada

The Fugitive Slave Act of 1850 imperiled the safety of many blacks in America. Former slaves, sometimes entire families, who had lived in freedom for years were suddenly subject to being arrested and forced back into slavery. Consequently, thousands of blacks sought freedom by fleeing to Canada.

In 1851 Mary Ann moved to Windsor, Canada West, and soon became one of the most outspoken proponents of black migration from America to Canada, where she believed her race would find greater freedom and safety. In 1852 she published a pamphlet, *A Plea for Emigration; or, Notes on Canada West, in Its Moral, Social, and Political Aspect*, which encouraged black American fugitives to move to Canada.

Her entire family settled in Windsor, where she and her brother Isaac taught at a segregated missionary school. Although many black leaders, such as Henry Bibb, then supported segregated communities and facilities, Mary Ann sought genuine integration in Canada.

Editor of the *Provincial Freeman*

In March 1853 Mary Ann issued the first edition of the *Provincial Freeman*, Canada West's first antislavery newspaper—and the first newspaper in North America to be edited by a black woman. Reflecting her influence as its editor, the paper's motto was "Self Reliance Is the True Road to Independence." Through the *Provincial Freeman* she attacked slavery, criticized the all-black settlements in Canada, and solicited funds to help fugitive slaves. The paper was necessary, she wrote in an early issue, to help black people decide "whether or not to leave Yankeedom with disenfranchisement and oppression" and settle "in a land of impartial laws and a Constitution having no distinctions of color."[1]

Originally published in Windsor, the paper was

moved in May 1854 to Toronto and in the summer of 1855 to Chatham, the headquarters of the Underground Raiload. By the spring of 1856 Mary Ann, her brother Isaac, and H. Ford Douglass shared editorial duties. However, in 1858 an economic depression in Canada forced the *Provincial Freeman* out of business.

Lecturer on Race Issues

Beginning in 1855 Mary Ann made periodic visits to the United States to speak to audiences about slavery and other subjects relating to race, such as the need for unity among abolitionists and among Canadian and American black communities. She criticized self-segregated black settlements and encouraged fugitives to integrate themselves into the larger social structure. Being absolutely committed to the principle of self-reliance, she attacked those who wanted to support fugitives through public begging.

Mary Ann was a pioneer on the speaking circuit and soon became widely recognized as the first educated black woman lecturer in North America. Even more than other black women antislavery lecturers, she faced danger from opponents because she publicly encouraged fugitive slaves to escape to Canada and because she actually offered them the material means to get there. She was often heckled as she lectured and insulted when she traveled.

Despite the antagonism she faced from slavery sympathizers, Mary Ann enjoyed great popularity as a lecturer and won praise for her logic, intelligence, originality, and persuasiveness. Her powerful language included the use of such expressions as "moral pest," "petty despot," "moral monsters," and "nest of unclean birds."[2] She objected to the use of the word *Negro* as being a loose, inaccurate term but accepted *colored people*.

In the summer of 1856, after her first season of lecturing, she married Thomas F. Cary of Toronto. They lived in Chatham and had a daughter, Sally, but her husband and daughter did not slow down her career or dedication to public affairs.

Return to Education

At the beginning of the 1860s Mary Ann Shadd Cary was teaching in Michigan, but in 1863 she returned to Chatham, where she became a naturalized British citizen and taught at another missionary school.

Meanwhile, the Civil War was raging in the United States. When President Lincoln called for half a million volunteers to increase the Union's military strength after the bloody battles of Gettysburg and Vicksburg, Cary relocated to Indiana in August 1863, so that she could aid the Union cause and thus the cause of freedom for black American slaves. Becoming a recruiting officer, she enlisted black volunteers to serve at the front for the federal forces.

After the war she stayed in America and taught, first in Detroit and then in Washington, D.C., where she served as a public school principal for seventeen years. During those years she also contributed articles to the *New National Era*, edited by Frederick Douglass, and to the *Advocate*, edited by John Cromwell.

Her Later Years

In her forties Cary became the first woman to enroll in the law department of Howard University, receiving an LL.B. degree in 1883. "Her determination in later life to build a second career as a lawyer," wrote Elise M. Lewis in *Notable American Women, 1607-1950*, "attests to her courage, will, and vitality."[3]

One of the post-Civil War causes to which Cary lent her skills as an orator and legal expert was woman suffrage. As early as the 1850s she was drawn to this issue, and in 1855 she became the first woman to be admitted as a corresponding member to one of the early African-American conventions held to discuss black suffrage. She argued before the Judiciary Committee of the United States House of Representatives that women had a right to vote under the Fourteenth and Fifteenth Amendments, which provided that right to good citizens and taxpayers. She pressed the legal point and actually became a registered voter in the District of Columbia, one of the few women to gain the franchise at that time. Cary joined the National Women's Suffrage Association and in 1878 addressed the group's convention.

In her last years she continued to lecture and write, never ceasing to stir up controversy in her pursuit of rights for blacks and women. Mary Ann Shadd Cary died in Washington, D.C., on June 5, 1893, leaving behind a unique legacy in a wide range of fields. As a pioneering African-American female journalist and lecturer, she opened doors for all those who have followed.

Shirley Chisholm

FIRST BLACK WOMAN IN CONGRESS

(1924–   )

A PIONEERING POLITICAL figure, Shirley Chisholm was the first African-American woman elected to the United States Congress, and she was both the first black and the first woman to seek the nomination of a major party for president. She inspired other blacks, women, and independently-minded citizens of all kinds to aspire to high political office.

She was born Shirley Anita St. Hill, in Brooklyn, New York, on November 20, 1924, to Charles and Ruby (Seale) St. Hill. When she was three years old, Shirley and her two younger sisters were sent to Barbados to live with their maternal grandmother. "Years later I would know what an important gift my parents had given me by seeing to it that I had my early education in the strict, traditional, British-style schools of Barbados," Chisholm said as an adult. "If I speak and write easily now, that early education is the main reason."[1]

After seven years, the three girls returned to Brooklyn to rejoin their parents and a new baby sister. Shirley was greatly influenced by both of her parents. Charles read voraciously and sparked her interest in black rights, while Ruby molded her daughters into well-rounded women: "We were to become young ladies—poised, modest, accomplished, educated, and graceful," Shirley recalled, "prepared to take our places in the world."[2]

In 1936 the family moved from the Brownsville section of Brooklyn to the Bedford-Stuyvesant district, where Shirley first experienced serious racial tensions. In Barbados she had lived in a black community, and in Brownsville, a primarily white, Jewish neighborhood, minorities were harmoniously integrated. Bedford-Stuyvesant was different. About half of its residents were black, and they were engaged in a continual power struggle with other groups. Here Shirley first began to hear racial slurs.

After graduating from high school she enrolled at Brooklyn College, where she majored in psychology and minored in Spanish. During her college years she joined the Harriet Tubman Society, whose ideas about black pride reminded her of her father's.

Educator

In 1946 she graduated cum laude from college and took a job as a teacher at the Mount Calvary Child Care Center in Harlem. Soon she enrolled at Columbia University, where she took night classes in early childhood education.

At Columbia she met Conrad Chisholm, a graduate student, whom she married in 1949. Her husband was a private investigator specializing in insurance claims cases, and because his work was often dangerous, Shirley persuaded him to take a safer, related job for New York City as a Medicaid claims investigator.

During the 1950s Shirley Chisholm made rapid progress in her career as an educator, receiving her M.A. degree in 1952, and becoming director of the Friend in Need private nursery school in Brooklyn the following year. Soon thereafter she took over the directorship of the Hamilton-Madison Child Care Center in Manhattan. This phase of her career peaked in 1959 when she became a consultant to the City Division of Day Care, where she supervised 10 day care centers in New York City till 1964.

Early Years in Politics

Chisholm's interest in politics had first been aroused during her college years, when she joined the Seventeenth Assembly District Democratic Club, of which she remained a member for several years after graduating from college. In 1953 she became part of a group called the Committee for the Election of Lewis S. Flagg, Jr., a black lawyer. After the committee successfully elected Flagg to a judgeship, the leader, Wesley ("Mac") Holder, reorganized the group in 1954 on a more permanent basis as the Bedford-Stuyvesant Political League. However, the league was torn by internal strife when Chisholm challenged Holder for the presidency, and she left it in 1958.

In 1960 Chisholm returned to politics by helping to form the Unity Democratic Club, a black rights political action group. It joined forces with the Nostrand Democratic Club, a nonracially motivated reform organization, and in 1962 wrested control of the Seventeenth Assembly District away from the traditional white political machine.

In 1964 Chisholm herself was elected to represent the district in the New York State Assembly, where she served for the next four years. While there, she sponsored two memorable bills, one creating a program enabling disadvantaged young people to go to college, and the other providing unemployment insurance for domestic and personal employees.

First Black Woman in Congress

In 1968 Chisholm, ready for bigger challenges, ran for the United States Congress in the primarily black Twelfth Congressional District of New York, located in the borough of Brooklyn. After winning the Democratic primary she faced the Republican candidate James Farmer, the former national chairman of the Congress of Racial Equality. Despite Farmer's considerable reputation in the black community and his support among both Republicans and liberals, Chisholm won the election by a comfortable margin. She became, in her words, "the first American citizen to be elected to Congress in spite of the double drawbacks of being female and having skin darkened by melanin."[3]

On joining the United States House of Representatives in early 1969, she was assigned to the Agricultural Committee but at her insistence was soon transferred to the Veterans' Affairs Committee, where she served for two years. In 1971 she switched to the Education and Labor Committee, where she fought for the poor, advocated minimum wage increases, and tried to obtain federal subsidies for day care centers.

In 1972 Chisholm put together a coalition of blacks, feminists, and other minority groups and ran for the Democratic nomination for president of the United States. The first black and the first woman to seek such a nomination, she won 151 votes at the 1972 Democratic National Convention. She compared her role with that of Al Smith, the unsuccessful Democratic presidential candidate in 1928. Smith, a Catholic, helped to pave the way for the victorious campaign of the Catholic John F. Kennedy in 1960. "What I hope most," Chisholm wrote after her run in 1972, "is that soon there will be others who will feel themselves as capable of running for high political office as any wealthy, good-looking white male."[4]

As the years passed, Chisholm moved up the seniority ladder and gained increasing stature in Congress. In 1977 she joined the powerful House Rules Committee. During her first two years in Congress she supported her party on only 97 of 127 bills (about 74 percent), but by 1979-80 she had become more conscious of the value of party loyalty, voting with the Democrats on 154 of 163 bills (about 94 percent). On one issue, however, she consistently sided with the Republicans against the Democrats: she refused to support strict environmental laws that she felt would cost people jobs.[5]

While her career in Washington was flourishing, however, her marriage at home was declining. In 1977 she divorced Conrad Chisholm and later that year married Arthur Hardwick, Jr., a black businessman whom she had met ten years earlier when both were members of the New York State Assembly. After Hardwick was in a nearly fatal car accident in 1979, over the next few years her desire to spend more time with her husband and her discomfort with the new conservative climate in Washington caused Chisholm to announce her retirement from Congress on February 10, 1982. She served till January 3, 1983.

Retirement Years

Retirement, however, did not mean inactivity. Soon Chisholm joined the lecture circuit, as well as becom-

The Schomburg Center / NYPL

SHIRLEY CHISHOLM

National Convention in 1984 she led the formation of the National Political Congress of Black Women. Elected its first leader, she used her national renown and her great organizational skills to expand the body from an initial group of 500 members at its first convention to 8,500 by 1988. In that year the group sent a delegation of one hundred women to the Democratic National Convention to demand that the party support civil rights and social programs. Chisholm also vigorously promoted Jackson's 1988 presidential campaign.

Other organizations with which Chisholm has been active include the League of Women Voters, the National Association for the Advancement of Colored People, the National Board of Americans for Democratic Action, and the National Organization for Women. On three separate occasions she appeared on the Gallup Poll's list of the Ten Most Admired Women in the World. In 1973 Clairol presented her with its Woman of the Year Award for Outstanding Achievement in Public Affairs. Many colleges have given her honorary degrees.

Chisholm has left a lasting record of her political and social career in two remarkable autobiographical books: *Unbought and Unbossed* (1970), which outlines her life up to her election to the House of Representatives, and *The Good Fight* (1973), which chronicles her run for the presidency.

"My significance, I want to believe," Shirley Chisholm wrote, "is not that I am the first black woman elected to the United States Congress, but that I won public office without selling out to anyone. . . . We need men and women who have far greater abilities and far broader appeal than I will ever have, but who have my kind of independence—who will dare to declare that they are free of the old ways that have led us wrong, and who owe nothing to the traditional concentrations of capital and power that have subverted this nation's ideals."[6]

ing the Purington Professor at Mount Holyoke College in Massachusetts, where she taught classes in political science and women's studies. In 1985 she was visiting professor at Spelman College in Georgia. In 1986 Arthur Hardwick died of cancer, and in 1987 Chisholm retired from teaching.

She never lost her zest for political action. In 1984 Jesse Jackson, following the path that Chisholm had blazed in 1972, ran for the presidency, and she assisted him in his campaign. After the Democratic

Johnnetta B. Cole

FIRST BLACK FEMALE PRESIDENT OF SPELMAN COLLEGE

(1936—   )

AFTER GAINING "a wealth of experience as an administrator, educator, activist, anthropologist, and expert in cross-cultural studies on race, sex, and class,"[1] in 1987 Johnnetta B. Cole became the first African-American woman president of Spelman College, the oldest and largest historically black college for women in the United States.

Born Johnnetta Betsch in Jacksonville, Florida, on October 19, 1936, she was the second of three children of John Thomas Betsch, Sr., and Mary Frances (Lewis) Betsch. Mary was a professor of English at Edward Waters College in Jacksonville and later treasurer and vice president of an insurance company that one of her grandfathers had helped to found. John was a mason, a civic activist, and eventually an executive in his wife's family's business.

College at Fifteen

Johnnetta acquired a love of reading at an early age, spending vast amounts of her time at the Jacksonville public library's black branch, which was named for her great-grandfather who had founded the family's insurance business. She excelled at the segregated high school she attended.

At the age of only fifteen Johnnetta entered the predominantly black Fisk University in Nashville, Tennessee, under its early admission program. The following year she transferred to Oberlin College in Ohio, where she experienced, in her words, "culture shock in the predominantly white world."[2] After receiving her B.A. degree in sociology from Oberlin in 1957, she enrolled at Northwestern University in Evanston, Illinois, where she earned an M.A. degree in anthropology in 1959.

Advocate for Women and People of Color

In 1960 she married Robert Cole, the son of an Iowa dairy farmer. The couple soon moved to the African nation of Liberia, where Johnnetta spent two years carrying out anthropological fieldwork. Later she also did fieldwork in Cuba, Haiti, and Grenada.

In 1967 Johnnetta B. Cole received her Ph.D. in anthropology from Northwestern University. Two years later she became assistant professor of anthropology at Washington State University in Pullman, where she also served as the director of the school's black studies program.

In 1970 Cole accepted the position of associate professor of Afro-American studies at the University of Massachusetts in Amherst, where she taught for the next thirteen years, eventually becoming a full professor of Afro-American studies and anthropology and also serving for a time as the school's associate provost for undergraduate education (1981-83). During this time she was also a visiting professor at Oberlin College, the University of California at Los Angeles, Williams College in Williamstown, Massachusetts, and Hunter College of the City University of New York. In 1984 Hunter appointed her full professor of anthropology and director of the school's Latin American and Caribbean Studies program.

"Through her teaching and research in the areas of cultural anthropology, African American studies, and women's studies, she became a steadfast advocate for people of color and women throughout the world.

Her passion and persistence for equality and self-enrichment through education and community service, paved the way for her appointment as the first African-American woman to serve as president of Spelman College since its founding in 1881."[3]

President of Spelman College

In 1986 Cole applied for the position of president of Spelman College in Atlanta, Georgia, the preeminent college for black women in the United States and one of the nation's most prestigious schools of any kind. She was selected for the job because, as she herself believed, the trustees wanted someone who was qualified, black, and female, "so they no longer needed to explain why, in 106 years, a sister president could not be found."[4]

Taking office on July 1, 1987, Cole soon found that she had to spend half of her time on fund-raising, at which she became expert. In 1992, under her leadership, Spelman completed a campaign that brought in $113.8 million, the largest sum ever raised by a black college or university.[5]

Cole directed Spelman to reflect her "belief in education as a powerful instrument for change." "If we do nothing to improve our world," she declared in her inaugural speech, "then we cannot call ourselves educated women."[6] She soon established the school's Office of Community Service, through which students volunteered for community projects; by 1993 about 40 percent of Spelman's students had volunteered for service.

Cole also instituted a mentorship program, which paired Spelman students with the chief executive officers of Atlanta companies. These pairings promoted, she believed, the "rediscovery of the nexus of leadership and service."[7]

Cole maintained a close one-on-one relationship with the students. Despite her heavy administrative schedule, she managed to teach an anthropology or women's studies course each year, and she made her-

JOHNNETTA B. COLE

Courtesy of Johnnetta B. Cole

self available to students for office visits. Because of her accessibilty, students nicknamed her their "sister president."[8]

During Cole's presidency Spelman rose to new heights. It became the first historically black college to receive a number one rating in *U.S. News and World Report*'s annual college issue. In 1996 *Money Magazine*, in its list of best buys, ranked Spelman College as the number one historically black college, the number one women's college, and the number seven college in America.

Author

Cole has written and edited textbooks used in classrooms throughout America's colleges and universities. She edited three textbooks on anthropology: *Anthropology for the Eighties: Introductory Readings* (1982), *All American Women: Lines That Divide, Ties That Bind* (1986), and *Anthropology for the Nineties: Introductory Readings* (1988).

In *Conversations: Straight Talk with America's Sister President* (1993) Cole discussed problems faced by African-American women, such as racism and sexism. These evils, she said, can be conquered; "though it is sometimes very difficult to imagine our nation totally free of racism and sexism, my intellect, my heart, and my experience tell me that it is actually possible."[9] In September 1997 she published *Dream the Boldest Dream: And Other Lessons of Life.*

Community and Business Activist

Cole has been an active participant in numerous community and civic organziations, including the American Anthropological Association, the Atlanta Rotary Club, the Carter Center of Emory University, the Feminist Press, the Fund for a Free South Africa, the National Council of Negro Women, and the United Way of Metro Atlanta. She served as chairperson of the presidents of the forty-one institutions of the United Negro College Fund, and she headed the board of the United States Department of Education's Fund for the Improvement of Post-Secondary Education.

Cole has established many ties with the business community. She became the first woman elected to the board of directors of Coca-Cola Enterprises and the first black woman to become a member of the Atlanta Chamber of Commerce. Currently she is a director on the boards of Coca-Cola, Merck and Company, Home Depot, and Management and Training Corporation.

Honors and New Horizons

Among Cole's many honors are the *Working Woman* Hall of Fame Award (1989), the American Anthropological Association Distinguished Service Award (1993), the YWCA Woman First Award (1993), and the Martin Luther King Distinguished Service Award (1994). She has received honorary degrees from over forty colleges and universities, including Fisk University, Princeton University, Yale University, and the University of Sussex in England.

From her marriage to Robert Cole, whom she divorced in 1982, she has three sons: David, Aaron, and Ethan. In 1987 she married Arthur J. Robinson, Jr., an administrator at the Centers for Disease Control and Prevention in Atlanta, by whom she has two stepsons.

In 1997, after a decade of service as the seventh president of Spelman College, Cole resigned, announcing that after a one-year sabbatical she would join the faculty at Emory University as Presidential Distinguished Professor of Anthropology, Women's Studies, and African-American Studies.

Anna Julia Haywood Cooper
PIONEERING SCHOLAR

(c. 1858/59—1964)

ONLY THE FOURTH KNOWN African-American woman to earn a doctoral degree, Anna Julia Haywood Cooper was one of the earliest serious scholars to tackle the issues of gender and racial discrimination in America. Her long life began in slavery in the 1850s and ended during the civil rights struggle of the 1960s. A dedicated educator and powerful writer, she instilled a sense of social fairness into generations of Americans.

Anna Julia Haywood was born in Raleigh, North Carolina, on August 10, 1858 or 1859. Her mother was Hannah Stanley (Haywood), a slave, and her father was probably Hannah's owner, George Washington Haywood. Cooper studied at Saint Augustine's Normal School and Collegiate Institute (now Saint Augustine's College), an Episcopalian institution in Raleigh. While there, during the early post-Civil War years, she tutored other students.

Lifelong Commitment to Education

Even at that early stage in her life, Anna's "faith in education as essential to true liberation was unshakable."[1] When she finished her studies at Saint Augustine's, she stayed there as a teacher.

In 1877 she married George A. C. Cooper, who had been born a free man in Nassau and entered Saint Augustine's in 1873 to study theology. In 1879, just three months after his ordination, he died. Anna Cooper never remarried.

After earning her A.B. degree from Oberlin College in Ohio in 1884, she taught modern languages at Wilberforce University in Ohio during 1884-85. The following year she returned to Raleigh to teach mathematics, Latin, and German at Saint Augustine's. Cooper received an M.A. degree in mathematics from Oberlin in 1887, and during that same year she accepted a job as a teacher in Washington, D.C., at the Preparatory High School for Colored Youth, which was renamed the M Street High School in 1891 and the Paul Laurence Dunbar High School in 1916. Here she spent most of the rest of her career as an educator.

In the 1890s Cooper joined other black intellectuals in a campaign to fight sexism and racism in America. She made speeches and presented papers to such groups as the American Conference of Educators (1890), the Congress of Representative Women (1893), the Second Hampton Negro Conference (1894), the National Conference of Colored Women (1895), and the National Federation of Afro-American Women (1896).

During that decade Cooper also expanded her personal horizons by visiting Canada and the Bahamas, and in 1900 she traveled to London to present a paper called "The Negro problem in America" at the first Pan-African Conference there. After the conference she toured Europe.

From 1902 to 1906 Cooper served as principal of the M Street High School, but when she objected to the board of education's plan to weaken the curriculum of black schools, she was removed from her position. From 1906 to 1910 she headed the department of languages at Lincoln University in Jefferson City, Missouri, after which she then returned to the M Street High School as a Latin teacher.

Cooper now decided to continue her own education. She studied at the Guilde Internationale in Paris, during the summers of 1911-13 and at Columbia

University in the summers of 1914-17. After completing her dissertation she earned her Ph.D. degree from the Sorbonne in Paris in 1925. To achieve this feat, she had to overcome not only the disadvantages of her gender and her race but also those of her age (she was in her mid-sixties), as well as the necessity of raising two foster children since her forties and her half brother's five orphaned grandchildren since her late fifties.

In 1930 she became president of Frelinghuysen University in Washington, D.C., a group of schools offering evening classes in academic, religious, and trade programs for blacks. After economic and accrediting problems caused the university to lose its charter in 1937, a few years later it became the Frelinghuysen Group of Schools for Colored Working People, of which Cooper served as registrar till 1950.

The principal event of Cooper's later years was her private publication in 1951 of a book on the lives and writings of the prominent African-American Grimké, family. The Grimkés, with whom Cooper was closely associated in her early years, included the Reverend Francis James Grimké,, a former slave and a graduate of Princeton Theological Seminary; his wife, Charlotte, a teacher and activist; and Archibald Grimké,, Francis's brother, a former slave and a graduate of Harvard Law School.

Writer on Gender and Race Issues

Cooper's earliest writings, mainly essays and papers, were collected into the book *A Voice from the South* (1892), illustrating her dual roles as feminist and black advocate.

Calling for the intellectual development of women, she wrote that through education a woman's "horizon is extended. Her sympathies are broadened and deepened and multiplied. She is in closer touch with nature. Not a bud that opens, not a dew drop, not a ray of light, not a cloud-burst or a thunderbolt, but adds to the expansiveness and zest of her soul!"[2]

Men, too, would benefit from women's development. "The cause of freedom," Cooper believed, "is not the cause of a race or a sect, a party or a class—it is the cause of human kind, the very birthright of humanity. . . . It would be subversive of every human interest that the cry of one-half of the human family be stifled."[3]

In *A Voice from the South*, Cooper attacked white America with brutal frankness, deploring "laws. . . in certain states requiring persons known to be colored to ride in one car, and persons supposed to be white in another."[4] Praising Canadians' politeness to black women, she felt "shame" and "mortification" that white Americans "offered such an unfavorable contrast."[5] She identified white America within a larger framework of Western civilizations that she often characterized as "barbarian."

Her principal work was *L'attitude de la France à l'égard de l'esclavage pendant la Révolution* (1925), her doctoral dissertation, translated by Frances Richardson Keller as *Slavery and the French Revolutionists* (1788-1805) (1988). Though labeled as a study of French racial attitudes, it covers a wide geographical and historical range and examines the topic from the slaves' point of view as well. Her opening words instantly establish the angry tone of the work: "Slavery in the European colonies of the Americas was an institution based solely upon an abuse of force. Created by a short-sighted and barbarous policy and maintained by violence, . . . it could be quickly abolished by a simple legislative measure when the people whom it dishonored realized that they could no longer violate moral law."[6]

Anna Julia Haywood Cooper, long a living legend, died in Washington, D.C., on February 27, 1964, at the age of 105. She was buried in Raleigh next to her husband, whom she had outlived by eighty-five years.

Fanny Jackson Coppin
FIRST BLACK WOMAN PRINCIPAL

(1837—1913)

WHEN SHE WAS NAMED principal of the Institute for Colored Youth in Philadelphia, in 1869, Fanny Jackson (later Coppin) became the first black woman to head an institution of higher learning in America. She also contributed to the black community as a church official, a political activist, and a missionary to Africa.

Fanny Jackson was born a slave in Washington, D.C., in 1837, the daughter of a slave named Lucy (Orr) Jackson, and an unknown father who may have been white. When she was a young child, her freedom was purchased by an aunt, Sarah Orr. Fanny then lived with relatives in New Bedford, Massachusetts, and Newport, Rhode Island. In Newport she worked as a domestic for George Henry Calvert, great-grandson of Lord Baltimore, the founder of Maryland. Calvert's wife, Mary, was descended from Mary, Queen of Scots.

Early in life Fanny understood the value of education. During her six years of employment with the Calverts, she studied with a private tutor and then attended the local segregated public schools. After further study at Rhode Island State Normal School in Bristol, Fanny traveled to Ohio and enrolled in the Ladies Department of Oberlin College, where she graduated in 1865 with an A.B. degree, only the second African-American woman to do so.

Innovative Educator

While attending Oberlin, Fanny was chosen as a student teacher of the preparatory department at the school, the first African-American to receive this honor. She also opened an evening school for former slaves. Because of her academic record at Oberlin and her successful evening school, she became well known in black communities throughout the United States.

Fanny's growing reputation resulted in her obtaining a good job soon after leaving Oberlin in 1865. She was appointed principal of the female high school department at the Institute for Colored Youth in Philadelphia, founded by the Society of Friends in 1837. Besides the girls' department, the institute had a preparatory department, a boys' high school department, and a teacher training course. In 1869 she was promoted to principal of the entire institute, at that time the highest educational position held by any black woman in the United States.

"A brilliant teacher and a daring innovator in black education," wrote Linda M. Perkins in *Black Women in America*, "Fanny Jackson Coppin advocated vocational training many years before Booker T. Washington while maintaining, as he did not, a firm commitment to the importance of liberal arts in black education."[1] In 1889, under her leadership, the institute opened an industrial department, which offered training in such occupations as bricklaying, carpentry, cooking, dressmaking, plastering, printing, and shoemaking. It was the first trade school for African-Americans in Philadelphia.

The institute was located near the historic Mother Bethel African Methodist Episcopal (AME) Church. In 1881 she married Levi Jenkins Coppin, an AME minister who pastored a church in Baltimore during their first three years of marriage, transferred to a Philadelphia church in 1884, edited the *AME Review* from 1888 to 1896, and then served as pastor of Mother Bethel till 1900.

The Schomburg Center / NYPL

FANNY JACKSON COPPIN

spoke at political rallies, served as a vice president of the National Association of Colored Women, and was a member of the board of managers for the Home for Aged and Infirmed Colored People in Philadelphia.

In 1896 she became ill with pleurisy and never fully recovered, though she remained principal of the Institute for Colored Youth till June 1902.

Missionary in South Africa

After her retirement Coppin went with her husband to South Africa, where he was to serve as bishop of the Fourteenth Episcopal District in Cape Town. The couple arrived in December 1902, and while there, Fanny developed missions among the women of the country. In gratitude, the African missions built the Fanny Jackson Coppin Girls Hall in her honor.

In December 1903 Coppin and her husband left South Africa, making some stops in Europe before returning to the United States in the spring of 1904.

When Levi Coppin was appointed bishop of the Seventh Episcopal District of the AME church, Fanny went with him to South Carolina, part of his district, but when her health declined further, she returned to Philadelphia. By 1905 she was so weak that for the rest of her life she rarely left her home. In her last years she prepared her autobiography, *Reminiscences of School Life, and Hints on Teaching* (1913).

Fanny Jackson Coppin died at her home in Philadelphia on January 21, 1913. Coppin State College in Baltimore is named for her.

Prior to leaving for Cape Town in 1902, Coppin said at a testimonial dinner in her honor that she had realized her life's dream: "to get an education and to teach my people."[2]

Fanny Jackson Coppin joined the AME church after her marriage, presiding over the local Women's Mite Missionary and later serving as national president of the Women's Home and Foreign Missionary Society of the AME Church. In 1888 she represented the church at the Centenary of Missions Conference in London.

While engaged in her profession and her church work, Coppin also found time to be a political activist. She supported the woman suffrage, often

Ellen Craft

RUNNER FOR FREEDOM

(1826—1891)

ALONG WITH HER HUSBAND, William Craft, Ellen Craft is known for having made what was probably the most dramatic escape from slavery ever recorded, told by William in his book *Running a Thousand Miles for Freedom* (1860). Ellen later became an active abolitionist and a school founder.

She was born in Clinton, Georgia, in 1826, the daughter of Major James Smith, a cotton planter, and his house slave, Maria. When Ellen was eleven, Smith gave her to Eliza, his daughter, as a wedding gift. Ellen moved to her new mistress's home in Macon, Georgia, where she met William Craft, a fellow slave.

The couple planned to marry, but Ellen wanted to wait till after they were free so that her children would not be born into slavery. Being separated from her own mother at an early age had a lasting effect on her. "She had seen," William later wrote, "so many other children separated from their parents in this cruel manner, that the mere thought of her ever becoming the mother of a child, to linger out a miserable existence under the wretched system of American slavery, appeared to fill her very soul with horror."[1] However, when a good plan of escape did not soon materialize and when their owners gave them permission to wed, they married in 1846.

The Great Escape

By 1848 the Crafts had designed a plan of escape. Since the distance from Georgia to northern freedom was too great to walk, they had to devise a subterfuge by which they could use public transportation. Ellen would pose as a young male slave owner who was trav-eling to Philadelphia for medical reasons with William as a slave valet. Ellen could pass for white because she was a quadroon, but she had to play a man because a white woman would not travel alone with a male slave. To cover her lack of a beard, she wrapped her face in handkerchiefs under the pretense of being sickly. She also cut her hair short, wore men's clothing, and covered her eyes with dark glasses. Finally, being illiterate at that time, she put her writing arm in a cast so that she would not be expected to sign in at hotels.

In December 1848 Ellen and William put their plan into action. It nearly failed right at the very beginning, when she boarded a train in Georgia and found herself sitting next to an old white man who knew her well. Turning her head away from him, she pretended to be deaf, and, when necessary, responded to his ever louder talk with a single word to avoid his recognizing her voice.

The Crafts successfully traveled through the slave states of Georgia, South Carolina, North Carolina, Virginia, and Maryland, reaching Philadelphia after eight days on Christmas Day of 1848.

Freedom—Temporarily

In Philadelphia the Crafts were aided by free blacks and white Quakers. The Barkley Ivens family, Quakers, took them in for a few weeks while they recuperated from their journey, and during this time Ellen and William also received tutoring in reading and writing.

The Crafts then moved to Boston, Massachusetts, where they stayed for two years, aided by abolitionists such as William Lloyd Garrison and William

Welles Brown, who arranged appearances for them. Meanwhile, Ellen established herself as a seamstress and studied with an upholsterer.

However, in 1850 the Crafts' new life was threatened by the passage of the Fugitive Slave Law, under which their former owners sent two slave catchers with warrants to arrest the Crafts and return them to slavery. Abolitionists sheltered the couple and helped them to get out of Boston, but before leaving the city on November 7, 1850, Ellen and William were married for a second time. Theodore Parker, the well-known abolitionist and Unitarian clergyman, performed the ceremony.

The Crafts then traveled by land to Canada, and in Halifax boarded a steamer bound for Liverpool, England.

Years in England

For six months after Ellen and William Craft arrived in England in December 1850, they toured England and Scotland with William Welles Brown to publicize the antislavery cause.

The Crafts then improved their literacy by studying at the Ockham School, a trade school for rural youth, near Ripley, Surrey. In return, they taught English students manual skills.

Ellen Craft gave birth to five children in England—Charles, Brougham, William, Ellen, and Alfred—thus fulfilling her early wish not to deliver any children into slavery.

In about 1852 the Crafts settled in London and became active on the antislavery lecture circuit and on the executive committee of the London Emancipation Committee. In 1860 William published their story as *Running a Thousand Miles for Freedom*, and during the Civil War he worked to undermine British support for the Confederacy. Ellen continued as a seamstress, raised funds for newly freed slaves, and helped to establish a school for girls in Sierra Leone.

Return to America

In 1869, four years after the end of the Civil War and the emancipation of all slaves, the Crafts returned to

ELLEN CRAFT.

Ellen Craft

The Schomburg Center / NYPL

the United States. After working for a time in Boston, they bought Woodville plantation in Ways Station near Savannah, Georgia, where they grew rice and cotton. Ellen also ran a school for local children, but the Crafts faced opposition from local white farmers and had difficulty in raising capital.

By the time Ellen died in 1891, the school had been closed for some time and the plantation was barely surviving. At her request she was buried near an oak tree on the plantation.

The Crafts' "escape dramatized the moral turpitude of American slavery, and their attempted recapture heightened sectional conflict in the years before the Civil War."[2] In an 1852 article in the *Boston Liberator*, an abolitionist newspaper, Ellen Craft wrote that she would "much rather starve in England, a free woman, than be a slave for the best man that ever breathed upon the American continent."[3]

Dorothy Dandridge

FIRST BLACK NOMINATED FOR BEST ACTRESS ACADEMY AWARD

(1922—1965)

ONE OF THE MOST accomplished actresses of her time, Dorothy Dandridge set a high on-screen standard for the African-American female film stars who followed her. Though Hollywood restricted her to playing stereotypes, she rose above her material and forced critics and audiences to take black actresses seriously. She was the first black to be nominated for an Academy Award as best actress.

Dorothy Jean Dandridge was born in Cleveland, Ohio, on November 9, 1922. Her father, Cyril Dandridge, was a cabinetmaker and minister. Her mother, Ruby Jean (Butler) Dandridge, was an aspiring entertainer. The parents separated at about the time of Dorothy's birth.

The Wonder Kids

Left with two girls to raise, Ruby turned to the field she knew best—entertainment. She formed, and wrote the material for, an act called the Wonder Kids, consisting of Dorothy and her older sister, Vivian. The girls toured the country, singing, dancing, and performing comedy skits at schools, churches, and social gatherings.

In the early 1930s the family settled in Los Angeles, where Ruby began to find work as an entertainer, eventually performing on radio and television as well as in films, including *Cabin in the Sky* (1943), *My Wild Irish Rose* (1947), and *Hole in the Head* (1959). Meanwhile, her daughters, while enrolled in school, also continued their careers. With another girl, Etta Jones, they became the three Dandridge Sisters, and appeared briefly in several films, including the Marx

Brothers movie *A Day at the Races* (1937). When Dorothy was sixteen, the girls traveled to New York City to perform at the famed Cotton Club, often on the same bill with Cab Calloway and Bill ("Bojangles") Robinson. Shortly after working in the film *Irene* (1940) the trio split up.

Aspiring Actress

Early in her solo career Dorothy Dandridge appeared in more than a dozen short musical films, notably as the dream girl of the Mills Brothers singing group in *Paper Doll* (1942). She also played bit parts in feature movies, such as *Sun Valley Serenade* (1941), *Drums of the Congo* (1942), *Lucky Jordan* (1942), and *Hit Parade of 1943* (1943).

In 1942 she married the dancer Harold Nicholas, whom she had met at the Cotton Club several years earlier. The marriage ended in divorce, and the couple's severely brain-damaged daughter, Harolyn, was eventually put into a private institution. In later years Dandridge said that it was her daughter's condition that motivated her to strive for success.

She had long aspired to be a film actress, and after the breakup of her marriage, she devoted herself to fulfilling that dream. To support herself and to make contacts, she first established herself as a nightclub singer, appearing at important clubs throughout the country. In 1951, for example, she performed with Desi Arnaz's band, and in 1952 her performances saved the New York City nightclub La Vie en Rose from bankruptcy.

DOROTHY DANDRIDGE

Breaking the Mold

Meanwhile she took acting lessons and auditioned for roles. Up to that time most black women in films, such as Hattie McDaniel*, had to play menial roles, especially servants. Dandridge wanted to break that mold.

A couple of low-budget films, *The Harlem Globetrotters* (1951) and *Tarzan's Peril* (1951), gave her good exposure. But her major breakthrough came when she was cast opposite Harry Belafonte in *Bright Road* (1953), in which she made a strong impression playing a southern schoolteacher.

Soon afterward she won the coveted title role in Otto Preminger's *Carmen Jones* (1954), an all-black adaptation of Georges Bizet's opera *Carmen*. Standing out in an all-star cast that included Harry Belafonte, Pearl Bailey*, Diahann Carroll*, and Brock Peters, she was brilliant as the self-destructive coquette. *Life* magazine put her on its cover. Major news magazines ran stories on her, among them *Newsweek*, which praised her performances as Carmen and as the teacher in *Bright Road*: "The range between the two parts suggests that she is one of the outstanding dramatic actresses of the screen."[1] Dandridge's performance in *Carmen Jones* won her an Academy Award nomination, the first time that a black woman had been nominated for an Oscar in a leading role (Hattie McDaniel had won an Oscar for her supporting role in the 1939 film *Gone with the Wind*).

Incredibly, though, her career stalled. "I was to reach a high and also the beginnings of a decline inevitable for a Negro actress for whom there was no place else to go," she wrote in her autobiography (with Earl Conrad), *Everything and Nothing: The Dorothy Dandridge Tragedy* (1970), "no higher or better role to play, no new story available, no chance to play roles meant for white only."[2] She continued to work in nightclubs, but it was three years before she made another film.

A New Stereotype

Hollywood did not know what to do with Dandridge. She was a major leading lady, but since very few black leading men were available with whom to team her, inevitably, she had to be cast opposite white actors. Filmmakers, however, handled her on-screen relationships with whites timidly, fearing the reaction of audiences.

Having earlier broken the servant mold in movies, Dandridge now faced the beginning of a new film stereotype—the black temptress. *Island in the Sun* (1957), *The Decks Ran Red* (1958), *Tamango* (Italian-French, 1958), and *Malaga* (British, 1960) dealt with interracial romances, but awkwardly. Her white "lovers" were not allowed to kiss her on screen.

One of her most important later roles was as Bess in Preminger's film version of George Gershwin's folk opera *Porgy and Bess* (1959). Again she was asked to play the temptress, but this time she tempted black men instead of white. Many felt that the film was insulting to black people, but Dandridge's dignified performance lifted her above criticism. She won the Golden Globe Award for best actress in a musical film.

In that same year, 1959, she married the white nightclub owner Jack Denison. However, in 1962 they divorced, and shortly thereafter she filed for bankruptcy. She could no longer afford the private institution for her daughter, who, after a brief and disastrous stay with Dandridge, was transferred to a state facility.

New Successes

By 1965 Dandridge's career was on the upswing again. She enjoyed a successful engagement at a New Mexico nightclub, was scheduled to open at the Basin Street East in New York City, was hired to make an American western film and two movies for a Mexican producer, and was finishing her autobiography, for which she had already found a publisher.

However, before she could take advantage of these new opportunities, she was found dead in her Hollywood apartment on September 4, 1965. She had died from an overdose of an antidepressant drug.

Dorothy Dandridge made historic contributions to her profession and her race despite being stereotyped and having only a small number of significant roles. She blazed a new path by showing that black women could handle starring roles in white-dominated films. By the end of her short life "Dorothy Dandridge had brought the black actress in films from behind the shadows and had emerged as Hollywood's first authentic movie goddess of color."[3]

Selected performances:

FILMS

The Big Broadcast of 1936 (Dandridge Sisters, 1935)
A Day at the Races (Dandridge Sisters, 1937)
It Can't Last Forever (Dandridge Sisters, 1937)
Going Places (Dandridge Sisters, 1939)
Irene (Dandridge Sisters, 1940)
Four Shall Die (or *Condemned Men*, 1941)
Bahama Passage (1941)
Lady from Louisiana (1941)
Sun Valley Serenade (1941)
Sundown (1941)
Easy Street (short, 1941)
Drums of the Congo (1942)
Lucky Jordan (1942)
Paper Doll (short, 1942)
Hit Parade of 1943 (1943)
Atlantic City (1944)
Since You Went Away (1944)
Pillow to Post (1945)
The Harlem Globetrotters (1951)
Tarzan's Peril (1951)
Bright Road (1953)
Remains to Be Seen (1953)
Carmen Jones (1954)
Island in the Sun (1957)
The Decks Ran Red (1958)
Porgy and Bess (1959)
Tamango (Italian-French, 1958 in Europe, 1959 in the United States)
Malaga (British, 1960 in Europe, 1962 in the United States)

Ruby Dee

ACTRESS OF ARTISTIC AND SOCIAL COMMITMENT

(1924–   )

STAR OF STAGE, SCREEN, radio, and television, Ruby Dee has become one of the most distinguished actresses of her time, respected and admired by both audiences and fellow actors. Often working with her husband, Ossie Davis (whom she married in 1948), she has sustained at the highest level a remarkably long career noted for its artistic integrity and social consciousness.

Originally named Ruby Ann Wallace, she was born in Cleveland, Ohio, on October 27, probably in 1924, one of four children (three daughters and one son) of Marshall Edward Wallace, a railroad porter and waiter, and Emma (Benson) Wallace, a schoolteacher.

When Ruby was a baby, the family moved to New York City and settled in Harlem. Her mother insisted that the children study music and literature instead of watching movies or listening to the radio. In the evenings family members read poetry aloud to one another, a practice that gave Ruby a head start in her later career as an entertainer. She was painfully shy as a youngster, but as she later admitted, "I had wild feelings churning inside me I wanted to express."[1] As a student at Hunter High School in New York City, she decided to become a professional actress after her reading of a play won her classmates' applause. Her mother supported the decision but urged her to become a "serious" actress.

After graduating from high school she took the stage name Ruby Dee and pursued two careers in New York City simultaneously: She enrolled at Hunter College, where she studied Romance languages; and she became an apprentice at the American Negro Theatre, where she studied acting from 1941 to 1944 and appeared in several plays, such as *Natural Man* (1941) and *Walk Hard* (1944).

Stage Actress

In December 1943, while still a student, Ruby Dee made her Broadway debut with a walk-on part as a native girl in a World War II drama called *South Pacific* (not the later Rodgers and Hammerstein musical hit of the same name). During her student years she also appeared in some radio plays and occasionally worked at odd jobs. After graduating from Hunter College with a B.A. degree in 1945, she used her knowledge of French and Spanish on a brief job as a translator for an import business.

In February 1946 Dee returned to Broadway, making a favorable impression in her substantial role of Libby George in *Jeb*. The play starred Ossie Davis as a black war hero facing trials and frustrations on his return home from World War II.

In June 1946 Dee took over the title role in the all-black Broadway production of *Anna Lucasta* (which had been running since August 1944), about a streetwalker redeemed by true love. She also starred with Ossie Davis in a national tour of the play. Later they costarred in *The Smile of the World* (1949).

During a break in rehearsals for *The Smile of the World*, Dee and Davis were married in December 1948. They had three children: Nora, LaVerne, and Guy.

In 1952 Dee appeared on the off-Broadway stage in her husband's one-act play *Alice in Wonder*. In 1953, through Jewish friends she had met while protesting the prosecution of Julius and Ethel Rosenberg for treason, Dee played the Defending Angel in *Bontche Schweig*, one of the three short plays making up *The World of Sholom Aleichem*. She credited that production with raising her consciousness about the power of theater and the universality of oppression.

During the 1950s she continued to hone her craft through further studies, including sessions at the Actors Workshop. From 1958 to 1960 she was coached by the famed Jewish actor Morris Carnovsky.

One of the highlights of Dee's stage career was her Broadway performance in Lorraine Hansberry's* prize-winning play *A Raisin in the Sun* from March 1959 to June 1960. As the patient, long-suffering Ruth Younger, a young wife and daughter-in-law in a black family struggling to rise above their circumstances in a Chicago tenement, she was universally acclaimed by reviewers.

Dee has named her role in *Purlie Victorious* (1961), written by Ossie Davis, as one of her favorites. A satire on southern black-white relationships, the play featured Dee as Lutiebelle Gussie Mae Jenkins, who helps the preacher Purlie, played by Davis, to outwit a white plantation owner.

In 1965 Dee became the first black actress to appear in major roles at the American Shakespeare Festival in Stratford, Connecticut, playing Cordelia in *King Lear* and Kate in *The Taming of the Shrew*. In Ypsilanti, Michigan, the following year she continued to draw on the classical repertory by performing in ancient Greek plays, including Aristophanes' *The Birds*, in which she played Iris. That same year she appeared in Ann Arbor, Michigan, as Julia Augustine in the modern play *Wedding Band*, which focuses on an interracial love affair.

In 1970 Dee gave one of her most powerful performances in the New York City production of *Boesman and Lena*, about South African people of mixed race, who are rejected by both blacks and whites. She played Lena, who struggles to earn a living while trying to coexist with her brutish husband. In this role Dee believed she finally put an end to her stereotyped image as "the Negro June Allyson."[2] For her portrayal of Lena, Dee won both the Obie Award and the Drama Desk Award in 1971.

At the New York Shakespeare Festival of 1972, she repeated her role as Julia Augustine in *Wedding Band*, winning another Drama Desk Award in 1973.

Dee's later theatrical roles included Gertrude in *Hamlet* (1975); the lead in the musical *Twin-Bit Gardens* (also known as *Take It from the Top*, 1979), which she also wrote and directed; and Amanda in *The Glass Menagerie* (1989). In 1988 she was inducted into the Theatre Hall of Fame.

In 1995 she and Davis starred together in *Two Hah Hahs and a Homeboy*, a two-act dramatic piece compiled by Dee. The work paid homage to the African-American writer Zora Neale Hurston* and presented an updated approach to black folktales.

In 1998 Dee starred in the one-person show *My One Good Nerve: A Visit with Ruby Dee*. Based on passages from her 1987 book of the same name, the show featured poetry, comedy, and reminiscences.

Motion Picture Career

Dee made her film debut in *The Jackie Robinson Story* (1950) as the baseball hero's wife. Over the next two decades she earned a reputation as a highly skilled actress in such movies as *Edge of the City* (1957), as Sidney Poitier's wife in a waterfront drama; *Take a Giant Step* (1959), as a compassionate family maid who comforts a black teenager; *A Raisin in the Sun* (1961), a film version of the play; *Gone Are the Days* (1963), a film version of the play *Purlie Victorious* under which title the film was rereleased in 1964); *The Balcony* (1963), as a prostitute; *The Incident* (1967), as a New York City subway passenger terrorized by hoodlums; *Uptight* (1968), which she coscripted, as a young mother on welfare who supplements her income by streetwalking; and *Black Girl* (1972), as Netta's mother.

Frustrated by her limited opportunities in motion pictures, however, Dee performed in hardly any films from 1973 through 1988. She returned to films costarring with Ossie Davis in Spike Lee's *Do the Right Thing* (1989), as an accomplished actress whose career is unfulfilled in white America. For her role in this film she won the National Association for the Advancement of Colored People (NAACP) Image Award for best performance by an actress in 1989. Her later pictures include *Jungle Fever* (1991) and *Just Cause* (1995).

Radio and Television Performer

In 1955 Dee played the nonblack title role in the daytime radio serial *This Is Nora Drake*. During the early stage of her hiatus from films, she teamed up with her husband on the radio series *The Ossie Davis and Ruby Dee Story Hour* (1974–75).

Dee made her television debut in 1960 when she appeared in "Actor's Choice" on the *Camera Three* anthology series. Since then she has appeared on the small screen in a wide variety of programs, guest-starring on such drama series as *The Fugitive* (1963), *The Defenders* (1965), and *Police Woman* (1975). For her role in an episode of *East Side, West Side* (1964), she received an Emmy nomination for best actress. She appeared in the "Slavery" segment of the documentary series *The History of the Negro People* (1965), starred in Lorraine Hansberry's "To Be Young, Gifted, and Black" on *NET Playhouse* (1972), and played the narrator and Zora Neale Hurston in "Zora Is My Name!" on *American Playhouse* (1990).

Dee also had some recurring roles in television series, such as Martha Frazier in *The Guiding Light* (1967). In the role of Alma Miles she became the first black actress featured in the popular serial *Peyton Place* (1968–69). Later Dee and her husband starred in their own series, *With Ossie and Ruby* (1981–82), and in 1992 she played Estelle Williams, the cleaning lady on the short-lived sitcom *Middle Ages*.

She has appeared in many television movies and miniseries, beginning with *Deadlock* (1969). In 1983 she played Mary Tyrone in an all-black television production of Eugene O'Neill's *Long Day's Journey into Night*, for which she received the ACE Award. In 1991 she won an Emmy for her supporting-actress role as an irascible housekeeper in *Decoration Day* (1990), a Hallmark Hall of Fame production. Other highlights of her television movie and miniseries career include *Roots: The Next Generations* (1979), *I Know Why the Caged Bird Sings* (1979), *Gore Vidal's Lincoln* (1988), and *Stephen King's The Stand* (1994).

Social Activist

Dee has devoted much of her private and professional life to helping others. She has aided the cause of racial equality by serving on national committees and raising money for the legal defense of civil rights work-

RUBY DEE

Ruby Dee, Emmalyn Enterprises, Inc.

ers arrested in demonstrations. Among the organizations with which she has been associated are various AIDS groups, the Congress of Racial Equality, the NAACP, the Southern Christian Leadership Conference, the Student Nonviolent Coordinating Committee, and the Urban League. She established the Ruby Dee Scholarship in Dramatic Art to help talented young black women enter the acting profession. Her other activities have included making records for the blind, raising money to fight drug addiction, and speaking out against the Vietnam War.

Dee has also expressed her thoughts through her writings. Besides contributing articles and columns to newspapers and magazines, she has written scripts, including the musical play *Twin-Bit Gardens;* the book *My One Good Nerve* (1987), a collection of stories and poems; and juvenile books, such as *Two Ways to Count to Ten* (1988), for which she won the 1989 Literary Guild Award.

Dee's husband, Ossie Davis, shares her artistic goals and political sensibilities. As a team the couple gave recitations while touring the United States in *A Treasury of Negro World Writing* (1964); recorded *The Poetry of Langston Hughes* (1969); founded the Institute of New Cinema Artists, where youths are trained for jobs in films and television, and the Recording Industry Training Program, where disadvantaged young people are prepared for careers in music; and lent their support to such civil rights leaders as Martin Luther King, Jr., Malcolm X, and Bayard Rustin. After half a century of living and working together, Dee and Davis have neither altered nor slowed down their energetic approach to art and social struggle.

While the nature of the civil rights movement has changed through the years, Dee's commitment and concern have not lessened. Whereas earlier objectives, such as voting rights, were clear and specific, she says, today's goals, such as economic structure and social order, are larger and more generalized. She worries about a consequent loss of vigilance in new generations. "We're forgetting how to fight," she says; "we're forgetting how to protest."[3]

Both artistically and socially, Dee has never forgotten how to fight and protest, and she has received many honors and awards for her achievements in these areas. In 1970 the New York Urban League presented Dee and Davis with the Frederick Douglass Award for bringing "a sense of fervor and pride to countless millions." In 1972 she received the Operation PUSH Martin Luther King, Jr., Award. In 1975 Actors Equity gave Dee and Davis the Paul Robeson Citation "for outstanding creative contributions both in the performing arts and in society at large." In 1995 President Clinton presented Ruby Dee with the prestigious National Medal of Arts.

Selected performances:

STAGE

Natural Man (1941)
Starlight (1942)
Three's a Family (1943)
South Pacific (1943)
Walk Hard (1944)

Jeb (1946)
Anna Lucasta (1946)
A Long Way from Home (1948)
The Washington Years (1948)
The Smile of the World (1949)
Alice in Wonder (1952)
The World of Sholom Aleichem (1953)
A Raisin in the Sun (1959)
Purlie Victorious (1961)
A Treasury of Negro World Writing (1964)
King Lear (1965)
The Taming of the Shrew (1965)
The Talking Skull (1965)
Wedding Band (1966)
Agamemnon (1966)
The Birds (1966)
Oresteia (1966)
Boesman and Lena (1970)
The Imaginary Invalid (1971)
Wedding Band (1972)
Hamlet (1975)
Twin-Bit Gardens (or *Take It from the Top* (1979)
Checkmates (1988)
The Glass Menagerie (1989)
Two Hah Hahs and a Homeboy (1995)
My One Good Nerve: A Visit with Ruby Dee (1998)

FILMS

The Jackie Robinson Story (1950)
No Way Out (1950)
The Tall Target (1951)
Go, Man, Go! (1954)
Edge of the City (or *A Man Is Ten Feet Tall*, 1957)
St. Louis Blues (1958)
Take a Giant Step (1959)
Virgin Island (1960)
A Raisin in the Sun (1961)
The Balcony (1963)
Gone Are the Days (or *The Man from C.O.T.T.O.N.*, 1963)
The Incident (1967)
Uptight (1968)
Black Girl (1972)
Buck and the Preacher (1972)
Countdown at Kusini (Nigeria, 1976)
Cat People (1982)
Do the Right Thing (1989)
Love at Large (1990)
Jungle Fever (1991)

Color Adjustment (narrator, 1992)
Cop and a Half (1993)
Just Cause (1995)

RADIO

This Is Nora Drake (1955)
The Ossie Davis and Ruby Dee Story Hour (1974–75)

TELEVISION MOVIES

Deadlock (1969); *The Sheriff* (1971)
It's Good to Be Alive (1974)
I Know Why the Caged Bird Sings (1979)
Roots: The Next Generations (1979)
All God's Children (1980)
Long Day's Journey into Night (1983)
The Atlanta Child Murders (1985)
Windmills of the Gods (1988)
Gore Vidal's Lincoln (1988)
Decoration Day (1990)
The Court-Martial of Jackie Robinson (1990)
The Ernest Green Story (1993)
Stephen King's The Stand (1994)
Tuesday Morning Ride (1995)

TELEVISION SERIES

The Guiding Light (1967)
Peyton Place (1968–69)
Watch Your Mouth (1978)
With Ossie and Ruby (1981–82)
Middle Ages (1992)

Selected writings:

FICTION

Twin-Bit Gardens (or *Take It from the Top*, musical
   play, 1979)
My One Good Nerve (stories and poetry, 1987)

JUVENILE FICTION

Two Ways to Count to Ten (reteller, 1988)
The Tower to Heaven (reteller, 1991)

Sarah Mapps Douglass
EDUCATOR AND ABOLITIONIST

(1806—1882)

SARAH MAPPS DOUGLASS was an outstanding representative of a special group of nineteenth-century African-Americans: those who were born to relative privilege but who were willing to forgo the comfortable life, risk censure, and dedicate themselves to helping their people. She became one of the most important black educators and activists for racial equality of her time.

Born into a prominent family of free blacks in Philadelphia in 1806, Sarah Mapps Douglass was the daughter of Robert Douglass and Grace (Bustill) Douglass. Sarah's maternal grandfather, a Quaker named Cyrus Bustill, owned a bakery, operated a school, and was an early member of the Free African Society, the first black benevolent organization. Her mother ran a millinery store next to the Bustill family bakery.

During Sarah's youth, females rarely received thorough educations. Few black women obtained schooling at the secondary level, and all women were denied admission to college. Douglass, however, received private tutoring for several years and later attended a school that her mother had founded along with the wealthy black shipbuilder James Forten. As a result Douglass received an exceptionally good education.

Educating Black Youth

She soon set out to share that education with the rest of the African-American community. In the 1820s she established a Philadelphia school for black children. The school was self-supporting for many years but eventually ran into funding difficulties. In 1838 the Philadelphia Female Anti-Slavery Society, which

her mother had helped to found in 1833, took over financial control of the school.

In 1853 Douglass was appointed head of the girls' primary department at the newly opened Institute of Colored Youth in Philadelphia. The institute was a Quaker-supported training school for public teachers. She set high scholastic standards for her students, many of whom achieved academic recognition and went on to become teachers themselves, thus spreading education to an ever larger number of black youth. Douglass retired from teaching in 1877.

Fighting Racism

When she was a teenager, she joined her mother's abolitionist organization, the Philadelphia Female Anti-Slavery Society. By 1838 Sarah Mapps Douglass had already served the society as a member of the board of directors, as a member of the education committee, as librarian, and as corresponding secretary. Through the society she developed friendships with other members, notably the white abolitionists Sarah and Angelina Grimké, who were the daughters of a South Carolina slave-owner.

Douglass and the Grimkés, not satisfied to battle only slavery, wanted to eliminate racial inequality of all kinds. They found prejudice even in the peaceful Quaker sect, to which the Grimkés, like Douglass and her maternal forebears, belonged. Quaker meeting-houses had segregated seating, with black members being placed under stairs or in a corner and guarded so that the races would not mix.

When the Grimkés and other white Quakers sought to end this segregation, Douglass helped. She supplied Sarah Grimké with information that the latter used in her 1837 written statement entitled "The Subject of Prejudice against Color amongst the Society of Friends in the United States."

In December 1837 Douglass sent a letter to William Basset of Lynn, Massachusetts, who was gathering information with which to convince his fellow New England Quakers to join the antislavery movement. In her letter to him she described her experiences in Philadelphia under the Arch Street Meeting's segregated seating practices. She confessed that "even when a child my soul was made sad with hearing five or six times during the course of one meeting this language of remonstrance addressed to those who were willing to sit by us. 'This bench is for the black people.'. . . And oftentimes I wept, at other times I felt indignant."[1]

In 1838 Douglass and her mother attended the wedding of Angelina Grimké and Theodore Weld, a prominent abolitionist. The Philadelphia press, expressing outrage at blacks socially mingling with whites, called the occasion an intolerable incident of "amalgamation" of the races.[2] Soon a mob burned down Pennsylvania Hall, the state antislavery society's newly built headquarters, and set fire to the Shelter for Colored Orphans. Douglass herself faced "various incidents of subtle and overt racial oppression and discrimination."[3] Nevertheless, firm in her convictions, she remained friendly with the Welds, whose home she frequently visited. She also continued to attend Quaker meetings, though it took decades before the sect changed its practice of segregation.

Following her conflict with the Quakers, which was the most dramatic of her career, Douglass devoted the rest of her life to working for her race in other ways as well. Through the early 1860s she participated in antislavery activities and wrote articles, contributing regularly to *The Anglo-African*, and after the Civil War she became a leader of the Woman's Pennsylvania Branch of the American Freedman's Aid Commission.

In 1855 she wedded William Douglass, rector of Saint Thomas Protestant Episcopal Church, but her married life was brief, as William died in 1861. It is not known if they were related, but because they both had the same surname, she is sometimes listed as Sarah Mapps Douglass Douglass.

She died in Philadelphia on September 8, 1882, having "lived her life according to her convictions that education would shape a better world for her race and that racism in society had to be eliminated."[4]

Rita Dove

FIRST AFRICAN-AMERICAN POET LAUREATE

(1952—)

WHEN RITA DOVE was named poet laureate of the United States in 1993, she became the first African-American and the youngest person to hold that position. She had already elevated herself to prominence in 1987 by winning the Pulitzer Prize for *Thomas and Beulah*, one of the finest books of lyric verse among contemporary American poets.

Rita Frances Dove was born in Akron, Ohio, on August 28, 1952, the second of four children of Ray and Elvira (Hord) Dove. Her father became the first black chemist at Goodyear Tire and Rubber Company, and probably in the whole tire and rubber industry. Through his drive to break barriers and achieve everything within his power, he served as a role model for Rita.

The family listened to a wide range of music. "Music was one of those first experiences I had of epiphany, of something clicking, of understanding something beyond, deeper than rational sense," Dove has said.[1] She began taking cello lessons when she was ten. Books, too, were a big part of her childhood. She spent countless hours at the local public library and even wrote some stories and plays that her classmates performed.

Becoming a Poet

In 1970 Dove was among one hundred high school seniors who were selected as Presidential Scholars, and taken for a visit to the White House. That fall she entered Miami University in Oxford, Ohio, where she majored in English. She was interested in fiction, but what fascinated her most was the word magic of

RITA DOVE

Fred Viebahn

poetry. When she revealed her intention to become a poet, however, both her parents and her teachers were incredulous.

Nevertheless, Dove pursued the rest of her education with that ambition in mind. She received a B.A.

degree from Miami University in 1973, studied as a Fulbright scholar at the University of Tübingen in West Germany during 1974–75, and then became a teaching and writing fellow in the Writers' Workshop at the University of Iowa, where she earned an M.F.A. degree in 1977.

That same year Dove published her first chapbook of verse, *Ten Poems*, followed by another chapbook, *The Only Dark Spot in the Sky* (1980); her first book-length poetry collection, *The Yellow House on the Corner* (1980), which was based on her master's thesis; and *Museum* (1983), a poetry collection inspired by her travels abroad from 1979 to 1981.

In 1981 Dove joined the faculty at Arizona State University at Tempe, where she was an assistant professor for six years and a full professor for two more years. In 1989 she became a professor at the University of Virginia at Charlottesville, where since 1993 she has held the position of Commonwealth Professor of English.

Poet Laureate

Dove's growing reputation as a poet and professor of poetry was officially acknowledged when she was named the nation's seventh poet laureate, the appointment taking effect on October 1, 1993. Her formal title was Library of Congress poet laureate consultant in poetry. The appointment was for one year, but she was asked to stay for another year, and she left the position in May 1995.

As poet laureate Dove was expected to participate in the Library of Congress's poetry and literature programs, advise the library on its literature collections and other literary matters, and draw other poets into the library's free public readings and lectures. She believed that her selection as poet laureate sent a message about the diversity of the nation's culture and literature. Consequently, during her tenure she consciously enlarged the range of poets and writers featured in the library's series of live readings. The number of people attending the readings increased dramatically.

Dove promoted poetry as an art among a wide audience, attempting to show that poets are "real people who write about real things."[2] She was particularly anxious to encourage children and teenagers to experience poetry in a positive way, as when

RITA DOVE

Fred Viebahn

she advocated the use of closed-circuit television to broadcast readings to students who would be free to ask, rather than forced to answer, questions about the poetry they heard.

Awards and Honors

Dove's best-known work is her forty-four-poem epic *Thomas and Beulah* (1986), which won her the Pulitzer Prize in 1987. Based on family stories that her mother and maternal grandmother told her, *Thomas and Beulah* narrates the story of Dove's family's migration from the rural South to the industrialized Midwest. The poet alternates descriptions of ordinary domestic scenes, such as polishing furniture, with profound events, such as a death in the family. This technique of linking everyday moments with deep human truths characterizes much of Dove's art.

Many of her poems deal with race. For example, "Crab-Boil" in *Grace Notes* (1989) recounts an experience she had in Florida in 1962, when her family was forced to stay on a beach reserved for blacks. However, not all her poems are about being black. Dove is also an avowed feminist, yet she never writes for didactic or propaganda purposes. Her aim is to write "poems about humanity" without "racial or gender partiality."[3]

Among Dove's other works are *Fifth Sunday* (1985), a collection of short stories; *The Siberian Village* (1991), a one-act play; *Through the Ivory Gate* (1992), a novel; and *The Darker Face of the Earth* (1994), a verse play in fourteen scenes. *Mother Love: Poems* (1995) is a cycle of poems relating the story of the mother and daughter Demeter and Persephone, respectively the goddess of the harvest and the goddess of spring in Greek mythology. Dove used this story as a springboard to examine modern mother-daughter relationships as well. She restricted herself to the sonnet form, whose confining nature she found appropriate. "The Demeter/Persephone cycle of betrayal and regeneration is ideally suited for the form," she wrote in her preface to the poems, "since all three— mother-goddess, daughter-consort, and poet—are struggling to sing in their chains."[4]

Besides her work as a writer, poet laureate, and educator, Dove has served as panelist (1984–86) of the National Endowment for the Arts Literature Program and chairperson (1985) of its poetry panel, as president (1986–87) and board member (1985–88) of the Associated Writing Programs, and as juror for the Pulitzer Prize and the National Book Award in poetry (both 1991). In the mid-1990s she was an associate editor of *Callaloo*; advisory editor for the *Gettysburg Review*, the *Georgia Review*, and *TriQuarterly*; and member of the Afro-American Studies Visiting Committee at Harvard University.

Among her many honors in addition to the Pulitzer Prize are two National Endowment for the Arts Creative Writing Fellowships (1978 and 1989), a National Endowment for the Humanities Portia Pittman Fellowship at Tuskegee University (1982), a Guggenheim Fellowship (1983–84), the Academy of American Poets' Lavan Younger Poet Award (1986), the Ohio Governor's Award (1988), a Mellon Fellowship (1988–89), induction into the Ohio Women's

Hall of Fame (1991), and *Glamour* magazine's Woman of the Year Award (1993). In 1993 Dove gave the first official poetry reading at the White House in over a dozen years, and the following year she won the Folger Shakespeare Library's Renaissance Forum Award, the American Academy of Achievement's Golden Plate Award, and the International Platform Association's Carl Sandburg Award. In December 1996 she received the Heinz Award, and in January 1997 President Clinton awarded her the prestigious Charles Frankel Prize for achievement in the humanities.

Dove married Fred Viebahn, a German writer, in 1979. He translated some of her poems into German, and these were published as a book in 1989. They have a daughter, Aviva Chantal Tamu Dove-Viebahn.

Music remains a major part of Dove's life. She still plays the cello, performs on the viola da gamba with the University of Virginia's Early Music Consort, and sings with the university's opera workshop.

"Poetry is language at its most distilled and most powerful," she has said. "It's like a bouillon cube: you carry it around and then it nourishes you when you need it."[5] Countless modern readers have found sustenance in the poetry of Rita Dove.

Selected writings:

FICTION

Fifth Sunday (short stories, 1985)
The Siberian Village (play, 1991)
Through the Ivory Gate (novel, 1992)
The Darker Face of the Earth (verse play, 1994)

POETRY

Ten Poems (1977)
The Only Dark Spot in the Sky (1980)
The Yellow House on the Corner (1980)
Museum (1983)
Thomas and Beulah (1986)
Grace Notes (1989)
Mother Love: Poems (1995)

Katherine Dunham

DANCING ANTHROPOLOGIST

(1909–   )

ONE OF THE MOST POPULAR and historically important dancer-choreographers of her time, Katherine Dunham led a troupe that performed Caribbean, African, and African-American movements to diverse audiences throughout the world from the 1940s to the 1960s. She had a scholarly, anthropological approach to ethnic dance. "Her concerts were visually and kinesthetically exciting and appealing; they were also based on a profound understanding of the peoples and cultures represented as well as on a keen knowledge of social values and human psychology."[1]

Katherine Dunham was born in Glen Ellyn, a suburb of Chicago, on June 22, 1909, the second of two children of Albert Millard Dunham and Fanny June (Taylor) Dunham. Fanny, of French-Canadian and Indian ancestry, died when Katherine was young. Albert, of Malagasy and West African descent, left Katherine and her brother, little Albert, with relatives in Chicago while he traveled as a salesman. It was during the time that she lived with her Aunt Lulu and Uncle Arthur, a voice coach and choral leader, that Katherine first developed her interest in the performing arts.

Her father later remarried and moved his family to Joliet, Illinois, where he ran a dry-cleaning business. Family tensions caused Katherine to cultivate her own world of imagination. During her years at Joliet High School and Joliet Junior College, she studied dance.

She then attended the University of Chicago, where she earned her way by giving dance lessons and working as an assistant librarian. While in Chicago, she studied modern dance and ballet. She also helped to found a black dance group that later became the Chicago Negro School of Ballet. Her troupe performed at the Chicago Beaux Arts Ball in 1931, and she danced a solo in a ballet based on Martinique folklore at the Chicago Civic Opera Theater in 1934.

During this early phase of her career, in 1931, she married Jordis McCoo, a dancer, but the marriage soon ended in divorce.

Dance Studies in the Caribbean

Katherine Dunham developed an interest in anthropology through a University of Chicago course she took with Robert Redfield, who introduced her to the idea of dance as a part of social and ceremonial life. She decided to make a thorough, scientific study of the forms and functions of African-based ritual dance as found in the Caribbean. With financial support from the Julius Rosenwald Foundation and a Guggenheim Award, she went to the Caribbean in 1935 and did fieldwork in Jamaica, Haiti, Trinidad, and elsewhere.

In Jamaica she visited the village of Accompong and was accepted by the local Maroons as one of the "lost peoples" of Africa. The Maroons, believing that her mission was to instruct her people in the Maroon heritage, allowed her to witness their sacred war dance. Later she wrote a book about her experiences in Jamaica, *Katherine Dunham's Journey to Accompong* (1946; revised edition, 1972).

In Haiti she soon developed a close, lifelong relationship with the people, participating in their secret rituals, performing in their public dances, and rising in their mystical culture to the highest level, seer.

Through her absorption of the spirit of Caribbean dance, Dunham became an avowed mystic. She began to believe in the power of dance to heal and transform lives.

In 1936 she graduated from the University of Chicago with a bachelor's degree in anthropology. Later she earned an M.S. degree at the same school and a Ph.D. at Northwestern University.

On the basis of her firsthand research, Dunham wrote a doctoral thesis, "Dances of Haiti" (published in Spanish in 1947, French in 1957, and English, in a revised edition, in 1983). In the ensuing years she continued to maintain contact with the academic world by giving lecture-demonstrations to anthropological societies in major cities, such as London, and at universities, including the University of Chicago. She also served as visiting professor at Case Western Reserve University in Cleveland, Ohio; artist in residence at Southern Illinois University in Carbondale; university professor and professor emerita at Southern Illinois University in Edwardsville; and visiting professor at the University of California at Berkeley.

Dunham Dance Troupe

While seriously engaged in these academic endeavors, Dunham nevertheless felt that dance was mainly for dancing, not studying. She therefore set out to convey her social convictions and cultural knowledge through dance performances.

Dunham founded a professional dance company in 1939, and over the next few years she scored major successes as both choreographer and performer in several shows, notably *Tropics* (1939) in New York City, *Cabin in the Sky* (1940–41) on Broadway and on tour throughout the United States, and *Tropical Review* (1943–44) in New York City and in another American tour.

In 1943 she founded the Katherine Dunham School of Arts and Research in New York City, where she and her staff taught dance, theater arts, literature, and world cultures. Besides members of the Dunham dance troupe, students at the school included well-known actors, such as Marlon Brando and James Dean. Some Dunham dancers, including Eartha Kitt* and Archie Savage went on to brilliant individual careers.

From the 1940s to the 1960s the troupe performed successfully throughout the world. As choreographer and performer, Dunham led her group in many programs, such as *Carib Song* (1945) in New York City; *Bal Negre* (1946–48) in New York City, on an Ameri-

can tour, in Mexico, and elsewhere; *Caribbean Rhapsody* (1950–60) on tours in Europe, Latin America, the Far East, and the Middle East; and *Bambouche* (1962–63) in New York City and on an American tour. She also choreographed and/or appeared in a number of films, including *Star-Spangled Rhythm* (1942), *Stormy Weather* (1943), *Green Mansions* (1958), and *The Bible* (1964).

During those years Dunham continued her anthropological studies. She often took members of her troupe into villages so that the dancers could become familiar not only with movements but also with cultural and social contexts of the dances.

In 1941, Dunham married John Pratt, a costume and set designer, who designed her productions till his death in 1986. The couple adopted a daughter, Marie Christine Columbier, who also became a designer.

In addition to her work in the field of dance, Dunham maintained an active literary career. She published an autobiography, *A Touch of Innocence* (1959; revised edition, 1980); coauthored a play, *Ode to Taylor Jones* (1967); issued the book *Kasamance: A Fantasy* (1974); and wrote magazine stories, sometimes under the pseudonym Kaye Dunn.

Performing Arts Training Center

Katherine Dunham's dance company performed for the last time in New York City in 1965, after which Dunham spent the next two years in Senegal representing the United States at the Festival of Black Arts in Dakar and training the National Ballet of Senegal.

She then moved to East Saint Louis, Illinois, to develop the Performing Arts Training Center of Southern Illinois University. "The need for objectives to replace crime and delinquency," she said about this project, "for disciplines for the leisure time of the young, the necessity in the face of increasing poverty to provide the essentials of human sustenance...are grave preoccupations." The center that she proposed would teach not only arts but also such subjects as languages, psychology, and anthropology. "The project presented reaches far beyond dance in the popular definition....Dance as it would serve the East Saint Louis project is concerned with the fundamentals of human society."[2]

To assist her in teaching this broad-based cultural heritage, she brought in artists and scholars from

Haiti, Brazil, Senegal, and elsewhere. The center also maintains a Children's Workshop, where youngsters learn folk arts of Africa, Latin America, and the Caribbean. The nearby Katherine Dunham Museum houses artifacts and art objects from her world travels.

The philosophy behind the Performing Arts Training Center reflected Katherine Dunham's lifelong commitment to social activism. Even as a child in grade school, she refused to sing a song that she felt was degrading to African-Americans. Throughout her career she promoted understanding and respect for African-based culture and fostered self-esteem among her black audiences and her students. She worked to end segregation in audiences and accommodations in the cities where she and her troupe performed, often working with the National Association for the Advancement of Colored People and the Urban League.

Dunham's artistry and social activism have brought her many awards and honors. The Haiti government gave her medals and citations in the 1950s and 1960s. Her book *Island Possessed* (1969) recorded her continuing relationship with the people of Haiti. She also received the *Dance Magazine* Award (1968), the University of Chicago Alumni Professional Association Achievement Award (1968), the National Center of Afro-American Artists Award (1972), the Albert Schweitzer Music Award (1979), the Kennedy Center Honor (1983), the Distinguished Service Award of the American Anthropological Society (1986), the National Medal of Arts (1989), the Capezio Dance Award (1991), and many honorary degrees.

In early 1992 Dunham fasted for forty-seven days to protest the treatment of Haitian refugees by the United States government. In 1994 she received many tributes in honor of her eighty-fifth birthday, including one at Town Hall in New York City, and an extended celebration sponsored by the Caribbean Cultural Center.

While being especially known for her anthropological approach to dancing, Katherine Dunham produced much more than just a new theory of dance and culture. She created a living, vibrant artistic legacy. "I would feel I'd failed miserably if I were doing dance confined to race, color, or creed," she explained. "I don't think that would be art, which has to do with universal truths."[3]

KATHERINE DUNHAM

The Schomburg Center / NYPL

Marian Wright Edelman

FOUNDER OF THE CHILDREN'S DEFENSE FUND

(1939–   )

AMERICA'S LEADING advocate for children's rights, Marian Wright Edelman is the founder and president of the Children's Defense Fund. Through her organization she educates the public and pressures lawmakers to improve conditions for those people with the greatest needs but the least power— children.

Named after the singer Marian Anderson*, Wright was born in Bennettsville, South Carolina, on June 6, 1939, the youngest of two daughters and three sons of Arthur Jerome Wright and Maggie Leola (Bowen) Wright. Her father, a Baptist minister, established the Wright Home for the Aged, the first such institution for blacks in South Carolina, and her mother ran it.

While growing up, Marian did exceptionally well at school, took piano and voice lessons, and became a drum majorette. After studying for two years at Spelman College in Atlanta, America's largest liberal arts college for black women, she won a scholarship to go abroad. Anticipating a career in the foreign service, she studied for one summer at the Sorbonne in Paris, attended the University of Geneva in Switzerland during the academic year, and then spent the following summer in Moscow, supported by another scholarship.

Civil Rights Activist

Returning to Spelman for her senior year, however, Mariam soon abandoned her plans to join the foreign service. Something of more immediate importance had arisen: the growing civil rights movement. During the next year she took part in the Atlanta sit-ins and spent a night in jail, and after graduating

from Spelman with a B.A. degree in 1960, she decided to study law so that she could use the law to help her people.

In 1963 Wright received an LL.B. degree from Yale and began a year of training with the National Association for the Advancement of Colored People (NAACP) in New York City. After learning how to deal with civil rights law, she went to Jackson, Mississippi, to work.

Arriving there in the summer of 1964, Wright soon found that her main task was to retrieve from jail the hordes of northern white students who had gone south to register black voters. It was during that summer that the civil rights workers James Chaney, Andrew Goodman, and Michael Schwerner were murdered in Mississippi.

Marian stayed in Mississippi for four years and became the first black woman admitted to the state bar. While working on civil rights cases, she began to realize that those rights were strongly linked to her clients' economic condition. What good would it do them to win the right to eat at a restaurant if they could not afford a meal there?

Working for the Poor

As counsel to the Child Development Group of Mississippi, Wright helped to restore federal funding of the Mississippi Head Start program. While visiting Washington, D.C., to lobby for this program, she learned firsthand that the poor, especially poor children, had no voice in the nation's capital.

During her stay in Mississippi she met Peter Edelman, a legislative assistant to Robert F. Kennedy, who had recently been elected senator from New York. She brought to Kennedy's attention the extreme poverty in Mississippi and was largely responsible for the senator's commitment to fight poverty throughout America.

In 1968 she married Peter Edelman and moved to Washington, D.C., to be near him and to begin her service as a voice for poor people on a national level. Marian Wright Edelman served as counsel to the Poor People's Campaign and established the Washington Research Project, a research and advocacy organization. During the next few years she lobbied members of Congress to expand Head Start to cover more children.

In 1971 the Edelmans moved to Boston, where Peter Edelman served as vice president of the University of Massachusetts and Marian directed the Center for Law and Education at Harvard University, as well as continuing to head the Washington Research Project. Meanwhile, growing within her was the increasing conviction that something more concrete had to be done for the huge numbers of American youngsters who felt they had no future.

Children's Defense Fund

In 1973 Marian Wright Edelman created the Children's Defense Fund (CDF) out of the Washington Research Project. A nonprofit, nonpartisan organization, the CDF acts as a voice for America's children, engages in research and public education, monitors federal agencies, assists with the drafting of legislation, and provides testimony before lawmakers.

Edelman herself keeps the issue of children's welfare before the public and the Congress with a heavy schedule of speaking and writing. She regularly talks to clubs, reporters, editorial boards, graduating classes, and other groups, citing dramatic statistics to make her point that America is neglecting its young people. According to her data, one in five children in the United States is poor—one in *two* among black children. A black baby is twice as likely as a white one to die before the age of one. Nearly a third of American children have no health insurance. Adequate day care is available to only a small percentage of mothers who need it. These statistics point to a "national tragedy."[1]

Edelman applies her speaking skills with particu-

MARIAN WRIGHT EDELMAN

Courtesy of Marian Wright Edelman

lar force when addressing members of Congress, many of whom have been known to hide at her approach. She speaks softly, but reels off her statistics and arguments at a staggering speed. Her lobbying skills are legendary, and she has won the support not only of liberals such as Senator Edward M. Kennedy of Massachusetts but also of conservatives, such as Senator Orrin G. Hatch of Utah.

Edelman helped to organize the June 1, 1996, Stand for Children rally in Washington, D.C., which attracted two hundred thousand people. The following month she showed her willingness to battle anyone in defense of children by publicly denouncing President Clinton's support for the welfare overhaul bill as making "a mockery of his pledge not to hurt children. . . . It will leave a moral blot on his presidency and on our nation that will never be forgotten."[2]

Besides making frequent contributions to professional journals, popular magazines, and newspapers, Edelman has written powerful books in behalf of children. In *Families in Peril: An Agenda for Social Change* (1987), she questioned the priorities of a world that permitted forty thousand children to die each day from hunger and disease while spending $2.7 billion each day on weapons of war. In *The Measure of Our Success: A Letter to My Children and Yours* (1992), she exhorted readers to turn away from selfish pursuits and find a way to commit themselves to helping others, especially children. Reflecting the early religious training she received from her father, she expressed her deepest personal thoughts and feelings in *Guide My Feet: Prayers and Meditations on Living and Working for Children* (1995).

Family and Future

Edelman's husband, Peter, shares her concern for America's poor and children; he served as an assistant secretary at the Department of Health and Human Services till he resigned in September 1996 in protest against the welfare reform bill signed into law in August by President Clinton. The Edelmans have three grown sons: Joshua Robert, Jonah Martin (after Martin Luther King, Jr.), and Ezra Benjamin. Since Peter is white and Jewish, the family considers itself a model for successful biracial, interfaith households. Each son has had what the family calls his "Baptist bar mitzvah."

Tolerance of diversity characterizes not only her family life but also much of her public work, including her address at the Call for Renewal rally in Washington, D.C., in September 1996. The Call for Renewal is a Christian political organization created as an alternative to the rising number of conservative Christian groups. She called for a future of charity toward others.

Indeed the call for charity toward others, especially the most defenseless members of society, has motivated Marian Wright Edelman's entire adult life. "As we face a new century and a new millennium," she has written, "the overarching challenge for America is to rebuild a sense of community and hope and civility and caring and safety for all our children."[3]

Myrlie Evers-Williams

FIRST WOMAN TO LEAD THE NAACP

(1933–   )

B EST KNOWN FOR MUCH of her life as the widow of the slain civil rights leader Medgar Evers, Myrlie Evers-Williams leaped into a prominence of her own in 1995 when she was elected the first female head of the National Association for the Advancement of Colored People (NAACP), her official title being "Chairman, National Board of Directors, NAACP."[1] She was, however, well prepared and well qualified for her new role, having spent, since her first husband's death in 1963, many years as an advertising executive, a director of corporate philanthropy, a leader in city government, and a member of the NAACP board.

Myrlie Louise Beasley was born in Vicksburg, Mississippi, on March 17, 1933. Soon after her birth her parents separated, and she was raised by one of her grandmothers, Annie McCain Beasley, and an aunt, Myrlie Beasley Polk. Both teachers, they influenced her to seek a college education, so in 1950 she enrolled at Alcorn Agricultural and Mechanical College (now Alcorn State University) in Lorman, Mississippi, as an education major and music minor.

With Medgar Evers

On her first day at the college, she met Medgar Evers, whom she married in December 1951. In 1952 he graduated from Alcorn, and Myrlie left school without a degree to move with him to Mound Bayou in the Mississippi Delta, where he took a job as an insurance agent. Appalled by the conditions suffered by local black sharecroppers, Medgar joined the NAACP, became a field secretary in 1954, and set up an office in Jackson, Mississippi, where his wife worked as his secretary.

During the rest of the 1950s and the early 1960s, white reaction against the civil rights movement in the South became increasingly violent. The couple received death threats, and Myrlie tried to persuade her husband to move the family, which now included three children, to California. When their house was firebombed in the spring of 1963, she put the flames out with a garden hose. "We lived with death as a constant companion, twenty-four hours a day," she later recalled.[2]

At 12:30 A.M. on June 12, 1963, Medgar Evers was shot on the front steps of his house as he returned from an NAACP meeting. He died less than an hour later at a hospital. A white supremacist, Byron De La Beckwith, was put on trial for the murder, but after two all-male, all-white juries failed to reach a verdict, he was freed.

New Directions

In 1964 Myrlie Evers moved with her children to Claremont, California, near Los Angeles. She gave speeches for the NAACP; earned a B.A. degree (1968) in sociology at Pomona College, one of the Claremont Colleges; and, after graduation, took a job as the assistant director of the Claremont College system's Center for Educational Opportunity, where she helped underprivileged high school dropouts obtain their diplomas and go on to college.

In 1967 Evers published a biography of her late husband, *For Us, the Living*, which she wrote with William Peters. In addition to describing the evolution of Medgar Evers's commitment to the civil rights movement, the work also movingly tells the couple's

The Schomburg Center / NYPL

MYRLIE EVERS-WILLIAMS

love story. In 1983 the book was made into a television movie starring Howard Rollins and Irene Cara.

Gaining Experience

Disturbed by the continuing polarization of the races in the United States, Myrlie decided to run for a vacant California congressional seat in 1970, believing that as a member of Congress she could help to bring about peaceful integration. Running on the Democratic ticket, she supported government subsidies for what she called "people-oriented" programs and advocated an immediate end to the Vietnam War. Though she lost the general election in the heavily conservative Republican district, she made a good showing, pulling a higher share of the vote, about 36 percent, than any Democrat had garnered in more than a decade.

In the early 1970s Evers served as a contributing editor of *Ladies' Home Journal* and as a vice president at Seligman and Lapz, a New York-based advertising firm. In 1975 she returned to California and settled in Los Angeles as director of corporate community affairs for the Atlantic Richfield Company (ARCO). At

ARCO she secured money for the National Women's Education Fund, for a group that supplied meals to disadvantaged people in Los Angeles, and for other worthy organizations. In 1987 Mayor Tom Bradley of Los Angeles appointed her the first black female commissioner of the city's Board of Public Works.

Reborn

While engaged in all these activities and enjoying a new marriage since 1976 to Walter Williams, a civil rights worker and union activist, Evers-Williams continued to feel haunted by the lack of justice handed out following her first husband's slaying. Through the years she kept track of developments in the case in Mississippi.

In 1989 a Mississippi newspaper began to uncover evidence that jury tampering had occurred during Byron De La Beckwith's second murder trial. Evers-Williams pressed for a new trial, at which new witnesses testified that the defendant had boasted of killing Medgar Evers. On February 5, 1994, a racially mixed jury convicted Beckwith of murder, and he was sentenced to life in prison. "I didn't realize how deeply implanted this need to clear everything up was," Evers-Williams told a writer. "I was reborn when that jury said, 'Guilty!'"[3] The story of how the assassin was brought to justice was told in the motion picture *Ghosts of Mississippi* (1996).

Leading the NAACP

Long a member of the NAACP board, Evers-Williams rose to become one of its vice chairs. By the mid-1990s, however, the organization was in a state of turmoil. In August 1994 Benjamin F. Chavis, the executive director, was dismissed for using NAACP funds to settle a sexual harassment suit. In January 1995 some NAACP board members brought a federal suit against the chairman, William F. Gibson, for his alleged misuse of NAACP money. Financial support for the organization plummeted.

In February 1995 Evers-Williams ran against Gibson in an election for the NAACP chair. She represented the group's traditionally mainstream wing, whereas Gibson, besides carrying the stigma of his alleged financial misdeeds, appealed more to extremists because of his friendly ties with the controversial

Nation of Islam leader Louis Farrakhan. Evers-Williams narrowly won the election but immediately began to heal the divisions within the organization by blowing her audience a kiss before her victory speech.

Only four days after Evers-Williams won the election, her second husband, Walter Williams, died. She has two sons, Darrell and James, and a daughter, Reena, from her first marriage.

As head of the NAACP Evers-Williams tried to attract more young people to membership in the organization, believing that African-American youth must be constantly alert to the danger of losing ground gained by earlier civil rights efforts. To prevent such slippage, she strongly defended affirmative action, organized voter registration drives, and spoke out against continuing discrimination in jobs, education, and housing.

Above all, Evers-Williams provided stable leadership for the NAACP during a critical period of internal strife. Besides Chavis and Gibson, several other high-level members of the NAACP, among them Henry Lyons and Hazel Dukes, were accused of financial improprieties. In November 1997 the NAACP accepted the resignation of Lyons, and the following month the organization's national board voted to remove Dukes. Evers-Williams kept the NAACP focused on its goals of social progress while at the same time resolving these disruptive personnel problems.

Early in 1998 she decided not to seek a fourth one-year term as chairman, feeling that she had accomplished her mission of helping to save the NAACP from its "financial, moral and organizational morass."[4] She was succeeded as chairman by Julian Bond.

Later in 1998 she received the Spingarn Medal, the NAACP's highest honor. In early 1999 she published her autobiography, *Watch Me Fly: What I Learned on the Way to Becoming the Woman I Was Meant to Be*.

"I know I wouldn't have had certain doors open to me if it hadn't been for Medgar," Myrlie Evers-Williams has said. "I also know if I hadn't had the intellect, I wouldn't be able to use it."[5]

Crystal Fauset

FIRST BLACK WOMAN ELECTED TO A STATE LEGISLATURE

(1893—1965)

CRYSTAL FAUSET WAS the first black woman elected to any American state legislature. She also served as an important race relations specialist on both the national and the international scenes.

She was born Crystal Dreda Bird in Princess Anne, Maryland, on June 27, 1893, the youngest of nine children of Benjamin Oliver Bird and Portia E. (Lovett) Bird. Her father served as the first principal of Princess Anne Academy (later a part of the University of Maryland), a school for young blacks. After he died in 1897 his wife, Portia, succeeded him as principal till her own death in 1900.

Orphaned at the age of seven, Crystal then moved to Boston, Massachusetts, to live with her maternal aunt, attending the city's integrated public school system and studying at Boston Normal School. After graduating in 1914, she taught school for three years.

In 1918 she joined the national board of the Young Women's Christian Association (YWCA) in New York City. As first secretary of the younger African-American girls in the YWCA, Crystal traveled all over the United States, Mexico, and Cuba to study black conditions. This experience taught her, she later said, that "problems cannot be segregated—wherever I went, they appeared as inter-racial problems."[1]

In 1927 she began to make speeches for an American Friends Service Committee program designed to communicate to white groups the aspirations of African-Americans. Over the next few years she studied at Columbia University's Teachers College in New York City, from which she received a bachelor's degree in 1931. During that time Crystal, an accomplished singer and pianist, repeatedly gave a lecture entitled "Music in the Life of America."

In 1931 she married Arthur Huff Fauset, principal of Singerley School in Philadelphia. The marriage eventually ended in divorce, but she kept his surname.

Early Political Ventures

In 1933 Crystal Fauset became associate secretary of the Institute of Race Relations at Philadelphia's Swarthmore College. Her work with the institute, which she helped to found, convinced her that if she wanted to educate the general public about the concerns of black Americans she would need to take direct political action.

Her first venture into politics came in 1935, when she became a member of the administrative staff of the Works Progress Administration (WPA) in Philadelphia. At about that time she also organized the Philadelphia Democratic Women's League, and in 1936 she became director of black women's activities for the National Democratic Committee.

Pennsylvania State Assembly

Fauset was now beginning to make a national name for herself, especially as an effective public speaker. In 1938 Democratic leaders urged her to run for the Pennsylvania state legislature. Disturbed by the low economic status of blacks, especially by the plight of those in breadlines, she decided to become a candidate so that, if elected, she could work to improve conditions.

Since her Philadelphia district was two-thirds white, Fauset based her campaign largely on telephone conversations. On November 8, 1938, she was elected to the Assembly of the Commonwealth of Pennsylvania, the first African-American woman ever elected to a state legislature. "My interest in people," she said soon after the election, "isn't in any sense limited to my race. . . . It is a universal interest in human beings."[2]

During her time as a legislator Fauset made her mark particularly as a public speaker. In her speeches she encouraged citizens, especially black women, to become involved in community programs through political action. In 1939 Pennsylvania Governor George Earle recognized her efforts by giving her the Meritorious Service Medal.

Race Relations Specialist

After less than a year in the legislature Fauset resigned in late 1939 so that she could become the assistant state director of the Education and Recreation Program of the WPA in Pennsylvania. She saw this job as a way of improving race relations in her state by educating both races to a more progressive point of view.

In 1941 Fauset, through her friendship with Eleanor Roosevelt and her leadership roles in the election campaigns of President Franklin D. Roosevelt, was appointed special consultant to the director of the Office of Civilian Defense. In that capacity she served as race relations adviser to Mayor Fiorello La Guardia of New York City, to Eleanor Roosevelt, and indirectly to the White House.

Early in 1944 Fauset resigned that position to join the Democratic National Committee in its election-year efforts. However, she found the chairman of the committee unwilling to deal fairly with African-Americans, so she left the Democratic party and supported the Republican candidate for president, Thomas E. Dewey.

In 1945 Fauset helped to establish the United Nations Council of Philadelphia, forerunner of the World Affairs Council. As an officer of that organization she attended the founding of the United Nations in San Francisco, in 1945. Now involved with world politics, she went on speaking tours in India, the Middle East, and Nigeria.

In 1955 Fauset received her second Meritorious Service Medal from the Commonwealth of Pennsylvania. Presented by Governor John S. Fine, the citation commended her for her efforts toward international friendship, especially through her leadership in the American-Korean Foundation.

Crystal Fauset, a major race relations activist and political pioneer, remained involved in public issues till her death in Philadelphia on March 28, 1965.

Ella Fitzgerald
FIRST LADY OF JAZZ

(1917—1996)

THE MOST CELEBRATED jazz singer of her generation, Ella Fitzgerald was known as the First Lady of Jazz (or Song), for her ability to perform with a virtuosity rivaling that of the greatest instrumentalists.

Ella Jane Fitzgerald was born in Newport News, Virginia, on April 25, 1917. Her parents, William Fitzgerald and Temperance ("Tempie") Williams, were unmarried, and before Ella was a year old, William, a wagon driver, left the family. Soon Tempie, a laundress, was living with Joseph Da Silva. They moved to Yonkers, New York, where Tempie had another daughter, Frances, and where Joseph worked in a sugarhouse.

Ella Fitzgerald loved to sing and dance. She learned to sing by imitating the vocal stylings she heard on radio and records, especially those of Louis Armstrong and Connee Boswell of the Boswell Sisters. "When I was a girl," she later said, "I listened to records by all the singers, white and black, and I know that Connee Boswell was doing things that no one else was doing at the time."[1] As a teenager Fitzgerald was better known in her neighborhood as a dancer than as a singer. In fact, her first professional performance as an entertainer was as a nightclub dancer when she was fifteen.

However, at about that time (1932) her mother died, and soon afterwards Ella moved out of her stepfather's home and went to live with her mother's sister in Harlem. Before long Fitzgerald dropped out of school, became involved with the numbers racket, and worked as a lookout at a brothel. Caught by the authorities, she was put into the Riverdale Children's Association, an orphanage and school, from which she ran away in 1934, determined to make a career in show business.

Discovered by Chick Webb

Fitzgerald made her stage debut in December 1934 when she won an amateur contest at the Apollo Theater in Harlem, singing "Judy" and "The Object of My Affection." The following month she performed "Judy" at the Harlem Opera House, where she won another contest and earned a week's work. She came to the attention of Charles Linton, lead singer for Chick Webb's band. Linton took her to Webb, who hired her in 1935.

Under Webb's musical guidance Fitzgerald honed her professional skills, developed confidence, and began recording. Among her best early recordings were "Sing Me a Swing Song" (1936) with Webb and "Did You Mean It?" (1936) with Benny Goodman.

In 1938 she collaborated with Al Feldman (who used the stage name Van Alexander), a pianist and arranger for Webb, on a new song, "A-tisket, A-tasket." Based on the well-known nursery rhyme, the novelty song became a tremendous hit when she issued her recording of it with Webb that year.

Fitzgerald went on to write many other songs, by herself or in collaboration with others. Among her works were "I Found My Yellow Basket," "Oh! But I Do," and "You Showed Me the Way."

When Chick Webb died in 1939, Ella took over the band and led it for the next three years under the billing Ella Fitzgerald and Her Famous Orchestra.

During that time, in December 1941, she impulsively married Benjamin ("Benny") Kornegay, a band hanger-on, but the marriage was annulled in mid-1942.

Solo Career

In 1942 Fitzgerald disbanded her group and embarked on her long, magnificent career as a soloist. Over the next few years she performed at various nightclubs and continued to make recordings, such as "Flying Home" (1945). In 1946 she became associated with the jazz impresario Norman Granz's Jazz at the Philharmonic concerts, which gave her an international following in the jazz community.

In 1947 Fitzgerald married Ray Brown, a bass player from Pittsburgh. From 1948 to 1952 she sang in a jazz group led by Brown. The couple adopted an infant named Raymond Brown, Jr., but in 1953 this marriage too ended, and Ella never remarried. Ray, Jr., continued to live with Fitzgerald, and in 1967 they moved to a house in Beverly Hills, California. Ray Brown, Jr., later became a successful musician and bandleader.

After her divorce from Brown, Fitzgerald was managed by her good friend Granz. In her prime she toured from forty to forty-five weeks each year, performing with small jazz groups, big bands, and symphony orchestras. She made frequent appearances at jazz festivals with Duke Ellington, Count Basie, Oscar Peterson, and other jazz giants. Her repertory included jazz songs, show tunes, novelties (such as "A-tisket, A-tasket"), and opera (*Porgy and Bess* excerpts). She also appeared in television specials and had a cameo role in the 1955 film *Pete Kelly's Blues*.

Fitzgerald won countless awards, among them popularity awards from jazz magazines; honorary doctorates; the American Music Award (1978); the Kennedy Center Award (1979) for her lifetime achievement in the performing arts; the National Medal of the Arts (1987), presented at the White House; and thirteen Grammy Awards, including one

ELLA FITZGERALD

in 1967 for her lifetime achievement. In 1989 she became the first recipient of the Society of Singers Lifetime Achievement Award, named "Ella" in her honor.

Prolific Recording Artist

Fitzgerald made more recordings than nearly anyone else in jazz history. She began her recording career, through Chick Webb, at Decca, where she recorded such classics as "How High the Moon" (1947) and *Ella Sings Gershwin* (1950).

In 1956 Norman Granz bought out her contract from Decca and began to record her on his own Verve label. At Verve she issued a series of great albums recorded live at concerts, beginning with *Jazz at the Opera House* (1957). Granz produced her fabulously successful songbook series of albums, each devoted to a single major American songwriter or songwriting team, including Cole Porter, Richard Rodgers and Lorenz Hart, Duke Ellington, and George and Ira Gershwin. "I never knew how good our songs were," Ira Gershwin once said, "until I heard Ella Fitzgerald sing them."[2] The series established her as one of the supreme interpreters of popular songs. From this point on in her career, she was universally acknowledged as the queen of both popular and jazz singing.

In 1961 Granz sold Verve to MGM. Fitzgerald continued to record for the label till the mid-1960s and then spent several uncongenial years at Capitol, attempting country music, and Reprise, singing rock and soul.

She was rescued in the early 1970s by Granz, who founded Pablo, a label dedicated to classic jazz. Fitzgerald's Pablo recordings included several duet albums with the guitarist Joe Pass, such as *Take Love Easy* (1973) and *Speak Love* (1983).

Unique Style

Fitzgerald had a small, light, girlish voice, but she offset that disadvantage with a number of assets. She possessed an extremely wide vocal range, cultivated impeccable diction, and was blessed with a perfect sense of intonation. Mel Tormé said she had "the best ear of any singer ever."[3]

Above all, Fitzgerald had a unique vocal agility. She was the ultimate master of scat singing—improvising on syllables with no textual significance, often in imitation of jazz instruments. Her 1945 recording of "Flying Home," one of the finest of all jazz vocal recordings, was a tour de force in which she first displayed her full powers as a scat singer. Through this recording she also completely aligned herself with a new style of jazz—bebop, a kind of jazz expressionism characterized by chromaticism, flexible rhythms, and irregular phrasing.

Fitzgerald had an innate, infectious cheerfulness

that leaped out at the audience as she scatted. Even her renditions of sad ballads "communicated a wistful, sweet-natured compassion for the heartache she described."[4]

She was admired and praised by other musicians of all kinds, including the jazz instrumentalist Charlie Parker and the classical singer Dietrich Fischer-Dieskau. The popular singer Bing Crosby summed up the musical legacy of Ella Fitzgerald: "Man, woman, or child, Ella is the greatest."[5]

Beginning in the early 1970s, Fitzgerald had eyesight problems complicated by diabetes. She also suffered from circulatory system complications. In 1986 she had heart surgery, but she returned to the concert stage the next year. Despite these illnesses, she continued to perform at least once a month into the early 1990s. In 1993 both of her legs were amputated below the knees. She died at her Beverly Hills home on June 15, 1996.

Selected recordings:

SINGLES
(under Chick Webb's name)

"Sing Me a Swing Song" (1936, Decca)
"There's Frost on the Moon" (1937, Decca)
"A-tisket, A-tasket" (1938, Decca)
"Undecided" (1939, Decca)

SINGLES
(under Benny Goodman's name)

"Did You Mean It?" (1936, RCA Victor)

SINGLES
(under Teddy Wilson's name)

"My Melancholy Baby" (1936, Brunswick)

SINGLES
(under Ella Fitzgerald's name)

"Into Each Life Some Rain Must Fall" (1944, Decca)
"I'm Beginning to See the Light" (1945, Decca)
"Flying Home" (1945, Decca)
"How High the Moon" (1947, Decca)
"The Tender Trap" (1955, Decca)
"Mack the Knife" (1960, Verve)

ALBUMS

Ella and Ray (1948, Jazz Live)

Ella Sings Gershwin (with pianist Ellis Larkins, 1950, Decca)

Lullabies of Birdland (compilation, 1954, Decca)

Ella Fitzgerald Sings the Cole Porter Songbook (1956, Verve)

Ella Fitzgerald Sings the Rodgers and Hart Songbook (1956, Verve)

Ella and Louis (1956, Verve)

Ella Fitzgerald Sings the Duke Ellington Songbook (1956–57, Verve)

Jazz at the Opera House (1957, Verve)

Like Someone in Love (1957, Verve)

Ella Fitzgerald Sings the Irving Berlin Songbook (1958, Verve)

Ella in Rome: The Birthday Concert (recorded 1958, first released 1988, Verve)

Ella Fitzgerald Sings the George and Ira Gershwin Songbook (1959, Verve)

Mack the Knife: Ella in Berlin (1960, Verve)

Ella Fitzgerald Sings the Songs from the Film "Let No Man Write My Epitaph" (with pianist Paul Smith, 1960, Verve, rereleased on CD as *The Intimate Ella*, 1991, Verve)

Ella Fitzgerald Sings the Harold Arlen Songbook (1960–61, Verve)

Ella Swings Brightly with Nelson (1961, Verve)

Ella Returns to Berlin (recorded 1961, first released 1991, Verve)

These Are the Blues (1963, Verve)

Ella and Basie: On the Sunny Side of the Street (1963, Verve)

Ella at Juan-les-Pins (1964, Verve)

Ella in Hamburg '65 (1965, Verve)

Take Love Easy (with guitarist Joe Pass, 1973, Pablo)

Fine and Mellow: Ella Fitzgerald Jams (1974, Pablo)

Ella in London (1974, Pablo)

Fitzgerald and Pass . . . Again (with guitarist Joe Pass, 1976, Pablo)

Lady Time (1978, Pablo)

Speak Love (1983, Pablo)

Easy Swing (with guitarist Joe Pass, 1986, Pablo)

Roberta Flack

POPULAR SINGER

(1939—   )

"ORIGINALLY SCHOOLED in classical music and devoted to high standards of professionalism and disciplined hard work, Roberta Flack is one of the few genuine artists in the contemporary popular music field."[1] With her soft but intense singing style she has recorded many hit singles and albums and has performed live to tumultuous applause all over the world.

Roberta Flack was born in Black Mountain, near Asheville, North Carolina, on February 10, 1939 (according to *Who's Who in America*, though other sources give 1937 and 1940), one of four children of Laron and Irene Flack. Her father was a draftsman, and her mother was a domestic servant. Both parents were talented, self-taught pianists. When Roberta was five years old, the family moved to Arlington, Virginia, and at the age of nine she began taking regular piano lessons from a local teacher.

After graduating from high school she enrolled at Howard University in nearby Washington, D.C., where she majored in music education, shifted her emphasis from piano to voice, and became the first undergraduate in the school's history to give a public recital in vocal music, performing art songs, opera arias, and spirituals. In 1958 she received her B.A. degree. While she was working on her master's degree the following year, her father died and she left school to help support the rest of the family.

For one year she taught English and music to children in kindergarten through high school at a black school in Farmville, North Carolina. Over the following seven years, besides teaching music in three different junior high schools in the District of Columbia public school system, she took advanced voice lessons from Frederick ("Wilkie") Wilkerson, who advised her to devote herself to popular music instead of opera technique.

Flack took his advice and gradually began to pick up jobs as a popular singer in Washington nightclubs. At the end of the 1966–67 school year she gave up teaching to concentrate on her singing career. In 1968 the jazz pianist Les McCann heard her at a club and arranged for her to obtain a contract with Atlantic Records in New York City.

Recording Career

Roberta Flack soon shot to the top of the popular music industry in the early 1970s. In 1970 she released her first two albums, *First Take* and *Chapter Two*, and in late 1971 she issued *Quiet Fire*. All three immediately sold well, but her greatest surge in popularity came when her recording of "The First Time Ever I Saw Your Face," a track from her first album, was heard in the Clint Eastwood film *Play Misty for Me* (1971). Reissued in 1972 as a single, both the song and the original album soared to the top of the charts. That same year saw the release of her fourth album, *Roberta Flack and Donny Hathaway*, as well as a single duet with Hathaway, "Where Is the Love?" In 1973 she issued the single "Killing Me Softly with His Song" and the album *Killing Me Softly*.

With these performances Flack dominated the major awards of the early 1970s. The *Down Beat* magazine reader poll named her the best female vocalist of 1971 through 1973. In March 1973 she won two Grammys: best record of 1972 for "The First Time Ever I Saw Your Face" and best vocal duet for "Where Is the Love?" The following year her "Killing

ROBERTA FLACK

Records. After her favorite duet partner, Donny Hathaway, committed suicide in 1979, she teamed up with Peabo Bryson for the duet single "Tonight I Celebrate My Love" (1983) and the album *Born to Love* (1983).

In 1988, after several years without making an album, Flack returned to Atlantic and recorded *Oasis* (1988), whose title track became a hit single. Her later recordings included the duet "Set the Night to Music" (1991), with Maxi Priest, and the albums *Set the Night to Music* (1991) and *Roberta* (1994).

Successes on Stage

During the early 1970s Flack matched her recording success with many triumphs in live performances. She appeared at most of the major jazz and pop festivals, sang in nightclubs, and gave concerts in New York City at Philharmonic Hall and Madison Square Garden. In 1973 she starred in her first television special, *The First Time Ever.*

In the late 1970s, however, Flack cut down on both her recordings and her live performances to pursue other interests, especially her work in various educational programs for disadvantaged youth. She spent nearly all of 1979 in mourning for her friend and singing partner Donny Hathaway.

In the 1980s Flack resumed her public appearances. In 1983 she toured around the world, performing in Europe, the Middle East, the Far East, and South America. She was honored in March 1984 with a music tribute in New York City, and the following April 22 was declared Roberta Flack Day in Washington, D.C. In 1988 she participated in the Madison Square Garden concert celebrating the fortieth anniversary of Atlantic Records.

She continued to enjoy an active concert career in the 1990s, often performing at benefits. In 1991, for example, she sang at Symphony Hall in Boston at a benefit for Cohen Hillel Academy to help families of critically ill children. In 1992 she performed at a concert for Amnesty International in March, appeared on a televised AIDS benefit special in September, gave a week of New York City concerts in October, and embarked on a tour of the Far East in November. In 1993 she began to appear in the annual Colors of

Me Softly with His Song" won in the category of best record and earned her the award for best female vocalist. She was the first artist to win Record of the Year at the Grammy Awards two years in a row.

During the next decade she continued to record many hits for Atlantic, including "Feel like Makin' Love" (1974), "If Ever I See You Again" (1978), and "Making Love" (1982). With Donny Hathaway she recorded the duets "The Closer I Get to You" (1978), "You Are My Heaven" (1980), and "Back Together Again" (1980). Among her albums were *Feel like Makin' Love* (1975), *Blue Lights in the Basement* (1978), and *I'm the One* (1982). During those years she also appeared in the film *Renaldo and Clara* (1978) and recorded the music track for the movie *Bustin' Loose* (1981).

In 1983 Flack moved from Atlantic to Capitol

Christmas tour. She toured with Judy Collins to benefit breast cancer organizations in 1997.

Flack married Stephen Novosel, a white jazz bassist, in 1966. After the marriage ended in divorce in 1972 she determined to "avoid combining marriage and the pursuit of a career like it was a case of leprosy."[2]

Her style is a perfect blend of popularity and artistry, of emotion and mind. "My kind of music," she has said, "could be called a combination of science and soul. Soul, because I'm able to communicate what I feel . . . and that to me is the expression of . . . one's soul. . . . The scientific part is the part that gets you over because you know how to do what it is that you're doin'."[3]

Selected recordings:

SINGLES

"The First Time Ever I Saw Your Face" (1972, Atlantic)

"Where Is the Love?" (with Donny Hathaway, 1972, Atlantic)

"Killing Me Softly with His Song" (1973, Atlantic)

"Feel like Makin' Love" (1974, Atlantic)

"If Ever I See You Again" (1978, Atlantic)

"The Closer I Get to You" (with Donny Hathaway, 1978, Atlantic)

"You Are My Heaven" (with Donny Hathaway, 1980, Atlantic)

"Back Together Again" (with Donny Hathaway, 1980, Atlantic)

"Making Love" (1982, Atlantic)

"Tonight I Celebrate My Love" (with Peabo Bryson, 1983, Capitol)

"Oasis" (1988, Atlantic)

"Set the Night to Music" (with Maxi Priest, 1991, Atlantic)

ALBUMS

First Take (1970, Atlantic)

Chapter Two (1970, Atlantic)

Quiet Fire (1971, Atlantic)

Roberta Flack and Donny Hathaway (1972, Atlantic)

Killing Me Softly (1973, Atlantic)

Feel like Makin' Love (1975, Atlantic)

Blue Lights in the Basement (1978, Atlantic)

Roberta Flack (1978, Atlantic)

Roberta Flack Featuring Donny Hathaway (1980, Atlantic)

Live and More (1980, Atlantic)

Bustin' Loose (1981, MCA)

I'm the One (1982, Atlantic)

Born to Love (1983, Capitol)

Oasis (1988, Atlantic)

Set the Night to Music (1991, Atlantic)

Roberta (1994, Atlantic)

Aretha Franklin

QUEEN OF SOUL

(1942–   )

Oᴺᴇ ᴏꜰ ᴛʜᴇ ᴏʀɪɢɪɴᴀᴛᴏʀꜱ of soul music in the 1960s, Aretha Franklin has been known since then as the Queen of Soul. She "is one of the icons of contemporary pop music. With her extraordinary range and incendiary, gospel-driven vocal phrasings, she is perhaps the most exciting singer of the rock era."[1]

Aretha Franklin was born in Memphis, Tennessee, on March 25, 1942, one of five children (three daughters and two sons) of Reverend C(larence) L. Franklin and Barbara (Siggers) Franklin. When Aretha was two years old, her father moved the family to Detroit, Michigan, where he served as minister of the New Bethel Baptist Church.

C. L. Franklin was a popular fire-and-brimstone preacher and singer who often traveled on the evangelical circuit. He was known for his "thunderous style and syncopated timing"[2] and for his celebrated church choir. Famous gospel and blues singers, such as Mahalia Jackson* and B. B. King, frequently visited the family home.

Aretha absorbed this musical atmosphere and began to sing at local churches, imitating her father's style, before she was ten years old. At fourteen, as the lead singer in her father's New Bethel choir, she made her first professional recording, *Songs of Faith* (1956), a gospel album for Chess Records. She also traveled with the choir as it accompanied C. L. Franklin on his revivalist tours.

The Columbia Years

In her late teens Aretha Franklin set out for New York City to become a pop singer, and in 1961 John Hammond, the legendary producer who discovered Billie Holiday*, Bob Dylan, and Bruce Springsteen, signed her to a contract with Columbia Records.

Over the next five years Franklin recorded many singles and albums, but she never developed a distinctive style at Columbia. Her producers alternated and blended gospel, blues, jazz, and heavily orchestrated pop material on her recordings. Nevertheless, her fabulous raw talent was clearly evident on such singles as "Cry like a Baby" (1965) and such albums as *The Tender, the Moving, the Swinging Aretha Franklin* (1962).

During those years Franklin also performed on the so-called chitlin' circuit, small nightclubs of predominantly black audiences. There she sang jazz, rhythm and blues, and bluesy versions of pop standards.

Stardom at Atlantic

In 1966 Columbia offered her a new contract, but she opted to sign with Atlantic Records, which specialized in the lean, southern-sounding rhythm and blues of artists such as Ray Charles and Wilson Pickett. Freed from rich pop orchestrations and allowed to draw on her gospel background, Franklin found her true style. Soon she and a few other artists—notably Otis Redding, the Supremes, and the Temptations—achieved mass popularity with their versions of rhythm and blues, which became known as soul.

Franklin's debut single for Atlantic, "I Never Loved a Man the Way I Love You" (1967) and her first album, of the same name (1967), each sold more than a million copies. There followed a long string of hits in the late 1960s, including the singles "Respect"

(1967), "Chain of Fools" (1967), and "Sweet Sweet Baby Since You've Been Gone" (1968). In the early 1970s some of her best recordings were of songs she had written, notably "Until You Come Back to Me" (1973), a collaboration with Stevie Wonder. Among her many outstanding albums during those years were *Lady Soul* (1968), *Aretha Now* (1968), and *Young, Gifted, and Black* (1972).

However, when popular taste changed in favor of disco music in the mid-1970s, Franklin faced a commercial decline because, she felt, the record company did not promote her work strongly enough. As a result, she left Atlantic in 1979.

Comeback with Arista

In 1980 Franklin appeared in the movie *The Blues Brothers*, and she stole the film with her powerful rendition of "Respect."

Also in 1980 she began releasing recordings for her new label, Arista Records. Her first great success for Arista was the album *Jump to It* (1982), for which she selected songs containing lyrics and emotions with which she could identify and music in a contemporary pop-rock idiom. She achieved even greater success with *Who's Zoomin' Who?* (1985), a pop-soul album containing three hit singles, including "Freeway of Love."

Throughout the late 1980s she continued to enjoy popular success. In July 1986 the Showtime cable network broadcast her first television special, *Aretha!*, a presentation of the singer in concert in Detroit. In 1987 she became the first female performer inducted into the Rock and Roll Hall of Fame. In 1988 the Public Broadcasting Service telecast the documentary *Aretha Franklin: Queen of Soul*. Her recordings included "I Knew You Were Waiting for Me" (1987), a duet with George Michael; *One Lord, One Faith, One Baptism* (1988), her first gospel album since 1972; and *Through the Storm* (1989), featuring duets with James Brown, Whitney Houston, and Elton John.

In 1991 Franklin dedicated her album *What You See Is What You Sweat* to her sister Carolyn, who died in 1988, and her brother Cecil, who died in 1989. The album "reflects as much of me as you can put on one record," [3] she has said. In 1992 Atlantic issued *Queen of Soul: The Atlantic Recordings*, a four-CD compilation of her classic work from the late 1960s and early 1970s. In 1994 Arista released another outstanding collection, *Greatest Hits, 1980–1994*.

Virtuoso Vocalist

Offstage Franklin likes to live a quiet, unexciting life. She enjoys cooking, fishing, and watching soap operas on television. "I like to do things with children and for the church," she has said, "which is even more important today than it ever was." [4]

Her first husband, Ted White, who served as her business manager, abused her. She divorced him and in 1971 married the actor Glynn Turman, whom she divorced in 1984. She is the mother of four sons: Clarence, Edward, Teddy, and Kecalf. After her first divorce her brother Cecil managed her career until his death in 1989. Shortly after her second divorce she was devastated by the death of her father, who had been in a coma since he was shot in 1979 by burglars invading his home. She had remained close to him throughout the years and had regularly sought his advice.

Her father's presence remains with her every time she performs with her "thunderous style" or wins another honor for the career that he inspired. In January 1993 she sang at the Lincoln Memorial in Washington, D.C., as part of President Clinton's inaugural celebrations. In March 1994 Franklin, the winner of over a dozen Grammy Awards, was given a lifetime achievement Grammy Award, and in December of that year she was presented with a lifetime achievement award at the Kennedy Center Honors in Washington, D.C. In June 1996 she performed in a concert at Carnegie Hall in New York City, and one year later she sang at the Washington, D.C., reception for Vice President Al Gore's daughter and her husband.

Aretha Franklin's greatest work is characterized by a "virtuoso, at times histrionic, vocal style." Her "voice, a robust yet crystalline alto, is remarkable for its reliable intonation, expressive vibrato, and great range of pitch, dynamics, and expression. She is able to execute changes of register, volume, and timbre with dexterity and fluency, often altering the entire color of her voice in successive verses of a song as the text demands." [5]

Increasing age has not diminished her powers. "My voice is better than ever, because of experience," she said in middle age. "At the risk of sounding egotistical—it just gets better. I am my favorite vocalist." [6]

Selected recordings:

SINGLES

"Today I Sing the Blues" (1960, Columbia);
    "Running Out of Fools" / "Cry like a Baby"
    (1965, Columbia)
"I Never Loved a Man the Way I Love You" / "Do
    Right Woman—Do Right Man" (1967, Atlantic)
"Respect" / "Dr. Feelgood" (1967, Atlantic)
"Baby, I Love You" (1967, Atlantic)
"Chain of Fools" (1967, Atlantic)
"Sweet Sweet Baby, Since You've Been Gone" /
    "Ain't No Way" (1968, Atlantic)
"Think" / "You Send Me" (1968, Atlantic)
"The House That Jack Built" / "I Say a Little
    Prayer" (1968, Atlantic)
"See Saw" / "My Song" (1968, Atlantic)
"Share Your Love with Me" (1969, Atlantic)
"Don't Play That Song for Me" (1970, Atlantic)
"Bridge over Troubled Water" / "Brand New Me"
    (1971, Atlantic)
"Spanish Harlem" (1971, Atlantic)
"Rock Steady" / "Oh, Me! Oh, My! I'm a Fool for
    You, Baby" (1971, Atlantic)
"Day Dreaming" (1972, Atlantic)
"Young, Gifted, and Black" (1972, Atlantic)
"Amazing Grace" (1972, Atlantic)
"Master of Eyes" (1973, Atlantic)
"Until You Come Back to Me" (1973, Atlantic)
"Ain't Nothing like the Real Thing" (1974, Atlantic)
"Something He Can Feel" (1976, Atlantic)
"Break It to Me Gently" (1977, Atlantic)
"Almighty Fire" (1978, Atlantic)
"Can't Turn You Loose" (1980, Arista)
"Hold On, I'm Comin'" (1981, Arista)
"Jump to It" (1982, Arista)
"Freeway of Love" (1985, Arista)
"Who's Zoomin' Who?" (1985, Arista)
"Sisters Are Doin' It for Themselves" (with Annie
    Lennox, 1985, RCA)
"Another Night" (1986 Arista)
"Jumpin' Jack Flash" (1986, Arista)
"I Knew You Were Waiting for Me" (with George
    Michael, 1987, Arista)
"Oh, Happy Day" (with Mavis Staples, 1988 Arista)
"Through the Storm" (with Elton John, 1989, Arista)
"Gimme Your Love" (with James Brown, 1989, Arista)
"It Isn't, It Wasn't, It Ain't Never Gonna Be" (with
    Whitney Houston, 1989, Arista)
"A Rose Is Still a Rose" (1998, Arista)

ARETHA FRANKLIN

New York Daily News

ALBUMS

Songs of Faith (1956, Chess)
Aretha (1961, Columbia)
*The Tender, the Moving, the Swinging Aretha
    Franklin* (1962, Columbia)
I Never Loved a Man the Way I Love You (1967,
    Atlantic)
Aretha Arrives (1967, Atlantic)
Lady Soul (1968, Atlantic)
Aretha Now (1968, Atlantic)
Aretha Live at Fillmore West (1971, Atlantic)
Spanish Harlem (1971, Atlantic)
Young, Gifted, and Black (1972, Atlantic)
Amazing Grace (1972, Atlantic)
Hey Now Hey (1973, Atlantic)
Sparkle (1976, Atlantic)
Something He Can Feel (1976, Atlantic)
Jump to It (1982, Arista)
Get It Right (1983, Arista)
Who's Zoomin' Who? (1985, Arista)
Aretha (1986, Arista)
One Lord, One Faith, One Baptism (1988, Arista)
Through the Storm (1989, Arista)
What You See Is What You Sweat (1991, Arista)
A Rose Is Still a Rose (1998, Arista)

Irene McCoy Gaines

CIVIL RIGHTS REFORMER

(1892—1964)

D EVOTED TO THE betterment of her race, especially its women and youth, Irene McCoy
Gaines followed every path she could to attain that goal: community and organizational leader,
social worker, political activist, clubwoman, and lecturer. Behind all her efforts was the urgent desire to
reform the American social structure to ensure civil
rights for all.

Irene McCoy was born in Ocala, Florida, on October 25, 1892, the younger daughter of Charles
Vivien Smith and Mamie (Ellis) Smith. Her older
sister died in childhood. Charles Smith was a barber
and postal carrier. As an infant Irene was taken to
Chicago, where, after her parents divorced in 1903,
she stayed with her mother.

Irene graduated from Wendell Phillips High School,
attended Fisk Normal School in Nashville, Tennessee
(1905–1910), and then returned to Chicago to work
as a typist for the Juvenile Court. Between 1910 and
1914 she won three oratorical essay contests.

In 1914 she married Harris Barrett Gaines, a law
student. They had two sons: Harris Barrett and
Charles Ellis.

Commitment to Reform

Through her own experiences and those of the people
she met at the Juvenile Court and elsewhere, Irene
McCoy Gaines began to understand the large-scale
problems and needs of her race. She felt that she had
a personal role to play in improving conditions for
blacks because, "despite many handicaps and obstacles, which I have had to face, I now know that my
unkind environment and obstacles were given me for

a purpose, and that I have been made stronger by
and through them."[1]

Gaines especially wanted to help black youth by
opening opportunities for them. She joined the War
Camp Community Service during World War I, became industrial secretary for the first African-American
branch of the Young Women's Christian Association in
Chicago in 1920, recruited for the Urban League in
the 1920s, worked as a social worker in the Cook
County welfare department from the early 1930s to
1945, and served as president of the Chicago Council
of Negro Organizations (CCNO) from 1939 to 1953.

Her protestations against the poor conditions in
segregated schools in Chicago led to such reforms as
improved educational facilities for pregnant teenagers and the establishment of an integrated nursery
school, one of the first in the city. Gaines also had
success in employment reform. She investigated the
working conditions of black women domestics and
helped to organize and set up training for them. In
March 1941, as president of the CCNO, she organized the first march on Washington, D.C., where
she and others protested discrimination against blacks
in employment. In June President Franklin D.
Roosevelt issued an executive order banning discrimination in federal and defense employment. On other
occasions Gaines testified before congressional committees that were considering legislation aimed at
ensuring fair employment practices.

Politician and Clubwoman

Seeing the great need for reforms through legislation,
Gaines actively supported political candidates who

agreed with her ideas. She served as president (1924–35) of the Illinois Federation of Republican Colored Women's Clubs and as Republican state central committeewoman from the First Congressional District (1928). In 1940 she became the first black woman to run for the state legislature (her husband served there from 1928 to 1936), and in 1950 she became the first black woman to be a party candidate for county office when she ran on the Republican ticket for county commissioner. Although she lost both elections, she gained credibility for her race simply by running for the offices.

Gaines was an active clubwoman. During her years with the welfare department, she started clubs for young people. As fine arts and literature chairperson of the Northern District Association of Club Women, she helped to organize events that encouraged racial cooperation, such as a Negro in Art Week. She also founded and headed the Chicago and Northern District Association of Club Women and Girls. After serving as historian and then recording secretary of the National Association of Colored Women's Clubs (NACWC), Gaines was elected as president for two terms (1952–56) and then reelected for an unprecedented third term (1956–58). As president of the NACWC she oversaw the establishment of a new clubhouse in Washington, D.C., and directed a neighborhood improvement program.

Gaines undertook speaking engagements throughout the United States, especially in her role as president of the NACWC. In her speeches she often drew on biblical stories and quotations, which reflected her deep religiosity. She was a member of three Protestant churches, the Theosophical Society, and Moral Re-Armament.

Gaines even took her fight for equality into the international arena, presenting United Nations Secretary General Trygve Lie with a statement in 1947 protesting the "inferior status" of the "colored women of America...[and] of the world."[2] In 1954 she called for women to participate in a "one world" program and to become "a part of a great sisterhood of all humanity."[3]

Gaines received many awards for her efforts. Among them were the George Washington Honor Medal in 1958 for her NACWC neighborhood improvement program, the Fisk University Distinguished Alumni Service Award in 1959, and an honorary degree from Wilberforce University in 1962.

Irene McCoy Gaines died in Chicago on April 7, 1964.

Sarah Garnet

EDUCATOR AND SUFFRAGIST

(1831—1911)

S ARAH GARNET WAS a pioneering principal in the New York City public school system and one of the most important early suffragists. As an educator she helped to integrate New York City schools, and as a suffragist she helped to organize the Equal Suffrage Club, which worked for women's rights beyond Garnet's own lifetime.

Sarah was born in Queens County, New York, in an area now in Brooklyn, in 1831, the eldest of ten (or eleven) children. She was named Minsarah J. Smith, but her first name was commonly shortened to the familiar Sarah. Her parents, Sylvanus, a prosperous pig farmer, and Ann Eliza (Springsteel or Springstead) Smith, were of mixed Native American, white, and African-American descent. Two of her brothers were killed in the Civil War, and one of her sisters was Susan Maria Smith McKinney Steward, a well-known physician.

Some details of Saraha's education are uncertain. However, in 1845, at the age of fourteen, she began teaching at a black school in Williamsburg, later a part of Brooklyn.

At an early age she married Samuel Tompkins (according to her obituary in the *New York Age* and statements by her student and friend Maritcha R. Lyons, though the name has also been recorded as James Thompson).[1] They had two children, both of whom died young.

School Principal in Manhattan

Sarah's teaching experience and additional training after her first job at the age of fourteen are unknown. However, by 1863 she had advanced far enough in her profession to earn an appointment as principal of two black schools in Manhattan: Grammar School Number Four (which became Public School Number Eighty-one) and Public School Number Eighty. She was the first black woman to be a principal in the New York City public school system, and she held both positions till she retired in 1900.

During her first twenty years as a principal, New York City maintained separate schools for blacks and whites. In 1883 the Board of Education proposed closing three of the black schools, but Sarah, among others, testified against the proposal before the state legislature. In 1884, to resolve the issue, the legislature passed a law allowing students of any race to attend either the previously all-white or the previously all-black schools. Separate staffs, however, remained in place at all schools. Sarah, then, had only black students from 1863 to 1883, after which she had integrated student bodies, while her staffs were all black throughout her tenure.

"She. . . won the fidelity of the teachers," the *New York Age* said in its obituary of her, "the regard of the patrons and the ready obedience of the pupils by her reasonableness, her serenity of temper, her tact and her rare combination of affability and dignity."[2]

Her students included many prominent success stories. Among them were Walter F. Craig, a violinist and conductor; Ferdinand L. Washington, a businessman; Harry A. Williamson, a podiatrist and author; and many successful teachers, such as Susan Elizabeth Frazier, who in 1896 became the first black appointed to a white-staffed school in New York City."The clustering of teachers is significant, for Garnet served as a powerful role model."[3]

During her years as a principal, her private life

underwent important changes. About 1879, her first husband having died, she married Henry Highland Garnet, a prominent abolitionist and Presbyterian clergyman. He was appointed United States minister to Liberia, but died shortly after his arrival there in 1882.

In 1883 Sarah Garnet opened a seamstress shop on Hancock Street in Brooklyn, a business she ran for the rest of her life.

Suffragist

In the late 1880s Garnet helped to form the Equal Suffrage Club, a Brooklyn-based black women's group that worked for women's rights. In 1907 the club supported the Niagara Movement, a forerunner of the National Association for the Advancement of Colored People. Garnet was the principal force behind the club, but it continued to function even after her death.

She also lent her support to other causes. An early member of the National Association of Colored Women, she headed the organization's suffrage department for years. In 1892, with her sister Susan Maria Smith McKinney Steward and other black women, Garnet formed a committee to raise money to replace the presses of Ida B. Wells-Barnett's* Memphis newspaper, which mobs had destroyed to punish her for her antilynching editorials. In the mid-1890s Garnet helped to found the Brooklyn Home for Aged Colored People.

In July 1911 she went to London, to attend the first Universal Races Congress, at which she and her sister Susan arranged a photographic exhibit of prominent African-American women. During her stay in England Garnet acquired suffragist literature.

Sarah Smith Tompkins Garnet turned eighty while she was abroad, and she appeared to be in good health when she returned to the United States in early September. However, on September 17, 1911, she died suddenly at her home in Brooklyn, having devoted her life to improving the status of black teachers and of women.

Althea Gibson

TENNIS TRAILBLAZER

(1927–   )

ALTHEA GIBSON WAS the first black international tennis champion. She also became the first black member of the Ladies Professional Golf Association.

Althea Gibson was born in Silver, South Carolina, on August 25, 1927, the eldest of five children of Daniel and Annie (Washington) Gibson. Her father was a sharecropper till, when Althea was a small child, the family moved to the Harlem section of New York City, where he became a handyman in a garage.

Althea Gibson had a troubled childhood. Growing up in a tough neighborhood where education was not highly valued, she often got into trouble for truancy, and in her early teens she dropped out of school altogether to work at a series of odd jobs. Restless and discontent, she kept losing the jobs, and when not working, she loitered in the streets of New York City.

It was during this period, however, that Gibson discovered she had a talent for paddle tennis, which she revealed in games sponsored by a local Police Athletic League. A league supervisor encouraged her to take up regular tennis and bought her two rackets. When she defeated some male players at the Harlem River Tennis Courts, she was invited to join the Cosmopolitan Club, a prestigious black tennis club. Cosmopolitan members, impressed by her natural ability, provided her with a junior membership to their club and financed her tennis lessons with the professional Fred Johnson.

Turning Point

The game of tennis gave Gibson a focus and purpose in life for the first time. Within a year after beginning her lessons with Johnson, she won the girls' singles at the New York State Open Championships in 1942. In 1944 and 1945 she won the national girls' singles championship of the predominantly black American Tennis Association (ATA).

Shortly thereafter, Gibson's talent attracted the attention of two black surgeons who were leaders in the ATA: Hubert Eaton of Wilmington, North Carolina, and Robert W. Johnson of Lynchburg, Virginia. When she accepted their offer for her to live with Eaton's family during the school year and Johnson's in the summer, each man providing her with advanced tennis instruction, beginning in the fall of 1946, the arrangement improved her game so much that in the summer of 1947 she won the first of her ten consecutive ATA women's championships.

Part of Gibson's agreement with the doctors was that she would attend high school and with her newfound sense of stability and direction, she found that she now actually enjoyed classes. In 1949 she graduated tenth in her class from Williston Industrial High School in Wilmington, and that fall she entered Florida Agricultural and Mechanical (A&M) College (now University) at Tallahassee on a tennis scholarship. There she kept up a full load of classes, played both tennis and basketball, worked as a student assistant in the physical education department, and played saxophone in the marching band.

Meanwhile, Gibson also began to make a good showing in predominantly white tennis tournaments, including the 1949 and 1950 eastern and national indoor championships. However, despite her demonstrated ability, she still could not get an invitation to the all-important outdoor national tournament sponsored by the United States Lawn Tennis Association

(USLTA). Then the highly respected former national champion Alice Marble published a lengthy editorial in the July 1950 issue of *American Lawn Tennis* protesting against racial discrimination in tennis and stating her belief that Gibson should be given a chance to play. Soon Gibson received word that if she applied to enter the nationals, she would be accepted. "I filled out the entry blank," she later said, "as fast as I could get hold of one."[1] The national grass court championship tournament, held at Forest Hills, New York, was the most prestigious event in American tennis. No African-American player had ever participated.

Breaking the Color Barrier

On August 28, 1950, when Gibson stepped onto the court at Forest Hills, she became the first black, male or female, to play in a major event sanctioned by the USLTA. She won the first round but lost in the second. "Her appearance at Forest Hills broke the color barrier in elite tennis and cleared the way for other black competitors, both female and male, in other world-class tennis events and other sports as well."[2] In 1951 she became the first African-American to play at the All-England Tennis Championships in Wimbledon, where she reached the quarterfinals.

During the next several years Gibson continued to win the national ATA (black) championship annually. She also did well in the white circuit, though without winning a major tournament. Meanwhile she graduated from Florida A&M (1953) with a degree in physical education and began teaching in the physical education department of Lincoln University in Jefferson City, Missouri.

In 1955 Gibson undertook an exhibition tour of

ALTHEA GIBSON

The Schomburg Center / NYPL

Asia for the State Department. The following year she increased her international reputation by playing in Mexico, Sweden, Germany, Egypt, and elsewhere. In 1956 she won the French Championship, the first time a black person had won a major tennis singles title, and was invited to compete again at the Wimbledon and Forest Hills tournaments that year, both of which she lost.

By 1957, however, after years of struggle and hard work, Gibson had finally perfected her game. In July of that year she became the first black player, man or woman, to win at Wimbledon, defeating Darlene Hard in the singles finals 6–3 and 6–2, and she teamed up with Hard to win the doubles championship as well. In September she became the first black to win at Forest Hills, defeating Louise Brough 6–3 and 6–2. The following year Gibson, now the number one female tennis player in the world, successfully defended the same three titles.

"I Was Born Too Soon"

In 1959, at the top of her game, Gibson announced her retirement. The reason for her departure was her need to earn a living, tennis being at that time not lucrative enough to support her.

For several years Gibson experimented with various projects. She recorded songs on the Dot label, toured in tennis exhibitions in conjunction with the Harlem Globetrotters basketball games, appeared in the John Wayne movie *The Horse Soldiers* (1959), worked in community relations as a representative of Ward Baking Company, and wrote the autobiographical books *I Always Wanted to Be Somebody* (1958) and *So Much to Live For* (1968).

In the mid-1960s Gibson returned to the world of sports by competing in golf tournaments. In 1964, once again proving her remarkable athletic skill, she became the first black to hold a Ladies Professional Golf Association (LPGA) player's card. However, golf, like tennis, could not support her. Years later, after professional women golfers and tennis players began to earn vast sums of money, Gibson lamented the fact that she had missed out on those financial opportunities: "I was born too soon."[3]

Since the 1970s she has been involved in directing and administering athletic activities. From 1975 to 1977 she served as the athletic commissioner of the state of New Jersey. In 1988 she became a special consultant to the New Jersey Governor's Council on Physical Fitness and Sports. She also worked for the Essex County, New Jersey, Park Commission as a programmer of girls' and women's activities and for the Valley View Racquet Club of North Vale, New Jersey, as a director of programs. In addition, she kept her connection with tennis by serving as a professional teacher from the 1970s to the 1990s.

During those years she was married twice. In 1965 she married William A. Darben, and in 1983 Sydney Llewellyn, who had been her tennis coach for many years, became her second husband.

Gibson has received many important awards and honors. In both 1957 and 1958 she was named the Associated Press Woman Athlete of the Year. She has been inducted into the Lawn Tennis Hall of Fame (1971), the Black Athletes Hall of Fame (1974), the International Women's Sports Hall of Fame (1980), the South Carolina Hall of Fame (1983), and the Sports Hall of Fame of New Jersey (1994).

Althea Gibson was one of the greatest athletes of her time, a pioneer who helped to open doors for future African-American sports stars, and "the benchmark by which other black women measure their achievement in the sport of tennis."[4]

Nikki Giovanni

A SPEAKER OF THE AGE

(1943—   )

"I BECAME A SPEAKER of the age inadvertently," the poet Nikki Giovanni has said. "I have always thought my job is to call what I see, to describe my world. When you are a speaker from a people who don't have a voice, then you are a spokesperson."[1]

She was born in Knoxville, Tennessee, on June 7, 1943, the younger of two daughters of Jones ("Gus") Giovanni, a probation officer, and Yolande Cornelia (Watson) Giovanni, a social worker. At birth she was given her mother's two given names along with the usually male tag *Jr.*, so that her original full name was Yolande Cornelia Giovanni, Jr. Her father's surname came from the Italian master of one of Jones's ancestors. She was nicknamed Nikki.

After graduating from Fisk University in Nashville, Tennessee, in 1967, Nikki undertook graduate studies at the University of Pennsylvania School of Social Work in 1967 and the Columbia University School of Fine Arts in 1968.

Budding Poet

As a child Giovanni heard stories from her maternal grandfather, John Watson, a teacher and Latin scholar who loved myths. From her mother she heard romantic tales. "I appreciated the quality and the rhythm of the telling of the stories," Giovanni later recalled, "and I know when I started to write that I wanted to retain that—I didn't want to become the kind of writer that was stilted or that used language in ways that could not be spoken."[2]

She began her writing career as a student involved in the black literary movement of the late 1960s. In the years since then she has become "famous for strongly voiced poems that testify to her own evolving awareness and experience."[3]

Each decade of her career has seen a new development. "In the sixties, militancy characterizes her writing; in the seventies, greater introspection and attention to personal relationships; in the eighties, a global outlook with a greater concern for humanity in general. However, the various themes reflect changes in emphasis rather than wholesale abandonment of one concern for another."[4]

While attending Fisk in the mid-1960s, Giovanni was a militant civil rights activist. She helped to found the university's Student Nonviolent Coordinating Committee chapter. During that time she captured the revolutionary spirit of her wing of the civil rights movement in her poetry collections *Black Feeling, Black Talk* (1968) and *Black Judgement* (1968). "Nikki-Rosa," in *Black Judgement*, her most famous poem, contains the often-quoted line "Black love is Black wealth," a central idea in her work.[5] She became known as the Princess of Black Poetry.

After the birth of her son, Thomas Watson, in 1969, Giovanni, who decided not to marry, changed her focus from public issues to private ones. She explored motherhood, womanhood, and personal relationships. Much of this new work, however, extended her earlier interests by speaking directly to black people, celebrating positive features of black life, and suggesting that personal values should be applied toward making the world a better place. Her poetry collections during this period included *Re: Creation* (1970), *My House* (1972), *Ego Tripping and Other Poems for Young People* (1973), *The Women and the Men* (1975), and *Cotton Candy on a Rainy Day* (1978).

She also published *Gemini: An Extended Autobiographical Statement on My First Twenty-five Years of Being a Black Poet* (1971).

In the 1980s Giovanni continued her evolution as an artist and person by using her writings to stress respect for all of humanity. *Those Who Ride the Night Winds* (1983) is a collection of poems dedicated to the courage of "those who ride the night winds" and who know that life "is a marvelous, transitory adventure—and are determined to push us into the next century, galaxy—possibility."[6] The central image of the book is contained in "This Is Not for John Lennon (and this is not a poem)," in which she questions and criticizes a society in which the John Lennons of the world are routinely destroyed.[7] *Sacred Cows... and Other Edibles* (1988), a collection of essays, examines the world from a larger perspective than in her earlier works. "About a Poem," for example, looks at the changes in the civil rights movement from the 1960s to the 1980s. The black point of view broadened between those two decades. The newer issue is how to accept the responsibilities of freedom because, for blacks as well as whites, "the self is... a part of the body politic."[8]

In 1987 Giovanni became a visiting professor of English at Virginia Polytechnic Institute and State University in Blacksburg, Virginia, a position that became permanent in 1989. "My son had just graduated from high school," she later explained, "and I thought it would be a good time for me to get away, for a new adventure."[9] She continued her writing, but at a reduced rate. "One thing teaching does," she said, "is slow down publication."[10]

Giovanni's writings in the 1990s reflect her maturation as an artist reaching her fifties. While still energetically tackling contemporary issues, she also developed an increasing interest in retrospection. In 1994 she published a new edition of *Ego Tripping and Other Poems for Young Readers*, with ten new poems added to her 1973 collection. She also issued the illustrated children's book *Knoxville, Tennessee* (1994), the text of which is her 1968 poem of the same name, describing her childhood joys of summer with her family in Knoxville. *Racism 101* (1994) is an important book of essays presented from her perspective as a university faculty member. In this work she indicts American higher education for perpetuating inequities, deplores the neglect of urban schools, reflects on the legacy of the 1960s, contemplates space exploration, and addresses a wide range of other issues. In

1996 she wrote a *New York Times* article on the burning of black churches.

Professional Activities, Awards, and Honors

Before making her long-term commitment at Virginia Tech, Giovanni taught for shorter periods at other institutions. She served as assistant professor of black studies at Queens College of the City University of New York in Flushing (1968–69); associate professor of English at Rutgers University, Livingston College, New Brunswick, New Jersey (1969–70); visiting professor of English at Ohio State University in Columbus (1984); and professor of creative writing at the College of Mount Saint Joseph on-the-Ohio in Mount Saint Joseph, Ohio (1985–87). She encouraged her students everywhere to be fearlessly creative, noting, "It's better to take a chance and be wrong than to be safe and dull."[11]

Giovanni has engaged in a wide range of other professional activities. She has written columns for, and contributed articles to, periodicals. As a commentator, lecturer, and poetry reader she has appeared on stage, radio, and television. She has recorded albums of her poetry readings, including *Truth Is on Its Way* (1971), *Like a Ripple on a Pond* (1973), *Legacies: The Poetry of Nikki Giovanni* (1976), and *Cotton Candy on a Rainy Day* (1978). In 1988 she became director of the Warm Hearth Writer's Workshop, in the early 1990s she was elected to the board of directors of the Virginia Foundation for the Humanities and Public Policy, and she began to participate in the Appalachian Community Fund and the Volunteer Action Center.

Giovanni has received many forms of recognition for her work. She was named one of the ten Most Admired Black Women by the *Amsterdam News* in 1969 and Woman of the Year by *Mademoiselle* in 1971. Among her other awards and honors were the Omega Psi Phi Fraternity Award for her outstanding contribution to arts and letters (1971), a life membership and scroll from the National Council of Negro Women (1972), the National Association of Radio and Television Announcers Award for best spoken word album (1972) for *Truth Is on Its Way*, the Woman of the Year Youth Leadership Award from *Ladies' Home Journal* (1972), election to the Ohio Women's Hall of Fame (1985), the Outstanding Woman of Tennessee citation (1985), the Ohioana Book Award (1988) for *Sacred Cows . . . and Other Edibles*, the Woman of the Year citation from the Lynchburg, Virginia, chapter of the National Association for the Advancement of Colored People, (1989), and many honorary doctorates. In 1988 the McDonald's Literary Achievement Award, a poetry award to be presented in her name in perpetuity, was established in her honor. In the same year the National Festival of Black Storytelling created the Nikki Giovanni Award for young African-American storytellers.

Nikki Giovanni has taken her role as a speaker of the age seriously. However, her approach to this role differs from that of many of her contemporaries, who, she says, thought they were supposed to change the world. "I don't think so," she maintains. "We're to put the truths as we see them and have enough respect for the truths as other people see them to see what good comes out of it."[12]

NIKKI GIOVANNI

Courtesy of Nikki Giovanni

Selected writings:

NONFICTION

Gemini: An Extended Autobiographical Statement on My First Twenty-five Years of Being a Black Poet (1971)
Sacred Cows . . . and Other Edibles (essays, 1988)
Racism 101 (essays, 1994)

POETRY

Black Feeling, Black Talk (1968)
Black Judgement (1968)
Re: Creation (1970)
My House (1972)

The Women and the Men (1975)
Cotton Candy on a Rainy Day (1978)
Those Who Ride the Night Winds (1983)

JUVENILE POETRY

Spin a Soft Black Song: Poems for Children (1971 revised edition, 1987)
Ego Tripping and Other Poems for Young People (1973 revised edition, 1994)
Vacation Time: Poems for Children (1980)
Knoxville, Tennessee (1994)

Whoopi Goldberg

MEGASTAR

(1955—   )

WHOOPI GOLDBERG, WHO overcame poverty, disability, and chemical dependency to win Oscar, Grammy, and Golden Globe awards, is one of the few true megastars in show business today.

Originally named Caryn Elaine Johnson, she was born in New York City on November 13, 1955. (Early in her career she lied about her age to make herself appear more mature, so some published reports list her birth year as 1949 or 1950.) She was the younger child of Robert James Johnson and Emma (Harris) Johnson. Robert abandoned the family early, and Emma supported her children with a variety of jobs.

Caryn attended Saint Columba, a Catholic school, for her general elementary education. She also participated in the acting program for children at the New Jersey arts center branch of Hudson Guild, a New York City settlement house where her mother was working as a Head Start teacher. After graduating from Saint Columba in 1969 Caryn briefly attended Washington Irving High School before dropping out. (She never attended the prestigious High School for Performing Arts as she later claimed.) Caryn struggled as a student due to dyslexia, but it was years later before she realized that she suffered from this disability.

In the early 1970s she lived as a hippie on the New York City streets and became involved with the drug culture. When she decided to abandon that world for a rehabilitation center, her drug counselor was Alvin Martin. In 1973 she married Martin, with whom she had a daughter, Alexandrea, in 1974. The couple both obtained clerical jobs at the Chase Manhattan Bank, but the marriage soon broke up, and they divorced in the late 1970s.

In 1974 Caryn Johnson moved with her daughter to San Diego, California, living for a time on welfare, though she briefly held a number of jobs, including one as a mortuary cosmetician.

Early Stage Work

It was in San Diego that Caryn Johnson began her stage career. (No evidence has been found to substantiate her later claim to have worked in the choruses of the Broadway productions *Hair, Jesus Christ Superstar,* and *Pippin* in the late 1960s and early 1970s.) She selected the whimsical Whoopi Cushion as a stage name, later giving it a French twist, recorded as Cushon and Coussin. However, her mother convinced her that nobody would take someone with such a name seriously, so Whoopi decided to use Goldberg, the name of a distant Jewish relative, as her new surname. "Goldberg's a part of my family somewhere," she later explained, "and that's all I can say about it."[1]

She joined the newly formed San Diego Repertory Theater, where she performed improvisational sketches and appeared in plays such as *A Christmas Carol* (1977) and *Mother Courage* (1981). During her years with that company she also did stand-up comedy; worked with improvisational groups, notably Spontaneous Combustion; and created a one-woman show whose original title was *More Than One Person,* later known by other titles, such as *The Whoopi Goldberg Show* and *The Spook Show.*

In 1981 Goldberg moved north to Berkeley, California, where she worked with the Blake Street Hawkeyes, a performance troupe. She performed throughout the San Francisco area and in 1983 took

WHOOPI GOLDBERG

Film and Television Star

Goldberg's Broadway success soon led to film and television offers. She made a spectacular movie debut as Celie, a victim of spousal abuse, in *The Color Purple* (1985), based on the novel by Alice Walker* and directed by Steven Spielberg. Since then she has appeared in a steady stream of films, both comedies and dramas. An early highlight was her role as Oda Mae Brown, the phony medium in *Ghost* (1990). Other memorable films include *The Long Walk Home* (1990); *Sister Act* (1992); *Sister Act 2: Back in the Habit* (1993); the animated *The Lion King* (1994), as the voice of Shenzi, the hyena; and the docudrama *Ghosts of Mississippi* (1996), as Myrlie Evers*, widow of the slain civil rights leader Medgar Evers.

Goldberg has also appeared in several made-for-television movies, including *Kiss Shot* (1989), *In the Gloaming* (1997), and *Rodgers and Hammerstein's Cinderella* (1997). Her recurring roles in television series have included Guinan in *Star Trek: The Next Generation* (1988–93), Brenda in the sitcom *Bagdad Café* (1990–91), and the voice of Gaia in the animated *Captain Planet and the Planeteers* (1990–93). During 1992–93 she hosted the talk program *The Whoopi Goldberg Show*. She has been one of the busiest personalities in American television specials, re-creating her stage show in *Whoopi Goldberg: Direct from Broadway* (1985) and hosting the Academy Awards and many other special programs.

In 1997 she replaced Nathan Lane in the leading role of Pseudolus in the Broadway revival of the musical comedy *A Funny Thing Happened on the Way to the Forum*, a part Zero Mostel and Phil Silvers had each performed decades earlier. Goldberg was the first woman ever to play Pseudolus, the lascivious ancient Roman slave who yearns for freedom.

Goldberg is also a talented writer. Besides creating much of her stage and television material, she has written two books: a children's book, with John Rocco, called *Alice* (1992), and an autobiographical work titled simply *Book* (1997).

Goldberg has used her star status to fight for causes in which she believes. For example, in 1986 she began her annual participation in the television show *Comic Relief* to benefit the homeless. She has also been a major fund-raiser for organizations involved in AIDS research.

her one-woman act to Europe, where the show was called *Whoopi Goldberg Abroad*. Returning to the United States, she created a new act, *Moms Mabley*, whose title character was a famed black comedienne. In January 1984 Goldberg took *The Spook Show* to New York City, and in October of that year she made her Broadway debut with a one-woman act called simply *Whoopi Goldberg*.

Her show consisted entirely of sketches involving her impersonations of a wide range of characters, among them an adolescent white Valley Girl who performs an abortion on herself, a little black girl who wants to be white, and a well-educated male junkie who is a burglar by profession.

"I know I'm supposed to say I do a lot of work on these characters," Goldberg confessed in 1987, "but I don't. They kinda live in me. It's a residence hotel. They say things and express stuff that I would never express. It's exactly like being schizophrenic. Whoopi disappears."[2]

Though Goldberg's first husband, Alvin Martin, was African-American, most of her subsequent boyfriends, including the actors Ted Danson (during 1992–93) and Frank Langella (beginning in the mid-1990s) have been white. Goldberg's second and third husbands, both of whom she divorced, were also white: the cinematographer David Claessen (married 1986–88) and the labor organizer Lyle Trachtenberg (married 1994–95). Trachtenberg, like some of her other companions, was Jewish.

Awards and Honors

Among Goldberg's many major awards and honors are a Grammy Award for best comedy album for *Whoopi Goldberg* (a recording of her 1984–85 Broadway show), and the best actress Golden Globe award for her performance in the film *The Color Purple* (1985). For her supporting role in *Ghost* (1990) she won an Academy Award, a Golden Globe Award, and a British Academy of Film and Television Arts Award. Among her other awards and honors were the Hans Christian Andersen Award for outstanding achievement by a dyslexic (1987), several Image Awards by the National Association for the Advancement of Colored People, the Woman of the Year honor from Harvard University's Hasty Pudding Theatricals (1993), and the Female Star of the Year Award from the National Association of Theater Owners (1993).

"With her trademark dreadlocks, widemouthed grin, and distinctive looks," wrote her biographer James Robert Parrish, "this talented performer [is] universally regarded as a great comedian, a fine dramatic actor, and a determined humanitarian."[3]

Selected performances:

STAGE

A Christmas Carol (1977)
Mother Courage (1981)
Whoopi Goldberg (1984)
A Funny Thing Happened on the Way to the Forum (1997)

FILMS

The Color Purple (1985)
Jumpin' Jack Flash (1986)
Burglar (1987)
Fatal Beauty (1987)
The Telephone (1988)
Clara's Heart (1988)
Beverly Hills Brats (1989)
Ghost (1990)
The Long Walk Home (1990)
Homer and Eddie (1990)
Soapdish (1991)
House Party Two (1991)
The Player (1992)
Sister Act (1992)
Wisecracks (1992)
The Magical World of Chuck Jones (1992)
Sarafina! (1992)
National Lampoon's Loaded Weapon One (1993)
Made in America (1993)
Sister Act 2: Back in the Habit (1993)
Naked in New York (1994)
The Lion King (animated, voice only, 1994)
The Little Rascals (1994)
Corina, Corina (1994)
Star Trek: Generations (1994)
The Pagemaster (1994)
Liberation (1994)
Boys on the Side (1995)
Moonlight and Valentino (1995)
Tales from the Crypt Presents Bordello of Blood (1996)
Eddie (1996)
Theodore Rex (1996)
Bogus (1996)
The Associate (1996)
Ghosts of Mississippi (1996)
Burn, Hollywood, Burn (1998)
How Stella Got Her Groove Back (1998)

TELEVISION MOVIES

Kiss Shot (1989)
The Celluloid Closet (1996)
In the Gloaming (1997)
Rodgers and Hammerstein's Cinderella (1997)
Boys on the Side (1998)

TELEVISION SERIES

Star Trek: The Next Generation (1988–93)
Bagdad Café (1990–91)
Captain Planet and the Planeteers (animated, voice only, 1990–93)
The Whoopi Goldberg Show (1992–93)

Emma Azalia Smith Hackley

CHAMPION OF BLACKS IN MUSIC

(1867—1922)

MUSICIAN, ACTIVIST, EDUCATOR, and philanthropist, Emma Azalia Smith Hackley played a major role in uplifting the cultural life of African-Americans. She promoted black spirituals among black people, many of whom wanted to forget such music because it reminded them of slavery; and she convinced both blacks and whites that blacks could appreciate and perform classical music.

Born Emma Azalia Smith in Murfreesboro, Tennessee, on June 29, 1867, the elder daughter of Henry and Corilla (Beard) Smith. Her father was a blacksmith, while her mother was a schoolteacher who established a school in Murfreesboro for freed slaves and their children.

When white hostility forced the closure of the school in 1870, the family moved north to Detroit, Michigan, where the Smiths were the first blacks to live in their neighborhood. Henry Smith ran a curio shop and held various other jobs. Corilla Smith now focused her teaching on little Emma, who began music lessons at the age of three and could read and write by six. At an early age she often sang and played the piano for visitors in the family home.

During her years at Miami Avenue Public School, where she was the first black student, she began taking voice and violin lessons, while attending Detroit Central High School, she played piano in local dance orchestras during the evenings. She joined the Detroit Musical Society, gave solo recitals, and composed a march played at her high school graduation ceremonies in 1883.

In the fall of 1883 Emma entered Washington Normal School, a teacher-training institution, where she was again the first black student. She helped to pay for her education there by playing piano and giving music lessons. After graduating in 1886 she began teaching second grade at Clinton Elementary School in Detroit.

In January 1894 she left her job and eloped with Edwin Henry Hackley, a lawyer, writer, and clerk in the Denver, Colorado, County Deeds Office. The couple settled in Denver.

Pursuing a Musical Career

Emma and Edwin had met at a Detroit concert featuring the singer Sissieretta ("Black Patti") Jones, whose performance inspired Emma to pursue a career in music. She therefore undertook studies leading to a bachelor of music degree at the University of Denver School of Music, where in 1900 (or 1901) she became the first black American to graduate.

In 1901 she began her first concert tour, making her debut in Denver. During those early performances a newspaper, the *Indianapolis Freeman*, described her voice as "a high soprano of great range and sweetness" and called her "the most thoroughly artistic and cultured singer the race has yet produced."[1]

When not touring, Hackley taught in the extension department of the University of Denver School of Music, sang in the Denver Choral Society, and conducted choral concerts. She also began to play the violin publicly.

Political Activist

Because Hackley had light skin and long, wavy auburn hair, some observers, including newspaper commentators, suggested that, to advance her career, she should abandon her race and pass as white. She refused to do so.

Experiencing discrimination in her travels, Hackley became a political activist, working tirelessly for racial equality. She organized a Denver branch of the Colored Women's League and served as its secretary. With her husband she established the Imperial Order of Libyans, a fraternal group that fought racial prejudice and promoted patriotism. Edwin edited the *Denver Statesman*, a black newspaper to which Emma contributed a regular column, "The Exponent."

However, while the Hackleys worked well together, they did not live well together. Late in 1901 they separated, and after Emma returned from a long concert tour, she settled in Philadelphia, and became music director at the Episcopal Church of the Crucifixion.

The People's Chorus

In 1904 Hackley organized the People's Chorus, consisting of a hundred excellent singers from the black community. Her concerts with the chorus featured black spirituals and classical works. At that time many black people, including musicians, had a negative attitude toward spirituals because of the genre's lingering associations with slavery. Hackley, however, persistently educated musicians and audiences to the musical beauty and rich cultural heritage embodied in African-American folk music.

On the other hand, her performances of standard classical works met with opposition from whites, many of whom believed that blacks were not suited to perform classical music, which required rigorous special training. Instead, according to the traditional white view of the time, blacks should perform only their own music, such as spirituals, because such music relied only on natural ability. Hackley, of course, knew better. "The masses of the colored people," she wrote, "if properly taught, can express the best music written. Of all the races the colored race could best express even Bach if they were taught to love Bach's music."[2]

In October 1905 Hackley and several members of the People's Chorus gave a successful concert in Philadelphia. With the proceeds from this event she studied under the well-known voice teacher Jean de Reszke in Paris, from late 1905 to late 1906. After another Philadelphia concert she returned to Paris the following year and remained in Europe till the fall of 1907.

Having benefited so much from her European training, Hackley determined to make the same experience available to other black American musicians. She established the Hackley Foreign Scholarship Fund with money from her own concerts and other fund-raising projects, identified deserving black performers through competitions, and sent the winners to study in Europe. The first recipient, in 1908, was the violinist and composer Clarence Cameron White, who chose to study in London. Hackley, too, went to London, where she studied, taught, and performed.

When she returned to the United States in 1909, she and her husband, with whom she had reconciled a few years earlier, finally separated for good. However, they never divorced, and they remained friendly.

Voice Culture for Black Masses

Hackley devoted most of the rest of her life to what she called "voice culture" (vocal training) for the African-American masses. She began to include in each of her performances "a lecture on vocal production, general musicianship, and even tips on stage presence and poise."[3] In 1909 she self-published a book version of her lectures, *A Guide in Voice Culture.*

In 1910 Hackley began an extensive series of farewell appearances, in which she sang, played the piano, led huge choruses of local singers, and continued her lectures on voice culture. Her goal was to promote the serious study of music among as many members of her race as possible. She became enormously popular, and her audiences often numbered in the thousands.

In late 1914 Hackley began to unite a series of eleven articles for the *New York Age* under the general heading "Hints to Young Colored Artists," covering a wide range of topics, including two pieces entitled "Demonstration of Voice Culture." In 1916 she published another collection of her lectures, *The Colored Girl Beautiful.*

While Hackley's lectures on voice culture were a great success, she knew that they alone could not turn people into well-trained black music teachers, of whom there was a significant shortage. To produce those teachers, she opened her own music school, the Normal Vocal Institute in Chicago, Illinois, where she and her assistants—Pauline James Lee and Hackley's sister, Marietta Smith Johnson—taught piano, theory, voice culture, and languages. The school experienced financial difficulties, however, and it survived only from late 1915 to early 1917. The short-lived Azalia Hackley Music Publishing House met the same fate soon afterward.

Meanwhile, Hackley came out of retirement and resumed touring. She organized large-scale folksong festivals in communities across the country, featuring spirituals and classical pieces by black composers, such as Samuel Coleridge-Taylor and Will Marion Cook. Hackley's only published composition, "Carola," was also performed.

During 1920–21 she visited Japan, and in 1922 she was in California planning a tour when she became ill. Her sister took her home to Detroit, where Hackley died on December 13, 1922.

In the mid-1930s her People's Chorus was renamed the Hackley Choral Society, and in 1939 A. Merral Willis founded a school in Hackley's name in New York City. In 1943 the E. Azalia Hackley Memorial Collection of Negro Music, Dance, and Drama was established at the Detroit Public Library.

Hackley's promotion of music in the black community was as important in elevating African-American culture as Booker T. Washington's promotion of industry was for the community's economic development. "The race," she once said, "needs daring, original people to think and speak."[4] Emma Azalia Smith Hackley was certainly one of those people.

Fannie Lou Hamer

"SICK AND TIRED" ACTIVIST

(1917—1977)

FAMED FOR HER recurring statement "I'm sick and tired of being sick and tired," Fannie Lou Hamer rose from being a doormat to being the doorkeeper of her own destiny. She shared the empowering effect of the civil rights struggle with all who would listen to her words, in the process becoming one of the most quotable women of her time. Her career was marked by a call to dismantle entrenched racist attitudes and seek to build positive programs in their place.

Born Fannie Lou Townsend in Montgomery County, Mississippi, on October 6, 1917, she was the twentieth child of sharecropper parents, Jim and Lou Ella Townsend. Raised in the grinding poverty typical of black sharecroppers in the South, Fannie went to work picking cotton at the age of six and continued to labor on the plantation for many years. Throughout her youth she received the equivalent of about six years of schooling, while absorbing the harsh lesson that blacks in Mississippi had virtually no rights and no future.

In 1942 she married Perry ("Pap") Hamer, a tractor driver from another plantation, the couple later adopted two girls.

Eventually Fannie Lou Hamer was promoted from cotton picker to timekeeper on the plantation. Her pay, however, was still low, and the family continued to suffer the pain of poverty and hopelessness.

Empowerment through Civil Rights Action

When Hamer attended a rally in August 1962 led by the Reverend James Bevel of the Southern Christian Leadership Conference (SCLC) and James Forman of the Student Nonviolent Coordinating Committee (SNCC), both of which groups were organizing people to fight for freedom in Mississippi, her life changed dramatically.

Hamer answered the call for volunteers to challenge the Mississippi voting laws that in effect excluded blacks. On August 31 she was among a group of eighteen blacks who traveled by bus to Indianola to register to vote, all of whom failed a literacy test requiring them to copy and interpret part of the constitution of the State of Mississippi.

Returning to the plantation in Ruleville, Hamer found the plantation owner angry about her attempt to register to vote: "The landowner said I would have to go back to withdraw or I would have to leave," she later recalled, "and so I told him I didn't go down there to register for him; I was down there to register for myself."[1] She left the plantation.

In December 1962 Hamer again failed the literacy test, but on her third try, in January 1963, she passed and became a registered voter. By now strongly committed to her role in the civil rights movement, she joined SNCC as a supervisor in Sunflower County, Mississippi, and devoted herself to teaching blacks how to pass the literacy test to become registered voters.

After attending a civil rights workshop in Charleston, South Carolina, Hamer and a group of other blacks were returning to Ruleville on a Trailways bus when they stopped at a bus terminal in Winona, Mississippi, to eat. When they refused to acknowledge the whites-only rule in the restaurant, they were arrested, and while in the Winona jail Hamer suffered a beating so terrible that it left her permanently injured.

"Sick and Tired"

Hamer's experience in Winona strengthened her resolve to change the racist system in Mississippi. She believed that one way to get the power to make that change was to acquire political leverage. When blacks in the state organized the Mississippi Freedom Democratic party (MFDP) in 1964, after unsuccessful efforts to become part of the Mississippi Democratic party, Hamer became its vice chair and she ran for Congress in the second congressional district of Mississippi on the MFDP ticket. At the 1964 Democratic National Convention in Atlantic City, the MFDP challenged the white Mississippi delegation for the right to be seated. Hamer drew national attention when she testified before the credentials committee and revealed the truth about the oppression of blacks in Mississippi. Ultimately only two of the sixty-eight MFDP delegates were seated at the convention, a decision with which Hamer strongly disagreed. "We didn't come all this way," she said, "for no two seats when all of us is tired."[2]

"All my life I've been sick and tired," she said on many occasions. "Now I'm sick and tired of being sick and tired."[3] She extended this idea beyond the civil rights movement. Of the Vietnam War, she said, "We are sick and tired of our people having to go to Vietnam and other places to fight for something we don't have here. . . . We want. . . to end the wrongs such as fighting a war in Vietnam and pouring billions over there, while people in Sunflower County, Mississippi, and Harlem and Detroit are starving to death."[4]

While spending much of her time trying to destroy the racist elements in American society, Hamer also devoted energy to creating positive programs. She helped to bring the Head Start program to Ruleville. However, she believed that such government programs eventually had the effect of keeping poor people dependent, so she concentrated her efforts on promoting self-reliance. In 1969 she founded the Freedom Farm Cooperative in Sunflower County and fed fifteen hundred people with the food grown there. She helped to raise funds for a low-income housing project in Ruleville, to start a low-income day care center, and to bring to Ruleville a garment factory that provided jobs.

Religious Motivation

Hamer often stated that her Christian faith was at the heart of her work. Her favorite biblical passage,

FANNIE LOU HAMER

The Schlomburg Center

Luke 4:18, convinced her that God and Jesus Christ favor the poor and oppressed: "The Spirit of the Lord is upon me, because he hath anointed me to preach the gospel to the poor; he hath sent me to heal the broken-hearted, to preach deliverance to the captives, and recovering of sight to the blind, to set at liberty them that are bruised." Acts 17:26 told her that we are all of one humanity: "And hath made of one blood all nations of men for to dwell on all the face of the earth, and hath determined the times before appointed, and the bounds of their habitation."

In this pursuit of a unified humanity, Hamer believed, all black women, whether middle class or working class, had a special obligation to support right and justice: "Whether you have a Ph.D., or no D, we're in this bag together. And whether you're from Morehouse or Nohouse, we're still in this bag together."[5]

She herself received honorary doctoral degrees from many institutions, among them Howard University, Morehouse College, and Tougaloo College.

Fannie Lou Townsend Hamer died in Mound Bayou, Mississippi, on March 14, 1977. During her speaking engagements she often sang her favorite song, "This Little Light of Mine," because she regarded herself as a "little light" that she hoped made a difference. She did.

Virginia Hamilton

INNOVATIVE CHILDREN'S AUTHOR

(1936—   )

VIRGINIA HAMILTON IS ONE of the most gifted, innovative authors of children's books writing today. Her richly textured works have challenged not only her young readers but also critics, who have had difficulty categorizing her as a traditional children's author. Hamilton's "inventive use of language, her complex weaving of theme, character, and form, and her use of various mythologies have raised children's literature to new heights of excellence."[1]

Virginia Esther Hamilton was born in Yellow Springs, Ohio, on March 12, 1936, the youngest of five children of Kenneth James Hamilton and Etta Belle (Perry) Hamilton. Her father was a mandolinist, and her mother was a homemaker. Virginia Hamilton grew up in a rural environment, her mother's family having long farmed in the Yellow Springs area.

Both parents, as well as many of her aunts and uncles, were wonderful storytellers. "Because I was around people who expressed themselves through stories, just everything became a story," Hamilton later explained. "I learned that telling had a beginning, a middle, and an ending, and it became very natural for me to speak in terms of narration or story and to write that way later on."[2]

After finishing high school Hamilton attended Antioch College (1952–55) in Yellow Springs but left without a degree. In 1955 she began spending her summers in New York City working as a bookkeeper, experiencing city life, and trying to become a writer. During 1957–58 she attended Ohio State University in Columbus, after which she moved to New York City and began studying at the New School for Social Research from 1958 to 1960.

In New York she met Arnold Adoff, a Jewish teacher and poet who became her literary agent. They married in 1960 and had two children, Leigh and Jaime.

Hamilton lived in New York City for about fifteen years, but after she became a successful writer she returned with her family to Ohio.

Zeely and Beyond

During the early 1960s Hamilton held various jobs and wrote constantly, submitting many manuscripts to magazines. Her first real success was the publication of her children's novel *Zeely* (1967), in which a girl named Elizabeth, who calls herself Geeder, is introduced to authentic African cultural images through an African-American woman, Zeely. This work was one of the earliest children's books to convey such imagery, as well as one of the first to portray a black American family that was not poverty-stricken.

Hamilton has become a prolific writer of books for young readers. She has published biographies, including *Paul Robeson: The Life and Times of a Free Black Man* (1974); folktale collections, such as *The People Could Fly: American Black Folktales* (1985); and a wide range of fiction, from the mystery of *The House of Dies Drear* (1968) to the science fiction of *Willie Bea and the Time the Martians Landed* (1983) to the historical fiction of *Anthony Burns: The Defeat and Triumph of a Fugitive Slave* (1988) to the fantasy of *Jaguarundi* (1995).

Hamilton won special praise for *M. C. Higgins, the Great* (1974). The book "chronicles the quests of Mayo Cornelius Higgins as he attempts to forge his identity as a young man, share a friendship with an outcast neighbor, experience a bittersweet first love, and save his family from a possible disaster."[3] *M. C. Higgins, the Great* "is arguably the best and most complex portrayal of a black American family in children's literature."[4]

Hamilton's artistry transcends racial pigeonholing, however. "The constant in my books," she maintained in 1983, "is that the characters are black and yet, the emotional content is simply human."[5]

Awards and Honors

Hamilton has won a huge number of awards and honors. *M. C. Higgins, the Great* was the first work in history to win both the National Book Award and the Newbery Medal (both 1975). She received the Nancy Block Memorial Award of the Downtown (New York City) Community School Awards Committee (1967) for *Zeely* ; the Edgar Allan Poe Award for juvenile mystery (1969) for *The House of Dies Drear*; the Newbery Honor Book Award (1971) for *The Planet of Junior Brown* (1971); the *Boston Globe-Horn Book* Award, the Coretta Scott King Award, and the Newbery Honor Book Award (all 1983) for *Sweet Whispers, Brother Rush* (1982); the Coretta Scott King Award and the *New York Times* Best Illustrated Children's Book Award (both 1986) for *The People Could Fly: American Black Folktales*; the *Boston Globe-Horn Book* Award (1988) and the Coretta Scott King Award (1989) for *Anthony Burns: The Defeat and Triumph of a Fugitive Slave*; the Newbery Honor Book Award (1989) for *In the Beginning: Creation Stories from Around the World* (1988); the Catholic Library Association Regina Medal (1990); the Laura Ingalls Wilder Medal of the American Library Association (1995); the John D. and Catherine T. MacArthur Fellowship, known as the Genius Award (1995); and other numerous awards and honors.

Challenging the Critics

One reason for Hamilton's great success is her willingness to challenge young readers with "complex stylistic features, for children's books, such as stream-of-consciousness ruminations, multiple settings, and shifting time periods, combinations of differing genres, and major characters in psychic and emotional distress."[6] *Anthony Burns*, *The Planet of Junior Brown*, and *Sweet Whispers, Brother Rush*, among other books, contain such elements.

Critics, too, have been challenged by her work. Some wonder if her techniques are suited only for adult readers, not children. Hamilton herself, however, knows that young readers can, and want to, grasp far more than is usually presented to them. Her goal, she says, is to respond "to their needs, fears, loves and hunger in as many new ways as possible."[7]

Besides giving her readers fresh methods of presentation, Virginia Hamilton offers them substantive ideas that can stimulate young minds to understand the world from an ever-larger point of view. "All of the children of Hamilton's books," according to Nina Mikkelsen in Virginia Hamilton, "...serve to urge, warn, and reveal to us, in subtle and artistic ways, that something needs to be done if our lives are not to be destroyed by environmental carelessness, universal greed, prejudice, ethnic quarrels, misuse of the earth's resources, and loss of ethnic heritage."[8]

Selected writings:

JUVENILE FICTION

Zeely (1967)
The House of Dies Drear (1968)
The Time-Ago Tales of Jahdu (1969)
The Planet of Junior Brown (1971)
Time-Ago Lost: More Tales of Jahdu (1973)
M. C. Higgins, the Great (1974)
Arilla Sun Down (1976)
Justice and Her Brothers (1978)
Jahdu (1980)
Dustland (1980)
The Gathering (1981)
Sweet Whispers, Brother Rush (1982)
The Magical Adventures of Pretty Pearl (1983)
Willie Bea and the Time the Martians Landed (1983)
A Little Love (1984)
Junius over Far (1985)
The People Could Fly: American Black Folktales (1985)
The Mystery of Drear House: The Conclusion of the Dies Drear Chronicle (1987)
A White Romance (1987)
In the Beginning: Creation Stories from Around the World (1988)

Anthony Burns: The Defeat and Triumph of a Fugitive Slave (1988)

Bells of Christmas (1989)

The Dark Way: Stories from the Spirit World (1990)

Cousins (1990)

The All Jahdu Storybook (1991)

Drylongso (1992)

Many Thousand Gone: African Americans from Slavery to Freedom (1993)

Plain City (1993)

Jaguarundi (1995)

Her Stories: African American Folktales, Fairy Tales, and True Tales (1995)

When Birds Could Talk and Bats Could Sing: The Adventures of Bruh Sparrow, Sis Wren, and Their Friends (1996)

A Ring of Tricksters: Animal Tales from America, the West Indies, and Africa (1997)

JUVENILE NONFICTION

(biographies)

W. E. B. Du Bois: A Biography (1972)

Paul Robeson: The Life and Times of a Free Black Man (1974)

Lorraine Hansberry

AUTHOR OF *A RAISIN IN THE SUN*

(1930—1965)

ONE OF THE MOST celebrated of all African-American playwrights, Lorraine Hansberry had a major impact on the professional theater despite her short life. Her first produced play, *A Raisin in the Sun*, has become an American classic.

Lorrain Vivian Hansberry was born in Chicago on May 19, 1930, the youngest of four children of Carl Augustus Hansberry and Nannie (Perry) Hansberry. Carl was a successful real estate broker who supported the Urban League and the National Association for the Advancement of Colored People and unsuccessfully ran for Congress as a Republican in 1940. Nannie was a schoolteacher and later a ward committeewoman. Both parents had migrated north from southern states, Carl from Mississippi and Nannie from Tennessee.

Raisin Seeds

Since Chicago's black neighborhoods had a serious housing shortage. Carl Hansberry made much of his money by buying large houses vacated by whites and dividing the structures into small apartments. Lorraine Hansberry later used this type of apartment as the setting for *A Raisin in the Sun*, much of whose action centers on the struggle for better housing.

After attending public schools in Chicago, she studied for three years at the University of Wisconsin-Madison where she developed liberal political views as she integrated her dormitory, worked for the Henry Wallace presidential campaign in 1948, and became president of the Young Progressive League in 1949. One experience at the university that had a lasting effect on her was a school production of Sean

O'Casey's play *Juno and the Paycock*. She was impressed by O'Casey's method of universalizing the suffering of a specific people, the Irish. A few years later she would apply the same technique to the African-American condition in *A Raisin in the Sun*.

Struggling Writer

In 1950, eager to experience real life outside the classroom, Hansberry left the university and moved to the Harlem section of New York City. She began working at a progressive newspaper, *Freedom*, founded by Paul Robeson. In 1952 she became associate editor of the newspaper.

Life in Harlem stimulated Hansberry to begin writing poetry, short stories, and plays. Her writing reflected her progressive politics, often focusing on how people reacted to their social wounds or struggled to overcome adversity.

"One cannot live with sighted eyes and feeling heart," she once explained, "and not know and react to the miseries which afflict this world."[1]

In 1953 Hansberry married Robert Barro Nemiroff, a white student of Jewish heritage at New York University, with whom she shared many political and cultural interests. In that same year she left her job at the *Freedom* to devote herself to creative writing, and over the next few years she held various jobs off and on, working as a typist, a program director at a progressive summer camp, and a recreation leader for the handicapped.

Then a stroke of luck came her way. In 1956 Nemiroff and his friend Burt(on) D'Lugoff (under the pseudonyms Bob Barron and Burt Long, respectively) wrote a hit song, "Cindy, Oh, Cindy." The money from the song enabled Hansberry to quit her jobs and concentrate full-time on writing.

A Raisin in the Sun

Like all good writers, Hansberry wrote about what she knew best. For her first major work she drew on her memories of the working-class black families who had rented apartments from her father in Chicago. She wrote a realistic play about specific characters struggling to improve their lives, but she cast the drama so that, like O'Casey's *Juno and the Paycock*, it could be understood and felt by any person from any background.

Originally she called the play *The Crystal Chair*. Then she reflected on a Langston Hughes poem, "Harlem," in which he asks: "What happens to a dream deferred?... Does it dry up like a raisin in the sun?... Or does it explode?"[2] The play became *A Raisin in the Sun*.

Major Broadway producers would not touch the work—a black story on Broadway would not "sell." So a family friend, Phil Rose, who employed Nemiroff in a music publishing firm, and David S. Cogan raised enough money to take the show on tour in New Haven, Connecticut; Philadelphia, and Chicago. The play was such a success that a Broadway production was inevitable, and *A Raisin in the Sun* opened at the Ethel Barrymore Theater on March 11, 1959. Audiences and critics immediately loved it. When the play won the New York Drama Critics Circle Award, Hansberry became the first black playwright, the youngest person, and only the fifth woman to win the honor.

Last Years

A Raisin in the Sun made Hansberry a celebrity, and she was soon in great demand as a speaker at various conferences and meetings. On March 1, 1959, before an audience of black writers at a conference sponsored by the American Society of African Culture in New York City, she delivered one of her most important speeches, "The Negro Writer and His Roots" (published in the *Black Scholar* in 1981). Declaring that "all art is ultimately social," she called on black writers to become involved in "the intellectual affairs of all men, everywhere."[3] Taking her own advice, she became deeply involved in the civil rights movement in the early 1960s, helping to raise funds for various organizations, including the Student Nonviolent Coordinating Committee (SNCC).

In 1960 NBC commissioned Hansberry to write the script for the opening segment of a five-part television series on the Civil War. After thoroughly researching the topic of slavery, she wrote *The Drinking Gourd*, which dramatized the horrible effects of the slave system not only on blacks but also on whites. In one scene, when a slave, Hannibal, is caught learning to read, he is blinded by a white overseer. NBC believed the play to be too controversial and shelved the entire project.

In 1961 Columbia Pictures released the film version of *A Raisin in the Sun*, while Hansberry busied herself writing several new plays.

However, in the spring of 1963 she had a fainting spell. Subsequent tests showed that she had cancer of the pancreas. Despite failing health she continued to write and to engage in political activities publishing *The Movement: Documentary of a Struggle for Equality*, a photographic essay on the civil rights issues of that time, in 1964. On October 15, 1964, her play *The Sign in Sidney Brustein's Window* opened on Broadway at the Longacre Theater. Having a primarily white cast, the drama exhorted intellectuals to become involved in social problems and world issues.

In May 1963 Hansberry joined other celebrities in raising funds for SNCC and supporting the southern freedom movement. In May 1964 she left her hospital bed to give a speech to the winners of a writing contest sponsored by the United Negro College Fund, in which she coined the now famous phrase "young, gifted, and black."

Lorraine Hansberry finally lost her battle with cancer on January 12, 1965. She died at University Hospital in New York City at the age of thirty-four.

Posthumous Renown

In her will Hansberry named her former husband, Robert Nemiroff (whom she had divorced earlier in the 1960s), as her literary executor. Through editing, publishing, and producing her work, he ensured that her reputation continued to grow after her death.

Hansberry left many finished and unfinished projects. In 1969 Nemiroff adapted some of her unpublished writings to create the play *To Be Young, Gifted, and Black*, an off-Broadway hit in New York City and a successful touring play throughout the United States during 1970–71. An expanded version was published in book form as *To Be Young, Gifted, and Black: Lorraine Hansberry in Her Own Words* (1969, with later editions).

In 1970 Nemiroff guided a Broadway production at the Longacre Theater of Hansberry's *Les Blancs* (The Whites). Her most political play, it is set in Africa during a revolution. Inspired by a vision of a female warrior figure, the black protagonist chooses to lead his people in battle against colonial oppression even though his choice means losing his white wife, killing his own brother, and accidentally causing the death of a white woman who has been like a mother to him.

Nemiroff edited and in 1972 published *Les Blancs: The Collected Last Plays of Lorraine Hansberry*. Besides *Les Blancs*, the book presents *The Drinking Gourd* and *What Use Are Flowers?*, the latter being a short play about a band of children struggling to survive after a nuclear holocaust, aided by a hermit who tries to reconnect them with the love of knowledge and beauty.

Further productions of her works added to Hansberry's prestige, especially *A Raisin in the Sun*, which in 1974 was turned into a Broadway musical, *Raisin*, that won an Antoinette Perry (Tony) Award. In 1987 the original drama was revived nationwide, and in 1989 it was presented on television. Nemiroff continued to guide these and other revivals and publications of Hansberry's works till his own death in 1991.

Contemporary feminists have found foreshadowings of their cause in Hansberry's works. In *A Raisin in the Sun*, for example, Mama shares the role of protagonist with Walter, Beneatha aspires to be a doctor, and abor-

tion is introduced as an issue for poor women. In *The Drinking Gourd* Rissa, the house slave, shows strength and independence by defying her master and arming her son for his escape from slavery.

Lorraine Hansberry, through the dramatic power of *A Raisin in the Sun*, forced the American professional theater to take black artists more seriously. The play, however, has more than just historical interest. Today it holds the stage as well as ever because its timeless characters—regardless of color—"affirmed life in the face of brutality and defeat."[4]

Selected writings:

FICTION

(plays unless otherwise indicated)

A Raisin in the Sun (play, 1959; film script, 1961)

The Sign in Sidney Brustein's Window (1964)

To Be Young, Gifted, and Black, adapted by Robert Nemiroff (1969)

Les Blancs, adapted by Nemiroff (1970)

Les Blancs: The Collected Last Plays of Lorraine Hansberry, edited by Nemiroff (book, 1972)

NONFICTION

"This Complex of Womanhood" (article, *Ebony*, August 15, 1960)

"A Challenge to Artists" (article, *Freedomways*, Winter 1963)

The Movement: Documentary of a Struggle for Equality (book, 1964)

To Be Young, Gifted, and Black: Lorraine Hansberry in Her Own Words, adapted by Nemiroff (book, 1969)

"The Negro Writer and His Roots: Toward a New Romanticism" (article, *Black Scholar*, March/April 1981, based on a 1959 speech)

Elizabeth Ross Haynes

PIONEER ACTIVIST

(1883—1953)

ORGANIZATION OFFICIAL, social reformer, civic activist, and author, Elizabeth Ross Haynes participated in many of the historic struggles and achievements of her race in the first half of the twentieth century. She is probably best remembered for breaking color barriers in the Young Women's Christian Association (YWCA).

Elizabeth Ross was born in Lowndes County, Alabama, on July 30, 1883, the daughter of former slaves Henry and Mary (Carnes) Ross. After studying at State Normal School (now Alabama State University) from 1896 to 1900 and graduating as valedictorian of her class, she earned an A.B. degree at Fisk University in Nashville, Tennessee, in 1903, attended summer sessions in the graduate school of the University of Chicago from 1905 through 1907, and received an A.M. degree in sociology from Columbia University in 1923.

Elizabeth began her professional career as a schoolteacher. She taught in Alabama, Missouri, and Texas.

In 1910 she married George Edmund Haynes, a sociologist and later a founder and executive director of the National Urban League. They had a son, also named George.

YWCA Trailblazer

From 1908 to 1910 Elizabeth served as the first black national secretary of the YWCA. She supervised the organization's activities at colleges and in cities with black branches, which under her leadership greatly increased in number. After her marriage she became a volunteer worker for the YWCA, achieving another breakthrough in 1924 when she became the first black woman elected to the national board of the YWCA, a position she held till 1934. In her roles as national secretary and national board member, she helped to build the YWCA movement. In a 1910 report, she wrote that through the YWCA young women were "being turned inward to their own beliefs and ideals, and outward to the part they can play in helping to better... social conditions."[1]

In spite of Haynes's lofty positions with the YWCA, the organization as a whole was highly segregated during most of her years with the group. Along with other notable activists, including Lucy Laney* and Charlotte Hawkins Brown,* she fought to end the YWCA's racist practices, such as having white women set policies for black branches and suppressing opportunities for black leadership, but full integration at the YWCA was not achieved till 1946.

Advocate for Black Women

Haynes's efforts on behalf of women extended far beyond her activities with the YWCA. During World War I, when she was living in Washington, D.C., she served as a volunteer for the Women's Bureau of the United States Department of Labor, where her husband was employed.

After the war, women in the work force attracted much national attention, and in 1919 the First International Congress of Working Women met in Washington, D.C. When it failed, however to address the specific needs of African-Americans, a group of prominent women, including Haynes, signed a petition calling for the congress to offer programs more relevant to black women.

From 1920 to 1922 she served as domestic service secretary for the United States Employment Service in Washington, D.C., and in 1922 prepared a report called "Two Million Negro Women at Work." In her research she found most black women engaged in three types of occupations: domestic and personal service, agriculture, and manufacturing and mechanical industries. Haynes was saddened by the plight of those in domestic service, "with all their shortcomings—their lack of training in efficiency, in cleanliness of person, in honesty and truthfulness, and with all of the shortcomings of ordinary domestic service; namely basement living quarters, poor working conditions, too long hours, no Sundays off, no standards of efficiency, and the servant 'brand.'"[2] Rural black women working in agriculture had to travel long distances to labor in hot fields, and they had little recreation. Black women with manufacturing jobs received low pay; worked in dirty, poorly ventilated factories; and had restricted opportunities because of a lack of training.

New York City Activist

In their later years Haynes and her husband lived in New York City, where Elizabeth continued to engage in various forms of social betterment. For many years she performed interracial work for the Federated Council of the Churches of Christ in America, for which her husband was secretary of the Commission on Race Relations. She was a member of the New York Planning Commission and the Harlem Better Schools Committee, chaired the Industry and Housing Department of the National Association of Colored Women, served as superintendent of the Junior Department of the Abyssinian Baptist Church School in New York, and was secretary of the board of managers of the Adam Clayton Powell Home for the Aged. In 1935 she was elected coleader of the Twenty-first Assembly District in New York County, in which capacity she attended to such problems as unemployment, legislation, and assistance to the elderly.

Besides writing her highly regarded report "Two Million Negro Women at Work" and her master's thesis, "Negroes in Domestic Service in the United States" (published in the *Journal of Negro History* in 1923), Haynes wrote two important biographies of blacks—*Unsung Heroes* (1921) presents the life stories of several celebrated blacks, including Sojourner Truth* and Phillis Wheatley.* *The Black Boy of Atlanta* (1952) relates the story of Major R. R. Wright, a black educator and banker.

Elizabeth Ross Haynes died in New York City on October 26, 1953, leaving behind a long record of accomplishments as a civil rights and women's rights pioneer.

Dorothy Height

PRESIDENT OF THE NATIONAL COUNCIL OF NEGRO WOMEN

(1912–   )

DOROTHY HEIGHT has been a central figure in the civil rights and women's rights movements of her time. No African-American woman has surpassed her ability as an organizational leader in her roles with the Young Women's Christian Association (YWCA), the Delta Sigma Theta sorority, and especially the National Council of Negro Women (NCNW).

Dorothy Irene Height was born in Richmond, Virginia, on March 24, 1912, to James Edward Height and Fannie (Burroughs) Height. She had one sister, a half sister, and a half brother. In 1916 the family moved to Rankin, Pennsylvania, a small mining town. Her father was a building contractor and a Sunday school superintendent. From her mother, a private nurse and an activist in various organizations, she derived the idea of organizing clubs.

In addition to being an outstanding student at Rankin High School, Dorothy Height became active in the YWCA, where she early on developed leadership skills. By the age of fourteen she was elected president of the Pennsylvania State Federation of Girls Clubs.

After graduating from high school Height enrolled at New York University, where she finished her undergraduate work in three years, in 1933 earning a master's degree in educational psychology at the end of her fourth year.

After leaving college she took a practice teaching position at Brownsville Community Center in Brooklyn. Shortly after, in 1935, she became a case worker for the New York City Department of Welfare, and was soon promoted to an advisory position to investigate the Harlem riots of that year. It was around this time that she joined the United Christian Youth

Movement and soon became one of the leaders of the organization.

YWCA Leader

Having been active as a member of the YWCA since girlhood, Height accepted a position with the organization in the late 1930s so that she could develop her skills working with a large-scale, internationally oriented body. Assigned to Harlem as assistant director of the Emma Ransom House, a place of lodging for black women, she soon recognized the most serious problem of the house's inhabitants and became a vocal, lifelong advocate of fair wages and dignified working conditions for domestic workers.

In 1939 Height moved to Washington, D.C., to become executive secretary of the YWCA Phillis Wheatley Home. The following year she directed the YWCA School for Professional Workers in Mount Carroll, Illinois.

In 1944 Height joined the national board of the YWCA in New York City. Her principal task was to develop training programs for YWCA staff and volunteers, but she also helped to plan the historic convention of 1946, at which the membership voted to support an interracial charter calling for complete integration of the YWCA.

Height then became the national board's interracial education secretary, and in this capacity she helped to lead the YWCA into the larger arena of the civil rights struggle of the 1960s and 1970s. In 1963, as secretary of the YWCA's Department of Racial Justice, she planned strategies to eliminate lingering segregation within the association. In 1970 she helped to formulate the famous YWCA One Imperative, a statement of the belief that the elimination of racism was of fundamental importance in ending oppression in society. Height herself believed that "the Y must get middle-class black and white liberals into the ghettos working not for, but with, minority groups."[1]

Head of Delta Sigma Theta

Soon after Height joined the Delta Sigma Theta sorority, in 1939, she took on a leadership role with the organization. In June 1940 she proposed the formation, and became head, of a nationwide job analysis project to study and improve employment opportunities and conditions for black women.

Height was elected vice president of Delta Sigma Theta in 1944, and in 1947 she became national president. During her tenure she expanded the scope of the sorority and drew national and international attention to its work. Under her leadership Delta Sigma Theta created international chapters, beginning with Haiti in 1950, and became actively involved in world affairs, for example, by meeting with members of the United Nations Department of Information and the Political and Economic Committee on the Rights of Women. In the United States her efforts included starting a bookmobile to serve the black people of Georgia and holding a series of nationally broadcast town meetings.

By the mid-1950s, feeling that she had accomplished her goals for Delta Sigma Theta, Height stepped down from the presidency in 1956 so that she could accept even larger challenges.

President of NCNW

In the late 1930s Height had met Mary McLeod Bethune*, founder and president of the National Council of Negro Women, an umbrella group for local and national organizations committed to uniting middle- and upper-class black women to fight for social action programs and humanitarian causes. Height soon joined the NCNW and in 1957 became its president.

Through her role in the NCNW she joined with Martin Luther King, Jr., Whitney Young, and others to lead the American civil rights movement in the

1960s and beyond. She held voter education drives in both the North and the South, and she arranged for the NCNW to raise funds to pay students who postponed their college education to participate in civil rights actions.

A strong advocate of self-reliance, she guided many NCNW-sponsored programs aimed at providing African-Americans with immediate relief as well as economic stabilty for the future. Such activities included food drives, child care and housing projects, and career and educational programs. One project, for example, concentrated on supplying seed and feed for farmers and starting food cooperatives in rural areas. While another used a federal grant to operate a job-training program for teenagers.

Height saw to it that the council developed many programs specifically designed to enhance the lives of black women. Through a Ford Foundation grant, the NCNW began Operation Woman Power, a project that helped women to open their own businesses. Today the council also operates the Bethune Museum and Archives for black women's history, publishes *Black Women's Voice*, maintains the Information Center for and about black women, and runs the Women's Center for Education and Career Advancement for women interested in nontraditional careers. Through the council, Height conceived and organized the Black Family Reunion Celebration of 1986 to reinforce the traditional values of the African-American family. It became an annual event.

Height has also made a major effort to link black Americans with people from Third World countries, especially Africa, where the NCNW has offices in both the west and the south. She has often spoken publicly about the need for the United States, the United Nations, and local organizations to improve the conditions of women in Third World countries. As early as 1960 she went to Africa to study women's organizations there, becoming a consultant on this issue to the American secretary of state soon thereafter. Her efforts in this capacity not only helped to win American aid for new black African nations, but also forged a strong cooperative feeling between blacks in Africa and the United States. In 1991 she attended the first ever summit of Africans and African-Americans, held to call for African development in the United States and to strengthen ties between Africans and black Americans.

During her years with the NCNW, Height also lent her leadership services to other organizations, serving as a member of the American Red Cross Board of Governors; chairing the Committee on the Status of Women, Equal Employment, and Employment of the Handicapped; and acting as a consultant to the New York State Social Welfare Board. In October 1997 she participated in the Million Woman March rally in Washington, D.C., to help unify black women in America.

Awards and Honors

Height's distinguished service and contributions to society have earned her innumerable awards and honors. They include Hadassah's Myrtle Wreath of Achievement (1964), the National Council of Jewish Women's John F. Kennedy Memorial Award (1965), the Ministerial Interfaith Association Award (1969), the *Ladies' Home Journal* Woman of the Year Award for her work in human rights (1974), the Congressional Black Caucus's William L. Dawson Award for "Decades of public service to people of color and particularly women" (1974), the Citizen's Medal Award from President Reagan (1989), the Caring Institute's Caring Award (1989), the Camille Cosby World of Children Award (1990), the Ambassador Award of the YWCA (1993), the Presidential Medal of Freedom (the highest American civilian honor) from President Clinton (1994), a citation by the TransAfrica Forum (1997), and over twenty honorary degrees.

Through her leadership roles in three influential women's organizations—the YWCA, Delta Sigma Theta, and the NCNW—Dorothy Height has exerted tremendous influence in favor of the pursuit of equal rights for black women around the globe. "Her life exemplifies her passionate commitment to a just society and her vision of a better world."[2]

DOROTHY HEIGHT

The Schomburg Center / NYPL

Anita Hill

LAWYER AND WRITER SPECIALIZING IN SEXUAL HARASSMENT

(1956–   )

IN OCTOBER 1991 Anita Hill was suddenly thrust into the limelight when she accused President Bush's Supreme Court nominee Clarence Thomas of having sexually harassed her when she worked for him in the early 1980s, first at the Department of Education and later at the Equal Employment Opportunity Commission (EEOC). Her action forced the issue of sexual harassment to the forefront of public debate. "Testifying," she later said, "has helped me understand that one individual's behavior and actions make a difference."[1]

Anita Faye Hill was born in Lone Tree, Oklahoma, on July 30, 1956, the youngest of thirteen children of Albert and Erma (Elliott) Hill. She grew up doing chores on a 250-acre farm.

A straight-A student, Anita Hill was valedictorian of her class at Morris High School in 1973. After going on to attend Oklahoma State University in Stillwater, from which she graduated with a B.S. degree in psychology in 1977, her interest in civil rights led her to study law at Yale University Law School, which awarded her a J.D. degree in 1980.

Working for Clarence Thomas

From August 1980 to July 1981 Hill was an associate in the prestigious law firm of Wald, Harkrader, and Ross in Washington, D.C. On the recommendation of one of the firm's partners, Clarence Thomas hired her as his special counsel when he became head of the Office of Civil Rights in the Department of Education. Within a few months, according to Hill, Thomas began harassing her by pressing her for dates and speaking to her in a lewd manner. She rejected his advances and objected to his language, but the harassment stopped only after several months when he became involved with another woman.

When Thomas became chairman of the EEOC in May 1982, Hill went with him as his assistant. That fall, she later alleged, he began to harass her again.

Academic Lawyer

In July 1983 Hill left the EEOC to begin teaching at the O. W. Coburn School of Law at Oral Roberts University in Tulsa, Oklahoma. Thomas himself had recommended her to the dean of the law school, Charles Kothe, who later worked as Thomas's special assistant at the EEOC. When the Coburn school closed in 1986, Kothe, still friendly with Thomas, recommended Hill for a teaching position in commercial law at the University of Oklahoma's College of Law in Norman. Because of the professional help she received from Thomas and his friend Kothe, Hill later explained, she was reluctant for many years to report the harassment she had experienced.

As her career at the University of Oklahoma progressed well, she helped minority student organizations and became involved with law school committees. In 1990 she was awarded tenure, and later her colleagues elected her to an important committee overseeing hiring, tenure, and salaries.

The Hearings and Their Aftermath

On July 1, 1991, the White House announced the nomination of Clarence Thomas, now a judge on the federal appeals court, to the Supreme Court. Later that month Hill privately confided her experience with Thomas to a friend and sought advice about whether or not to come forward. Her confidant, however, told some friends the story without naming Hill, and the rumor then began to spread from person to person and from government department to government department. Soon it was clear that Hill was the person whose career fit the description in the story. On October 6 the journalist Nina Totenberg interviewed her on National Public Radio, and the resulting publicity induced the Senate Judiciary Committee to subpoena Hill to testify during Thomas's confirmation hearings that month.

She appeared before the committee for seven hours. "After approximately three months of working there [the Department of Education]," she said in her opening statement, "he asked me to go out socially with him. What happened next and telling the world about it are the two most difficult things, experiences of my life. It is only after a great deal of agonizing consideration and a number of sleepless nights that I am able to talk of these unpleasant matters to anyone but my close friends."[2] She then gave graphic testimony her alleging Thomas's sexual harassment. When Thomas himself addressed the committee, he denied the charges and characterized the hearings as a "high-tech lynching for uppity blacks."[3] On October 15 the full Senate confirmed his nomination to the Supreme Court by a vote of 52 to 48.

When the hearings concluded, Hill received so many letters from women detailing their experiences of sexual harassment that she began to research the topic and then to give lectures on her findings.

Her efforts to raise national awareness about the problem of sexual harassment brought her accolades from women's groups. The editors of *Glamour* magazine named her the Woman of the Year for 1991, and in 1992 the American Bar Association's Commission on Women in the Profession gave her the Margaret Brent Women Lawyers of Achievement Award.

In December 1993 Hill signed a million-dollar agreement with Doubleday to write her autobiography and a historical account of sexual harassment. After first taking an unpaid leave of absence from her teaching position to work on the first book, in October 1996 she resigned from the University of Oklahoma so that she could spend more time on her writing projects. In early 1997 she became a visiting scholar at the University of California in Berkeley.

ANITA HILL

New York Daily News

Her autobiography, *Speaking Truth to Power*, was published in 1997.

Early in that book she clearly summarized her position in the national dialogue over sexual harassment. "To my supporters," she wrote, "I represent the courage to come forward and disclose a painful truth—a courage which thousands of others have found since the hearing. To my detractors I represent the debasement of a public forum, at best, a pawn, at worst, a perjurer. Living with these conflicting perceptions is difficult, sometimes overwhelming."[4]

Anita Hill, through her failure to stop the Clarence Thomas Supreme Court confirmation and her subsequent success in sensitizing people to the issue of sexual harassment, has become a symbol of both the frustrations and the accomplishments of the women's rights movement on this issue.

Billie Holiday

LADY DAY

(1915—1959)

WHILE SUFFERING THROUGH a tormented life, Billie Holiday poured out her heartache in song performances that were both emotionally poignant and musically brilliant. She earned the title of Lady Day and attained legendary status as the most influential female singer in jazz history.

For many years there was confusion about her early years, confusion that Donald Clarke finally cleared up in his book *Wishing on the Moon: The Life and Times of Billie Holiday* (1994).

Born in Philadelphia on April 7, 1915, she was given the name Elinore Harris on her birth certificate. Throughout her life her first name was spelled in various ways, the most common one being Eleanora. Her parents, Sara ("Sadie") Harris and Clarence Holiday, were not married, so Sadie gave her surname to the baby on the birth certificate but listed another man, Frank DeViese, probably a family friend, as the father. Sadie was herself an illegitimate child, whose mother's surname was Harris and whose father's surname was Fagan. When Eleanora was still a small child, Sadie took her to Baltimore, Maryland, Sadie's hometown, where, in fact, she had become pregnant. There Sadie took the surname Fagan as a way of becoming closer to her father, thus giving rise to the erroneous idea that Billie Holiday was born in Baltimore with the name Eleanora Fagan.

Her parents never married each other and in fact probably never even lived together. In 1920 Sadie married Philip Gough, a longshoreman, who abandoned the family three years later.

Caught playing hooky from school once too often, Eleanora was sent to the House of Good Shepherd for Colored Girls, a Catholic reformatory, in January 1925. Soon after being released to her mother in October, the preteen girl was back on the streets, now working as a prostitute.

During that time, at a madam's house and elsewhere, Eleanora listened to blues and jazz recordings and imitated the styles she heard. Music had always been a central part of her life. Her father, Clarence Holiday, was an accomplished rhythm guitarist who, at various times in his career, worked with Fletcher Henderson, Benny Carter, and other jazz greats before dying in 1937. In the late 1920s Eleanora began singing in Baltimore nightclubs.

Sometime between 1927 and 1929 Eleanora moved to New York City, where her mother had already gone to work as a domestic, and was soon placed by Sadie in a Harlem brothel, but after being arrested for prostitution, she worked for a time as a waitress in a gambling house.

By the early 1930s she was singing regularly at various Harlem nightclubs. After one year at the Nest she moved to the nearby Pod's and Jerry's.

It was about this time that she took the stage name Billie Halliday. She later claimed to have derived the first name from a screen star, Billie Dove, but she also had a good friend named Billie and had herself long been called Bill or William by her father and her close friends. The surname Halliday was a tribute to her musical father. She changed the spelling at first because she did not want to trade on his reputation, but within a few years she adopted his form of the name, Holiday.

Because she was reluctant to take tips off the tables, as other nightclub singers did, she was sometimes called Lady. In the mid-1930s she became good friends with the saxophonist Lester Young. She called him Prez (that is, president of the saxophone), so he

BILLIE HOLIDAY

The Emperor Jones (1933); scored great successes during two engagements at the Apollo (November 1934 and April 1935), a Harlem theater famed for its performances by black entertainers; and had a singing role in the short film *Symphony in Black* (1935).

In 1935 Holiday began to make a series of celebrated recordings with ensembles of great musicians led by the pianist Teddy Wilson. Among the best known of those recordings were "Miss Brown to You" (1935), "I Cried for You" (1936), and "Mean to Me" (1937). In 1936 she started to record under her own name, issuing such classic performances as "Did I Remember?" (1936), "Billie's Blues" (1936), and "Fine and Mellow" (1939). These recordings brought her national fame, and soon other singers were imitating her style.

Meanwhile, she also began to make her first major appearances outside New York City. In 1937 she toured with the Count Basie Orchestra and the following year with Artie Shaw's group, with whom she became one of the first black singers to be featured onstage with a white band.

From January to September 1939 Holiday had an extended engagement at Café Society Downtown, an interracial Greenwich Village nightclub popular with intellectuals and the political left. There she created an especially strong impression with her interpretation of the antilynching song "Strange Fruit," which she recorded that same year.

called her Lady Day (that is, Lady [Holi]Day, the president's First Lady). Fans and coworkers soon adopted these nicknames for the pair.

Early Recordings and Stage Triumphs

In 1933 Billie Holiday was working at another Harlem club, Monette's, where the music producer John Hammond discovered her. He soon arranged her first recording sessions, under the leadership of the clarinetist Benny Goodman, including "Your Mother's Son-in-Law" (1933) and "Riffin' the Scotch" (1933).

Soon Holiday's career was taking off in other directions as well. She appeared as an extra in the movie

Commercial Peak

During the 1940s Holiday reached the peak of her commercial popularity. She performed at nightclubs in major American cities throughout the decade, and she conquered three great New York City concert halls: the Metropolitan Opera House (1943), Town Hall (1946), and Carnegie Hall (1948). From 1943 to 1947 she won many awards from jazz critics and fans.

As a result of her popularity Holiday was invited to Hollywood to appear in a film, *New Orleans* (1947), which also featured the jazz trumpeter Louis Armstrong. However, her role turned out to be that of a maid, and the racial stereotyping humiliated her so much that she never made another picture.

One of her most popular recordings was "Lover Man" (1944). Others included "Body and Soul" (1940), "Gloomy Sunday" (1941), and "Now or Never" (1949).

The Last Decade

In the early and 1950s Holiday kept a busy schedule. She fulfilled many club and concert engagements; toured Europe (1954); performed at the first Newport Jazz Festival (1954); published her autobiography, *Lady Sings the Blues* (1956), which was ghost-written by the journalist William Dufty; and recorded albums, including *Billie Holiday at Jazz at the Philharmonic* (1954), *Body and Soul* (1957), and *Lady in Satin* (1958).

During that decade, however, she also experienced a decline in both her health and her voice. As a teenager she had begun smoking marijuana, and later she graduated to opium and heroin. In May 1947 she was convicted of a narcotics charge in Philadelphia and served time at the Federal Reformatory for Women in Alderson, West Virginia, till March 1948. When she was released, she resumed her drug habit, simultaneously doing herself additional harm by drinking excessive amounts of liquor.

While battling those addictions (she committed herself to sanitoriums for treatment in 1947 and 1956), she also endured painful personal relationships with men. Holiday had a propensity for choosing men who physically abused her, lived on her money, and encouraged her drug habit. She had many such relationships, but only two led to marriage. In 1941 she married James N. ("Jimmy") Monroe, a club manager, from whom she was divorced after many years of separation in 1956, just before she married Louis ("Louie") McKay, her personal manager since 1951. They separated in 1957 but never divorced.

Holiday gave her last performance at the Phoenix Theater in New York City on May 25, 1959. Shortly thereafter, suffering from liver cirrhosis and other ailments, she entered the Metropolitan Hospital in Harlem, where she died on July 17, 1959.

Influential Style

Holiday sang with a unique musical style and vocal quality. However, she often acknowledged her indebtedness to the blues singer Bessie Smith* and the jazz trumpeter Louis Armstrong.

From Smith she absorbed a blues feeling in her work, though she seldom performed classically structured blues songs, and she never sang in Smith's heavy, powerful manner. Nevertheless, Holiday masterfully applied her light vibrato voice to blues singing, as on her recording of "Fine and Mellow" (1939), in which she expressed the doleful text through her continual use of blue (lowered) thirds descending to seconds.

Armstrong, the first to develop jazz improvisation into a true art form, profoundly influenced Holiday. It was from him that she learned to improvise and phrase in the manner of an accomplished jazz instrumental soloist, yet she never distorted the vocal line or failed to convey the deepest meaning of the lyric. "I don't think I'm singing," she once explained. "I feel like I'm playing a horn. I try to improvise like Les Young, like Louis Armstrong, or someone else I admire. What comes out is what I feel."[1] Like an instrumentalist, she would detach her line from the basic beat and elongate or condense the melodic cells in a stunning display of rhythmic subtlety and flexible phrasing, as on her recording of "Did I Remember?" (1936). "She sometimes recomposed a song to suit herself," wrote her biographer Donald Clarke, "but even when she did not do that, she subtly altered it harmonically, making it a personal vehicle, all the elements of the art of singing at the service of swing."[2] Holiday was the first important, influential vocalist to adopt this improvisational manner of performance.

Through her recordings and the biographical film *Lady Sings the Blues* (1972), based on her autobiography, Billie Holiday has continued both to inspire and influence jazz singers and to command the highest level of reverence among jazz fans.

Selected recordings:

SINGLES

(under Benny Goodman's name)

"Your Mother's Son-in-Law" (1933, Columbia)
"Riffin' the Scotch" (1933, Columbia)
"Love Me or Leave Me" (1933, Columbia)

SINGLES

(under Teddy Wilson's name)

"Miss Brown to You" (1935, Brunswick)
"I Cried for You" (1936, Brunswick)
"I'll Get By" / "Mean to Me" (1937, Brunswick)
"Foolin' Myself" / "Easy Living" (1937, Brunswick)
"My Man" (1937, Brunswick)
"When You're Smiling" (1938, Brunswick)
"More Than You Know" / "Sugar" (1939, Brunswick)

SINGLES

(under Billie Holiday's name)

"Did I Remember?" / "No Regrets" (1936, Vocalion/Okeh)
"Billie's Blues" (1936, Vocalion/Okeh)

"Me, Myself, and I" (1937, Vocalion/Okeh)
"A Sailboat in the Moonlight" (1937, Vocalion/ Okeh)
"On the Sentimental Side" (1938, Vocalion/Okeh)
"Back in Your Own Back Yard" / "When a Woman Loves a Man" (1938, Vocalion/Okeh)
"Strange Fruit" / "Fine and Mellow" (1939, Commodore)
"Body and Soul" (1940, Vocalion/Okeh)
"Loveless Love" (1940, Okeh)
"God Bless the Child" (1941, Okeh)
"I Cover the Waterfront" (1941, Columbia)
"Gloomy Sunday" (1941, Okeh)
"Lover Man" (1944, Decca)
"Now or Never" (1949, Decca)
"My Sweet Hunk o' Trash" (with Louis Armstrong, 1949, Decca)

ALBUMS

Billie Holiday at Jazz at the Philharmonic (1954, Clef)
Lady Sings the Blues (1956, Clef)
Body and Soul (1957, Verve)
All or Nothing at All (1959, Verve)
Lady in Satin (1958, Columbia)
Billie Holiday (1959)

Lena Horne

DISTINGUISHED VOCALIST

(1917–   )

LENA HORNE IS ONE of the greatest singers in the history of American popular music. "Her earthy, husky voice is highly distinctive and capable of considerable depth of expression," wrote one critic.[1] Her classic performance is the title track of the film *Stormy Weather* (1943).

Lena Mary Calhoun Horne was born in Brooklyn, New York City, on June 30, 1917, to Teddy and Edna Louise (Scottron) Horne. At one time her father was a clerk for the New York State Department of Labor, but he was also heavily involved with numbers rackets. Her mother was an aspiring actress.

In 1920 Teddy Horne deserted the family, and soon thereafter Edna also departed, leaving little Lena in the care of Teddy's parents. Teddy's mother, Cora Calhoun Horne, who was active in the women's suffrage movement, the Urban League, and the National Association for the Advancement of Colored People (NAACP), she greatly influenced her granddaughter's later interest in the civil rights movement, actually registering the two-year-old Lena as a member of the NAACP.

In about 1924 Lena rejoined her mother, and over the next few years they lived a nomadic existence along the East Coast while Edna continued to struggle as an actress. During that time Lena moved back and forth between her mother and her grandmother. In 1927-28 Lena lived with her Uncle Frank Horne in Fort Valley, Georgia, with her mother in Atlanta, Georgia, and with a family acquaintance in Atlanta. In early 1929 Lena returned to Brooklyn to live with her grandparents, later moving with her mother to the Bronx and then to Harlem.

These unsettled years profoundly affected Lena.

"For me the problem of defining just what it meant to be a Negro was compounded because for many years I was to be virtually rootless in the world" of both whites and blacks. "Neither world was ever to be totally mine because I would never stay long enough in either of them to acquire that ultimate, bred-in-the-bones knowledge of them that comes from having roots so deep that you cannot see or even trace some of them."[2]

Early Career

At the age of sixteen Lena Horne quit school and went to work as a singer and dancer in the chorus at the famous Cotton Club in Harlem, where the ownership and patrons were white but the entertainers were black. She took this step with the blessing of her mother who in fact, called on a friend at the club to arrange the audition. At the Cotton Club, Lena Horne worked with some of the greatest names in black entertainment, such as Cab Calloway, Duke Ellington, Billie Holiday,* and Ethel Waters.*

In the beginning Horne, by her own admission, could not carry a tune. Using some of her early earnings to take music lessons, however, she improved rapidly. In 1934, while still at the club, Horne attracted the attention of a producer and as a result briefly appeared on Broadway as a quadroon girl in *Dance with Your Gods*. Soon afterward she left the sleazy atmosphere of the Cotton Club to tour with Noble Sissle's Society Orchestra. Under his leadership she also issued recordings, including "That's What Love Did to Me" (1936).

At about this time her father, now operating a hotel in Pittsburgh came back into her life. In early 1937 Lena Horne married a friend of her father's, Louis Jones, a registrar in the Pittsburgh coroner's office. They had two children, Gail and Teddy, before they separated in 1941 and divorced in 1944.

Turning Point

In 1938 Horne costarred in the all-black musical film *The Duke Is Tops*, and early the next year she had a leading part in the all-black Broadway revue *Blackbirds of 1939*.

But the real turning point in her career came in late 1940, when Charlie Barnet made her the chief vocalist with his all-white band. Horne now began to make a national name for herself through tours with the band and through recordings with the group, especially the hit "Good-for-Nothin' Joe" (1941).

In 1941 she left Barnet's band and became the featured singer at Café Society Downtown, the only nonsegregated nightclub in New York City outside Harlem. There she met Paul Robeson, the great black singer, and Walter White, executive director of the NAACP, both of whom helped her to develop an appreciation for the need of racial solidarity. Soon she moved to Hollywood, where she appeared at the Little Troc Club.

In 1942 Horne signed a movie contract with Metro-Goldwyn-Mayer (MGM), becoming only the second black American to be contracted by a Hollywood movie company. Since her contract stipulated that she would not be asked to play stereotyped roles, over the next several years most of her screen assignments were brief guest appearances as a singer, as in *Panama Hattie* (1942), *Swing Fever* (1943), *Broadway Rhythm* (1944), and *Ziegfeld Follies* (1946). The most important film Horne did for MGM was the all-black musical *Cabin in the Sky* (1943), in which she played the temptress Georgia Brown.

LENA HORNE

Stormy Weather and Beyond

With no other major projects on hand for Horne, MGM lent her to Twentieth-Century Fox, where she made another all-black musical, *Stormy Weather* (1943), playing Selma Rogers and singing the title song, which soon became her signature number.

During World War II, when Horne performed on United Service Organizations tours, she insisted that both black and white soldiers be permitted in her audiences. She became the pinup girl for thousands of black American GIs.

Returning to MGM, Horne resumed her small parts in white musicals, for several years, during which she met Leonard ("Lennie") Hayton, a studio music director who won acclaim for his scoring of *The Harvey*

Girls (1946) and *Singin' in the Rain* (1952) and Academy Awards for *On the Town* (1949) and *Hello, Dolly!* (1969). She secretly married Hayton, who was white, in 1947, but when the marriage became publicly known in 1950, the couple received hate mail from whites and bitter comments from blacks.

Under Hayton's tutelage Horne continued to develop her singing talent from the 1940s through the 1960s. She recorded many albums, including *This Is Lena Horne* (1952), *Lena Horne at the Waldorf Astoria* (1956), *Porgy and Bess* (with Harry Belafonte, 1959), and *Lena...Lovely and Alive* (1962). Her films included *Words and Music* (1948) and *Meet Me in Las Vegas* (1956), and she made her Broadway debut as a star in the musical *Jamaica* (1957). She also guest-starred on television variety shows hosted by Perry Como, Frank Sinatra, and others; headlined the television special *Lena in Concert* in 1969; and gave innumerable concerts throughout the world.

Horne became increasingly active in the civil rights movement during the 1960s and participated in the famous March on Washington in August 1963. During that period she issued *Lena* (1965), an autobiographical book in which she revealed the strain she had been under since her earliest days in show business. Influential blacks wanted her to be a "symbol of Negro aspirations," while whites wanted to exploit her as "an exotic sexual symbol."[3] "But now I am free," she wrote. Blacks "no longer need a handful of successful people to symbolize their hopes.... I can, at last, try to be myself."[4]

The 1970s, however, began darkly. Her father, a stablizing force in her life since her move to Hollywood, died in 1970. Just a few months later her son died, and in 1971 she lost her husband. She spent the next few years regathering her emotions by living quietly in Santa Barbara, California.

In 1974 she returned to Broadway in the show *Tony Bennett and Lena Horne Sing*, and in 1978 she appeared in the movie *The Wiz*, an all-black version of *The Wizard of Oz*.

Reaping Rewards

By the 1980s Horne had attained legendary status in the entertainment world. She gave what was billed as a farewell concert tour in 1980, but the following year she returned to the New York City stage in *Lena Horne: The Lady and Her Music*, which became the longest-running one-woman show in Broadway history. Her performance won her a special Tony Award, the New York City Handel Medallion, the Drama Desk Award, and a Drama Critics Circle citation. A recording of the show won a Grammy Award, in 1982 she went on tour with it throughout the United States, and in 1984 Showtime cable television broadcast the show.

Among the later highlights of her career was a 1993 appearance at the USJVC Jazz Festival, at which she performed songs by Billy Strayhorn. The Blue Note label issued her albums *We'll Be Together Again* (1994) and *An Evening with Lena Horne* (1995), the latter of which won her another Grammy.

Among Horne's many major awards and honors are the NAACP's Spingarn Award (1983), the Kennedy Center Honors Award for Lifetime Contribution to the Arts (1984), the Paul Robeson Award from the Actors' Equity Association (1985), a Grammy Lifetime Achievement Award (1989), the Marietta Tree Award from the Citizens Committee for New York (1997), and the Ella Award for Lifetime Achievement from the Society of Singers (1997). The Public Broadcasting Service televised a 1996 American Masters documentary called *Lena Horne: In Her Own Voice*, and the Society of Singers presented an eightieth-birthday tribute to her at Avery Fisher Hall in New York City in 1997.

Lena Horne, having weathered the personal storms of her youth and endured the "Stormy Weather" years of unwanted symbolism, lived to become one of the most distinguished and highly honored popular singers of the twentieth century.

Selected recordings:

SINGLES

(under Noble Sissle's name)

"That's What Love Did to Me" (1936, Decca)
"I Take to You" (1936, Decca)

SINGLES

(under Charlie Barnet's name)

"Good-for-Nothin' Joe" (1941, Bluebird)
"Haunted Town" (1941, Bluebird)
"You're My Thrill" (1941, Bluebird)

SINGLES

(under Henry Levine's name)

"Memphis Blues" / "St. Louis Blues" (1941, Victor)

SINGLES

(under Artie Shaw's name)

"Love Me a Little" / "Don't Take Your Love from Me" (1941, Victor)

SINGLES

(under Teddy Wilson's name)

"Out of Nowhere" (1941, Columbia)

ALBUMS

Birth of the Blues (1940, RCA)
Moanin' Low (1940, RCA)
Little Girl Blue (1942, RCA)
Till the Clouds Roll By (1946, MGM)
Words and Music (1948, MGM)
This Is Lena Horne (1952, RCA)
It's Love (1955, RCA)
Stormy Weather (1956, RCA)
Lena Horne at the Waldorf Astoria (1956, RCA)
Jamaica (1957, RCA)
Give the Lady What She Wants (1958, RCA)
Porgy and Bess (with Harry Belafonte, 1959, RCA)
Lena Horne at the Sands (1961, RCA)
Lena on the Blue Side (1962, RCA)
Lena . . . Lovely and Alive (1962, RCA)
Lena and Gabor (with Gabor Szabo, 1970, Skye)

Lena Horne: The Lady and Her Music (1981, Qwest/Warner Bros.)
The Men in My Life (1988, Three Cherries)
We'll Be Together Again (1994, Blue Note)
An Evening with Lena Horne (1995, Blue Note)

Selected performances:

STAGE

Dance with Your Gods (1934)
Blackbirds of 1939 (1939)
Jamaica (1957)
Tony Bennett and Lena Horne Sing (1974)
Lena Horne: The Lady and Her Music (1981)

FILMS

Duke Is the Tops (1938)
Panama Hattie (1942)
Cabin in the Sky (1943)
Stormy Weather (1943)
Swing Fever (1943)
I Dood It (1943)
Thousands Cheer (1943)
Two Girls and a Sailor (1944)
Broadway Rhythm (1944)
Till the Clouds Roll By (1946)
Ziegfeld Follies (1946)
Words and Music (1948)
Duchess of Idaho (1950)
Meet Me in Las Vegas (1956)
Death of a Gunfighter (1969)
The Wiz (1978)

Whitney Houston
RECORD-BREAKING POP-GOSPEL SINGER

(1963—   )

"THE RESILIENCE AND metallic fiber of Miss Houston's voice," critic Stephen Holden observed in the *New York Times*, "suggest the pop-gospel equivalent of an Olympic athlete."[1] Her controlled, gospel-influenced vocal power earned her a unique distinction in pop music history: between 1985 and 1988 she became the first performer to record seven number one hit singles in a row.

Whitney Elizabeth Houston was born in Newark, New Jersey, on August 9, 1963, the younger child of John and Emily (Drinkard) Houston. Her father was the executive secretary of the Newark Central Planning Board. Her mother was a gospel and rhythm and blues singer who also had a son by an earlier marriage. Emily, known as Cissy, directed the choir at the New Hope Baptist Church in Newark and led various combinations of her relatives in a series of vocal ensembles known as the Gospelaires, the Drinkard Sisters, Cissy's Girls, and the Sweet Inspirations. Her groups sang backup in live performances and/or recordings with such stars as Elvis Presley and Aretha Franklin.*

Franklin, who often visited the Houston home, became Whitney's musical idol. "I remember being in the studio and how moving it was to see Aretha work," she later recalled. "She brought such great emotion to her music. I decided then that if I was going to sing, I wanted to make people feel the same way about my music."[2]

Early Singing Career

At the age of nine Whitney began singing in her mother's New Hope Baptist Church choir. Later Cissy coached Whitney in singing, and mother and daughter sang together in clubs and, as backups, on recordings by Lou Rawls and others. At the same time the teenaged Whitney established a career as a fashion model, appearing in *Vogue*, *Seventeen*, and *Cosmopolitan* magazines.

After graduating in 1981 from Mount Saint Dominic Academy in Caldwell, New Jersey, she signed with Tara Productions, a talent management company. While continuing to appear as a model in magazines, such as *Harper's Bazaar*, she concentrated now on a recording career. She sang some advertising jingles and briefly performed on albums by other artists, such as Paul Jabara.

An important step forward for her was signing a recording contract with Arista Records, whose founder and president, Clive Davis, began to establish a national audience for her through television appearances, showcase engagements, and other promotions. During this time her personal manager was Gene Harvey, of Tara Productions, but soon much of her career was handled by family members: her father served as her business manager, her half brother, Gary, backed her in her stage act, and her full brother, Michael, became her road manager.

Hit Recording Artist

In February 1985 Arista released her first album, *Whitney Houston*, which she promoted to commercial success through television appearances and a national tour beginning in June 1985 and culminating at Carnegie Hall in New York City in November of that year. Arista also released single tracks from the album, along with videos to match the singles.

WHITNEY HOUSTON

mat, not to mainstream pop stations.)

Houston's later albums include *Whitney* (1987), *I'm Your Baby Tonight* (1990), *The Bodyguard* (1992), and *The Preacher's Wife* (1996). Among her best-known singles are "Love Will Save the Day" (1988), "I'm Your Baby Tonight" (1990), "I Will Always Love You" (1992), "I'm Every Woman" (1993), "Exhale (Shoop Shoop)" (1995), and "I Believe in You and Me" (1997). She has won many Grammys and American Music Awards.

Houston has appeared as a guest singer on innumerable television programs and has performed on many Grammy Awards and American Music Awards shows. On July 4, 1986, she sang "Greatest Love of All" before a national television audience for a Statue of Liberty centennial celebration. She also appeared on a program celebrating Frank Sinatra's seventy-fifth birthday (1990), another celebrating Muhammad Ali's fiftieth birthday (1992), her own *Whitney Houston: This Is My Life* (1992), and other television specials.

While pursuing her music career, she fell in love with another singer, Bobby Brown, whom she married in 1992. They had a daughter, Bobbi Kristina Houston Brown.

Budding Actress

Whitney Houston has also expanded her career into acting. After making brief appearances as a singer in the films *Perfect* (1985) and *School for Vandals* (1986), she made her film acting debut in the role of Rachel Marron, a pop singer, in *The Bodyguard* (1992), whose music track formed the basis of her album of the same name. She later had roles in *Waiting to Exhale* (1995) and *The Preacher's Wife* (1996), a remake of the Christ-

Three of those singles—"Saving All My Love for You," (1985), "How Will I Know?" (1985), and "Greatest Love of All" (1986)—rose to number one on popular-recording sales charts. Houston's next four singles—"I Wanna Dance with Somebody Who Loves Me" (1987), "Didn't We Almost Have It All?" (1987), "So Emotional" (1987), and "Where Do Broken Hearts Go?" (1988)—also reached number one, making her the first recording artist to have seven consecutive number one singles. (Most music historians do not count "Thinking About You," released between "Saving All My Love for You" and "How Will I Know?," because Arista promoted "Thinking About You" only to radio stations with a black urban formas classic *The Bishop's Wife*. The music track of *The Preacher's Wife* was released as an album in 1997. In November 1997 she played the fairy godmother in a multi-ethnic television version of Rodgers and Hammerstein's musical play *Cinderella*.

Whitney Houston is a pivotal figure in the history of modern pop-gospel music. Her style blends characteristics drawn from such role models as Gladys Knight, Deniece Williams, and especially Aretha Franklin. "She combines and streamlines the accomplishments of her predecessors," wrote Stephen Holden, "dispensing with the decorative ornamentation that many gospel-trained singers have traditionally brought to pop music."[3] Her record-breaking string of number one hit singles is a testimony to her dramatic impact on the contemporary music scene.

Selected recordings:

SINGLES

"You Give Good Love" (1985, Arista)
"Saving All My Love for You" (1985, Arista)
"How Will I Know?" (1985, Arista)
"Greatest Love of All" (1986, Arista)
"I Wanna Dance with Somebody Who Loves Me" (1987, Arista)
"Didn't We Almost Have It All?" (1987, Arista)
"So Emotional" (1987, Arista)
"Where Do Broken Hearts Go?" (1988, Arista)
"Love Will Save the Day" (1988, Arista)

"One Moment in Time" (1988, Arista)
"I'm Your Baby Tonight" (1990, Arista)
"All the Man That I Need" (1991, Arista)
"Miracle" (1991, Arista)
"I Will Always Love You" (1992, Arista)
"I'm Every Woman" (1993, Arista)
"I Have Nothing" (1993, Arista)
"Queen of the Night" (1993, Arista)
"Exhale (Shoop Shoop)" (1995, Arista)
"I Believe in You and Me" (1997, Arista)

ALBUMS

Whitney Houston (1985, Arista)
Whitney (1987, Arista)
I'm Your Baby Tonight (1990, Arista)
The Bodyguard (1992, Arista)
The Preacher's Wife (1996, Arista)

Selected performances:

FILMS

Perfect (1985)
School for Vandals (1986)
The Bodyguard (1992)
Waiting to Exhale (1995)
The Preacher's Wife (1996)

TELEVISION MOVIE

Rodgers and Hammerstein's Cinderella (1997)

Addie Waites Hunton
CRUSADER "CRYING FOR RIGHT"

(1866—1943)

EDUCATOR, ORGANIZATION official, race and gender activist, suffragist, and clubwoman, Addie Waites Hunton crusaded tirelessly to provide blacks with the same rights and privileges accorded to whites in America. Her life's work was like that of other Southern-born black women, about whom "the air is surcharged with the smoke of battle," she wrote. "Around them they hear the heartthrobs and sighs of a people crying for right."[1]

Addie D. Waites (also recorded as Waits), was born in Norfolk, Virginia, on June 11, 1866 (some sources give 1875), the eldest of three children of Jesse, a successful businessman, and Adeline (or Adelina) (Lawton) Waites, who died when Addie was a young child.

Addie received a fine education. After her mother died she lived with a maternal aunt in Boston, Massachusetts, where she earned her high school diploma at Boston Latin School. In 1889 she became the first black American woman to graduate from Spencerian College of Commerce in Philadelphia.

Like many educated black women of the time, she turned immediately to teaching. For one year she taught school in Portsmouth, Virginia. Then she served as principal at State Normal and Agricultural College in Alabama (now Alabama Agricultural and Mechanical University).

In 1893 she married William Alphaeus Hunton, who was a pioneer in establishing Young Men's Christian Association (YMCA) services for blacks. They had four children, but only two survived infancy: William Alphaeus Hunton, Jr., and Eunice Hunton (Carter*), who became a well-known lawyer.

Bringing Black Women into the YWCA

Addie and William began their married life in Norfolk, where she taught school and helped her husband with his YMCA work. After a brief time in Richmond, Virginia, the couple moved to Atlanta, Georgia, after William was transferred to the YMCA there. Addie worked as a secretary and bursar at Clark College in Atlanta, simultaneously serving as her husband's secretary, travel companion, and adviser.

The Atlanta race riot of 1906 made the Huntons feel unsafe, so in December 1906 they moved to Brooklyn, New York. In 1907 the Young Women's Christian Association (YWCA), taking notice of Addie Waites Hunton's work for the YMCA, appointed her special secretary to work among black people. She soon began a tour of the South and Midwest to conduct a survey for the association and Hunton personally drew a number of valuable black women into YWCA work, including Elizabeth Ross Haynes,* who became the first black national secretary of the organization.

After spending 1909 to 1910 with her children in Europe, where she studied at the Kaiser Wilhelm University in Strasbourg, Addie rejoined her husband in Brooklyn and enrolled in courses at the College of the City of New York. Two years after the family moved to Saranac Lake, New York, in 1914 William died. Addie later published a book about his life and work, *William Alphaeus Hunton: A Pioneer Prophet of Young Men* (1938).

With Black Troops in France

During World War I Hunton performed war work with the YWCA and then volunteered for overseas service with the association. In the summer of 1918 she and two other women, Helen Curtis and Kathryn Johnson, became the only three African-American women workers supporting two hundred thousand segregated black troops stationed in France.

The women functioned mostly as morale builders for the men. Hunton taught soldiers to read and write and offered a discussion program on race leaders, music, religion, and other topics. Even after the war ended there was much work for the women volunteers to do.

In February 1919, when the Pan-African Congress met in Paris, Hunton, still in France, addressed the congress and encouraged the delegates to give women important roles during the postwar period of reconstruction.

In the spring of 1919 sixteen more black women joined Hunton and her two coworkers as volunteers in France, while Hunton continued giving her literacy course and helping to organize religious, athletic, and cultural programs.

In May she was assigned to the military cemetery at Romagne, where surviving black soldiers reburied the dead from the battlefield at Meuse-Argonne. "It would be a gruesome, repulsive and unhealthful task," she later wrote, "requiring weeks of incessant toil during the long heavy days of summer."[2] While performing this duty, the men faced "trials of discriminations and injustices that seared their souls like hot iron, inflicted as they were at a time when these soldiers were rendering the American army and nation a sacred service."[3]

After Hunton returned to America in the autumn of 1919, she and her coworker Kathryn Johnson wrote of their experiences with the troops in the book *Two Colored Women with the American Expeditionary Forces* (1920).

Addressing Issues of Race and Gender

For the rest of her life Hunton actively pursued justice and equality for her race and gender. She had already begun this course as early as her Richmond years in the 1890s when she became involved with the National Association of Colored Women (NACW). While living in Atlanta, she was state organizer for the Georgia Federation of Colored Women's Clubs.

In her essay "Negro Womanhood Defended," published in the July 1904 issue of *Voice of the Negro*, she shredded the common portrayal of black women as morally weak. "For centuries the Negro woman was forced by cruelty too diverse and appalling to mention to submit her body to those who bartered for it," she wrote. "She was voiceless, and there was no arm lifted in her defense."[4] Black women, then, were being blamed for wrongs perpetrated by men.

From 1906 to 1910 Hunton served as a national organizer for NACW, writing articles about the organization for *The Colored American Magazine* (July 1908) and *Crisis* (May 1911).

Hunton was also active in other women's organizations. She presided over the International Council of the Women of Darker Races, belonged to the Brooklyn Women's Club, and became a leading suffragist. When the National Woman's party held its national convention in 1921, Hunton was among the group of black women who presented the convention with a resolution asking the party to support black women voters in the South. The resolution failed to pass, but the effort brought the issue to public attention. From 1926 to 1930 she served as president of the Empire State Federation of Women's Clubs.

Hunton was an outspoken member of the Women's International League for Peace and Freedom. In 1926 she wrote a report on Haiti, condemning the United States occupation of the country and calling for restoration of its independence. She was president of the Circle for Peace and Foreign Relations.

Hunton served as a vice president and field secretary of the National Association for the Advancement of Colored People and helped to organize the Fourth Pan-African Congress, held in New York City in 1927. In 1939 she attended her last known public event, a ceremony honoring great African-American women at the New York World's Fair.

Addie D. Waites Hunton died in Brooklyn on June 21, 1943. Using her incredible energy to bring blacks into the YWCA, help black troops in Europe, and address a broad range of issues concerning race and gender inequality, she served her people well as a powerful voice "crying for right."

Zora Neale Hurston

PIONEER FOLKLORIST

(1891—1960)

ZORA NEALE HURSTON was the first black American woman to collect and publish African-American and African-Caribbean folklore. Her study of folklore dramatically affected her career as an essayist and creative writer.

She was born in Eatonville, Florida, on January 7, 1891, one of eight children of the Reverend John and Lucy Ann (Potts) Hurston. Her father was three times elected mayor of Eatonville, the first incorporated black township in the United States. Lucy, a former schoolteacher, taught Sunday school in her husband's Baptist church. When Zora was thirteen her mother died, and after her father remarried she lived with various relatives.

Growing up in Eatonville, America's first all-black, self-governing town, strongly influenced Zora's later life. The experience fostered within her a sense of independence in her opinions, an independence that often put her at odds with the majority of her own race. During those early years in Eatonville she encountered what she called "lying sessions," daily exchanges of folk stories by the adults gathered on Joe Clark's store porch.

At the age of fourteen Zora Neale Hurston left Eatonville to work as a maid and wardrobe assistant with a traveling Gilbert and Sullivan theatrical troupe. In Baltimore, Maryland, she left the troupe to enter Morgan Academy, a predominantly black high school from which she graduated in June 1918. That fall she began to take courses at Howard University in Washington, D.C., where she studied off and on till 1924. During that time, in 1921, her first published story, "John Redding Goes to Sea," came out in Stylus, the university's literary magazine.

Pursuing a Literary Career

In 1925 Hurston moved to New York City, where she joined the Harlem Renaissance, a literary and cultural movement that celebrated black folk life. During this time in New York City she published stories in two important journals associated with the movement, *Opportunity: A Journal of Negro Life* and *The New Negro*, and also attended Barnard College, from which she received a B.A. degree in 1928.

In an important essay, "How It Feels to Be Colored Me" (1928), Hurston stated her fundamental attitude toward being black in America: "I do not belong to the sobbing school of Negrohood who hold that nature somehow has given them a lowdown dirty deal and whose feelings are all hurt about it. Even in the helter-skelter skirmish that is my life, I have seen that the world is to the strong regardless of a little pigmentation more or less. I do not weep at the world—I am too busy sharpening my oyster knife."[1] This statement, as Alice A. Deck observed in *Notable Black American Women*, reflected Hurston's lifelong "belief in the fundamental equality between the races: there were good and bad, strong and weak individuals among both races, and no one group was perfect."[2]

Collecting Black Folklore

After leaving Barnard College, Hurston pursued graduate studies at Columbia University under the direction of the anthropologist Franz Boas, who encouraged her to return to Eatonville to collect black folklore. A private grant from Mrs. Osgood Mason, a New York socialite, enabled Hurston to undertake the project.

Folklore-Inspired Novelist

Hurston's novels were strongly influenced by her folklore studies. Just as *Mules and Men* presented characters as individuals, her first novel, *Jonah's Gourd Vine* (1934), examines the protagonist, John Buddy Pearson, as an example of humanity, not of a race. A Southern Baptist preacher given to adultery, he symbolizes all men who struggle with their consciences. Like the folklore collection, the novel shows how African and European-American views conflict in the black American mind, most notably in this story the traditional African view that expressing human sexuality is a spiritual act and the Puritan view that such expression is a sinful act.

In 1937 Hurston published *Their Eyes Were Watching God*, regarded by many as her best novel. The main character, Janie (Crawford) Killicks Starks Woods, seeks an identity for herself beyond the role of dutiful wife expected of her in her small rural town. By the end of the novel she has realized her sexual and intellectual potential on her own terms. Forming a backdrop to the story is an examination of the language, stories, and habits of black folk.

Hurston published her second collection of folklore, *Tell My Horse*, in 1938. She gathered the stories during trips to the islands of Haiti and Jamaica. Besides presenting transcriptions of the tales, she made comparisons between the black cultures as she found them at that time in the Caribbean and the United States.

The Schomburg Center / NYPL

ZORA NEALE HUSTON

From 1929 to 1931 she collected black folk stories in Florida and Alabama. She issued the results in the book *Mules and Men* (1935), the first collection of black folklore published by an African-American woman.

In *Mules and Men* Hurston made a valuable contribution to folklore studies by presenting material that vividly reveals American black life as an amalgamation of African and European traditions. She drew characters as individuals, not as racial representatives. However, her basically affirmative point of view was taken to task by some black critics, who wanted to see more evidence of racial bitterness in the stories. She continued to face this type of criticism throughout her career.

Hurston's passionate pursuit of folklore interfered with her relationships with men. In 1927 she married Herbert Sheen, a musician, and in 1939 she married Albert Price III, with whom she had worked on Works Progress Administration projects. Both marriages ended in divorce, mainly because she kept leaving home to travel throughout the southern United States and the Caribbean to find folklore.

Her third novel, *Moses, Man of the Mountain*, came out in 1939. In it Hurston drew on her folklore studies to retell the biblical story of Moses from an African-American point of view, casting Moses as a black voodoo doctor and the Israelites as dialect-speaking southern blacks. In the pre-Civil War South slaves developed the Moses-as-voodoo-doctor legend as a way of Africanizing the Christianity taught to them by southern whites.

Autobiography and Later Writings

Hurston's autobiography, *Dust Tracks on a Road*, published in 1942, incorporated folk narratives into her personal story, reemphasized her bicultural identity (which was reinforced by her folklore studies), and still resisted complaining about the condition of blacks in America. "I too yearn for universal justice," she wrote, "but how to bring it about is another thing. It is such a complicated thing, for justice, like beauty, is in the eye of the beholder."[3] *Dust Tracks on a Road* won the Anisfield-Wolf Award for its contribution to better race relations.

During the rest of the 1940s Hurston wrote articles for several magazines, including the *Journal of American Folklore* and the *Saturday Evening Post*, still focusing her attention primarily on the links between African-American culture and white American culture. For *Negro Digest*, however, she finally issued some statements about the mistreatment of blacks in the United States. In "My Most Humiliating Jim Crow Experience" (1944), she described being given a superficial examination by a white doctor in Manhattan. In "Crazy for This Democracy" (1945) she complained that some American ethnic groups were excluded from the democratic process. In "What White Publishers Won't Print" (1950), she criticized white publishers for not issuing works that showed blacks fully assimilated into mainstream American culture. Her tone in these articles, however, is more rational and analytical than angry and vindictive.

In 1948 Hurston published her fourth and last novel, *Seraph on the Suwanee*, a story about a working-class Southern white woman, Arvay Henson, who, like the black John Buddy Pearson in *Jonah's Gourd Vine*, faces an internal struggle, and, like the black Janie (Crawford) Killicks in *Their Eyes Were Watching God*, "'grows' into a woman with a positive sense of self."[4]

In the 1950s Hurston's income as a writer declined sharply. The royalties from her books dropped, she published no new books, and she wrote only a few articles and reviews. To earn a living, she took a series of menial jobs while living in southern Florida.

On August 11, 1955, the *Orlando Sentinel* published a letter Hurston had written to express her disapproval of the 1954 United States Supreme Court's decision to desegregate public schools. Unlike most African-Americans she felt there was no reason to desegregate. She believed the black schools, given the

tools, could educate just as well as white schools. "The Supreme Court would have pleased me more if they had concerned themselves about enforcing the compulsory education provisions for Negroes in the South as is done for white children," she wrote. She defiantly defended her opinion to civil rights readers: "Them's my sentiments and I am sticking by them. Ethical and cultural desegregation. It is a contradiction in terms to scream race pride and equality while at the same time spurning Negro teachers and self-association."[5]

Zora Neale Hurston died in poverty in Fort Pierce, Florida, on January 28, 1960, having enriched American black culture tremendously through her pioneering work as a folklorist and as an independent-minded essayist and novelist.

Selected writings:

FICTION

(novels unless otherwise indicated)

Jonah's Gourd Vine (1934)
Mules and Men (folklore, 1935)
Their Eyes Were Watching God (1937)
Tell My Horse (folklore, 1938)
Moses, Man of the Mountain (1939)
Seraph on the Suwanee (1948)
Spunk: The Selected Stories of Zora Neale Hurston
   short stories (1985)

NONFICTION

(essays unless otherwise indicated)

"How It Feels to Be Colored Me" (*World Tomorrow*, May 1928)
"Hoodoo in America" (*Journal of American Folklore*, October-December, 1931)
"Characteristics of Negro Expression" (*Negro: An Anthology*, edited by Nancy Cunard, 1934)
"Spirituals and Neo Spirituals" (*Negro: An Anthology*)
Dust Tracks on a Road (autobiography, 1942)
"My Most Humiliating Jim Crow Experience" (*Negro Digest*, June 1944)
"Crazy for This Democracy" (*Negro Digest*, December 1945)
"What White Publishers Won't Print" (*Negro Digest*, April 1950)

Mahalia Jackson

GOSPEL QUEEN

(1911—1972)

AMERICA'S MOST FAMOUS gospel singer, Mahalia Jackson, created a unique style through her blending of Baptist hymn tradition, Holiness fervor, and blues. More than anyone else, she established gospel music as a genre distinct from classical black spirituals,[1] earning the title of the Gospel Queen.

Mahalia Jackson was born in New Orleans, Louisiana, on October 26, 1911. Her father, Johnny Jackson, a barber, longshoreman, and Baptist preacher, was never a presence in the family home. Her mother, Charity Clark, was a maid and laundress who died when Mahalia was five. The orphaned girl grew up in a household with her brother, several half brothers and half sisters (her father's children), and six aunts. Some of her relatives played dance music at white people's parties, and some played blues and rags with the blues singer Ma Rainey.

Early Musical Influences

New Orleans, then as now, was filled with vibrant music of all kinds. Early in her life Mahalia Jackson absorbed the conservative music tradition of hymn singing at the Mount Moriah Baptist Church, where her family worshipped, and she was also attracted to the strong rhythms and emotional abandon evident in the music of a nearby Holiness church. In addition, she was inspired by the secular music all around her, including a new popular form to which New Orleans was giving birth—jazz. Jackson enjoyed the blues recordings of Bessie Smith*, Mamie Smith, and Ma Rainey, to which, however, she had to listen secretly because her peers—southern churchgoing blacks—associated the blues with the Devil.

As a child she dropped out of elementary school to help support the family. As a teenager she moved to Chicago, where she sang professionally with the choir of the Greater Salem Baptist Church and with the Johnson Gospel Singers, one of the first professional touring gospel groups.

At that time, however, music was just a sideline for Jackson. She worked as a laundress, studied beauty culture at Madam C. J. Walker's* and at the Scott Institute of Beauty Culture, and opened her own beauty shop, the first of her several business ventures.

Touring with Thomas A. Dorsey

In 1929 Jackson met the composer Thomas A. Dorsey, known as the Father of Gospel Music. He gave her musical advice, and in the mid-1930s they began a fourteen-year association of touring, with Jackson singing Dorsey's songs in church programs and at conventions. His "Precious Lord Take My Hand" became her signature song.

In 1936 Jackson married Issac Hockenhull, a college-educated entrepreneur who tried to persuade her to abandon her church singing so that she could earn more money performing blues and popular music. She refused, and the marriage ended in divorce, as did a later marriage, to the musician Sigmond Galloway.

In 1937 the great jazz trumpeter Louis Armstrong also tried to persuade Jackson to turn to the blues, but again she refused. When she sang, she felt compelled to express her deepest religious convictions.

the Gospel Queen.

By the mid-1950s she had her own radio and television shows in Chicago and appeared frequently on national programs. During this time she also owned a flower shop in Chicago and toured as a concert artist, appearing more frequently in concert halls and less often in churches. As a consequence of this change in her venues, her arrangements expanded from piano and organ to orchestral accompaniments. In 1950 she became the first gospel singer to perform at New York's Carnegie Hall, and in 1958 the first to sing at the Newport Jazz Festival.

Though Jackson was often invited to appear in nightclubs and to sing secular music, she always rejected such offers. However, in the early 1960s she did apply her gospel gifts to secular purposes. In 1961 she sang at President John F. Kennedy's inauguration. She stirred the audience with "How I Got Over" at the famous 1963 March on Washington rally, in which Martin Luther King made his "I Have a Dream" speech. Jackson strongly supported the civil rights movement and featured "We Shall Overcome" at her concerts.

The Schomburg Center / NYPL

MAHALIA JACKSON

Meanwhile, her tours with Dorsey became increasingly successful, especially in the South. In the North some black church members were uncomfortable with Jackson's Holiness emotionalism and jazzy worldliness. However, as the years passed, more and more people accepted her style of musical worship. "I believe that the gospel, and the singing of it," she once explained, "can be both commercial and uplifting at the same time."[2]

America's Gospel Queen

By 1947 Jackson had become the official soloist of the National Baptist Convention. Recordings further extended her fame, especially "Move On Up a Little Higher" (1947) and "Let the Power of the Holy Ghost Fall on Me" (1949). She was now well established as

Worldwide Success

Jackson first toured Europe in 1952, and was hailed by critics as the world's greatest gospel singer. In Paris she was called the Angel of Peace, and throughout the continent she sang to capacity audiences. She toured Europe again in 1962 and 1963-64, and in 1970 she performed in Africa, Japan, and India.

Jackson also had a spectacular recording career. From 1946 to 1954 she issued many popular singles for Apollo, including "Move On Up a Little Higher." Later, with Columbia, she recorded albums and won several Grammys, including two awarded posthumously: one for her lifetime achievement (1972) and one for the album *How I Got Over* (1976).

Jackson devoted much of her time and energy to helping others. She encouraged the careers of Aretha Franklin,* Della Reese,* and others, and she established the Mahalia Jackson Scholarship Foundation for young people who wanted to attend college. For her efforts in helping international understanding she received the Silver Dove Award.

A Joyful Sound

For most music fans Jackson symbolized gospel music. She spoke softly, but when she sang she mesmerized her audiences with her large, rich contralto voice and her total commitment to the gospel idiom. "The blues, baby, is when you're feelin' low . . . ," she once explained to Dinah Shore, "when you're down in the mouth. But gospel is always happy, a joyful sound."[3]

Mahalia Jackson died in Chicago on January 27, 1972. Through her recordings she left behind a glorious legacy—a truly joyful sound.

Selected recordings:

SINGLES

"He Knows My Heart" (1946, Apollo)
"Move On Up a Little Higher" (1947, Apollo)
"Even Me" (1947, Apollo)
"I Have a Friend" (1947, Apollo)
"Tired" (1947, Apollo)
"Amazing Grace" (1947, Apollo)
"I Can Put My Trust in Jesus" (1949, Apollo)
"Let the Power of the Holy Ghost Fall on Me"
   (1949, Apollo)

"Walk with Me" (1949, Apollo)
"Just over the Hill" (1950, Apollo)
"I Walked into the Garden" (1950, Apollo)
"Go Tell It on the Mountain" (1950, Apollo)
"The Lord's Prayer" (1950, Apollo)
"How I Got Over" (1951, Apollo)
"I Bow on My Knees" (1951, Apollo)
"God Spoke to Me" (1952, Apollo)
"In the Upper Room" (1952, Apollo)
"I Believe" (1953, Apollo)
"Hands of God" (1953, Apollo)
"Down to the River" (1953, Apollo)
"I'm on My Way" (1954, Apollo)
"Nobody Knows" (1954, Apollo)
"Every Time I Feel the Spirit" (1961, Columbia)

ALBUMS

Newport 1958 (1958, Columbia)
Great Gettin' Up Morning (1959, Columbia)
Come On, Children, Let's Sing (1960, Columbia)
The Power and the Glory (1960, Columbia)
Sweet Little Jesus Boy (1961, Columbia)
I Believe (1961, Columbia)
Great Songs of Love and Faith (1962, Columbia)
Recorded Live in Europe (1962, Columbia)
Silent Night—Songs for Christmas (1962, Columbia)
Make a Joyful Noise unto the Lord (1963, Columbia)
Let's Pray Together (1964, Columbia)
Mahalia Sings (1966, Columbia)
You'll Never Walk Alone (1968, Columbia)
Guide Me, O Thou Great Jehovah (1969, Columbia)
How I Got Over (released 1976, Columbia)

Judith Jamison

PIONEER OF MODERN DANCE

(1943–   )

JUDITH JAMISON IS ONE of the most popular, innovative dancers in American history. In 1989 she became the first African-American woman to head a major modern dance company when she was named artistic director of the Alvin Ailey American Dance Theater.

Judith Jamison was born in Philadelphia on May 10, 1943, the younger child of John Henry Jamison, a sheet-metal worker and pianist-singer, and Tessie Belle (Brown) Jamison, a teacher and former athlete. Both parents loved, and introduced her to, classical music, and her father gave her piano lessons.

When Judith was six, her parents enrolled her in the Judimar School of Dance in Philadelphia, where she studied for the next eleven years. There she received lessons in ballet, tap, jazz, primitive, and other dance forms, as well as absorbing musical and spiritual influences at her family's historic Mother Bethel African Methodist Episcopal Church in Philadelphia.

Jamison graduated from Germantown High School and then attended Fisk University in Nashville, Tennessee, with the intention of majoring in psychology. After three semesters, however, she returned to her hometown and enrolled at the Philadelphia Dance Academy (now the University of the Arts), determined to pursue a career in dance. She also attended classes in the Lester Horton technique at Joan Kerr's Dance School.

In 1964 Jamison attracted the attention of the great choreographer Agnes de Mille, who was teaching a master class at the Philadelphia Dance Academy. She invited Jamison to dance in a new ballet she had choreographed, *The Four Marys*. The performances took place in New York and Chicago during the spring of 1965.

Premier Dancer for Alvin Ailey

Later in 1965 Jamison auditioned for a Harry Belafonte television special. She failed to get the job but impressed an observer, Alvin Ailey, who asked her to join his American Dance Theater, a company of black dancers whose performances were infused with jazz, modern, classical, and African influences. She immediately agreed and stayed with him for the next fifteen years, performing in the United States, Europe, Russia, India, Japan, and elsewhere.

Jamison soon became the company's premier dancer. "To her exceptional stature of five feet ten inches and her elegant, imperial manner she applies an impeccable technique—an amalgam of classical ballet discipline and the best of several modern dance methods—producing a striking individual style," observed *Current Biography* in 1973.[1]

Jamison made her debut with Alvin Ailey in *Congo Tango Palace* (1965). One of her most memorable roles came in *Pas de "Duke"* (1976), a pas de deux that Ailey choreographed to tunes by Duke Ellington, which she performed with the great ballet star Mikhail Baryshnikov.

Jamison's signature piece was *Cry*, a sixteen-minute solo dance choreographed by Ailey as a birthday present for his mother and premiered by Jamison in 1971. In her interpretation of the work, Jamison later wrote, the character "represented those women before her who came from the hardships of slavery, through the pain of losing loved ones, through overcoming extraordinary depressions and tribulations. Coming out of a world of pain and trouble, she has found her way—and triumphed."[2]

After winning the coveted *Dance Magazine* Award

Courtesy of the Alvin Ailey Theater Foundation

JUDITH JAMISON

choreographed *Just Call Me Dance* (1984), *Time Out* (1986), *Time In* (1986), and *Into the Life* (1987)—all performed by different companies. The Alvin Ailey Repertory Ensemble staged her *Tease* in 1988.

Jamison went on to found her own dance company, the Jamison Project, which made its debut in November 1988. The troupe's repertory consisted largely of her own preexisting works, such as *Divining* and *Tease*. She also created a new piece, *Forgotten Time*, which the Jamison Project premiered in 1989.

Artistic Director of the Ailey Company

By the late 1980s Alvin Ailey was plagued by ill health, and in mid-1989 he asked Jamison to take over his company. She agreed, and three weeks after he died on December 1, 1989, Jamison was officially named his successor as artistic director of the Alvin Ailey Dance Theater. For six months she directed both the Ailey company and the Jamison Project before disbanding the latter.

Jamison has kept Ailey's presence in the company alive by reviving his choreographic works and by continuing the spirit of his artistic vision, which was to preserve both the heritage of American modern dance and the uniqueness of black American cultural expression. Jamison has also created new pieces of her own on a regular basis, including *Rift* (1991), *Hymn* (1993), *Initiative* (1994), *Riverside* (1995), and *Sweet Release* (1996). In 1998 the company celebrated its fortieth anniversary.

"I'll always be a dancer," Judith Jamison, the greatest African-American dancer of her time and the first black woman to head a major modern dance company, said in 1993; "I was born that way. I've never stopped. That's what I was supposed to be doing in life. I'm still connected through my choreography."[3]

in 1972, in December Jamison married fellow Ailey soloist Miguel Godreau, but the marriage did not last.

By the end of the 1970s she had performed in over seventy ballet productions for Ailey. Feeling the need for a change, she left his company to star in a Broadway musical, *Sophisticated Ladies* (1980). Later she also performed with the San Francisco Ballet and the Ballet of the Twentieth Century.

In the 1980s Jamison became interested in choreography. Ailey encouraged her in this new pursuit and let her use his troupe for the premiere of her first work, *Divining* (1984). Over the next few years she

Mae C. Jemison

FIRST BLACK WOMAN ASTRONAUT

(1956–   )

IN SEPTEMBER 1992 Mae C. Jemison made history as the first African-American woman to fly in space. She achieved her trailblazing success by following her credo: "Don't be limited by others' limited inaginations."[1]

Mae Carol Jemison was born in Decatur, Alabama, on October 17, 1956, the youngest of three children of Charlie and Dorothy Jemison. Her father was a roofer, carpenter, and maintenance supervisor. Her mother was an elementary schoolteacher.

Mae grew up in Chicago, where she early became hooked on the idea of traveling in outer space. "I recall looking at the stars," she later said, "wondering what was up there, knowing I'd go up there some day, though I didn't know how."[2] Mae read astronomy books and often visited the Museum of Science and Industry, and her interest in space was heightened in July 1969 when the *Apollo 11* astronauts landed on the moon.

After graduating from Morgan Park High School in 1973 at the age of just sixteen, Jemison entered Stanford University, from which she graduated in 1977 with a B.S. degree in chemical engineering and an A.B. degree in African and Afro-American studies. She then studied at Cornell University Medical College in New York City. While there she served as president of the Cornell Medical Student Executive Council and president of the Cornell Chapter of the National Student Medical Association.

Physician and Engineer

After she earned her medical degree in 1981, she interned at the Los Angeles County-University of South-ern California Medical Center till July 1982, after which she worked briefly as a general practitioner in Los Angeles.

From January 1983 till the summer of 1985 Jemison served with the Peace Corps as a medical officer in the western African countries of Sierra Leone and Liberia, administering health-care programs for Peace Corps volunteers and American Embassy personnel.

Returning to the United States in 1985, Jemison went to work in Los Angeles as a general practitioner at CIGNA Health Plans of California, a health maintenance organization. After caring for patients during the days, she spent her evenings taking further engineering courses at the University of California in Los Angeles.

Though her career as a physician was progressing well, she never forgot her early desire to go into space. She applied for admission into the National Aeronautics and Space Administration (NASA) space program, and in the summer of 1987, after intensive examinations and interviews, NASA accepted her.

Astronaut

Jemison was the first African-American woman ever admitted into the astronaut training program. She and her fellow astronaut candidates went through a rigorous one-year training program, studying space shuttle hardware and procedures. After she completed the program in August 1988, Jemison became a mission specialist astronaut and continued to work at the agency for the next several years.

In September 1992 Jemison participated in her first space mission, officially called STS-47 Spacelab. She later recalled preparing to take off in the space shuttle *Endeavour* at the Kennedy Space Center in Florida; "I was so excited. ... This is what I had wanted to do for a very long time.... It was the realization of many, many dreams of many people."[3] Jemison, with six other astronauts, remained aboard the shuttle for eight days, from September 12 till September 20.

Her assignment was to conduct experiments on weightlessness, tissue growth, and the development of semiconductor materials. In one experiment she used frogs to determine the effects of weightlessness, if any, on fertilization and embryologic development. In another experiment she used her own body to test the effectiveness of biofeedback techniques in alleviating motion sickness. She also investigated the loss of calcium in bones in space: "In space humans lose calcium from the bones," she explained, "and women lose more the longer we stay up there."[4]

After completing 127 orbits of the earth and 190 hours in space, the *Endeavour* returned to the Kennedy Space Center. Jemison expressed the hope that her historic flight would help people to appreciate the abilities of both women and members of minority groups.

MAE C. JEMISON

Awards and Honors

The many awards and honors Jemison has received for her accomplishments include the *Essence* Science and Technology Award (1988), the Gamma Sigma Gamma Woman of the Year Award (1989), the *Ebony* Black Achievement Award (1992), a Montgomery Fellowship from Dartmouth College (1993), and several honorary doctorates. In 1992 the Mae C. Jemison Academy, an alternative public school in Detroit, Michigan, was named after her.

In March 1993 Jemison resigned from the astronaut corps to return to the practice of medicine. She also established the Jemison Group, a company devoted to researching, developing, and marketing advanced technologies, such as a space-based telecommunication system designed to improve health care delivery in Third World countries.

As the first black woman astronaut, Mae C. Jemison opened doors of opportunity for other women and minorities and inspired many with her spirit of adventure. "I'd go to Mars," she has said, "at the drop of a hat."[5]

Barbara Jordan

ORATOR AND CONGRESSWOMAN

(1936—1996)

WIDELY REGARDED as one of the twentieth century's greatest orators, Barbara Jordan is especially remembered for her 1974 speech calling for the impeachment of President Nixon and for her 1976 keynote address at the Democratic National Convention. A pioneer politician, she chalked up many firsts, including being the first woman elected to the Texas Senate and the first woman and first black elected to Congress from Texas.

Barbara Charline Jordan was born in Houston, Texas, on February 21, 1936, the youngest of three daughters of Benjamin and Arlyne (Patten) Jordan. Her father was a warehouse clerk and Baptist minister. She developed a special closeness with her maternal grandfather, John Ed Patten, from whom she learned to act and think independently and to rise above mediocrity. "Life," he told her, "is not a playground, but a schoolroom."[1]

Barbara Jordan took his advice to heart, becoming an outstanding student at the Phillis Wheatley High School in Houston. A Career Day speech by the attorney Edith Sampson persuaded her to become a lawyer. Jordan, too, tried public speaking, and in 1952 she placed first in a statewide oratory contest, winning a trip to Chicago, where she won the national contest.

After graduating from high school in 1952 Jordan enrolled at Texas Southern University. She led the school's debating team in a tie against mighty Harvard University, a feat of which she remained proud for the rest of her life.

After taking a degree in government in 1956, for the next three years she studied at Boston University Law School in Massachusetts. In 1959 she earned her law degree, one of only two women, both black, in a graduating class of 128. Later that year she passed two bar exams: first one in Massachusetts and the other in Texas. She was offered a job in Massachusetts, but she opted to return to her native state, opening a private practice in Houston.

Texas State Senator

Soon Jordan became involved in politics, directing one of Houston's first voter drives in support of the 1960 Democratic ticket of John F. Kennedy for president and the Texan Lyndon B. Johnson for vice president. She put her speaking ability to use for the Harris County Democratic party, but she lost her bids for the Texas House of Representatives in 1962 and 1964.

In 1965, however, state legislative districts were redrawn, and Jordan found herself in the newly created Eleventh State Senatorial District, which was demographically favorable to the election of black political candidates. The following year she won election as the district's representative to the Texas Senate, thus becoming the first black elected to that body since 1883 and the first woman ever elected.

During her six years in the Texas Senate, Jordan sponsored most of the state's environmental legislation, wrote the first Texas minimum wage law, was responsible for the inclusion of antidiscrimination clauses in all state business contracts, and guided the passage of the state's first urban legislation. She was elected president pro tem of the Senate, and for one day, June 10, 1972, when the governor and the lieutenant governor were unavailable, she served as acting governor of the state.

United States Congresswoman

In 1972 Jordan became the first black since Reconstruction and the first woman ever elected to the United States Congress from Texas.

With strings pulled by former President Lyndon B. Johnson, the freshman Jordan was assigned to the important House Judiciary Committee, which soon had to deal with the matter of the possible impeachment of President Nixon for his role in the Watergate scandal.

On July 25, 1974, she mesmerized the nation with her eloquent speech in favor of impeachment, basing her opinion on the constitutional issues at stake. "I am not going to sit here and be an idle spectator in the diminution, the subversion, the destruction of the Constitution," she said.[2] Regarding Nixon himself, she went to the heart of the case: "Has the president committed offenses and planned and directed and acquiesced in a course of conduct which the Constitution will not tolerate? That is the question. We know that. We should now forthwith proceed to answer the question. It is reason and not passion which guide our decision."[3] Nixon finally resigned during the course of the impeachment hearings later that summer.

In 1976 Jordan became the first black woman to deliver a keynote address at a Democratic National Convention. Speaking from the stage at Madison Square Garden, in New York, she riveted her audience: "There is something special about tonight. What is different? What is special? I, Barbara Jordan, am a keynote speaker. . . . I feel . . . that my presence here is one additional bit of evidence that the American Dream need not forever be deferred. . . . Many fear the future. Many are distrustful of their leaders and believe that their voices are never heard. . . . More is required of public officials than slogans and handshakes and press releases. More is required. We must hold ourselves strictly accountable. We must provide the people with a vision of the future."[4]

Educator and National Spokesperson

In 1978 Jordan decided not to run for reelection to the Congress. "I felt some necessity to address national issues," she later explained. "I thought that my role now was to be one of the voices in the country defining where we were, where we were going, what the policies were that were being pursued, and where

BARBARA JORDAN

The Schomburg Center / NYPL

the holes in those policies were. I felt I was more in an instructive role than a legislative role."[5]

After leaving the House in January 1979, Jordan taught political ethics at the Lyndon B. Johnson School of Public Affairs at the University of Texas in Austin. She also served as a faculty adviser and a minority recruiter.

For ten weeks in 1982 she hosted a television show on the Public Broadcasting System, *Crisis to Crisis with Barbara Jordan*. In 1984 she received the Eleanor Roosevelt Humanities Award, was voted the Best Living Orator by the International Platform Association, and was elected to the Texas Women's Hall of Fame.

In the 1990s she continued to have an impact on national affairs through her great talent for public speaking, despite suffering for many years from multiple sclerosis, which meant that she often had to speak from a wheelchair. In 1994 she received the Presidential Medal of Freedom, the nation's highest civilian honor. In 1995, as chairwoman of the Commission on Immigration Reform, she returned to Congress to speak against a proposal to deny automatic citizenship to the children of illegal immigrants in this country. "To deny birthright citizenship would derail this engine of American liberty," she warned.[6]

Barbara Jordan died in Austin, Texas, on January 17, 1996, having achieved the distinction of becoming one of America's greatest orators and a political pioneer for blacks and women.

Florence Griffith Joyner

WOMEN'S TRACK RECORD BREAKER

(1959—1998)

BREAKING OLYMPIC AND world sprinting records, Florence Griffith Joyner rose to capture the unofficial title of world's fastest woman in 1988. At the same time she brought unprecedented glamour to the world of women's track with her striking makeup, designer fingernails, and sexy racing costumes. "Looking good is almost as important as running well," she once said. "It's part of feeling good about myself."[1] She brought new interest to her sport: "Her flamboyant style and meteoric rise to sprinting excellence put women's track and field in the spotlight."[2]

Originally named Delorez Florence (some sources say Florence Delorez) Griffith, she was born in Los Angeles on December 21, 1959, the seventh of eleven children of Robert and Florence Griffith. To avoid confusion with her mother, young Florence was nicknamed Dee Dee. Her father, an electronics technician, and her mother, a seamstress, divorced when Dee Dee was little. Mrs. Griffith then moved with her children from the Mojave Desert, where they were then living, to the Watts section of Los Angeles.

In elementary and junior high school, Dee Dee participated as a sprinter in competitions sponsored by the Sugar Ray Robinson Youth Foundation. She sometimes practiced by chasing jackrabbits when she visited her father in the Mojave Desert. When she was fourteen and fifteen, she won sprinting championships at the annual Jesse Owens National Youth Games. At Jordan High School in Los Angeles she set school records in sprinting and the long jump.

Florence Griffith graduated from high school in 1978, and the following year she enrolled at California State University at Northridge. There she was helped by Bob Kersee, an assistant track coach whose emphasis on technique enhanced her natural ability.

Near Misses

In 1980 Bob Kersee became an assistant coach at the University of California at Los Angeles (UCLA), where Griffith soon followed him. The increased level of competition at UCLA pushed her to new heights of achievement, and she became one of America's best sprinters, though she narrowly missed making the 1980 American Olympic team.

In 1982 Griffith won the National Collegiate Athletic Association (NCAA) 200-meter crown. At the 1983 NCAA championships she placed second in the 200 meters and won the 400 meters. It was during her college career that she began to show her distinctive fashion flair, sporting, for example, long fingernails painted in rainbow colors.

To intensify her preparations for the upcoming Olympics, Griffith began training with Kersee at his World Class Track Club. At the 1984 Olympics in Los Angeles she won the silver medal in the 200 meters and further entertained the American spectators with her 6½-inch fingernails patriotically painted red, white, and blue.

Disappointed by her second-place finish in the Olympics, Griffith went into semiretirement. While working days as a customer service representative for Union Bank in Los Angeles and nights as a hair stylist, she began to gain weight, slowing her sprint times down considerably.

Then in 1987 she asked Kersee to help her get into shape for the 1988 Olympics. He put her on a rigorous regimen, and she received moral support from her new boyfriend, Al Joyner, the 1984 Olympic triple jump gold medalist and the brother of her World Class Track Club teammate Jackie Joyner-Kersee*, wife of Bob Kersee. Florence Griffith and Al Joyner were married in October 1987. They had a daughter, Mary, who was born in 1991.

With continued help from Kersee and Joyner, Griffith Joyner lost weight and improved her speed, taking second place in the 200 meters at the 1987 World Championships in Rome, Italy, and helping the United States women's 4 x 100-meter relay team to win a gold medal.

Commitment to Be the Best

Instead of being happy with her fine comeback, Griffith Joyner was angry that once again in a big meet she was the runner-up. "When you've been second-best for so long," she said in a later interview, "you can either accept it, or try to become the best. I made the decision to try and be the best in 1988."[3]

Emulating Ben Johnson, the new world record holder in the men's 100 meters, Griffith Joyner worked on improving her start from the blocks and went on an extensive weightlifting program. She trained hard on the track every day, including lunch-hour sessions away from her day job and evening workouts after her second job. Eventually, to have more time for training, she switched from her full-time bank job to a part-time position in employee relations for Anheuser-Busch.

1988–Record Year

Griffith Joyner's extraordinary commitment paid off. At the United States Olympic track and field trials in July 1988, she broke the world 100-meter record of 10.76 an astonishing four times, recording a best of 10.49 in the second round and 10.61 in her gold-medal performance in the finals. A few days later she set an American record of 21.77 seconds in the 200 meters in a preliminary round and went on to win the event in 21.82 seconds.

She attributed her success partly to learning how to run relaxed: "When you're trying to go fast, you're fighting against your body instead of letting go."[4] Maturity, too, played a part: "It takes experience—time—to get strength, technique, to learn to concentrate on what you have to do, to be able to go to that line, confident that nobody else in that race can run with you."[5]

At the Olympic trials her costumes once again made news. Among her outfits were a purple one-legged suit and white bikini bottom with purple squiggles, a black bodysuit with yellow stripes on the side, and a white fishnet bodysuit. One day her long fingernails were painted orange with stripes on the tips, another they were fuchsia. Her sexy uniforms had a practical as well as an aesthetic purpose: "I like high-cut legs and low-cut tops that give me more movement,"[6] she explained.

A few weeks after the trials, Griffith Joyner changed coaches replacing Kersee with her husband. Joyner set up a program designed to have her in peak condition by the Olympic Games later that year.

At the Olympics held in September 1988 in Seoul, South Korea, Griffith Joyner won a gold medal in the 100 meters with an Olympic record time of 10.54 seconds. In the 200 meters she did even better, not only winning the gold medal but also breaking the world record of 21.71 twice, once in the semifinals with 21.56 and again in the finals, with 21.34. In the 200-meter finals she wore one red and one blue sneaker and a white belt.

On October 1 she won another Olympic gold medal by running the third leg of the American women's victorious 4 x 100-meter relay, after which she anchored the American women's 4 x 400-meter relay team to a silver medal—just forty minutes after the earlier relay.

During 1988 and 1989 Griffith Joyner received many major awards in honor of her Olympic achievements. The Associated Press and United Press International news services named her sportswoman of the year. Tass, the Soviet press agency, named her athlete of the year. She also received the Harvard Foundation Award for outstanding contributions to society, the International Jesse Owens Award as the year's outstanding track and field athlete, the James E. Sullivan Memorial Award as the top American amateur athlete, and the United States Olympic Committee Award.

New Priorities

On February 25, 1989, Griffith Joyner announced that she was retiring from track to devote more time to the many business and creative opportunities being offered to her. "It's a matter of priorities," she said in an interview. "With all I want to do—designing, writing, acting, modeling—I realized there would be no time to train."[7]

Over the next several years Griffith Joyner hosted sports events; endorsed products, such as American soft drinks and Japanese cosmetics; designed personal sportswear under her trademarked nickname, FloJo, as well as uniforms for the Indiana Pacers professional basketball team; appeared as a guest on television talk shows and as an actress in commercials and various entertainment programs, including the television soap opera *Santa Barbara* (1992); and became co-owner of NUCO Nails of Camarillo, California (1994). Her interest in young people was reflected in the foundation she established to help inner-city youths.

In 1993 Griffith Joyner became cochair of the President's Council on Physical Fitness and Sports, which comprises twenty members who advise the president on ways to promote fitness and sports programs for all Americans. One of her goals was to "educate children about eating healthy, exercise, and the importance of fun in sports, downplaying all this competitive stuff." More broadly she wanted to make all "Americans healthier and fitter. That would mean as much, if not more to me, than winning Olympic medals."[8] In 1997 her position on the council was reaffirmed. On September 21, 1998, Florence Griffith Joyner died suddenly in her sleep at her home in Mission Viego, California, when an epileptic seizure caused her to be suffocated by her bedding.

She "had an enormous influence on women's track and field in 1988," wrote Janet Woolum in *Outstanding Women Athletes*, "bringing a certain style and flair to women's track with her dramatic racing outfits and

FLORENCE GRIFFITH JOYNER

New York Daily News

outrageous makeup and fingernails, but it is her world-record time of 10.49 in the 100 meters that will keep her in track and field record books for years to come."[9]

Jackie Joyner-Kersee

WORLD'S GREATEST FEMALE ATHLETE

(1962–   )

W IDELY REGARDED AS THE best woman athlete of her time, Jackie Joyner-Kersee excelled at basketball, long jumping, hurdling, and other track and field events. She dominated her specialty, the grueling seven-event heptathlon, from the mid-1980s till the mid-1990s.

Jacqueline Joyner was born in East Saint Louis, Illinois, on March 3, 1962, one of four children of Alfred and Mary Joyner. She was named after Jacqueline Kennedy, the First Lady, because her grandmother predicted that "someday this girl will be the first lady of something."[1] Jackie's father was a construction worker and later a railroad switch operator. Her mother was a nurse's assistant.

The Joyners lived across the street from the Mayor Brown Center, where Jackie began running and jumping in track competitions when she was nine years old. Her success inspired her older brother, Al(fred), to go out for the same sport, and he eventually became a world-class triple jumper. A coach at the Mayor Brown Center convinced Jackie to take up the five-event pentathlon because mastering a variety of specialties would give her the best chance at the Olympics someday. At the age of fourteen she won the first of four consecutive National Junior Pentathlon Championships.

While attending Lincoln High School, Jackie set a state high school record of 20'7½" in the long jump. She also played volleyball and became a basketball star. After graduating in 1980 she accepted a basketball scholarship from the University of California at Los Angeles (UCLA).

Discovering the Heptathlon

At UCLA Joyner became an outstanding forward on the basketball team, while during track season she concentrated on long jumping.

However, an assistant track coach, Bob Kersee, saw her tremendous athletic potential. At his urging, she agreed to take up the heptathlon, a two-day ordeal consisting of the 200-meter dash, the 100-meter hurdles, the high jump, the shot put, the long jump, the javelin throw, and the 800-meter run. "I like the heptathlon," she once said, "because it shows you what you're made of."[2]

By 1982 Bob Kersee could see that she would someday break the world record. However, her progress was set back when she pulled a hamstring at the 1983 world championships, and her career was further adversely affected when she suffered another hamstring injury the following year just a few weeks before the Los Angeles Olympic Games. Her brother, Al, won the triple jump at the Olympics, but Jackie, hampered by her injury, narrowly lost the gold medal, finishing the heptathlon in second place.

In 1985 she turned in the world's best heptathlon mark of the year and set an American record with a long jump of 23'9". During that year she also graduated from UCLA with a B.A. degree in history. In January 1986 she married her coach, Bob Kersee.

Breaking the World Record

The marriage seemed to cement their working relationship as well, and Jackie Joyner-Kersee soon developed into an unstoppable force in the heptathlon. In July 1986, at the Goodwill Games in Moscow, she

JACKIE JOYNER-KERSEE

Elite International Sports Marketing

turned in a personal best in almost every event and set an American record of 12.85 seconds in the 100-meter hurdles. She not only won the heptathlon but also shattered the world record by 200 points, finishing with 7,148. Joyner-Kersee was the first American woman to hold a multi-event world record since Mildred ("Babe") Didrikson set a triathlon mark fifty years earlier.

Less than a month later, at the United States Olympic Festival in Houston, Texas, she staggered the sports world by breaking her own record with 7,161 points. Everyone knew that she was a world-class long jumper, but in this competition she established marks in the 200 meters, the hurdles, and the high jump that placed her among the top ten American individual specialists in those events.

In 1987 Joyner-Kersee won the overall points championship in the Grand Prix track and field indoor series despite having to compete against specialists in individual events, the heptathlon not being included in the meets. Later that year she won the

heptathlon at the USA/Mobil Outdoor Track and Field Championships and both the long jump and the heptathlon at the World Track and Field Championships. At the Pepsi Invitational track meet she unofficially broke the American 100-meter hurdles record with a hand-timed 12.6-second performance. During the Pan American Games that year she equaled the world record in the long jump with a leap of 24'5½".

Winning Olympic Gold

Joyner-Kersee's performances at the 1988 Olympic Games, held in Seoul, South Korea, unequivocally raised her to a level of her own in the sports world. She not only won the heptathlon, setting yet another world record with 7,291 points, but also took the gold medal in the open long jump with a mark of 24'3½". Both events had long been dominated by Soviet bloc women athletes. Joyner-Kersee was the

Elite International Sports Marketing

JACKIE JOYNER-KERSEE

Olympic Games, held in Atlanta the following month, she had to withdraw from the heptathlon after injuring her right hamstring on the first day of competition. A few days later, however, despite her injured leg, she courageously performed in the open long jump, in which she managed to take third place and win her sixth career Olympic medal.

Awards and Honors

Joyner-Kersee has won many awards and honors. Among them are the Jesse Owens Award (1986), the Sullivan Award as America's outstanding amateur athlete (1986), the *Track and Field News* Athlete of the Year Award (1986), the *Ebony* American Black Achievement Award (1987), the *Sporting News* first Female Athlete of the Year Award (1988), the Jim Thorpe Award (1993), the International Amateur Athletic Federation Female Athlete of the Year Award (1994), and the Jackie Robinson ("Robie") Award (1994).

In 1996, after the Olympics, Joyner-Kersee returned to basketball by joining the American Basketball League, a new women's professional organization. In 1997 she published *A Kind of Grace: The Autobiography of the World's Greatest Female Athlete* (written with Sonja Steptoe). To encompass her increasingly wide range of business and philanthropic interests, she founded the JJK and Associates, Inc., and JJK Community Foundation.

In 1998 her remarkable atheltic career came to an end. That summer she won the heptathlon at the Goodwill Games, and a few days later the tired champion placed sixth in the long jump at the United States Open. She then retired.

For her unparalleled achievements in the all-around test of the heptathlon and her world-class marks in individual running and jumping events, Jackie Joyner-Kersee has been praised by sports authorities as the best female athlete in the second half of the twentieth century. "You're the greatest athlete in the world," Bruce Jenner, the former Olympic champion in the men's decathlon, told her when she won her second consecutive Olympic heptathlon in 1992, "Man or woman, the greatest athlete in the world."[3]

first American woman to win an Olympic gold medal in the long jump and the first athlete in sixty-four years to win both a single event and a multi-event in the Games.

Her dominance continued over the next four years. In 1989, for example, she set a world indoor record of 7.37 seconds in the 55-meter hurdles.

At the 1992 Olympic Games in Barcelona, Joyner-Kersee became the first woman in Olympic history to win back-to-back gold medals in the heptathlon, taking first place with 7,044 points. Once again she entered the open long jump, placing third and receiving a bronze medal.

In 1993 she won the heptathlon at the World Track and Field Championships. In 1994 she won the event at the Goodwill Games in Saint Petersburg, Russia, and also became the Grand Prix outdoor champion.

At the United States Olympic Trials in June 1996, she was defeated in the heptathlon for the first time since 1984, losing to Kelly Blair, and during the

Coretta Scott King

FOUNDER OF THE CENTER FOR NONVIOLENT SOCIAL CHANGE

(1927—)

PRINCIPALLY KNOWN AS the widow of Martin Luther King, Jr., Coretta Scott King has long been a highly influential civil rights leader in her own right. She is especially noted for founding the Martin Luther King, Jr., Center for Nonviolent Social Change and for helping to establish a national holiday in honor of her husband.

Born Coretta Scott in Marion, Alabama, on April 27, 1927, she was one of three children of Obadiah ("Obie") Leonard Scott and Bernice (McMurry) Scott. Her father was a trucker, farmer, barber, and storekeeper.

In 1947, after graduating from Marion Lincoln High School, Coretta moved to Yellow Springs, Ohio, to study music and elementary education at Antioch College, where her sister, Edythe, had been the first black student in the school's history. An exceptional singer, Coretta made her concert debut in 1948, performing at a Baptist church in Springfield, Ohio. During her student years she was encouraged by the great Paul Robeson to continue singing, and after she graduated with an A.B. degree from Antioch College, in 1951, she entered the New England Conservatory of Music in Boston.

Marriage to Martin Luther King, Jr.

In Boston at that time too was the young Martin Luther King, Jr., a doctoral student at Boston University. One of his friends was Mary Powell, a Boston resident from his hometown of Atlanta, Georgia. "Mary, I wish I knew a few girls from down home to go out with," he confided to her. "I tell you, these

Boston girls are something else. The ones I've been seeing are so reserved."[1] In 1952 Powell introduced him to Coretta Scott.

On June 18, 1953, Coretta Scott and Martin Luther King, Jr., were married at her family's home in Marion, Alabama. They had four children: Yolanda, Martin, Dexter, and Bernice.

In June 1954 Coretta Scott King received a Mus.B. degree in voice from the New England Conservatory of Music. She then moved with her husband to Montgomery, Alabama, where he had already accepted the position of pastor of the Dexter Avenue Baptist Church.

Supporter of Her Husband's Work

In late 1955 Martin Luther King, Jr., became the leader of the historic Montgomery bus boycott, precipitated by Rosa Parks's* refusal to surrender her bus seat to a white man. Coretta Scott King joined her husband in this endeavor and supported him in all his future civil rights activities.

In addition to standing beside him in his meetings and demonstrations in the United States, she accompanied him on his foreign travels. In 1957 the couple went to Ghana to attend the country's independence celebrations, and in 1959 they visited India. When King was awarded the Nobel Peace Prize in December 1964, she shared the moment with him at the ceremony in the Norwegian captial, Oslo. Together they worked to ensure the passage of the Voting Rights Bill, signed into law by President Lyndon B. Johnson in August 1965.

Courtesy of The King Center

CORETTA SCOTT KING

Independent Civil Rights Activist

Coretta Scott King also attended civil rights events on her own, often representing her husband. In 1967, for example, she traveled to Chicago, to participate in Jesse Jackson's Operation Breadbasket program.

Just four days after Martin Luther King, Jr., was assassinated in Memphis, Tennessee, on April 4, 1968, she and her children led a huge demonstration in Memphis, where she called for a peaceful society.

In June of that year she took part in the famous Poor Man's March in Washington, D.C., giving the keynote speech for the event at the Lincoln Memorial before more than fifty thousand people.

In 1969 she founded the Martin Luther King, Jr., Center for Nonviolent Social Change in Atlanta, a living memorial to her husband that preserves, expands, and acts on his philosophy. At the center, she explained in the 1990s, "we have been working with young people since the seventies and we teach non-

violence as a way of life. Some arrive at the center very angry and disbelieving, but they come around because they see that nonviolence works. At first it begins to work inside them. We teach that nonviolence first changes the individual."[2]

In 1971 Coretta Scott King received a doctorate in music from the New England Conservatory. Throughout the rest of the 1970s she raised her children, worked for the civil rights cause, and guided the Center for Nonviolent Social Change. In 1977 she accepted the Presidential Medal of Freedom, the nation's highest civilian honor, on behalf of her late husband.

By the 1980s she had become one of the country's most influential African-American leaders, regularly delivering speeches and writing nationally syndicated newspaper columns. In 1980, largely through her efforts, the neighborhood around her husband's birthplace in Atlanta was declared a National Historic Site by the National Park Service. In 1983 she led a rally of half a million people in Washington, D.C., to commemorate the 1963 March on Washington, at which her husband delivered his famous "I Have a Dream" speech. As chairperson of the Martin Luther King Holiday Commission, established by an act of Congress, she formulated the plans for the first formal celebration of the holiday honoring her husband in 1986. In later years she continued to coordinate the public observance of the holiday at home and abroad.

During the 1980s Coretta Scott King also actively opposed the apartheid system in South Africa. She participated in Washington, D.C., protests that sparked nationwide demonstrations against South African racial policies, and in 1986 she traveled to South Africa to investigate apartheid firsthand. Later she met with President Reagan to urge him to approve sanctions against South Africa.

Her interest in universal freedom extended to other countries as well. In 1990, for example, she visited the southern African nations of Namibia, Zambia, and Zimbabwe and met with the recently released African National Congress leader, Nelson Mandela. In 1993 she attended the African/African-American Summit in Libreville, Gabon, held to boost economic relations between Africans and black Americans.

By the early 1990s Coretta Scott King had received over one hundred honorary doctorates and had become involved with many organizations outside her Center for Nonviolent Social Change. She served, for example, as cochair of the Full Employment Action Council and as an active member of the Black Leadership Forum.

In 1993 she led the rally marking the thirtieth anniversary of the 1963 March on Washington. In October 1994, at Coretta Scott King's urging, the board of the Martin Luther King, Jr., Center for Nonviolent Social Change unanimously elected Dexter Scott King to succeed his mother as head of the organization. The passing of the baton took place in early 1995.

However, she continued to speak out on public matters. In 1996, when some Californians claimed that Martin Luther King, Jr., would have disapproved of affirmative action programs, she vehemently denied that assertion, declaring that her husband would in fact have backed affirmative action. In 1997 and 1998 she and her family publicly called for a trial for James Earl Ray, who confessed to killing Martin Luther King, Jr., was sentenced without a full trial, and later recanted his confession. A trial, she felt, would not only clarify Ray's guilt or innocence but also bring out information about possible coconspirators. Unfortunately Ray died in April 1998 before being granted a new trial.

Coretta Scott King made a monumental contribution to the civil rights movement and to the nation when she founded the Martin Luther King, Jr., Center for Nonviolent Social Change. She conveyed the spirit of the center in *My Life with Martin Luther King, Jr.* (1969, revised 1993), a book that she hopes will "inspire a new generation to take up their own nonviolent fight for freedom, dignity and human rights around the world."[3]

Daisy Elizabeth Adams Lampkin

SOCIAL REFORMER AND FUND-RAISER

(1888—1965)

A LEADING ACTIVIST FOR civil rights and women's rights, Daisy Elizabeth Adams Lampkin performed her work through many organizations, most notably the National Association for the Advancement of Colored People (NAACP). She had a special gift for organizing fund-raising and membership campaigns.

According to most published sources, she was born Daisy Elizabeth Adams in Reading, Pennsylvania, on August 9, 1888. However, her marriage certificate lists the year as 1883,[1] and the 1900 census records the city as Washington, D.C., and the date as March 1884.[2] She was the only child of George S. Adams and Rosa A. (Proctor) Adams.

In 1909 Daisy moved to Pittsburgh, and in 1912 she married William L. Lampkin, a restaurateur. She was a pioneer proponent of combining career and marriage. "The woman who is pursuing a career makes a more successful wife," she said. "She is more broadminded. She has too much on her mind to have room for petty unpleasantness."[3] The Lampkins continued to live in Pittsburgh, where she was one of the city's most prominent black citizens for over half a century.

Wide-Ranging Activist

Lampkin actively worked for social reform by assuming leadership roles in a wide range of organizations. She served as vice president (1929-65) of the *Pittsburgh Courier* Publishing Company; as president for over forty years of the Lucy Stone Civic League (which awarded scholarships to students); as national organizer, vice president, and chairperson of the executive board of the National Association of Colored Women; as a founder and life member of the National Council of Negro Women; and as the first black woman alternate delegate-at-large to a Republican National Convention (1933). Lampkin was also a member of the Links, a black women's community and social society. In 1947 she was inducted as an honorary member of Delta Sigma Theta, a predominantly black sorority involved in community service. She often took leading roles in fund-raising for these organizations. For example, in 1952 she headed the fund-raising drive to purchase a national headquarters for Delta Sigma Theta in Washington, D.C.

Because of the national reputation she developed, Lampkin was often called on to participate in social reform campaigns that transcended her roles within particular organizations, most notably in 1935 when she, along with such prominent black women as Charlotte Hawkins Brown* and Mary McLeod Bethune*, attended a meeting in Atlanta, Georgia, of the Association of Southern Women for the Prevention of Lynching (ASWPL), a white organization. Lampkin felt that the ASWPL's position against lynching was not strong enough and that the group should firmly endorse legislation allowing federal intervention in lynching cases ignored by local authorities.

NAACP Leader

Her best-known accomplishments resulted from her leadership roles with the NAACP. From 1927 to 1947 she served as a field secretary for the organization. In 1935 she became national field secretary, a position she held till health problems forced her to resign in

1947, after which she served on the board of directors of the NAACP for the rest of her life.

Among the many valuable services that Lampkin performed for the NAACP on many levels, one of her great achievements was to bring Thurgood Marshall to the NAACP to join its Legal Defense Committee.

She was one of the most articulate spokespersons for integration: "No man is ready to meet the challenge of integration unless he is certain that he and his people have earned their place in an integrated society... and the Negro has earned his place. Living in an integrated society is his right; it is not a privilege extended to him by others."[4]

She strongly supported the organization of women's groups within the NAACP. "Our male leadership," she declared, "...is so busy with their private interests that nothing is done unless the women do it."[5]

Lampkin's greatest contribution to the NAACP may have been the innovative techniques she instituted for implementing highly successful membership and fund-raising drives. Her basic principle was to make each drive a team effort. "Cities were divided into four areas, each assigned a director. The directors held meetings twice a week and relied on churches throughout the cities to host the campaign efforts."[6] As a result of this procedure, Lampkin almost doubled the Pittsburgh chapter's membership by between 1962 and 1963. During the same period she raised nearly eleven thousand dollars in the Camden, New Jersey, chapter. Such success stories were repeated many times in NAACP chapters throughout the United States.

In these campaigns Lampkin helped to solidify the NAACP's long-term viability by enlisting the efforts of youth divisions. She knew that young people who took part in membership and fund-raising drives would develop a stake in the organization's future. At the same time the NAACP would reciprocate by teaching the young people about their history "so that they may be proud of their heritage."[7]

While conducting a membership drive for the NAACP in Camden on October 6, 1964, she suffered a stroke. She died at her home in Pittsburgh on March 10, 1965.

In 1983 the Pennsylvania Historical and Museum Commission set up a ten-foot-high marker in front of it and officially recognized the home as a historical landmark. She was the first black woman so honored by Pennsylvania. "Daisy Lampkin courageously sought full equality for blacks and women throughout the country," Governor Dick Thornburgh said in a statement issued for the ceremony. "Today her work stands as an inspiration for countless citizens."[8]

Lucy Craft Laney

SCHOOL FOUNDER

(1854—1933)

EDUCATIONAL REFORMER Lucy Craft Laney "devoted her entire life to assuring black people—particularly women—the freedom to be educated and to educate others."[1] As the founder and head of Haines Normal and Industrial Institute, she established new educational opportunities for her people and led the way for future black women educators, such as Mary McLeod Bethune,* Charlotte Hawkins Brown,* and Nannie Helen Burroughs.*

Lucy Craft Laney was born in Macon, Georgia, in April 1854, one of ten children of David and Louisa Laney. David, born a slave, became a free carpenter and a Presbyterian minister, while Louisa was a slave of the Campbell family of Macon until David purchased her freedom after their marriage so that their children would be free.

Louisa continued to work for the Campbells as a domestic servant, however. One of her duties was to dust the library, where little Lucy, whom she had taught to read and write at the age of four, would sit and read books. After Lucy attended Lewis High School (later known as Ballard-Hudson High School), the Campbells enabled her to enter Atlanta University, where she received a classical liberal arts education and graduated in 1873. Her further education consisted of some graduate studies at the University of Chicago during succeeding summers.

School for Black Youth

After graduating from Atlanta University, Lucy Laney taught in the public schools of several Georgia cities, including Savannah and Augusta, where the Reverend William J. White of the Harmony Baptist Church persuaded her to open a school for the city's black youth.

In 1883 Laney opened her school, using the lecture room of Christ Presbyterian Church for a classroom. She started with only five students and virtually no funds, but by the end of the second year enrollment had grown to 234 pupils, mostly female, because of Laney's belief that women would be the primary force in uplifting the black race. In 1886, when the school was chartered by the state of Georgia as a normal and industrial school, Lucy moved it to its own quarters on Gwinnett Street, and the new site soon had to be enlarged because of the increasing number of students.

The school survived fire and flood, but financial difficulties tested Laney most of all. Her greatest help came from Francine E. H. Haines, corresponding secretary of the Women's Executive Committee of Home Missions of the Presbyterian Church, who encouraged her friends to assist the school. Her efforts were so helpful that Laney named the school the Haines Normal and Industrial Institute in her honor. The Presbyterian Board of Missions also offered financial help.

In the early 1890s Laney established a kindergarten and a nurse education department at Haines. A Canadian-trained graduate nurse headed the nursing program, which later developed into the school of nursing at Augusta's University Hospital.

By 1914 the school had more than nine hundred students and over thirty teachers. In contrast to the approach to education favored by most black educators of the time, based on Booker T. Washington's program for industrial training, Laney emphasized a liberal arts curriculum to prepare her students to enter college and become teachers. Laney's success was outstanding, Haines Institute being widely regarded as one of the best secondary schools in the South and its graduates being favorably compared with white students in ability.

In 1917 a United States government report on Haines Institute noted, "The management is effective" and stated, "The administration of the principal has won for the school the confidence of both white and Colored people. The teachers are well prepared and doing thorough work."[2]

In the 1930s Haines Institute eliminated its elementary grades, offering instead a high school program plus a year of college courses. However, financial straits caused by the Great Depression forced the Presbyterian church to withdraw its support, and the school struggled for some years before finally closing in 1949. Its buildings were torn down, and a modern public school, the Lucy C. Laney High School, was built on the site.

Social Concerns

Laney measured the success of her work not only by what occurred within the classroom but also by the kind of young people she turned out into the world. She and other women, she felt, had a special role to play in molding the next generation of young people. "To women has been committed the responsibility of making the laws of society, making environments for children," she wrote in 1897. "She has the privilege and authority, God-given, to help develop into a noble man or woman the young life committed to her care. There is no nobler work entrusted to the hands of mortals."[3]

In her paper "The Burden of the Educated Colored Woman," which she delivered at the 1899 Hampton Negro Conference, Laney exhorted educated women to do even more. "Not alone in the schoolroom can the intelligent woman lend a lifting hand," she said, "but as a public lecturer she may give advice, helpful suggestions, and important knowledge that will change a whole community and start its people on the upward way."[4]

Laney took her own advice to heart and often spoke out on issues relating to social justice and cultural enrichment in the black community. In 1916, for example, she attended a conference called by Joel Spingarn, a leader of the National Association for the Advancement of Colored People, to establish a united block for fighting racism in the United States. She once urged black writers to go to the Sea Islands of Georgia and South Carolina to "study the Negro in his original purity."[5]

Never married, she devoted her life to her work and her young people. She was often referred to as the "mother of the children of the people."[6]

Lucy Craft Laney died in Augusta on October 23, 1933. She is still remembered as a pathbreaking school founder and as one of the most important African-American female educators in the history of the South.

Marjorie McKenzie Lawson

FIRST BLACK WOMAN JUDGE APPOINTED BY A PRESIDENT

(1912–)

MARJORIE MCKENZIE LAWSON had a long, varied career as a lawyer, journalist, and civic activist. She is best known for her historic role as the first black woman appointed to a judgeship by a president of the United States.

Born Marjorie McKenzie in Pittsburgh, Pennsylvania, on March 12, 1912, she was raised, after her father died when she was five years old, by her mother. Marjorie attended public schools in Pittsburgh, where she was the only black in her classes, and then earned a bachelor's degree in sociology (1933) and a certificate in social work (1934) at the University of Michigan. Moving to Washington, D.C., she earned a law degree at Terrell Law School (1939) and passed the District of Columbia bar examination (1939).

In 1939 she married Belford V. Lawson, Jr., a University of Michigan graduate who had become a member of the District of Columbia bar in 1933. They had one son, Belford V. Lawson III, who also became an attorney.

Law Practice with Her Husband

Marjorie McKenzie Lawson and her husband practiced law together in Washington, D.C., she specializing in administrative law, while he handled civil rights cases. In 1950 she helped him to win the Supreme Court case *Henderson* v. *United States*, which abolished segregation in railroad dining cars. During that same year she received a J.D. degree from Columbia University in New York, where she studied so that she could improve the status of her professional credentials.

While living in the nation's capital, Marjorie

Lawson became fully aware of the extent of discrimination against blacks in America. Having previously lived in basically nonsegregated northern cities, she was unprepared for her experiences in blatantly segregated Washington, D.C. "This abrupt contrast with her early life, as well as her training in social work and law, caused her to make a lifelong commitment to improving conditions in the black community."[1]

Living in Washington, D.C., Lawson soon decided to find a position with the federal government so that she could act on her social concerns. From 1943 to 1946 she served as assistant director and then director of the Division of Review and Analysis of the President's Commission on Fair Employment Practices.

Lawson also joined the National Council of Negro Women (NCNW), serving as NCNW vice president from 1952 to 1954. Later she served for many years as the organization's general counsel.

While continuing to practice law with her husband, she began a career as a journalist. For about fourteen years during the 1950s and 1960s, she wrote a column for the *Pittsburgh Courier*, "Pursuit of Democracy," in which she discussed federal policies that affected blacks.

Juvenile Court Judge

The peak of Lawson's career, her presidential appointment to a judgeship, came about through her personal friendship with John F. Kennedy. In 1956 her husband met Kennedy at the Democratic National Convention, where Kennedy first came to prominence. Both Lawsons soon became friends with

Kennedy, advised him on matters relating to the black community, and introduced him to prominent black leaders. In 1960, when Kennedy was running for president, he placed Marjorie Lawson at the head of a campaign unit that advised him on civil rights and campaign issues. After Kennedy was elected she served him yet again as a member of the inauguration committee.

Shortly after Kennedy took office in 1961 he signed a bill to add two juvenile courts to the existing single court in the District of Columbia. When he offered Lawson one of the new courts, she hesitated because "she did not wish to serve under the sole and senior judge, Orem Ketchum, a Republican appointee."[2] She asked Kennedy to appoint as chief judge either her or someone who shared her views on how to handle court cases. After Kennedy appointed Morris Miller chief judge, Lawson accepted the ten-year appointment as an associate judge in the District of Columbia Junveile Court. It was the first time in history that an American president had appointed a black woman judge.

She stayed on the bench from 1962 till 1965, and soon after she submitted her resignation to President Lyndon B. Johnson, he appointed her United States representative to the Social Commission of the United Nations Economic and Social Council, where she served till 1969.

Community Activist

Lawson devoted her later years to local politics and community activism. In 1966, with Walter Fauntroy, she founded the Model Inner City Community Organization, aimed at helping to rebuild communities in Washington, D.C. She also served on the board of the Washington Urban League, the District of Columbia Crime Commission (1966), the President's Task Force on Urban Renewal (1969), the Committee on the Organization of the District of Columbia Government (1970), the Mayor's Committee on Economic Development (1971), and the board of the National Bank of Washington and the Madison National Bank (1971).

In 1985 Belford Lawson died, having supported his wife's involvement in politics throughout the years of their marriage. After his death Marjorie McKenzie Lawson continued to practice law into the 1990s, still committed to the profession through which she had attained her historic position as America's first presidentially appointed African-American judge.

Edmonia Lewis

PIONEER SCULPTRESS

(c. 1843—1911 or later)

EDMONIA LEWIS WAS THE first major sculptress of African-American and Native American heritage. She "represented a fresh approach to the neoclassical sculpture tradition, injecting as she did timely yet universal human rights issues and developing a more emotional, naturalistic style than her contemporaries."[1]

Many details about her early life are uncertain. She claimed to have been born in 1854, but that birth date would have put her in college at the age of five. Her birth probably occurred in 1843 or 1845. The location, too, is in doubt—possibly Greenhigh, Ohio; Greenbush, New York; or the vicinity of Albany, New York.

Her father, a gentleman's servant, was a full-blooded African-American, while her mother was a Chippewa American Indian. Lewis, orphaned before she was five, lived with her mother's tribe, among whom she was known as Wildfire, till she was about twelve. She made baskets, embroidered moccasins, and sold her crafts as the tribe traveled about New York state.

Lewis left the Chippewas when her brother Sunrise, a California gold miner, arranged for her to receive schooling in Albany, New York. In 1859 his financial assistance made it possible for her to enter Oberlin College in Oberlin, Ohio. It was at Oberlin that she assumed the name Mary Edmonia Lewis, but throughout the rest of her life she seldom used the name Mary.

"The Form of Things"

As Lewis pursued liberal arts studies at college, she discovered her talent for art. "I had always wanted to make the form of things," she later recalled; "and while I was at school I tried to make drawings of people and things."[2] In 1862 she drew *Muse Urania* (now in the Oberlin College Archive), her only extant drawing, which she created as a wedding present for her classmate Clara Steele Norton.

Lewis left Oberlin under a cloud: In 1862 two white female students accused her of poisoning them, and a year later she was accused of stealing art supplies. Though neither case was proved against her, the college refused to let her graduate.

Lewis then moved to Boston, where, inspired by Richard Greenough's life-size statue of Benjamin Franklin, she began to establish herself as a sculptress receiving advice from the portrait sculptor Edward Brackett. With the Civil War raging, for her first sculptures she chose medallion portraits, modeled in plaster and clay, of war heroes and white antislavery leaders. During the war she also executed her first portrait bust, the subject being Colonel Robert Gould Shaw, a white Boston native who was killed as he led his black troops to battle. Most of Lewis's early works, including the bust of Shaw, have not been located.

Classical Studies in Europe

In 1865 Lewis moved to Europe to be near the roots of Western artistic tradition. At first she thought about living in England because of its abolitionist community. However, after visits to London, Paris, and Florence, she settled in Rome during the winter of 1865-66. For many years American sculptors had been drawn to Italy's classical sculpture, plentiful marble, and low-cost artisan labor. Lewis found Rome especially attractive because of its nonsexist treatment of women artists.

Following traditional practice, she learned to carve in marble by copying classical sculptures, many of which she sold to American tourists.

Her most consistent income resulted from commissions by admirers living in America, especially Boston. For those patrons Lewis produced, and shipped to them, small portrait busts in terra cotta and marble as well as "'conceits' or 'fancy pieces'—sculptures that used mythological children to convey human, often sentimental themes."[3] Her best-known conceit is *Poor Cupid*, also called *Love Ensnared*, completed in 1876 (National Museum of American Art, Washington, D.C.).

Unlike many of her peers, she did not hire artisans to enlarge her small clay and plaster models and to carve the final marble versions. Lewis carved the marbles herself. She created at least forty-six pieces, most of them unfortunately still missing.

Her Great Works

Because of her dual heritage and her classical studies, Lewis developed a unique style. Like other neoclassical artists of her time, she based her sculpting technique on an adaptation of classical models. Unlike the others, however, she eschewed ideas and images from classical art, history, and literature. Her subject matter and emotional content reflected her interest in the burning racial issues of the nineteenth century.

The Freed Woman and Her Child of 1866 (location unknown) and *Forever Free* of 1867 (Howard University, Washington, D.C.) both deal with the subject of emancipation. The latter work evokes the newly freed slaves' powerful emotions through a standing male figure, whose left arm holds a broken chain, and through a kneeling female figure who is praying. The eyes of both figures look upward.

In 1868 Lewis sculpted *Hagar*, or *Hagar in the Wilderness* (National Museum of American Art). Hagar, the Egyptian (and therefore, in nineteenth-century interpretation, black) biblical concubine of to Abraham, served as a means for Lewis to comment on both racial and gender oppression. She described as her motivation for this work "a strong sympathy for all women who have struggled and suffered."[4]

Some of Lewis's work reflected her Native American heritage. From 1869 to 1871 she carved a portrait bust of Henry Wadsworth Longfellow (Harvard University portrait collection), whose poem "The Song of Hiawatha" greatly influenced her. In 1872 she finished

EDMONIA LEWIS

The Schomburg Center / NYPL

Old Arrow Maker, or *The Old Arrow Maker and His Daughter* (National Museum of American Art), a sentimental portrait designed to counteract the period's stereotyped image of Native Americans as savages.

From 1870 to 1876 Lewis made several return visits to the United States and exhibited her works in Boston and elsewhere. In 1876 she exhibited her ambitious sculpture *The Death of Cleopatra* (Forest Park Historical Society, Forest Park, Illinois) in Philadelphia at the Centennial Exposition, where the work won a medal.

Lewis's last major commission was *Adoration of the Magi* (location unknown), which she worked on for a Baltimore church in 1883. The sculpture probably reflected her conversion to Catholicism in Rome in 1868.

As the vogue for neoclassical sculpture declined, so did the demand for Lewis's work. She drifted into obscurity, little being known of her final decades. The last recorded report of her existence in Rome was in 1911, and the date and place of her death are unknown.

In her heyday in the 1860s and 1870s, however, Lewis was one of the most popular attractions for Americans and Europeans who visited artists in Rome. In her red cap and mannish clothing, she made a colorful impression, and as a classically oriented female artist of African-American and Native American heritage based in Italy, she was clearly a novelty. But as early as 1863 Lewis asked that her work not be praised solely because of her background. Mary Edmonia ("Wildfire") Lewis earned her place in art history through the true merits of her emotionally charged neoclassicism, and in social history as the first woman of mixed African-American and Native American heritage to attain international stature in the art of sculpting.

Hattie McDaniel

FIRST AFRICAN-AMERICAN TO WIN AN OSCAR

(1895—1952)

FOR HER MEMORABLE PORTRAYAL of Mammy in the film classic *Gone with the Wind* (1939), Hattie McDaniel became the first black performer to win an Academy Award. "I hope that my winning the award will be inspiration for the youth of my race," she said, "that it will encourage them to aim high and work hard, and take the bitter with the sweet."[1]

Hattie McDaniel was born in Wichita, Kansas, on June 10, 1895, the youngest of thirteen children of Henry and Susan (Holbert) McDaniel. Her father often performed in minstrel shows. In 1900 the family moved to Colorado, living first in Fort Collins and then in Denver, where Hattie grew up.

Early Career as a Singer

McDaniel dropped out of high school after her sophomore year to enter show business. For the next several years she toured the West in music and comedy shows, mostly with her father's own Henry McDaniel Minstrel Show, which costarred her two brothers, Sam and Otis. After Otis died in 1916, and her father semiretired, Hattie McDaniel went solo.

From 1916 to 1920 she continued her western tours with various groups. During 1920-25 she appeared with Professor George Morrison's Melody Hounds, a touring black ensemble, and in the mid-1920s she embarked on a radio career, singing with the Melody Hounds on station KOA in Denver. In the late 1920s she performed extensively on both black and white entertainment circuits, such as the Orpheum, the Pantages, and the Theater Owners Booking Association (TOBA). During this time she wrote the lyrics and music to many of the songs she performed.

While her career was advancing in the 1920s, her personal life took some hard hits. Her husband, George Langford, died soon after she married him in 1922, and her father died the same year.

After the stock market crashed in 1929, her entertainment circuit, TOBA, went out of business, and for a while McDaniel had to work as a washroom attendant at the Club Madrid in Milwaukee, Wisconsin. Fortunately, one night when the club was short on entertainment, she got a chance to sing, was an immediate success, and became a regular at the club.

Becoming Established in Hollywood

In 1931 her remaining brother, Sam, who had settled in Hollywood as a bit-player in films and a radio performer (he later played credited parts in dozens of movies from the 1930s to the 1960s), persuaded Hattie to join him there. Her first significant mark in Hollywood came in her recurring role as Hi-Hat Hattie, a bossy maid, on the KNX radio show *The Optimistic Do-Nut Hour* (1931), on which Sam already had a job. Ironically, because her weekly pay for the show was so low, only five dollars, she had to moonlight as a real maid to support herself.

After playing several uncredited small parts in movies, notably *The Golden West* (1932), Hattie began to attract attention and finally landed larger film roles that began to win her screen credits. In her career she would eventually appear in about three hundred films, earning credits in over eighty of them. In most of these movies she played a maid or a cook.

An important early picture for her was *Judge Priest* (1934), starring Will Rogers in the title role. As Priest's washerwoman, Aunt Dilsey, Hattie McDaniel had a leading part in the film and demonstrated her singing talent.

Some of her roles tended to emphasize servility, for example, *The Little Colonel* (1935). Her real forte, however, and the type of role for which she became best known, was the sassy, independently minded servant she played in *Alice Adams* (1935), *Another Face* (1935), *Gentle Julia* (1936), and *The Mad Miss Manton* (1938).

McDaniel enjoyed her fame and, by now, fortune. She moved into an upscale Los Angeles neighborhood and began to donate to charity. Her personal life, however, still stumbled. After sixteen years of widowhood, she married Howard Hickman in 1938 but divorced him later the same year.

Gone with the Wind

In 1939 McDaniel played the key role of Mammy in *Gone with the Wind*, the film adaptation of Margaret Mitchell's best-selling novel about life in the Old South. Having lived most of her own life in the West, McDaniel had to be coached to develop a Georgia accent for the film. In this picture she portrayed her quintessential sassy-servant character, who repeatedly scolds her mistress, Scarlett O'Hara, and scoffs at Scarlett's suitor, Rhett Butler. "I love Mammy," McDaniel said. "I think I understand her because my own grandmother worked on a plantation not unlike Tara."[2]

Her performance in *Gone with the Wind* remains one of the most memorable in film history. One scene, in particular, stands out. As Mammy and Melanie Wilkes climb a stairway, Mammy, through flowing tears, chillingly tells Melanie that Rhett Butler will not let his dead little daughter, Bonnie, be buried, because the child was afraid of the dark. Largely because of that powerful scene, McDaniel won an Oscar for the best performance by a supporting actress in 1939. She was the first African-American to win an Academy Award.

In the 1940s she was frequently called on to play characters in the Mammy mold in other period films, such as *Maryland* (1940), *The Great Lie* (1941), and *Song of the South* (1946). She also continued to play sassy maids in modern settings, such as *Affectionately*

Yours (1941), *George Washington Slept Here* (1942), and *Family Honeymoon* (1948).

One film during that time was different, however. The revolutionary *In This Our Life* (1942) was the first movie to represent black characters as multidimensional persons coping with racism. McDaniel played Minerva Clay, a household servant whose son is falsely accused of a hit-and-run killing. Minerva Clay is not a comical, servile, or even sassy character, she is a realistic mother in pain. At one point she utters a now famous line: "Well, you know those policemen. They won't listen to what a colored boy says."[3]

McDaniel and other black actors and actresses formed the Fair Play Committee, which tried to improve the portrayals of blacks in films. She felt that she and her fellow professionals could bring about this change more effectively than outside political organizations could because "you can best fight any existing evil from the inside," she wrote in a 1945 letter. She and her friends were "speaking out against lines and types that we think objectionable, and both directors and producers are cooperative."[4]

In 1941 McDaniel married Lloyd Crawford, but this marriage, too, ended in divorce, in 1945.

Beulah

McDaniel's principal work in the last years of her life was the title role in the radio series *Beulah* (1947-52). She had been a frequent guest on radio programs ever since the 1920s. It now seems fitting that just as she achieved her first big success on radio, as the maid Hi-Hat Hattie, so her final triumph was in the same medium, as Beulah, another maid. Beulah, however, represented a great advance on McDaniel's earlier role. The character did not speak in dialect, was not servile, and displayed great intelligence by solving other characters' problems. On this show McDaniel "influenced the civil rights movement by proving to listeners that a black person could have a comedy role without degradation."[5]

In the late 1940s and early 1950s she began to experience health problems. Her brief fourth marriage to Larry Williams in 1949-50 contributed to her weakened condition. She suffered weight loss and had a series of slight strokes and heart attacks. Nevertheless, she kept recovering enough to continue working into 1952, when she was diagnosed with breast cancer. Hattie McDaniel died on October 26, 1952, at the Motion Picture Country Home and Hospital in Woodland Hills, California.

Her contribution to film history went far beyond being the first black to win an Oscar. "It is usually when people *see* the possibilities of upward mobility that they begin to remove the obstacles in their way. Hattie showed that it could be done, and her example certainly was not ignored by the generations that followed."[6]

Selected recordings:

SINGLES

"Quittin' My Man Today" / "Brown-Skin Baby Doll" (1926, Merritt)

"I Wish I Had Somebody" / "Boo Hoo Blues" (1926, Okeh)

"I Thought I'd Do It" / "Just One Sorrowing Heart" (1927, Okeh)

"That New Love Maker of Mine" / "Any Kind of a Man Would Be Better Than You" (1929, Paramount)

Selected performances:

FILMS

The Golden West (1932)
The Blonde Venus (1932)
Hello, Sister (1933)
I'm No Angel (1933)
The Story of Temple Drake (1933)
Imitation of Life (1934)
Judge Priest (1934)
Operator 13 (1934)
Alice Adams (1935)
Another Face (1935)
China Seas (1935)
Harmony Lane (1935)
The Little Colonel (1935)
Little Men (1935)
Lost in the Stratosphere (1935)
Murder by Television (1935)
Music Is Magic (1935)
The Traveling Saleslady (1935)
The Bride Walks Out (1936)
Can This Be Dixie? (1936)
First Baby (1936)
Gentle Julia (1936)
Hearts Divided (1936)
High Tension (1936)
Libeled Lady (1936)
Next Time We Love (1936)
Postal Inspector (1936)
Show Boat (1936)
Star for a Night (1936)
Valiant Is the Word for Carrie (1936)
We're Only Human (1936)
The Crime Nobody Saw (1937)
Don't Tell the Wife (1937)
Nothing Sacred (1937)
Over the Goal (1937)
Racing Lady (1937)
Saratoga (1937)
True Confession (1937)
Forty-five Fathers (1937)
Battle of Broadway (1938)
Carefree (1938)
The Mad Miss Manton (1938)
Quick Money (1938)
The Shining Hour (1938)
Shopworn Angel (1938)
Vivacious Lady (1938)
Everybody's Baby (1939)
Gone with the Wind (1939)
Zenobia (1939)
Maryland (1940)
Affectionately Yours (1941)
The Great Lie (1941)
George Washington Slept Here (1942)
In This Our Life (1942)
The Male Animal (1942)
They Died with Their Boots On (1942)
Johnny Come Lately (1943)
Thank Your Lucky Stars (1943)
Hi Beautiful (1944)
Janie (1944)
Since You Went Away (1944)
Three Is a Family (1944)
Janie Gets Married (1946)
Margie (1946)
Never Say Goodbye (1946)
Song of the South (1946)
Family Honeymoon (1948)
The Flame (1948)
Mickey (1948)

RADIO

The Optimistic Do-Nut Hour (1931)
Beulah (1947–52)

Mary Mahoney
PIONEER NURSE

(1845—1926)

MARY MAHONEY WAS the first black professional nurse in the United States. She provided expert nursing care for forty years and "worked for the acceptance of black women in the nursing profession and for the improvement of the status of the black professional nurse."[1]

Mary Eliza Mahoney was born in Dorchester, a part of the city of Boston, on May 7, 1845, the eldest of three children of Charles and Mary Jane (Stewart) Mahoney. She grew up in the nearby Roxbury section of the city.

At the age of eighteen Mahoney began working at the New England Hospital for Women and Children in Boston as a cook and cleaning woman. Long interested in becoming a nurse, she was finally accepted as a student nurse at the hospital in 1878, when she was thirty-three. The School of Nursing put its trainees through a rigorous schedule that many could not complete. Of the forty-two students who entered the program in 1878, only four finished, including Mahoney, who graduated on August 1, 1879.

Private-Duty Nurse

She soon registered with the Nurses Directory at the Massachusetts Medical Library in Boston, which provided nurses' names and references to potential employers who required the services of private-duty nurses. When families began employing Mahoney again and again, she firmly established herself as America's first African-American professional nurse. "Her well-known calm and quiet efficiency instilled confidence and trust, which in some instances overcame the racial barrier."[2] She earned an ever-widening reputation, being called to nurse patients as far away as New Jersey, Washington, D.C., and North Carolina.

Her alma mater took note of her success. "Miss Mahoney's excellent record evidently paved the way for the admission of other Negro women despite the rigid patterns of discrimination then prevailing in most nursing schools."[3] By 1899 the School of Nursing at the New England Hospital for Women and Children had produced five other black graduates.

Mahoney joined the Nurses Associated Alumnae of the United States and Canada, which later became the American Nurses Association (ANA). She was one of the few black nurses in the ANA at the time.

Advocate of Black Nurses' Rights

Because of Mahoney's efforts more and more black women became professional nurses, but they were not always given the same privileges accorded to white nurses. In 1908 Mahoney supported the organization of the National Association of Colored Graduate Nurses (NACGN), founded by Martha Franklin to give black nurses a united voice. Mahoney delivered the welcoming address at the NACGN's first annual convention in Boston in August 1909.

She became deeply involved with local and national NACGN affairs. Elected national chaplain in 1911, she gave opening prayers and instructed new officers in their duties. Also in 1911 she was honored with a life membership in the organization.

Mahoney's role as national chaplain for the NACGN was a natural outgrowth of her deep religiosity. She regularly attended People's Baptist Church, a historic black church in Roxbury.

Never married, Mahoney treated her patients like family. She loved to cook, and she often cooked for those in her care.

In 1911 she moved to New York to head the Howard Orphan Asylum for black children in Kings Park, Long Island. After holding this position for over a year, she retired in 1912 and returned to the Boston area.

In her later years Mahoney supported the women's suffrage movement, and in 1921, at the age of seventy-six, she became one of the first women in her city to register to vote.

Mahoney died in Boston on January 4, 1926. She was buried in Woodlawn Cemetery in Everett, Massachusetts, where her grave was made into a shrine by nursing organizations.

After her death Mahoney was honored in many ways. Several local NACGN chapters were named after her. In 1936 the organization established an award in her name; and when the NACGN merged into the American Nurses Association (ANA) in 1951, the ANA continued the award. The New England Hospital for Women and Children which became the Dimock Community Health Center, houses the Mary Mahoney Health Care Clinic.

In 1976 Mary Eliza Mahoney, a pioneer in the acceptance of black women in the nursing profession, was inducted into nursing's Hall of Fame.

Victoria Earle Matthews

FOUNDER OF WHITE ROSE MISSION

(1861—1907)

AUTHOR, CLUBWOMAN, and social activist, Victoria Earle Matthews was a tireless worker for her people in the 1890s and early 1900s. She performed her greatest service as the founder of the White Rose Mission, a settlement house for black girls.

Victoria Smith was born into sl;avery in Fort Valley, near Macon, Georgia, on May 27, 1861, one of nine children of a slave named Caroline Smith. According to family tradition Victoria and her older sister, Anna, were fathered by Caroline's white master, and after Caroline fled from slavery, her two fair-skinned daughters were raised as white in the master's household. When the Civil War set her free, Caroline returned to Georgia, regained custody of Victoria and Anna, and later moved with them to New York City in 1873.

Victoria attended public school in New York City only briefly, leaving to take work as a domestic. However, the family for whom she worked allowed her to use their library, where she read avidly.

In 1879 she married William Matthews, a coachman. They settled in Brooklyn and had one son, Lamartine.

Literary and Club Work

Her marriage proving to be unhappy, Victoria Matthews turned her attention to writing, submitting her childhood reminiscences to the *Brooklyn Eagle* and the *Waverley Magazine*. Under the pen name Victoria Earle she published *Aunt Lindy: A Story Founded on Real Life* (1893), a short novel set in Georgia, about an elderly ex-slave who resists the temptation to murder her former master.

Matthews took a deep interest in black women's clubs. In 1892 she became the first president of a new club, the Woman's Loyal Union of New York and Brooklyn. In 1895 she helped to found the National Federation of Afro-American Women, and the following year, as chairperson of its executive committee, she played a leading role in merging the federation with the National Colored Women's League to form the National Association of Colored Women (NACW), of which she served as national organizer from 1897 to 1899. A dramatic speaker, Matthews often lectured to black audiences on such topics as "The Awakening of the Afro-American Woman" and "The Value of Race Literature."

White Rose Mission

The death of her son at the age of sixteen precipitated a turning point in her career. When he died, "my heart went out to other people's boys and girls..." she explained. "I found that this was my field so I began to visit families."[1] She decided to devote herself to social welfare among young people.

Matthews had long been concerned about black girls who needed work and were being lured into prostitution. In 1896 she toured the South to investigate the techniques that unscrupulous men used to entrap girls who wanted to get jobs in the North. On February 11, 1897, in New York City, she founded the White Rose Industrial Association, which established "a working girls' home where newly arrived Negro girls were befriended, counseled, and prepared for employment through courses in cooking, sewing, and housekeeping."[2] Matthews even sent White Rose agents to New York City and Norfolk, Virginia, docks to prevent criminals from getting their hands on young female travelers.

White Rose Mission, as it was commonly called, moved in 1900 to larger quarters on Eighty-sixth Street, where she enlarged its activities into a kind of settlement house, with recreational activities, mothers' clubs, and a kindergarten. Matthews herself taught a class in black history and created a large library of books by and about African-Americans.

In 1907 a *New York Age* reporter described her as "a Salvation Army field officer, a College Settlement worker, a missionary, a teacher, a preacher, a Sister of Mercy, all in one, and without being in the least conscious of it."[3] However, tuberculosis gradually weakened her, and her assistants eventually took over her duties.

Victoria Earle Matthews died in New York City on March 10, 1907, at the age of only forty-five. The White Rose Mission, which later moved to 136th Street, became a lasting legacy of her dedication to helping defenseless African-American girls.

Cheryl Miller

BASKETBALL PIONEER

(1964–   )

CHERYL MILLER SET scoring records, won championships, and earned an Olympic gold medal during her basketball career. She became famous, however, not only for *what* she did but also for *how* she did it. A 6'3" forward, she "showed fans that women could play with the quickness and speed most often associated with the men's game."[1] Many still regard her as the greatest women's basketball player of all time.

Cheryl DeAnne Miller was born in Riverside, California, on January 3, 1964, the daughter of Saul and Carrie Miller. Her father, a former high school and college basketball player, taught her the basics of the game early on, and by the age of seven she was already playing on the Riverside courts with her brothers, one of whom, Reggie, became an outstanding professional player with the Indiana Pacers. In fifth grade she played on the boys' basketball team. "The boys on the other teams laughed at me in the beginning," she said of those days, "but then they'd see the score at the end of the game and they weren't laughing anymore."[2]

High School Phenom

During her four years at Riverside Poly High School (from 1978–79 through 1981–82), Miller averaged 32.8 points per game, setting California Interscholastic Federation records for the most points scored in one season (1,156) and in a career (3,405). In one game she scored an incredible 105 points.

A member of the American Junior National Team in 1981, the following year she played with the senior United States National Team. Miller was named to high school All-American teams for four consecutive years,

and in her senior year many sports authorities rated her the nation's top high school basketball player.

After being offered scholarships by nearly 250 colleges and universities, she finally chose the University of Southern California (USC), which not only had a good basketball program but also offered a first-rate education in her academic field of interest, communications and broadcasting.

Collegiate and Olympic Champion

Miller had no difficulty adapting to college-level competition. In her freshman year she led the USC Lady Trojans in scoring, steals, and blocked shots. She helped the team to win the 1983 National Collegiate Athletic Association (NCAA) Championship over Louisiana Tech, the defending champions, scoring 27 of USC's 69 points in the title game. The following year she led the Lady Trojans to yet another NCAA championship, and was voted the most valuable player in both tournaments.

During those two seasons Miller also participated in international competition. She was a member of the victorious United States National Team at the 1983 Pan American Games, and at the Los Angeles Olympics the following year she led the United States women's basketball team to a gold medal with a scoring average of 16.5 points per game.

Her best personal season at USC was her junior year, 1984–85, during which she averaged 26.8 points and 15.8 rebounds per game. In her senior year, 1985–86, she averaged 25.4 points per game and led the Lady Trojans all the way to the NCAA title game, which the team lost to the University of Texas.

During her college career Miller won nearly every major basketball award, including All-American honors (all our years), the Female College Athlete of the Year Award (1984), the Broderick Award as the player of the year (1984, 1985), the Naismith Trophy as the player of the year (1984, 1985, 1986), the Wade Trophy of the National Association for Girls and Women in Sports (1985), the Women's Basketball Coaches Association Player of the Year Award (1985, 1986), and the *Sports Illustrated* Player of the Year Award (1986).

Miller finished her college career as USC's all-time leader in several categories, including scoring and rebounding, with marks of 3,018 (23.6 average) and 1,534 (12.0 average) respectively. In March 1986 USC retired her number 31, making her the school's first basketball player, male or female, to be so honored. She was subsequently named Player of the Decade of the 1980s by the Women's Basketball Coaches Association and the United States Basketball Writers Association, and later she was inducted into the International Women's Sports Hall of Fame (1991), the Naismith Memorial Basketball Hall of Fame for men and women (1995), and the Women's Basketball Hall of Fame (1998).

After Miller graduated from USC with a B.A. degree in broadcast jouralism in 1986, she played on the United States National Team that summer, winning gold medals at the Goodwill Games and the World Basketball Championships. Shortly thereafter, however, a severe knee injury put an end to her playing career.

Coach Miller

Taking advantage of both her basketball experience and her broadcasting degree, Miller joined ABC television's sports staff, working on the sidelines at football games and providing color commentary for men's and women's college basketball games.

In September 1993 a golden opportunity came her way when USC hired her to coach her old team, the Lady Trojans. In two seasons she coached the team to a fine 44–14 record (26–4 and 18–10), a Pacific Ten Conference title (1994), a seventh-place national ranking (1994), and two NCAA tournament berths— remarkable achievements for a first-time coach, and especially for a former great player. Former stars tend to expect too much from their players, but Miller made the adjustment well. "I've been very fortunate," she later said, ". . . because once you hang around enough people, it rubs off on you, and I've been around a lot of good coaches,"[3] including her own USC coach, Linda Sharp.

After leaving her USC coaching job in September 1995, Miller returned to broadcasting. She served as a TNT sports commentator at the Atlanta Olympic Games in 1996, and later she covered National Basketball Association (NBA) games.

In 1997 she became the coach and general manager of the Phoenix Mercury of the Women's National Basketball Association (WNBA). One of her opponents was her former USC coach, Linda Sharp, now the coach of the WNBA's Los Angeles Sparks. In the league's record season, 1998, Miller coached the Mercury all the way to the championship series, which they lost to the defending champions, the Houston Comets.

As a player Cheryl Miller revolutionized women's basketball, using her athletic approach to introduce a more entertaining style to the game in the 1980s. "She electrified audiences all over the country and helped to transform women's basketball into an exciting spectator sport."[4]

Toni Morrison

FIRST AFRICAN-AMERICAN NOBEL PRIZE WINNER IN LITERATURE

(1931–   )

THROUGH HER BOOKS, small in number but gigantic in effect, the novelist and essayist Toni Morrison has transformed the way in which American readers view United States history and literature. More clearly and forcefully than any other writer, she has shown that America, past and present, cannot be understood without consideration of the African-American presence. For her literary achievement and for her championing of the importance of African-American writings, she was awarded the 1993 Nobel Prize for literature, the first African-American writer, male or female, to be so honored.

Originally named Chloe Anthony Wofford, she was born in Lorain, Ohio, on February 18, 1931, the second of four children of George and Ella Ramah (Willis) Wofford who had both migrated from the South with their families in the early 1900s. Her father, a welder, told her black folktales, and her mother sang traditional black songs to her. From her parents Morrison early absorbed the black southern heritage, especially an awareness of how African-Americans have reacted to displacement in their lives—first from Africa to America and then from the South to the North. In each of her later novels a protagonist leaves home to discover his or her true inner self and to connect that self to a larger community.[1]

After graduating from Lorain High School in 1949 Morrison entered Howard University in Washington, D.C., where she majored in English and minored in the classics. At Howard she changed her first name to Toni because many people had difficulty pronouncing Chloe. During her years as a student there she made her first trips to the South. The similarities she saw between black cultural life in the South and the North influenced her later novels, which are known for conveying a sense of African-American cultural unity. She graduated from Howard in 1953 and went on to earn a master's degree in English at Cornell University in Ithaca, New York, in 1955.

Morrison then worked as an English instructor at Texas Southern University in Houston from 1955 to 1957, after which she returned to Howard University to take up a similar position from 1957 to 1964. While teaching in Washington she met a Jamaican architect, Harold Morrison, whom she married in 1958. They had two sons, Harold and Slade.

Teacher and Editor

In the mid-1960s many book publishers, under pressure from civil rights groups, began to revise their textbook selections to reflect the contributions of African-Americans. Eager to participate in this effort, Morrison went to work as a textbook editor at a Random House subsidiary in Syracuse, New York, soon after leaving Howard University in 1964, and moved to New York City four years later to become a trade book editor with the parent company. At Random House she rose to become a senior editor, nurturing the writings of such important black authors as Toni Cade Bambara, Wesley Brown, Angela Davis, and June Jordan. Morrison also edited *The Black Book* (1974), an anthology of African-American history.

While continuing to work as an editor, she occasionally taught as well. During 1971–72 she was an associate professor of English at the State University of New York at Purchase, and during 1976–77 she was a visiting lecturer at Yale University. By 1985, ready to return to teaching full-time, she left Ran-

The Schomburg Center / NYPL

TONI MORRISON

dom House to accept a professorship at the State University of New York at Albany, where she had already begun to teach in 1984. Since 1989 she has been the Robert F. Goheen Professor in the Council of the Humanities at Princeton University.

While holding these jobs, Morrison pursued her creative writing career, the impetus for which was the breakdown of her marriage, which ended in divorce in 1964. She has said that she began writing to forestall "melancholy."[2]

Writer

Morrison's first novel was *The Bluest Eye* (1970), a story about a little black girl who wants blue eyes so that she will be beautiful. Morrison here exposes the psychological effects of racism as the girl's family is destroyed and the girl herself goes mad because black society has negated its own sense of beauty and black identity.

Sula (1973), Morrison's second novel, explores the relationship between two black women, Nel Wright and Sula Peace, as well as their relationship to the community. The two women represent characteristics that African-American women have long combined: Nel is the traditional nurturing woman, and Sula is the modern independent woman who defies the values of the community. Ultimately the story affirms the importance of black community allegiance over individuality.

Morrison achieved national recognition with her third novel, *Song of Solomon* (1977), the story of Milkman Dead, a young man who sets out to find a family fortune in the caves of Virginia but finds instead the songs and folklore of his ancestors. In this work Morrison, inspired by her editing of *The Black Book*, derived her prose from African-American oral and musical tradition. *Song of Solomon* was the first book by a black author since Richard Wright's 1940 novel *Native Son* to be a Book of the Month Club main selection.

Tar Baby (1981), Morrison's fourth novel, focuses on the conflict between blacks who pursue modern material success and those who embrace traditional African-American village values. The clash is personified by two characters: a black woman enjoying the benefits of money and fame, and a black man longing to return to the past. These two characters come together but eventually part because, symbolically, they cannot resolve their differences.

Morrison's next project was a trilogy about different kinds of love and black life in various periods of American history: *Beloved* (1987), *Jazz* (1992), and *Paradise* (1997). *Beloved*, her fifth novel, explores mother love and is based on a true nineteenth-century story she read while editing *The Black Book*. When Sethe, a runaway slave, is caught, she kills her daughter, Beloved, rather than allow her to be returned to slavery. Sethe eventually accepts her guilt, seeks forgiveness, and, with her family and community, tries to live a better life because of her experience. Into this story Morrison also weaves an examination of the American obsession with ownership, including slavery.

Jazz, her sixth novel, deals with black American city life of the 1920s and 1930s. Like *Beloved*, it was sparked by a historical event—a photograph by the great African-American photographer James Van Zee. It is a picture of a dead young woman who was shot by her lover at a party but who, before she died, refused to name her attacker. The story revolves around a love triangle, but much of the interest in the book centers on the way the story is told, with the narrator slipping in and out of the text like a clicking camera.

Morrison's seventh novel, *Paradise*, set in 1976 Oklahoma, interweaves love in multiple forms, from the destructive love of a woman's relationship with her spouse and children to the spiritual love among a group of women. A young mother, Mavis, distraught at being abused by her husband, leaves her infant twins in a car with the windows up on a hot day, and the babies die. She joins a group of other lost women in a former convent, where they practice a blend of Christian and African rituals. Men in the nearby all-black town of Ruby, suspecting the women of unnatural behavior, take guns to the convent and begin to shoot.

"The book coalesced around the idea of where paradise is, who belongs in it," Morrison has said. "All paradises are described as male enclaves, while the interloper is a woman, defenseless and threatening. When we get ourselves together and get powerful is when we are assaulted."[3] *Paradise* is Morrison's most overtly feminist novel.

Like the two earlier books in her love trilogy, *Paradise* was based on what Morrison originally believed to be a true story. She had heard that a group of men had murdered a convent of black nuns in Brazil. However, she later learned that the event never took place.

"The last word in the book, 'paradise,' should have a small 'p,' not a capital P," Morrison explained after the book was published with a capital P on the final word. "The whole point is to get paradise off its pedestal, as a place for anyone, to open it up for passengers and crew. I want all the readers to put a lowercase mark on that 'p.'"[4]

Playing in the Dark: Whiteness and the Literary Imagination (1992) is a collection of her Massey Lectures in American Civilization, which she delivered at Harvard University in 1990. In those lectures she presented her thesis that Europeans developed an ideology of whiteness in the United States so that they could unite in their opposition to blacks. She demonstrated that thesis by analyzing the works of such authors as Willa Cather, Ernest Hemingway, Herman Melville, and Mark Twain.

"Her work," according to *The Norton Anthology of African American Literature*, "always engages major contemporary social issues: the interrelatedness of racism, class exploitation and sexism, domination, and imperialism; the spirituality and power of oral folk traditions and values; the mythic scope of the imagination; and the negotiation of slipping boundaries, especially for members of oppressed groups, between personal desire and political urgencies. Her work also articulates perennial human concerns and paradoxes: how are our concepts of the good, the beautiful, and the powerful related; what is goodness and evil; how does our sense of identity derive from community while maintaining individual uniqueness?"[5]

Morrison herself has said that if her work "isn't about the village or the community or about you, then it is not about anything. I am not interested in indulging myself in some private, closed exercise of my imagination that fulfills only the obligation of my personal dreams—which is to say yes, the work must be political."[6]

Awards and Honors

Morrison has received many honorary degrees, has served as cochair of the Schomburg Commission for the Preservation of Black Culture, and has been a member of the National Council of the Arts. She won the National Book Critics Circle Award and the American Academy and Institute of Arts and Letters Award (both 1977) for *Song of Solomon*, the New York State Governor's Arts Award (1986), and the Washington College Literary Award (1987), of which she was the first recipient. *Beloved* earned her several honors, including the Pulitzer Prize (1988) and the Elizabeth Cady Stanton Award from the National Organization for Women.

In 1993 Toni Morrison won the highest honor for a writer, the Nobel Prize for literature, becoming only the eighth woman and the first African-American to receive the award. In 1996 the National Book Foundation presented her with a medal for her distinguished contribution to American letters.

Selected writings:

FICTION

(novels unless otherwise indicated)

The Bluest Eye (1970)
Sula (1973)
Song of Solomon (1977)
Tar Baby (1981)
Dreaming Emmett (play, 1986)
Beloved (1987)
Honey and Rue (lyrics for operatic piece, 1992)
Jazz (1992)
Paradise (1997)

NONFICTION

Playing in the Dark: Whiteness and the Literary Imagination (lectures, 1992)

Lucy Moten

HEAD OF MINER NORMAL SCHOOL

(1851—1933)

As PRINCIPAL of Miner Normal School in Washington, D.C., Lucy Moten became one of the most influential black educators in the United States. Her system produced teachers who were highly sought after by state superintendents throughout the nation.

Lucy Ellen (also recorded as Ella) Moten was born in Fauquier County, Virginia, in 1851. Her parents, Benjamin and Julia (Withers) Moten, were free blacks who moved to Washington, D.C., so that Lucy could receive a good education. She studied for a time in tuition schools for free blacks and then attended black public schools when they opened in 1862. For her secondary education she studied for two years in Howard University's normal and preparatory departments.

Teacher and Principal

Lucy Moten's first teaching job was at Washington's O Street School, a public grammar school where she taught primary classes from 1870 to 1873. She then sought more training for herself, studying at the State Normal School in Salem, Massachusetts, from which she graduated in 1875. Later she resumed teaching and also attended Spencerian Business College, graduating in 1883.

The great abolitionist and social reformer Frederick Douglass recommended Moten for the position of principal at Miner Normal School, a Washington, D.C., training school for black American elementary teachers. At first the Miner School board, of which Douglass was a member, balked because of her attractive appearance, which caused some board mem-

bers to fear that her character was not strong enough. When Douglass asked her if she would give up dancing, card playing, theater, and certain other recreations, she agreed. The board then appointed her to the position.

Miner Normal School

As principal at Miner Normal School (now part of the University of the District of Columbia), Moten stressed three major factors: health, training, and character. She wanted to ensure the good health of her students, and she wanted to establish a hygiene course in the school's curriculum. Having a strong sense of personal responsibility for both issues, she decided to study medicine at Howard University Medical School, where she received her M.D. degree in 1897. She then gave lectures at Miner on health and hygiene before bringing in another physician to conduct classes on those topics, and beginning in 1903 she brought in a doctor to give her students regular checkups.

Moten believed in providing her students—future teachers themselves—with the fullest possible education. She extended the school's program to two years, added a student teaching plan, and started a special one-year training course for college graduates who wanted to become teachers in Washington's elementary schools. Practicing what she preached, Moten further enriched her own training by taking graduate courses in education at New York University and by spending several summers in Europe.

The third issue of concern to Moten at Miner was moral character. "The teacher must be first class in every particular," she said, "a professionally trained person whose personality will impress itself on... pupils always for their best good. The aesthetic must be looked after as well as the moral and the physical."[1]

Moten's success with her three-pronged approach to education at Miner Normal School earned her a national reputation. The *Colored American* praised her: "It is conceded by those best posted on educational affairs that the explanation of the art of teaching by Miss Moten is equal to any of either race in this country."[2]

In 1920 Moten retired from Miner and moved to New York City about four years later. After being struck by a taxicab in Times Square, she died from her injuries on August 24, 1933.

In her will she left the bulk of her estate of more than $51,000 to her alma mater, Howard University, "for the education by travel of students of said university regardless of sex, color, or creed."[3] In 1954 a Washington elementary school was named in honor of Lucy Ellen Moten, whose innovations at Miner Normal School influenced and upgraded black education in America.

Constance Baker Motley

FIRST AFRICAN-AMERICAN WOMAN FEDERAL JUDGE

(1921–   )

AFTER WINNING many historically important civil rights victories as a lawyer for the National Association for the Advancement of Colored People (NAACP), Constance Baker Motley became the first black woman elected to the New York State Senate and the first to hold the office of New York City borough president. In 1966 she became the first African-American woman appointed to a federal judgeship.

Constance Baker was born in New Haven, Connecticut, on September 14, 1921, one of nine children of Willoughby Alva Baker and Rachel (Huggins) Baker, who had both migrated to the United States from the Caribbean island of Nevis.

Constance attended elementary and high schools in New Haven. She was also active in two organizations established to promote civil rights: the New Haven Youth Council, on which she served as president, and the New Haven Adult Community Council, of which she became secretary.

After graduating from high school in 1939 Constance attended Fisk University in Nashville, Tennessee, from 1941 to 1942. She then transferred to New York University, from which she graduated in 1943 with a major in economics. In 1946 she received her law degree from Columbia University Law School in New York City.

During that same year, 1946, she married Joel Wilson Motley, a real estate and insurance broker. They had one son, also named Joel, later a graduate of Harvard Law School.

NAACP Lawyer

During her senior year at Columbia, Motley became a law clerk for Thurgood Marshall, then the chief counsel of the NAACP Legal Defense and Education Fund and later an associate justice of the United States Supreme Court. Motley herself became an associate counsel for the NAACP, and from the late 1940s to the early 1960s she appeared before state and federal courts in eleven southern states and the District of Columbia in cases involving public school desegregation, public housing, and other civil rights issues.

She helped to write the briefs filed in the United States Supreme Court for the famous *Brown* v. *Board of Education* (1954) school desegregation case. The Supreme Court declared school segregation unconstitutional in this case and went on, in other cases, to strike down segregation in other areas of American life. "The Brown decision," Motley later wrote, "was the catalyst which changed our society from a closed society to an open society and created the momentum for other minority groups to establish public interest law firms to rescue their rights."[1]

Motley argued ten civil rights cases before the Supreme Court, winning nine. One of her best-known cases was *Meredith* v. *Fair*, in which, largely through her efforts, James Meredith gained entrance to the University of Mississippi in 1962.

State Senator and Borough President

To further the cause of civil rights, Motley entered politics. In February 1964 she was elected a member of the New York State Senate, the first black woman to hold that office.

Her stay in the Senate was brief however, because in February 1965 she was elected to fill a one-year vacancy as president of the borough of Manhattan, the first woman and only the third black to hold the presidency of any New York City borough. In November 1965 she was elected to a full four-year term, but again something more important came along to cut short her stay in office.

Federal Judge

In 1966 President Lyndon B. Johnson appointed Motley to the United States District Court for the southern district of the state of New York, including Manhattan, the Bronx, and several counties north of New York City. She was the first African-American woman named to a federal judgeship. In 1982 she became chief judge of her court, and in 1986 she took senior status.

As a federal judge in New York City, Motley has made many legal decisions of national importance. In 1991, for example, she ruled that it is illegal for a company to make photocopies of articles and book excerpts and to assemble them into anthologies for sale to college and university students. The ruling resulted from a case involving eight publishing companies against Kinko's Graphics Corporation, a company based in Ventura, California.

In 1996 Motley signed a judicial order barring Amtrak police from ejecting vagrants from Pennsylvania Station in New York City without evidence that the vagrants had committed a crime. She did, however, allow the arrest or ejection of people on the floor of the station or loitering in areas reserved for travelers holding tickets.

Motley has added to her stature by publishing many articles in legal and professional journals, including the *Brooklyn Law Review*, the *Harvard Blackletter Journal*, *Law and Inequality: A Journal of Theory and Practice*, and the *North Dakota Law Review*. She has received honorary degrees from some of the nation's most prestigious institutions, such as Brown University, Princeton University, Spelman College, and Yale University. Her awards include the Elizabeth Blackwell Award of Hobart and William

CONSTANCE BAKER MOTLEY

The Schomburg Center / NYPL

Smith Colleges (1965), the Columbia Law School Medal for Excellence (1987), and the New York State Bar Association Gold Medal Award (1988).

"The most pressing need among blacks," she has said, "is the need for greater political power.... More and more blacks will become involved in policy making agencies, in government, in politics, in business and diplomacy—in areas where blacks have not been before and where decisions and changes are going to be made."[2] As the first African-American woman New York State senator, New York City borough president, and federal judge, Constance Baker Motley has done more than her share of entering those decision-making realms where her people "have not been before."

Jessye Norman

SINGER WHO COMBINES SCHOLARSHIP AND ARTISTRY

(1945–   )

JESSYE NORMAN, a soprano opera star who can easily sing mezzo-soprano and even true contralto parts, commands an unusually wide repertory of songs, from seventeenth-century art pieces to spirituals to modern popular music. She also performs, with complete understanding, in at least eight languages. "This combination of scholarship and artistry contributed to her consistently successful career as one of the most versatile concert and operatic singers of her time."[1]

Jessye Norman was born in Augusta, Georgia, on September 15, 1945, one of five children of Silas and Janie (King) Norman. Her father was an insurance salesman, and her mother was a secretary for the Democratic party and an auditor for a local church. Both parents were musical, her father being a singer in the church choir and her mother an amateur pianist.

Jessye Norman, like her siblings, took piano lessons from an early age, and though she did begin to study voice seriously till her college years, her family always encouraged her to sing. As a young girl she fell in love with concert music and opera, the latter especially through the Metropolitan Opera's radio broadcasts. Her musical heroines were the great black singers Marian Anderson* and Leontyne Price*. With her high school choral director giving her special voice lessons, Norman sang arias for Girl Scout and PTA meetings and performed in local choirs.

After graduating from high school she enrolled at Howard University in Washington, D.C., where she studied voice under Carolyn Grant. After receiving a bachelor of music degree from Howard in 1967, Norman continued her voice studies with Alice Duschak at the Peabody Conservatory of Music in Baltimore, Maryland, and with Pierre Bernac and Elizabeth Mannion at the University of Michigan at Ann Arbor, where she earned her master's degree in 1968.

During her college years she made important progress toward her singing career. In 1965, for example, she won first prize in a vocal competition sponsored by the National Society of Arts and Letters, and in 1968 she was selected to participate in a State Department tour of South America. That year she also received a scholarship from the Institute of International Education to compete in the International Music Competition in Munich, Germany. As a result of winning first prize in that competition, she landed a contract with the Deutsche Oper in West Berlin, Germany.

Operatic Performer

Norman made her opera debut in the role of Elisabeth in Wagner's *Tannhäuser* at the Deutsche Oper in December 1969. As she continued to perform there over the next few years, she also made her opera debut in other major European cities. In Florence, for example, she debuted in 1971 as Sélika in Meyerbeer's *L'africaine* (The african maid). In 1972 she made her first appearances at La Scala in Milan, singing the title role in Verdi's *Aida*, and at Covent Garden in London, as Cassandra in Berlioz's *Les troyens* (The trojans).

Norman's first major appearance in the United States was a concert performance of *Aida* at the Hollywood Bowl in 1972. In 1982 she made her American stage debut as Jocasta in Stravinsky's *Oedipus rex*

JESSYE NORMAN

of the world have accompanied her, including those in Berlin, Boston, Chicago, Los Angeles, London, New York City, and Vienna.

Norman has become especially popular in France, where she is held in such great esteem there that she was invited to Paris to sing the French national anthem, "La marseillaise," at the July 14, 1989, bicentennial celebration of the French Revolution.

Just two months later, on September 20, 1989, she was the featured soloist under the baton of Zubin Mehta at the opening concert of the 148th season of the New York Philharmonic Orchestra, which was telecast live from Lincoln Center.

Norman has, in fact, made appearances in numerous television programs, among them *Kathleen Battle and Jessye Norman Sing Spirituals* (1991) and a concert telecast at Avery Fisher Hall in New York City (1994). She has also often been called on to sing at special occasions. For example, on May 23, 1994, she movingly performed two hymns at the funeral of former First Lady Jacqueline Kennedy Onassis.

Norman's vast repertory includes music from the seventeenth century (Purcell), the eighteenth century (Handel, Mozart), the nineteenth century (Schubert, Wagner), the twentieth century (Schoenberg, Messiaen), and American popular music (George Gershwin, Richard Rodgers). She is equally adept at handling a range of styles, from the light French fare of Satie to the heavy Russian sounds of Mussorgsky, from the rich romanticism of Brahms to the spare modernity of Stravinsky, and from the religious fervor of spirituals to the sophistication of Cole Porter. Her trademark is the gospel song "He's Got the Whole World in His Hands."

(King Oedipus) and Dido in Purcell's *Dido and Aeneas* in a double bill with the Opera Company of Philadelphia.

On September 26, 1983, Norman followed in the footsteps on Marian Anderson and Leontyne Price when she made her Metropolitan Opera debut as Cassandra in *Les troyens*. Her later roles with the company have included Ariadne in Richard Strauss's *Ariadne auf Naxos* (Ariadne on Naxos), Dido in *Les troyens*, Elisabeth in *Tannhäuser*, and Madame Lidoine in Poulenc's *Dialogues des carmélites* (Dialogues of the carmelites).

Concert and Recital Artist

Since the early 1970s Norman has sung in concerts, recitals, and festivals all over the world, including Canada, England, the Far East, France, Germany, Holland, Israel, Italy, Mexico, South America, Spain, and the United States. Most of the major orchestras

Recordings, Awards, and Honors

Many of Norman's dozens of recordings, which cover much of her opera, concert, and recital repertory, have won Grammys or Grammy equivalents, notably *Ravel: Songs of Maurice Ravel* (1984).

Norman's other distinctions include being named the Outstanding Musician of the Year by *Musical America* magazine (1982) and receiving honorary doctorates from many universities. In December 1997 she was awarded the Kennedy Center Honor for her lifetime achievement in the performing arts.

Dramatic Voice

Though Norman's commanding stage presence has made her a major operatic personality, "her special distinction lies in her ability to project drama through her voice as well as histrionically—a signal asset for concert and recital work."[2] In operas, concerts, and recitals, Norman's "opulent and dark-hued soprano... reveals uncommon refinement of nuance and dynamic variety."[3]

Her voice, usually described as a dramatic soprano, actually spans the soprano, mezzo-soprano, and contralto ranges. "When I began singing," she said in 1989, "I had three separate voices. My work over my professional life has been to connect them. I feel that I've made some progress in that respect, and it's now more comfortable to use all parts of my voice."[4]

Norman has an exceptional talent for languages and she sings in English, French, German, Hebrew, Italian, Latin, Russian, and Spanish. Unlike many other singers, she does not merely memorize sounds but actually understands every word she sings. "I love watching the faces of the people who are listening as I sing these songs and know that they understand," she has said of her performances of French songs in France. "I think that's what every performer wants:

to communicate, to be understood in many ways and on many levels."[5]

Through her scholarly preparations and her artistic presentations, Jessye Norman has become one of the great musical communicators.

Selected recordings:

ALBUMS

Wagner: Tristan und Isolde (1975, Philips)
Berg: Der Wein (1980, Columbia)
Berlioz: La Mort de Cleopatre (1982, Deutsche Grammophon)
Ravel: Songs of Maurice Ravel (1984, CBS)
Mahler: Symphony no. 2 in C Minor ("Resurrection") (1984, CBS)
Brahms: A German Requiem (1985, Angel)
Richard Strauss: Lieder (1987, Philips)
Handel/Schubert/Schumann: Lieder (Jessye Norman—Live at Hohenems) (1988, Philips)
Bizet: Carmen (1989, Philips)
Jessye Norman and James Levine: Salzburg Recital (1992, Philips)
Berg: Songs (1995, Sony)

Rosa Parks

THE SPARK THAT LIT THE MODERN CIVIL RIGHTS MOVEMENT

(1913–   )

ON DECEMBER 1, 1955, Rosa Parks was arrested for refusing to give up her seat to a white man on a Montgomery, Alabama, bus. Her arrest for violating Montgomery's segregation laws precipitated a mass boycott of the city's buses. The successful boycott brought its leader, Martin Luther King, Jr., to national prominence and paved the way for innumerable future protests and demonstrations against racial injustice. Rosa Parks, then, played a crucial role in sparking the modern civil rights movement.

She was born Rosa Louise McCauley in Tuskegee, Alabama, on February 4, 1913, the elder of two children of James and Leona (Edwards) McCauley. Her father was a carpenter, and her mother was a teacher. At the age of two she moved to her grandparents' farm in Pine Level, Alabama, with her mother and her younger brother.

After several years of schooling in Pine Level and nearby Spring Hill, Rosa, moved to Montgomery at the age of eleven and was enrolled in the Montgomery Industrial School for Girls, a private school whose philosophy of self-worth had a lasting effect on her. She completed the fifth through eighth grades at the Industrial School, the ninth grade at Booker T. Washington Junior High School, and the tenth and eleventh grades at the laboratory high school division of the state teacher-training college in Montgomery (now Alabama State University). After her junior year she dropped out of school to take care of her ill grandmother.

In 1932 Rosa married Raymond Parks, a barber who was active in black voter registration and other civil rights causes. At about that time she went back to Alabama State, earning her high school diploma in 1933.

During the following decade Rosa Parks held a variety of jobs, for example, at Saint Margaret's Hospital and at Maxwell Field, a local army base. Usually she supplemented those jobs by taking in sewing.

Early Work for Civil Rights

In 1943 and 1944 Rosa Parks tried to register to vote but was denied both times. To push forward the quest for black voting rights, she joined the Montgomery Voters League. In 1943 she was elected secretary of the Montgomery branch of the National Association for the Advancement of Colored People (NAACP), and in 1945 she became an adviser for the NAACP Youth Council. In the summer of 1955 she met Martin Luther King, Jr., the young pastor of Dexter Avenue Baptist Church in Montgomery, who was in the early stages of his interest in civil rights activism.

During the 1940s and 1950s Rosa Parks earned a living mainly by sewing, and by December 1955 she was employed as a seamstress at the Montgomery Fair department store. To get to and from work, she depended on the Montgomery City Lines buses.

The Montgomery Bus Boycott

The Montgomery buses, like other buses throughout the South at that time, were segregated, the first ten seats of every bus being reserved for white passengers. If the white section was filled to capacity when more white patrons boarded the bus, passengers in the black section were required to give up their seats to the whites.

ROSA PARKS

The Schomburg Center / NYPL

push us around?' He answered, 'I don't know, but the law is the law and you're under arrest.'"[1]

Rosa Parks was taken to jail, booked, fingerprinted, and locked up. One of the three civil rights activists went to the jail to bail her out with a one-hundred-dollar bond was E. D. Nixon, who together with other leaders was looking for a case like hers to challenge segregation laws in the courts. Nixon asked Parks if she would be willing to use her own case for that purpose. She replied, "If you think it will mean something to Montgomery and do some good, I'll be happy to go along with it."[2]

On December 5 Rosa Parks, represented by Fred Gray, one of Montgomery's two black lawyers, was tried, convicted, and fined fourteen dollars—ten dollars for her infraction and four dollars for court costs. Her attorney immediately started the appeal process.

The city's black organizations, headed by the Women's Political Council (WPC), began a boycott of Montgomery's buses on that very day. That night a large group of black ministers and citizens met at a local church and resolved to continue the boycott till the bus company provided fair service to blacks. The meeting led to the formation of the Montgomery Improvement Association (MIA), which elected Martin Luther King, Jr., as its president.

In the following weeks the MIA and the WPC repeatedly met with city and bus company representatives to no avail. Many boycotters, including Rosa Parks, lost their jobs. Blacks were harassed and attacked. On January 30, 1956, King's house was bombed while he was away. Still the boycott continued.

"In February 1956, after the appeal of Parks's conviction was dismissed on a technicality, lawyers filed suit in U.S. district court on behalf of five women, including Parks, who had been mistreated on the buses. The suit claimed that bus segregation was un-

On December 1, 1955, Rosa Parks and three other black passengers were asked to vacate an entire row of seats-the first row behind the white section—so that one white man could sit down. The three other blacks stood up, but Rosa Parks refused. The bus driver was James F. Blake, who coincidentally had evicted her from his bus in 1943 for boarding through the front door instead of the back. "'I'm going to have you arrested,' the driver said," Parks later recalled. "'You may do that,' I answered. Two white policemen came. I asked one of them, 'Why do you all

constitutional."[3] On June 5 a three-judge panel of a United States district court in Alabama voted two to one in favor of the plaintiffs. The city of Montgomery appealed the case, called *Browder* v. *Gayle*, to the United States Supreme Court, which on November 13 upheld the lower court's decision. On December 20, 1956, therefore, United States marshals served an order on city officials compelling them to desegregate the bus system, and the next day blacks, after a 382-day boycott, began riding on integrated buses.

Because of her role in the boycott and the desegregation of the buses, Rosa Parks and her family were continually threatened by Montgomery whites. Her husband suffered a nervous breakdown and became unable to work.

Working for Congressman Conyers

In August 1957 Rosa and Raymond Parks, both without employment and without local prospects, moved from Montgomery to Detroit, Michigan. Their first few years in Detroit were difficult. She took in sewing, and he worked as caretaker of a building.

Meanwhile, Rosa Parks continued her civil rights activities. She raised funds at rallies for the NAACP around the country, and she worked with Martin Luther King, Jr., and his Southern Christian Leadership Conference (SCLC) for nonviolent social change. In 1963 she participated with King in the March on Washington, D.C., and spoke at the SCLC's national convention.

In 1965 she joined the Detroit staff of Democratic United States Congressman John Conyers, Jr., and worked for him in various clerical capacities for over twenty years.

During those years she remained active with the NAACP, the SCLC, and other groups. She frequently gave speeches at churches, conventions, and official celebrations of the anniversaries of such events as the Montgomery civil rights actions and the birthday of Martin Luther King, Jr.

In 1987 she founded the Rosa and Raymond Parks Institute for Self-Development, which offers career and leadership guidance to black youth. Her husband had died ten years earlier, but she wanted to memorialize his name with hers in this project.

Retirement Years

Rosa Parks retired from her job with Congressman Conyers in September 1988 at the age of seventy-five. She attended ceremonies at the White House marking the twenty-fifth anniversary of the Civil Rights Act on June 30, 1989, was present at the dedication of the civil rights memorial in Montgomery, in November 1989, and was honored on her seventy-seventh birthday in 1990 at the Kennedy Center in Washington, D.C. A bust of her was unveiled at the Smithsonian Institution in Washington, D.C., in February 1991. Parks was honored in Montgomery on December 1, 1995, the fortieth anniversary of her refusal to give up her bus seat. In June 1997 she announced plans to set up one of the first charter schools in Detroit, the Raymond and Rosa Parks Academy for Self-Development.

Since 1963 the SCLC has annually sponsored the Rosa Parks Freedom Award, and beginning in 1979 the Virginia-based organized Women in Community Service has issued its own annual Rosa Parks Award. Parks herself has received the NAACP's Spingarn Award (1979), *Ebony* magazine's Service Award (1980), the Martin Luther King, Jr., Award (1980), the Martin Luther King, Jr., Nonviolent Peace Prize (1980), and the Martin Luther King, Jr., Leadership Award (1987). In September 1996 she was presented the Presidential Medal of Freedom, the nation's highest civilian honor.

"I had no idea when I refused to give up my seat on that Montgomery bus that my small action would help put an end to the segregation laws in the South," Rosa Parks wrote. "I only knew that I was tired of being pushed around."[4]

Leontyne Price

FIRST INTERNATIONALLY RENOWNED BLACK DIVA

(1927–   )

LEONTYNE PRICE was the first African-American soprano to achieve international diva status, an accomplishment that also opened doors for other aspiring black women in the field of opera.

She was born Mary Violet Leontine (later Leontyne) Price, in Laurel, Mississippi, on February 10, 1927, the elder of two children of James Anthony Price and Katherine ("Kate") (Baker) Price. Her father worked in a lumber company, and her mother served as a midwife. Both parents displayed musical talent in their Methodist church, James as a tuba player in the band and Kate as a singer in the choir. At the age of three Leontyne began to take piano lessons, and soon she added singing to her studies.

Inspiration from Marian Anderson

Her mother believed in Leontyne's talent and encouraged the child in every way possible. When Leontyne was nine, Kate took her to hear the great African-American contralto Marian Anderson* at a concert in Jackson, Mississippi. Anderson's performance "was just a vision of elegance and nobility," Leontyne Price later recalled. "It was one of the most enthralling, marvelous experiences I've ever had. I can't tell you how inspired I was to do something even similar to what she was doing. That was what you might call the original kickoff."[1]

Motivated by Anderson and aided by her parents, Price made rapid musical progress. By the age of eleven she was playing piano at church services, as well as playing and singing at weddings, funerals, and private gatherings. In high school she sang first soprano in the choral group and played the piano at school

concerts, and on December 17, 1943, she played and sang at her first formal public recital.

After graduating from high school in 1944 Price enrolled at the College of Education and Industrial Arts in Wilberforce, Ohio (also known as Wilberforce College, now divided into Wilberforce and Central State universities), where she studied voice with Catherine Van Buren, graduating with a B.A. degree in 1948. She then accepted a scholarship to the prestigious Juilliard School of Music in New York City, where she received advanced vocal training from Florence Page Kimball, a former concert singer.

Operatic Performer

While a student at Juilliard, Price saw live opera performances for the first time in her life, attending productions at the City Center and at the Metropolitan Opera. Tremendously excited, she determined to become an opera singer, and as a sophomore she joined Juilliard's Opera Workshop under the direction of Frederic Cohen. When the composer-critic Virgil Thompson heard her perform the role of Mistress Ford in an Opera Workshop performance of Verdi's *Falstaff*, he invited her to sing in a revival of his opera *Four Saints in Three Acts*. Her portrayal of Saint Cecilia in that work at the Broadway Theater in New York City in the spring of 1952 marked her professional debut as an opera singer. Leaving Juilliard, she then traveled to Paris to repeat the performance.

Later in 1952 she began an extended American and, under State Department auspices, European tour as Bess in a revival of George Gershwin's opera *Porgy and Bess*. Her highly praised portrayal of Bess gave

LEONTYNE PRICE

sionate artistry. She often returned to the San Francisco Opera for various roles up to 1971.

Price selected Aida as the role for several of her important European debuts: the Verona Arena (1958), the Vienna State Opera (1958), London's Covent Garden (1958), and Milan's famed La Scala (1960). Throughout the 1960s she remained exceptionally active as a performer of various roles with many opera companies, adding Chicago, Berlin, Paris, Salzburg, and other cities to her schedule.

On January 27, 1961, Price fulfilled a long-cherished dream by making her debut at New York City's Metropolitan Opera, singing Leonora in Verdi's *Il trovatore* (The troubadour) and receiving an unprecedented forty-two-minute ovation. She went on to be a resident member of the Metropolitan Opera company for the next twenty-four years, giving 164 performances in sixteen roles. In 1966 she was selected to open the new Metropolitan Opera House at Lincoln Center, playing Cleopatra in the world premiere of Samuel Barber's *Antony and Cleopatra.* At her PBS-televised farewell performance on January 3, 1985, she re-created her favorite role, Verdi's Aida. Her other roles included Leonora in Verdi's *La forza del destino* (The force of destiny), Doña Anna in Mozart's *Don Giovanni*, Doña Elvira in Verdi's *Ernani*, Amelia in Verdi's *Un ballo in maschera* (A masked ball), Cio-Cio-San in Puccini's *Madama Butterfly*, Tatiana in Tchaikovsky's *Eugene Onegin*, the title role in Puccini's *Tosca*, Pamina in Mozart's *Die Zauberflöte* (The magic flute), and Ariadne in Richard Strauss's *Ariadne auf Naxos* (Ariadne on Naxos).

Recitals, Concerts, and Recordings

While pursuing her career in opera, Price also won recognition for her recitals, concerts, and recordings. Her "first love," she said, was recitals. The "challenge of bringing to life nineteen or twenty characters in one recital is greater than only one over several hours."[2] In the early 1950s, while busily engaged in performing Bess, she found time to give recitals at, among

her an important foothold in the world of international opera.

However, the performance that truly revealed the enormous range of her operatic capability was her sensational singing of the title role in Puccini's *Tosca* on NBC television in early 1955. The first black to appear in opera on television, she won the admiration of millions of viewers and earned leading roles in subsequent NBC television opera productions up to 1964.

In September 1957 Price made her stage debut with a major American opera company when she appeared as Madame Lidoine in the American premiere of Poulenc's *Dialogues des carmélites* (Dialogues of the carmelites) with the San Francisco Opera. The following month, with the same company, she performed, for the first time, the title role in Verdi's *Aida*, which proved to be especially congenial to her pas-

other places, the Museum of Modern Art and the Metropolitan Museum of Art in New York City and Constitution Hall and the Library of Congress in Washington, D.C. In those early recitals she showed herself to be an outstanding interpreter of works by Samuel Barber, Igor Stravinsky, and other modern composers. On November 14, 1954, she gave her first Town Hall, New York City, recital. She gave further recitals during her opera-performing years, increasingly from the late 1970s till her retirement from opera in 1985, after which she pursued her recital career with even more vigor.

Price was also active in concerts with major symphony orchestras in the United States, Canada, Australia, India, Europe, and elsewhere. In December 1954, for example, she sang at the first performance of Barber's *Prayers of Kierkegaard* with the Boston Symphony Orchestra. From 1955 to 1960 she often appeared at the Hollywood Bowl in Los Angeles. In March 1971 she won praise for her interpretation of Richard Strauss's *Four Last Songs* with the Minnesota Orchestra at Carnegie Hall in New York City. After retiring from opera she continued her concert career along with her recitals, appearing with great success in the major music centers worldwide.

Since 1958 Price has recorded almost exclusively with RCA Victor. Her recordings include complete opera roles, aria collections, art songs, hymns, Christmas carols, popular songs, and black spirituals. She has won over a dozen Grammy Awards. Among her most highly prized recordings are the Grammy-winning *A Program of Song* (1960), *Prima Donna* (1966), *Leontyne Price Sings Robert Schumann* (1971), *Verdi: Arias* (1982), and *Leontyne Price and Marilyn Horne in Concert at the Met* (1983). In 1996 RCA issued the monumental eleven-CD set *The Essential Leontyne Price*, covering her opera and solo career from 1959 to 1991.

Awards and Honors

Price has received many awards and honors, including the Musician of the Year Award from *Musical America* magazine (1961), the Presidential Medal of Freedom (1964), the Spingarn Medal from the National Association for the Advancement of Colored People (1965), the National Medal of Arts (1985), and the Grammy Lifetime Achievement Award (1989). In 1998 she was one of a select inaugural

LEONTYNE PRICE

group of inductees into the American Classical Music Hall of Fame.

In 1952 Price married the bass-baritone William Warfield, Porgy to her Bess in her performances of *Porgy and Bess* in the early 1950s. They separated in 1959 and divorced in 1973.

Price's voice has the same rich color throughout her wide vocal range. "To the sensuously husky tone of Price's spinto soprano," wrote one critic, "a fast vibrato imparted a distinctive shimmer, and its registers and colors were well equalized and controlled. In the roles (notably Verdi) that most strongly engaged her sympathies, she was uniquely compelling in her intensity and directness of expression."[3]

Leontyne Price has long understood her important role as a pathbreaker in opera. "I feel that if God sees fit to make this possible, in the various turmoils and misunderstandings that exist," she said when she opened the new Met in 1966, "that being given this opportunity as one of my people may be the beginning of a certain dimension, that anyone who wants to aspire to be so completely free artistically as I have been, to be chosen to have what is so important to others on one's artistic merit alone, is truly an American act, and it makes me proud to be an American."[4]

Selected recordings:

SINGLES

"God Bless America" (1982, RCA)

ALBUMS

A Program of Song (1960, RCA)

Operatic Arias (1961, RCA)

Great Scenes from Gershwin's Porgy and Bess (1963, RCA)

Berlioz: Nuits d'été, / *Falla: El amor brujo* (1964, RCA)

Strauss: Salome (Dance of the Seven Veils, Interlude, Final Scene) / *Strauss: The Egyptian Helen* (Awakening Scene) (1965, RCA)

Prima Donna (1966, RCA)

Prima Donna, Volume 2 (1967, RCA)

Barber: Two Scenes from "Antony and Cleopatra" / *Barber: Summer of 1915* (1969, RCA)

Prima Donna, Volume 3 (1970, RCA)

Leontyne Price Sings Robert Schumann (1971, RCA)

Five Great Operatic Scenes (1972, RCA)

Puccini: Heroines (1973, RCA)

Leontyne Price Sings Richard Strauss (1974, RCA)

Verdi and Puccini Duets (with Placido Domingo, 1975, RCA)

Lieder by Schubert and Richard Strauss (1979, Angel)

Prima Donna, Volume 5 (1980, RCA)

Verdi: Arias (1982, RCA)

Noel! Noel! (1983, London)

Leontyne Price and Marilyn Horne in Concert at the Met (1983, RCA)

The Essential Leontyne Price (eleven-CD set, 1996, RCA)

Elreta Alexander Ralston

JUDICIAL REFORMER

(1919–)

A FTER EARNING a reputation as a respected criminal lawyer, Elreta Alexander Ralston became one of the first black women elected to the judiciary in the United States. She brought about many judicial reforms during her tenure as a judge.

Born Elreta Narcissus Melton in Smithfield, North Carolina, on March 21, 1919, she was the youngest of three children of Joseph C. Melton, a teacher and Baptist minister, and Alain A. (Reynolds) Melton. Elreta graduated from James B. Dudley High School in Greensboro, North Carolina, in 1934, received a B.A. degree from North Carolina Agricultural and Technical College (now University) in Greensboro in 1937, taught history and mathematics and directed music in South Carolina and North Carolina for several years, and in 1945 became the first black woman graduate from Columbia University School of Law.

In 1938 she married Girardeau Alexander, a surgeon. They had one son, also named Girardeau. After her husband's death in 1979, she married John D. Ralston, a retired judge.

Lawyer in Greensboro

Following her graduation from law school, Elreta Alexander worked as a law clerk in the firm of Dyer and Stevens in New York City from 1945 to 1947. Then from 1947 to 1968 she practiced law in Greensboro, becoming the first black female attorney active in North Carolina.

Alexander had a dramatic impact as a criminal lawyer. She became the first black woman to try a case in the state supreme court; she represented a group that brought suit against the Greensboro City Council in a rezoning issue that eventually resulted in the granting of a federal housing project to blacks; and she served as attorney for the incorporation of the first city-owned golf course for blacks in Greensboro. Alexander represented both blacks and whites in state and federal courts, including "a number of Ku Klux Klan men, who, after their trials, left the Klan because of her fair and effective representation of them."[1]

District Judge

In 1968 a new law required that most judges in North Carolina be elected. Alexander ran for one of the six district court judgeships in Guilford County. Without actively campaigning she won a seat on the bench, becoming one of the first African-American women to do so.

Alexander, previously a Democrat, switched parties and ran on the Republican ticket because she wanted to help build a viable opposition to the Democratic Party and thereby pressure the Democrats, who controlled state politics, into appointing qualified minorities to governmental positions, especially in the courts. Her plan worked, and soon the Democrats began to appoint black men as well as both white women and women of color to state executive and judicial positions.

Nevertheless, Alexander did not expect special treatment for blacks, and she certainly did not practice such treatment in her courtroom. "I don't practice ethnic law. . . ," she said in an interview in 1971. "I don't consider myself a black judge. I think of We, the People. I don't want Black Power or White Power.

. . . The duty of the judge is to interpret the law fairly, impersonally and accurately...to the end that the judge does not make law, but causes other people to abide by the law."[2]

Alexander effected many judicial reforms while she was in office. It was due to her efforts that judges and other officials stopped publicly addressing minority lawyers by their first name as a means of demeaning them. She established the practice of assigning probation officers to offenders regardless of either's color or gender. In 1969 she began a deferred-sentencing rehabilitation program called Judgment Day, a special day set aside for those in the program to report on their progress, which, if sufficient, enabled the offenders to avoid incarceration and a criminal record. Participants supported each other in a fashion similar to that used in Alcoholics Anonymous. Some people in North Carolina, including high state officers, attacked Judgment Day, but much of her program was later enacted into state law.

After being elected to four consecutive terms as a judge, Alexander Ralston retired from the bench in April 1981 to practice law in the integrated firm of Alexander Ralston, Pell, and Speckhard.

Awards and Honors

As busy as her career has been, Alexander Ralston has always found time for community involvement. She often speaks to youth, civic, religious, fraternal, governmental, educational, and senior citizens organizations. She has served on the board of advisers of the North Carolina Symphony, the Board of Disadvantaged Students at the University of North Carolina at Greensboro, the board of the Drug Action Council, and the board of visitors at Appalachian State University.

Alexander Ralston has earned many honors for her judicial and community work. In 1969 she received the Dolly Madison Award from the Greensboro Chamber of Commerce for her contribution to the empowerment of women. Guys and Dolls, Inc., a national family organization, named her the most admired black citizen of Greensboro in 1969 and 1970. Also in 1970 she received the Citizenship Award from the Cherokee Council of the Boy Scouts of America. She was awarded the Brotherhood Citation from the Greensboro Chapter of the National Conference of Christians and Jews in 1976. In 1977 the North Carolina Federation of Women's Clubs named her one of the twenty-five most distinguished women in the state. In 1980 she attended a reception at the White House for distinguished African-American women.

Elreta Alexander Ralston has firmly etched her name in history for her substantial achievements as a lawyer, a pioneer in opening doors for black women in the American judiciary, and a judge committed to judicial reform.

Charlotte E. Ray

FIRST BLACK WOMAN LAWYER IN AMERICA

(1850—1911)

CHARLOTTE E. RAY became the first black American woman, and only the third woman of any race, admitted to the practice of law in the United States. She earned a special reputation as an authority on corporation law.

Born in New York City on January 13, 1850, she was one of seven children of Charles Bennett Ray and Charlotte Augusta (Burroughs) Ray. Her father, who was of mixed African-American, Native American, and white ancestry, was a Congregational minister, abolitionist, and conductor of the Underground Railroad. Her mother came from Savannah, Georgia. After Charlotte completed her studies at the Institution for the Education of Colored Youth in Washington, D.C., in 1869, she became a teacher in the Normal and Preparatory Department at Howard University in the same city.

Brilliant Law Student

Ray decided to study law at Howard University. Knowing that schools at that time did not want to admit women to the study of law, she gained admission to Howard's law school by submitting her application under the name C. E. Ray.

After she was accepted and began her course of study in 1869, she soon impressed others at the school with her diligence and capability. James C. Napier, a classmate and later a registrar of the United States Treasury, remembered her as "an apt scholar."[1] General O. O. Howard, the founder and first president of Howard University, praised her as "a colored woman who read us a thesis on corporations, not copied from the books but from her brain, a clear incisive analysis of one of the most delicate legal questions."[2] Specializing in commercial law, Ray wrote a paper entitled "Chancery," which established her as one of the ablest young experts on corporation law in the country.

Soon after receiving her law degree from Howard University in February 1872, Ray was admitted to the practice of law in the District of Columbia.

Attorney Thwarted by Prejudice

Because of her academic accomplishments, Ray expected to have a future in law. Most observers felt the same way. A May 1872 article in *Woman's Journal* reflected that feeling: "In the city of Washington, where a few years ago colored women were bought and sold under sanction of law, a woman of African descent has been admitted to practice at the bar of the Supreme Court of the District of Columbia. Miss Charlotte E. Ray, who has the honor of being the first lady lawyer in Washington, is a graduate of the Law College of Howard University, and is said to be a dusky mulatto, possessing quite an intelligent countenance. She doubtless has a fine mind and deserves success."[3]

However, corporate leaders in Washington, D.C., simply could not accept the idea of doing business with a black woman lawyer. Despite her recognized stature as an authority on corporation law, she could not attract enough clients to maintain her law practice, so in 1879 she closed her office and returned to her native New York City.

The loss of her legal expertise was lamented for some years to come. Monroe A. Majors, in *Noted Negro Women* (1893), wrote that Ray's "special endowments make her one of the best lawyers on corporations in this country: her eloquence is commendable for her sex in the court-room, and her advice is authoritative."[4] In an 1897 interview the Wisconsin lawyer Kate Kane Rossi said that Ray, "although a lawyer of decided ability, on account of prejudice was not able to obtain sufficient legal business and had to give up... active practice."[5]

After returning to New York City, Ray taught in the Brooklyn public school system. She also attended the annual convention of the National Women's Suffrage Association, became an active member of the National Association of Colored Women, and married a man with the surname Fraim, about whom little is known.

By 1897 Ray was living in Woodside, Long Island, where she died on January 4, 1911.

Today the Greater Washington Area Chapter (GWAC), Women Lawyers Division of the National Bar Association recognizes Ray's contributions. The GWAC, a group of black women lawyers in the District of Columbia, presents an annual award named in her honor.

"In becoming a lawyer Charlotte Ray justified the dreams of many abolitionists, woman suffragists, and free black Americans...," Dorothy Thomas wrote in *Black Women in America*. "She remains an unsung pioneer."[6]

Sarah Parker Remond

ANTISLAVERY LECTURER

(1826—1894)

ALMOST ENTIRELY SELF-EDUCATED, Sarah Parker Remond became one of the most articulate, compelling public speakers of her time. Before the Civil War she movingly called for the abolition of slavery, during the war she asked Great Britain to support the Union cause, and after the war she made fund-raising speeches on behalf of the newly freed slaves.

Sarah Parker Remond was born in Salem, Massachusetts, on June 6, 1826, one of eight children of John and Nancy (Lenox) Remond. She had little formal schooling but educated herself by reading books, pamphlets, and newspapers she borrowed from friends or purchased at a low cost from the Anti-Slavery Society.

Her family and their friends included many abolitionists, and Sarah personally witnessed some of the effects of slavery when she observed incidents involving the Underground Railroad. She also attended antislavery lectures in Massachusetts, and Charles Lenox Remond, her older brother, became a well-known abolitionist lecturer.

Fighting Prejudice in America

Because her family heritage taught her that blacks had a right to liberty and justice, Sarah Remond did not take it kindly when, in May 1853, she was not permitted to take her seat at an opera performance at the Howard Athenaeum in Boston despite the fact that she had a ticket. Refusing to sit in the segregated gallery, she was forcibly ejected and pushed down a flight of stairs, but she won a significant legal victory when she sued and was awarded five hundred dollars, in a ruling that upheld the principle of desegregated seating in the hall.

In 1856 the American Anti-Slavery Society hired a team of lecturers, including Remond, her brother Charles, and Susan B. Anthony, to tour New York state and address antislavery meetings. The famed abolitionist William Lloyd Garrison, describing Remond's onstage effect, wrote of her "calm, dignified manner, her winning personal appearance, and her earnest appeals to the conscience and the heart."[1]

Over the next two years she spoke to antislavery gatherings in New York, Massachusetts, Ohio, Michigan, and Pennsylvania. She and her brother often encountered hotels and boardinghouses that refused to provide them with accommodations, and in those cases white antislavery friends had to find rooms for the two black abolitionists in private homes.

During this time Remond was acutely aware of her lack of formal education, and she constantly tried to make up for it through personal study. "Although my heart was in the work, I felt that I was in need of a good English education," she wrote to a friend in 1858. "... And when I consider that the only reason why I did not obtain what I so much desired was because I was the possessor of an unpopular complexion, it adds to my discomfort."[2]

Lecturing in Great Britain

In late December 1858 Remond left Boston for an extensive lecture tour in Great Britain, where she hoped to obtain British support for the American antislavery movement. In January 1859 she arrived in Liverpool, and over the next two years she gave over forty-five lectures in eighteen cities and towns in England, four cities in Ireland, and three cities in Scotland. She often drew large audiences and considerable press coverage.

Remond spoke movingly about the mistreatment of slaves in the United States, including the sexual abuse of females by their owners. She brought tears to the eyes of many listeners. "I appeal on behalf of four millions of men, women, and children who are chattels in the Southern States of America," she said during a lecture in 1859. "Not because they are identical with my race and color, though I am proud of that identity, but because they are men and women. The sum of sixteen hundred millions of dollars is invested in their bones, sinews, and flesh—is this not sufficient reason why all the friends of humanity should not endeavor with all their might and power, to overturn the vile systems of slavery."[3]

While giving those lectures, Remond still found time to attend classes at Bedford College for Ladies in London (later a part of the University of London) from October 1859 to mid-1861. She studied French, Latin, English literature, music, history, and elocution.

During the Civil War she remained in Great Britain and worked to influence British public opinion to support the Union blockade of the Confederacy's ports. After the war, as a member of the London Emancipation Society and the Freedmen's Aid Association in London, she solicited funds for the relief of ex-slaves.

Last Years in Italy

While living in England, Remond visited the Italian cities of Rome and Florence several times. In 1866 she moved to Italy, entered the Santa Maria Nuova Hospital in Florence as a medical student, and in 1871 she received a diploma that allowed her to provide professional medical services. She then practiced medicine in Florence for over twenty years.

Little is known of her later years, but during that time, in 1877, she married Lazzaro Pintor, a native of Sardinia. Sarah Parker Remond, one of the most effective of all antislavery lecturers, died in Italy on December 13, 1894, and was buried in Rome.

Rubye Doris Smith Robinson

LEADER OF SNCC

(1942—1967)

ACCORDING TO JAMES FORMAN, with whom she worked in the Student Non-Violent Coordinating Committee (SNCC), Rubye Doris Smith Robinson was "one of the few genuine revolutionaries in the black liberation movement."[1] Bernice Johnson Reagon, in *Notable American Women* (1980), wrote that in Robinson's short life she became "the key figure in managing the unwieldy and unpredictable existence of SNCC, the most radical of the civil rights organizations in the 1960s."[2]

Born Rubye Doris Smith in Atlanta, Georgia, on April 25, 1942, she was the second of seven children of John Thomas Smith and Alice (Banks) Smith. Her father was a self-employed mover and later a minister. Her mother was a beautician.

An exceptionally bright youngster, Rubye started kindergarten at the age of three and first grade at four. Throughout her school years she was ahead of her age group. At sixteen she finished high school and enrolled at Spelman College in Atlanta.

Joining the Civil Rights Movement

By the time she entered college Rubye was already determined to be politically active. Her commitment began when, at the age of thirteen, she watched on television as blacks in Montgomery, Alabama, protested segregation by boycotting the bus system. She was moved by the sight of old people walking instead of submitting to the practice of segregation on buses.

In early 1960, when she was a sophomore at Spelman, Rubye personally began to participate in the civil rights movement by joining a sit-in campaign against restaurants in Atlanta. In April she and other Atlanta students went to Raleigh, North Carolina, to help found SNCC.

Rubye's involvement with the civil rights struggle deepened when in February 1961 she went with a SNCC group to Rock Hill, South Carolina, where they joined a demonstration and were arrested. When she and the others spent their full sentence, thirty days, in jail, this marked the first time that sit-in protesters had opted for the jail-without-bail tactic.

That spring Rubye helped the Freedom Riders, protesters who were challenging the concept of legal segregation in interstate travel throughout the South. She joined a group of them in Alabama, where they boarded a bus for Jackson, Mississippi. In Jackson they were arrested for trying to use whites-only restrooms. Again, rather than pay a fine, Rubye chose to go to jail.

After her release she spent the summer on a voter registration project organized by SNCC in Mississippi. She also attended a training seminar for student activists at Fisk University in Nashville, Tennessee.

At about this time Rubye, along with SNCC as a whole, began to adopt a more tolerant attitude toward those blacks who physically struck back during demonstrations. Nonviolence, she and many at SNCC believed, was a useful tactic but not necessarily a way of life. This view separated her and SNCC from the completely nonviolent philosophy of Martin Luther King, Jr.

In the fall of 1961 Rubye returned to her studies at Spelman, where she eventually earned a bachelor's degree. However, her commitment to SNCC increased. She took part in demonstrations in Albany, Georgia, in December 1961; worked on SNCC projects in Cairo, Illinois, in the summer of 1962; and became a full-time staff member of SNCC, serving as administrative assistant to executive secretary James Forman, in the spring of 1963.

Guiding SNCC

For the next four years Rubye became SNCC's principal administrative force, answering the daily needs of the field staff, organizing student recruits, responding to emergencies, and supervising the Sojourner Motor Fleet (cars used in rural voter registration drives).

During the summer of 1964 Rubye led the recruitment of black volunteers to participate in the Mississippi Summer Project, a major voter registration drive. When she and nine other SNCC staff members visited Africa that fall, her experience there profoundly affected her, and on her return to the United States she strengthened her commitment to black nationalism. During that same period she joined other SNCC women in a sit-in at James Forman's office to demand that women be given more positions of responsibility in the organization. Other than Rubye herself, women were mostly assigned to clerical tasks.

In November 1964 she married Clifford Robinson, a veteran who became chief mechanic for the Sojourner Motor Fleet. They had a son, Kenneth.

Her new family life did not deflect Robinson from her work, however, and in the summer of 1966 she succeeded James Forman as executive secretary of SNCC. Led by her and chairman Stokely Carmichael, SNCC became more overtly committed to black nationalism, whose rallying cry was "black power."

Robinson was ambivalent about her goal, however, believing that its attainment might lead to "the extinction of the African type in America. . . because I want black people to have their own businesses and hold high political offices, but I know that when they do, they are going to become more and more a part of the American character. And the black soul is going to die in the middle of the white soul."[3]

Rubye Doris Smith Robinson remained active till a few months before her death from lymphoma in Atlanta on October 7, 1967, at the age of only twenty-five. Into her short years she packed a full lifetime of achievement as a civil rights reformer at SNCC. Perhaps her greatest legacy was as a role model. Southern blacks up to her time were taught to be submissive, but Robinson "just stood up to *anybody*," her coworker Stanley Wise remembered. "...As a result, she made you stand taller."[4]

Wilma Rudolph

OLYMPIC SPRINTER

(1940—1994)

WILMA RUDOLPH grew from a sickly child unable to walk into a champion sprinter who became the first American woman to win three gold medals in track and field in one Olympics.

Wilma Glodean Rudolph was born in the Saint Bethlehem section of Clarksville, Tennessee, on June 23, 1940, the twentieth of twenty-two children of Ed Rudolph, a railroad porter, from two marriages. Her mother, Blanche, worked as a domestic. Wilma weighed only 4½ pounds at birth, and by the age of four she had battled double pneumonia, scarlet fever, and polio, which left her left leg paralyzed.

Overcoming Paralysis

Once a week for the next two years Wilma's mother took her on a ninety-mile round trip to Nashville for special heat-and-water treatments. On the other days of the week her mother and other family members massaged the leg. Gradually Wilma began to show progress, aided by a leg brace and an orthopedic shoe, and by the age of eleven she was walking and running on her own.

At first her illness depressed her because she could not engage in the same physical activities that the other children enjoyed. Eventually, however, her depression turned to anger, which she channeled into a competitive spirit. She challenged herself to get better, and in later years that spirit enabled her to reach the top of the sports world.

Her father encouraged her to participate in organized athletics. "My father pushed me to become competitive," she later recalled. "With so many children, when you did something with one, you always had

another along. He felt that sports would help me overcome the problems."[1]

At Burt High School in Clarksville, Wilma Rudolph participated in both basketball and track. She became one of the best basketball players in the state, one year averaging over 32 points per game. Her exploits on the track were even more astonishing. She won the state sprint titles at 50, 75, and 100 yards. In the summer of 1956, after her junior year, she made the United States Olympic team. At the Olympic Games, held that year in Melbourne, Australia, she was eliminated from the 200 meters in the heats but won a bronze medal as a member of the women's 4 X 100-meter relay team.

After graduating from high school in 1957 she entered Tennessee State University (TSU) in Nashville, to which its famous track coach, Ed Temple, had personally recruited her. During her college years she added much-needed bulk to her previously gaunt six-foot frame. As she added weight she also added strength, endurance, and speed. Her unique running style was noted for its exceptional fluidity.

In 1959 Rudolph won the first of four consecutive Amateur Athletic Union (AAU) 100-meter titles. Then in early 1960 she became extremely ill after a tonsillectomy, but by the Olympic trials in July of that year she had recovered enough to set a new world record in the 200 meters—22.9 seconds. She made the United States Olympic team not only for the 200 meters but also for the 100 meters and the 4 X 100-meter relay.

Winning Olympic Gold

At the 1960 Olympics in Rome, Italy, Rudolph narrowly avoided disaster. The day before her semifinal in

easily in 24.0 seconds while running into a stiff wind.

As the anchor in the 4 X 100-meter relay, Rudolph helped the American women to set a world record of 44.4 seconds in their semifinal. In the final she received a bad baton pass and began her leg with a two-yard deficit, but she soon overcame the leading runner and shot ahead to a three-yard victory in 44.5 seconds, earning her third gold medal.

No other American woman in track and field had ever won three gold medals in a single Olympics. (An American woman had won three golds in swimming in 1920, and a Dutch woman had won four golds in track and field in 1956.)

Over the next two years Rudolph continued to show her championship form. At the February 1961 Millrose Games in New York City's Madison Square Garden, she tied her own world record of 6.9 seconds in the 60-yard dash. Two weeks later, at a New York Athletic Club meet, she broke the record again, running the distance in 6.8 seconds. Later that season, at Louisville, Kentucky, she ran one of her most memorable races, setting a world record of 7.8 seconds in the 70-yard dash and thus shattering the old record of 8.2 seconds, which had stood since 1935. In July 1961, at a meet in West Germany, she ran the 100 meters in 11.2 seconds—yet another world record. The following year she won her fourth straight AAU 100-meter title.

The Schomburg Center / NYPL

WILMA RUDOLPH WITH PRESIDENT JIMMY CARTER

the 100 meters she stepped into a hole in the practice area and twisted an ankle, which became swollen and discolored. The next day, however, she overcame the injury and won the semifinal in 11.3 seconds, equaling the world record. She went on to win the final in 11.0 seconds, but the following wind was too great for the record to be allowed as an official world record.

In the 200 meters Rudolph set an Olympic record of 23.2 seconds in her first heat. She won the final

Retiring on Top

In 1962 Rudolph retired from competitive running. "I couldn't top what I did," she later explained, "so I'll be remembered for when I was at my best."[2]

She had a practical reason for retiring—earning a living. At that time amateurs truly earned no money, and there was no professional track. However, she never regretted having competed in the era of pure amateurism. In later years she often appeared as a spokesperson for Olympic causes and looked back fondly at her experiences. "I love what the Olympics stand for," she said. "They'll always be a part of me."[3]

After graduating from TSU with a degree in education in 1963, Rudolph held a variety of jobs. She worked as a teacher and coach at several different grade levels in many cities, became involved with a job corps program, and assisted the Watts Community Action Committee in Los Angeles, California. The great legacy of her later years was the Wilma Rudolph Foundation, which she established to help youngsters attain an education.

During those years Rudolph's personal life did not go smoothly. Her 1961 marriage to William Ward ended in divorce the following year. Then in 1963 she married Robert Eldridge, whom she had known since second grade. They had four children—daughters Yolanda and Djuana and sons Robert and Xurry—before divorcing in 1976.

Rudolph's athletic career brought her many honors and awards, both before and after her retirement. She was named the United Press Athlete of the Year (1960); the Associated Press Woman Athlete of the Year (1960, 1961); the James E. Sullivan winner (1961) as America's outstanding amateur athlete, male or female; and the Babe Didrickson Zaharias Award

winner (1962). In her later years she was elected to the Black Sports Hall of Fame (1973), the National Track and Field Hall of Fame (1974), the International Women's Sports Hall of Fame (1980), the United States Olympic Hall of Fame (1983), and the Black Athletes Hall of Fame (1988). In 1984 the Women's Sports Foundation selected her as one of America's five greatest women athletes of all time. In 1990 she became the first woman to receive the Silver Anniversary Award of the National Collegiate Athletic Association (NCAA), even though she competed before the NCAA sponsored women's sports championships.

Her autobiography, *Wilma: The Story of Wilma Rudolph* was published in 1977, and that year her life story was also told in a television movie, *Wilma.*

In July 1994 she learned that she had a malignant brain tumor, from which she died on November 12, 1994, at her home in Brentwood, near Nashville, Tennessee.

Wilma Rudolph permanently changed track and field in the United States. It was largely because of her popularity that girls began to demand their own track programs in school across America. She also forced previously all-male meets, such as the Millrose Games, to add women's events to their programs. Her brief but spectacular career was highlighted, and epitomized, by her courageous efforts in overcoming illness and injury to star at the 1960 Olympic Games.

Josephine St. Pierre Ruffin
BLACK WOMEN'S CLUB LEADER

(1842—1924)

JOSEPHINE ST. PIERRE RUFFIN "was a leader in the club movement among black women and active in both the struggle for racial equality and the movement for women's rights."[1] Her greatest achievements were founding the Woman's Era Club in Boston, and inspiring the movement for a national organization of black women.

Josephine St. Pierre was born in Boston in 1842, the fifth daughter and youngest of six children of John St. Pierre and Elizabeth Matilda (Menhenick) St. Pierre. Her father, a clothes dealer of African, French, and Native American heritage, founded the Zion Church in Boston. Her mother came from Cornwall, England.

After attending public schools in Charleston and Salem, Josephine studied at a private school in New York to avoid the segregated schools in Boston. Returning to Boston in 1855 after schools there were desegregated, she finished her studies at Bowdoin School.

In 1858 she married George Lewis Ruffin, who studied law at Harvard, developed a thriving law practice, and in 1883 became Boston's first black municipal judge. They had five children: Hubert, a lawyer; Florida, a teacher and clubwoman; Stanley, an inventor and manufacturer; George, a musician; and Robert, who died in infancy.

Josephine St. Pierre Ruffin and her husband became involved in many community and national projects. During the Civil War they recruited black soldiers for the Union army, joined the Home Guard, and worked for the Sanitary Commission. After the war she organized the Kansas Relief Association, which collected money and clothing to help ex-slaves traveling from the South to Kansas, and following

her husband's death in 1886, she became even more active in clubs, charities, and associations. She also worked as an editor of a black weekly newspaper, the *Boston Courant*.

Woman's Era Club

In February 1893 Ruffin, with her daughter, Florida, and Maria Louise Baldwin,* principal of the Agassiz High School in Cambridge, founded the Woman's Era Club (also called the New Era Club), one of the earliest black women's clubs in America. It was a local club established mainly to promote the interests of blacks, though membership was also open to whites.

The club sponsored a variety of projects designed to encourage social reforms and racial uplift. For example, it awarded scholarships to deserving students, aided a hospital for black women through a sewing circle, and helped to support a black kindergarten in Georgia.

Ruffin and her daughter also founded the club's monthly illustrated magazine, *Woman's Era*, first published in March 1894. *Woman's Era*, which contained articles dealing with women's issues as well as political and economic matters, was the first significant periodical in the United States to be owned and operated by black women.

Ruffin's great gift was as a planner and organizer. In 1895 she issued the manifesto *A Call: Let Us Confer Together*, through which she proposed the first national conference of black women, held in Boston at the end of July 1895 under her leadership.

In her opening address to the conference, Ruffin

called for a national black women's organization: "These women's clubs, which have sprung up all over the country, built and run upon broad and strong lines, have all been a... general preparation for a large union such as it is hoped this conference will lead to."[2] Black women, she said, had "to teach an ignorant and suspicious world that our aims and interests are identical with those of all good aspiring women."[3]

National Association of Colored Women

This first national conference of black women led to the founding of the National Federation of Afro-American Women (NFAAW). With Ruffin's endorsement, Margaret Murray Washington, wife of the educator Booker T. Washington, was selected as president of the new national organization. Under her Ruffin's editorship, *Women's Era* became the official journal of the NFAAW.

At about the same time, however, another national organization of black women was formed, the National League of Colored Women (also called the Colored Women's League). In 1896 the two organizations merged into the National Association of Colored Women (NACW), with Mary Church Terrell as president and Ruffin as one of the seven vice presidents. *Woman's Era*, edited by Ruffin and her daughter till 1900, published news for the association.

After the NACW was formed, local clubs began to interconnect through a system of regional federation. In 1896 Ruffin organized the Northeastern Federation of Women's Clubs, the first such federation in the NACW, and was elected its vice president.

The Ruffin Incident

In May 1900 Ruffin decided to attend the biennial convention of the General Federation of Women's Clubs (GFWC), a predominantly white group that had just issued a certificate of membership for the Woman's Era Club to join the organization. However, when Ruffin arrived at the GFWC convention in Milwaukee, Wisconsin, the officers of the GFWC on learning that they had admitted a black club, retracted their offer of membership to the Woman's Era Club forthwith and refused to let Ruffin enter the convention as a representative of a black group.

Widely publicized throughout the country, the "Ruffin incident" sparked many favorable newspaper reports on Ruffin's stand for equal rights and many protests against the GFWC's racial policies. The episode had little impact on the GFWC, which kept its discriminatory practice for many years to come, but it had a tremendously positive effect on black women's clubs, which were inspired to work harder than ever to develop their own goals and organizations.

"I did not feel angry," Ruffin herself said of the incident. "It was an issue clearly set before the women of the country. It was an opportunity which I did not seek, but which I did not shirk."[4]

Much of Ruffin's organizational skill in forming black women's clubs resulted from her many years of association with well-established, predominantly white organizations. She did volunteer work for Associated Charities, served on the executive board of the Massachusetts Moral Education Association, helped a women's group called the Massachusetts School Suffrage, served on the executive board of the Massachusetts State Federation of Women's Clubs after her Woman's Era Club became affiliated with the federation, and became the first black member of the prestigious New England Woman's Club.

Besides the Woman's Era Club, Ruffin helped to establish other Boston civic organizations, both black and racially mixed. She was an organizer and vice president of the American Mount Coffee School Association, which raised money to assist a school in Mount Coffee, Liberia. She founded the Association for the Promotion of Child Training in the South. She helped to found, and later became chairperson of, the League of Women for Community Service, which opened homes where black women directed social service work. She was among the fifty-six charter members of the National Association for the Advancement of Colored People (NAACP), of which the Boston NAACP, organized in 1910, was first branch. In her later years she was elected to the board of management of the Sedalia Club of Boston.

Josephine St. Pierre Ruffin participated in public affairs virtually up to the end of her life, attending the annual meeting of the League of Women for Community Service only two weeks before she died at her home in Boston on March 13, 1924. She was one of the most profoundly influential forces in bringing national unity to the black women's club movement.

Edith S. Sampson

FIRST IN MANY FIELDS

(1901—1979)

EDITH S. SAMPSON'S CAREER was marked by a series of trailblazing achievements. She was the first woman to earn a law degree from Loyola University of Chicago, the first black person appointed a United States delegate to the United Nations, and the first black woman elected as a judge in Illinois.

Edith Spurlock was born in Pittsburgh, Pennsylvania, on October 13, 1901, one of eight children of Louis and Elizabeth (McGruder) Spurlock. Her father managed a cleaning and dying establishment, and her mother earned money by making buckram hat frames and switches of false hair.

After graduating from Peabody High School in Pittsburgh, she obtained a job with Associated Charities, which later helped her to gain admission to the New York School of Social Work. Completing her studies there, she moved to Chicago, to become a social worker at the Illinois Children's Home and Aid Society, while studying at John Marshall Law School during the evenings. Later she attended Loyola University of Chicago, and in 1927 she became the first woman to earn an LL.M. from that prestigious institution. She was admitted to the Illinois bar the same year.

Lawyer and Social Worker

For much of the next twenty years Edith successfully maintained dual careers in law and social work. While she was in law school, she performed social work for the Young Women's Christian Association and the Illinois Children's Home and Aid Society. In 1925 she became a probation officer, and later she served for eighteen years as a referee for the Juvenile Court of Cook County.

Meanwhile, she also practiced law, specializing in criminal law and domestic relations. In 1934 she became one of the earliest black women admitted to practice before the Supreme Court of the United States. Her office supplied legal help to thousands of poor black people who otherwise would have had no legal advice. "I talk from my heart," she said of her courtroom manner at the time, "and let the law take care of itself."[1] Her effective style won her many admirers, and in 1947 she was appointed assistant state's attorney of Cook County.

During her years as a lawyer and social worker she had a full personal life as well. Although her early marriage to Rufus Sampson, a field agent for Tuskegee Institute in Alabama, ended in divorce, in 1934 she married the attorney Joseph E. Clayton, who joined her in her practice in Chicago, and this marriage lasted until his death in 1957. However, Sampson continued to use her first husband's name in her public life. She had no children.

United Nations Delegate

In 1949 the National Council of Negro Women, whose executive committee Sampson chaired, selected her as its representative on a world tour undertaken by members of various types of American interest groups. The tour was part of the Cold War propaganda contest between the United States and the Soviet Union. "Wherever we went," she later reported, "we found that people had been misled into believing that fifteen million American Negroes lived behind barbed wire. They were amazed that I had a law degree, attended a white church, and had never been to a segregated school."[2] To an Indian heckler's comments about racial tensions in the United States, she admitted that life in her native country was not perfect, but claimed that she "would rather be a Negro in America than a citizen in any other land."[3]

When the trip was over the delegates organized the World Town Hall Seminar and elected Sampson its president. "My decision to make the Town Hall trip proved to be the turning point of my life," she later wrote. "After visiting and talking with the peoples of other countries, I knew that I could never make my law practice the primary business of my life; I would have to devote myself to... world brotherhood and world peace."[4]

Sampson therefore eagerly accepted President Truman's appointment as an alternate United States delegate (substituting for Eleanor Roosevelt) to the United Nations General Assembly in 1950. She was the first African-American, male or female, to be appointed a regular member of the United States delegation at the United Nations. Serving on the Social, Humanitarian, and Cultural Committee, she worked in many fields, including land reform, prisoner release, and human rights. "I was used to defending one man," she said; "now it's all people."[5]

In 1952 she was reappointed to her position, and the following year, early in President Eisenhower's administration, she served as member-at-large of the United States Commission for the United Nations Educational, Scientific, and Cultural Organization (UNESCO). During her years with the United Nations she also traveled abroad and spoke about the status of blacks in America.

After Sampson left the United Nations she continued to maintain a deep interest in international affairs. In 1961 and 1962 she served on the United States Citizens Commission on the North Atlantic Treaty Organization (NATO).

Judgeship in Illinois

In 1962 Sampson was elected associate justice of the Municipal Court of Chicago, becoming the first African-American woman elected to a judgeship in Illinois. Later she became judge of a branch of the Circuit Court of Cook County. Presiding over domestic relations, landlord-tenant disputes, and other matters, she developed a reputation as a superior mediator, known especially for her sincerity and her humanistic approach to making judgments.

Sampson retired from the bench in 1978 and died in Chicago the following year, on October 8, 1979.

As an African-American woman who attained many firsts for her people, Edith S. Sampson helped to weave black people more firmly into the fabric of American life. "When we Negroes achieve first class citizenship in America," she said, "we will not drape our mantles over our shoulders and return anywhere; we are already there."[6]

Betty Shabazz
SYMBOL OF PERSEVERANCE
(1936—1997)

AFTER WITNESSING the assassination of her husband, Malcolm X, struggling to support her six children while earning a Ph.D., and tirelessly preserving his memory and teachings, Betty Shabazz "became a symbol of perseverance to black America."[1] Before her own life, too, was abbreviated by a violent end, she rose to a prominence in her own right as a college official and a voice in the civil rights movement.

Born Betty Sanders in Detroit, Michigan, on May 28, 1936, she was adopted by an upper-middle-class Methodist family, who raised her and sent her to Tuskegee Institute in Alabama. Later she moved to New York City, to study nursing.

Life with Malcolm X

In 1956, while attending the Nation of Islam's Mosque No. 7 in Harlem, she met Malcolm X, the charismatic minister in charge. Two years later they married, and she became Mrs. Malcolm X Little (his original name being Malcolm Little). They had six daughters: Attallah, Qubilah, Ilyasah, Gamilah, and the twins Malikah and Malaak.

Through the early 1960s Malcolm X espoused the Nation of Islam's militant black nationalism and strongly antiwhite views. In 1964, however, he broke with the Nation of Islam and began to adopt a more moderate attitude toward black self-determination and possibly even cooperation with whites. He went on a pilgrimage to Mecca, became a Sunni Muslim, and changed his name to El-Hajj Malik El-Shabazz, which signified rebirth. His wife became Betty Shabazz or, in full, Hajj Bahiyah Betty Shabazz.

When he returned home and formed his own Muslim group, Malcolm X was vilified by the Nation of Islam, especially Louis Farrakhan, who succeeded him at Mosque No. 7. Farrakhan was quoted as saying that Malcolm X was "worthy of death."[2]

By early 1965 Betty Shabazz was worried. Her husband received death threats, and the family's house in Elmhurst, Queens, was firebombed.

On February 21, 1965, Betty Shabazz, pregnant with the twins, sat with her four daughters in the Audubon Ballroom in Washington Heights, New York City, as her husband began to deliver an address to an audience of four hundred people. Suddenly shots rang out. As she covered her children, she saw Malcom X slump to the floor. Three Black Muslim zealots were eventually convicted of the murder.

Betty Shabazz saw to it that her children learned about their father's key characteristic—self-discipline. "I taught them about him by myself being disciplined and strict," she said in a 1993 interview. "My children think my persona is me, when actually it is their father's."[3]

A Role of Her Own

After her husband's death Betty Shabazz struggled to earn a living and find a new identity while raising six children on her own. She received royalties from *The Autobiography of Malcolm X*, which was told to Alex Haley and published in 1965, and she earned fees for consulting at various institutions, including Malcolm X College in Chicago. In the long run, however, she knew she needed to upgrade her own education.

Shabazz therefore returned to Brooklyn State Hos-

Owensby & Co. Communications

BETTY SHABAZZ

such as school commencements; women's rights, civil rights, and black history conferences; and cultural tributes—plays, films, and so on—to Malcolm X. She addressed the issues of health and education for disadvantaged children, and she spoke of Malcolm X and the cause of black self-determination. "I'm private," said Shabazz, who never remarried, after Spike Lee's 1992 film *Malcolm X* brought her increased publicity. "But there were some public things I had to do, because of his commitment to the cause. I loved him, and he loved the people."[4]

A Fight for Life

The suspicion of a conspiracy beyond the three convicted assassins of Malcom X lingered in her mind for many years. In a 1994 television interview Shabazz clearly indicated her belief that Louis Farrakhan had been involved in the assassination, though Farrakhan denied it.

pital School of Nursing, where she earned certification as a registered nurse. Later she earned both a B.A. and an M.A. degree at Jersey City State College, and in 1975 she received her doctorate in education administration from the University of Massachusetts at Amherst.

From 1976 till her death Shabazz worked at Medgar Evers College in Brooklyn, a part of the City University, serving as assistant professor, director of communications and public relations, and director of institutional advancement, her principal duty being to raise funds for books and scholarships.

Shabazz also devoted much of her time to community affairs. She served as director of the African-American Foundation, director of the Day Care Council of Westchester County, a trustee of the National Housewives League, a PTA worker in a high school for pregnant students, a volunteer on the Sickle-Cell Telethon Advisory Board (her master's thesis was on sickle-cell anemia), and a member of the board of education of the Union Free School in New York City.

Shabazz was a frequent speaker at various events

In 1995 Qubilah Shabazz was charged in Minneapolis, Minnesota, with plotting to kill Farrakhan because she believed that he had not only played a role in her father's death but was also still a threat to her mother. After the arrest, Betty Shabazz took some of the heat off her daughter by announcing a reconciliation with Farrakhan.

To obtain her freedom, Qubilah agreed to a two-year probationary period during which she would undergo psychological and substance-abuse counseling in lieu of a trial. The agreement also required that Betty care for Qubilah's son, Malcolm Shabazz, and become the boy's legal guardian. He spent most of the next two years living with his grandmother.

In early 1997 Malcolm rejoined his mother in Texas, but after several months she sent him back to stay with his grandmother in Yonkers, New York. On May 1, 1997, a federal judge dismissed the indictment against Qubilah Shabazz because she had successfully completed her two-year probation. Malcolm, however, remained with his grandmother.

On June 1, 1997, Betty Shabazz suffered third-degree burns over 80 percent of her body during a fire at her Yonkers apartment. When police found twelve-year-old Malcolm Shabazz wandering in a daze near the apartment smelling of gasoline, they arrested him, and he later told police that he purposely set the fire, intending to kill his grandmother so that he could return to his mother.[5]

Over the next three weeks Betty Shabazz fought for her life with a courage that mirrored the strength she had shown in the years after her husband's death. She underwent five operations to replace burned tissue, defying medical experts by surviving day after day.

Finally, however, she succumbed at a Bronx, New York City, hospital on June 23, 1997. The following month her troubled grandson pleaded guilty to the juvenile equivalent of second-degree manslaughter and second-degree arson for the fire that killed her.

By rising to great heights of achievement after suffering the tragic early loss of her husband and by exemplifying a strength that passed understanding in her own final days, Betty Shabazz earned a special place in African-American history as a "symbol of perseverance."

Lucy Diggs Slowe

PIONEER BLACK DEAN OF WOMEN

(1885—1937)

———————————

AS THE FIRST BLACK woman dean at Howard University, Lucy Diggs Slowe raised the status of women deans in black institutions and "became the foremost spokesperson for black women's higher education and leadership training."[1] In the process she helped to win equality with whites and with black men for black women, both administrators and students, in the field of education.

Lucy Diggs Slowe was born in Berryville, Virginia, on July 4, 1885, the youngest of seven children of Henry and Fannie (Porter) Slowe. An orphan by the age of six, she was raised by a paternal aunt in Lexington, Virginia. At thirteen she moved with her family to Baltimore, Maryland, where she attended public schools and graduated from the Colored High School in 1904.

Later that year she enrolled at Howard University in nearby Washington, D.C., where in her senior year she became a founder and vice president of Alpha Kappa Alpha Sorority, the first Greek-letter organization for black women students.

After graduating from Howard University in 1908, Slowe returned to Baltimore's Colored High School as an English teacher. She earned an M.A. degree in English from Columbia University in New York in 1915 and then taught at a Washington, D.C., high school till 1919. In that year she was appointed principal of Shaw, a junior high school for blacks in the District of Columbia.

Dean of Women at Howard University

In 1922 Slowe was named dean of women at Howard University. At that time American education for white women emphasized well-rounded development of the student, that is, not only academic matters but also athletics, food service, health services, career guidance, and cultural activities. Slowe felt that black women students had not yet benefited from that movement and was determined that in her new position she would see that they did.

While expanding the education of her students, she also enlarged her own role as dean. Previously a dean of women at black institutions had served primarily as a chaperone who watched over the morals of women students. Slowe immediately changed that image at Howard University. In January 1923 she requested that J. Stanley Durkee, the white president of Howard, allow her to deal with all disciplinary matters concerning women students. This new authority not only elevated the status of the women's dean but also provided the women students with a role model of leadership.

Slowe diligently cultivated the qualities of independence and leadership in her students. She often spoke out against old rules of conduct imposed on women students, saying that the regulations were degrading and insulting. For example, "when a college woman cannot be trusted to go shopping without a chaperone she is not likely to develop powers of leadership."[2]

Slowe also criticized the traditional black church for its tendency to restrict the growth of women. "It is to be remembered, too, that much of the religious philosophy upon which Negro women have been nurtured has tended toward suppressing in them their own powers," she wrote. "Many of them have been brought up on the antiquated philosophy of Saint Paul in reference to woman's place in the scheme of things, and all too frequently have been influenced by the philosophy of patient waiting, rather than the philosophy of developing their talents to the fullest extent."[3]

Slowe took a personal hand in helping to broaden the horizons of her students. For example, she saw to their cultural needs by establishing a Cultural Series that exposed the young women to the highest forms of the fine arts. She encouraged the students' social skills by organizing teas at the women's dormitories and by giving an annual garden party at her home.

When Mordecai W. Johnson, a Baptist minister, became the first black president of Howard in September 1926, he and Slowe often clashed. One of the most serious confrontations occurred in January 1927, when she complained to the president about a male professor's use of vulgar language in a class of women students. When Johnson seemed to support the male professor, Slowe threatened to resign, and the issue was finally dealt with by the board of trustees, who put the professor on half-salary leave of absence. Because of this conflict, Slowe faced continued lack of cooperation from the president in the future, but she had upheld the dignity of her women students and had once again provided them with a role model of leadership.

Leader of National Women's Organizations

In 1933 Slowe became the first president of the National Association of College Women (NACW), an organization of black women college graduates. In her inaugural address she stated that the organization was formed to raise the standards of black women's higher education, to improve conditions and opportunities for black women faculty members, and to encourage advanced scholarship among women.

Slowe, through the NACW, influenced the presidents of black colleges to appoint women deans who were well trained and committed to establishing programs that would prepare young black women for leadership. In 1929 she organized the National Association of Deans of Women and Advisors to Girls in Negro Schools as part of the NACW. In 1935 the new group became an independent body.

Slowe was also active in many other women's and civic organizations. She was a member of the predominantly white National Association of Deans of Women, helped to found the National Council of Negro Women and became its first executive secretary, and served on the advisory board of the National Youth Administration. A strong advocate of the peace movement, she encouraged other black women to support this cause and became a member of the Women's International League for Peace and Freedom.

In addition to her professional activities, Slowe sang contralto in Saint Francis Catholic Church and in her own Madison Street Presbyterian Church in Baltimore, and she also won many prizes for her skill at tennis. During the last fifteen years of Slowe's life, her companion and housemate was the teacher and playwright Mary Burrill.

Lucy Diggs Slowe died in her Washington, D.C., home on October 21, 1937. At Howard University a stained glass window in the chapel and a dormitory are named in her memory. Slowe's transformation of the position of dean of women from that of a matron to a well-trained specialist in women's education inspired a similar change in black colleges nationwide.

Amanda Berry Smith

THE SINGING PILGRIM

(1837—1915)

INTERNATIONALLY ACCLAIMED as a leader of the Holiness revival in the late nineteenth century, Amanda Berry Smith was a Protestant evangelist, missionary, and advocate of children's welfare and women's rights. Because she often sang as she preached, newspapers and organizers of camp meetings called her "the singing pilgrim."[1]

She was born Amanda Berry in Long Green, near Baltimore, Maryland, on January 23, 1837, one of thirteen children of Samuel and Miriam (Matthews) Berry. Her parents were slaves till Samuel was allowed to purchase his and his family's freedom. The Berrys moved north to a farm in York County, Pennsylvania, where their home became a station on the Underground Railroad.

Growing up in this environment, Amanda dreamed of getting an education and helping the freedom movement. She received little formal education, but she learned to read from her parents and taught herself at every opportunity. Because of the great number of children in the family, the Berrys faced financial hardship and Amanda soon had to go to work as a domestic.

In 1854, at the age of seventeen, she married Calvin Devine of Columbia, Pennsylvania, but the marriage proved to be unhappy. They had two children, only one of whom, Mazie, survived.

Spiritual Conversion

While working as a domestic servant, Amanda was encouraged by some of her female employers to attend camp meetings and tent revivals. Empty from her marriage, she gladly absorbed the religious fervor at these events and underwent a Christian conversion in Columbia in 1856.

Her spiritual rebirth gave her strength when she separated from her husband, who was later killed while serving with the Union forces in the Civil War. She then married James Henry Smith, an ordained deacon at Bethel Church in Philadelphia, the founding congregation of the African Methodist Episcopal (AME) church. They had three children, none of whom survived.

While attending Sunday services at the Fleet Street AME Church in Brooklyn, New York, in November 1870, Amanda Berry Smith experienced the pivotal moment of her life. As the preacher spoke, she saw over his head a star, which seemed to change into the shape of a large white tulip. "And then I leaned back and closed my eyes," she wrote in her autobiography. "Just then I saw a large letter G, and I said, 'Lord, do you want me to read in Genesis or in Galatians? Lord, what does this mean?' Just then I saw the letter O. I said, 'Why, that means Go.' And I said, 'What else?' And a voice distinctly said to me, 'Go preach.'"[2]

Smith enthusiastically heeded the call to the Christian ministry. At about that time her second husband died, so she began to devote herself completely to evangelistic work. She gave her first sermon in Salem, New Jersey, and soon displayed an extraordinary aptitude for communicating with her listeners, enhancing her spiritual message through the power of her beautiful singing voice.

Because of her second husband's affliation with the AME church, Smith became associated with the same group. Some of the male pastors in the church strongly opposed her work because they were against allowing women in the pulpit. She persisted, however, and soon won the support and admiration of many in her church and in other denominations.

Missionary Abroad

In 1872 Smith learned that the AME church was sending missionaries to Africa. Believing that she was intellectually unqualified for such work, she began to prepare her daughter, Mazie, for the undertaking, but when Mazie eventually decided to marry and remain in the United States instead, Smith resolved to undertake the missionary work herself after all.

She began in 1876 by going to England, where her reputation spread quickly. For the next three years she toured European countries, especially France and Italy.

In October 1879 a friend persuaded Smith to go to India, where her missionary work was a great success even though other evangelists there struggled. Her religious fervor drew large audiences. James M. Thoburn, Methodist Episcopal bishop of India, said that from Smith he learned more "of actual value to me as a preacher of Christian truth... than from any other one person I had ever met."[3]

During her ministry abroad, just as in the United States, Smith faced initial prejudice against her as a woman preacher and evangelist. But her sincere, compelling presence as a speaker and singer soon overcame any doubts about her suitability as a missionary.

After a brief return to America, she finally set out in 1881 for her great goal—Africa. When Smith was a child, her parents had instilled in her a concern for the spiritual and material welfare of that continent. Now she hoped to make a positive contribution to uplifting the people there, especially in such western areas as Liberia and Sierra Leone. She observed many practices in Africa that troubled her, particularly cruelties inflicted on native women, and she wanted not only to save souls but also to improve standards of conduct. According to Lois L. Dunn in *Notable Black American Women*, Smith "was convinced that the culture of America, tempered by the presence of Christian belief, was superior to the habits and requirements of the people to whom she ministered. Part of the conversion that she strove to bring about was con-cerned with the transfer of these cultural values to their own daily lives."[4]

Among the missionaries with whom Smith worked in Africa was William Taylor, Methodist Episcopal bishop of Africa. He admired her achievements and openly stated his belief that she had done more for the missionary cause than all of her predecessors combined.

Smith adopted two native children, a boy and a girl, and in 1890 took them to Great Britain with the intention of educating then so that they could return to Africa and carry on her missionary work. The girl became ill in England and soon went back to Africa, but the boy studied in England as planned and did later return to his homeland as a missionary.

Home for Orphans

After ensuring the well-being of her adopted children—the girl in Africa and the boy in England—Smith returned to the United States, which she had left fourteen years earlier. After preaching along the eastern seaboard, she moved to Chicago, and in 1893 published *An Autobiography: The Story of the Lord's Dealings with Amanda Smith, the Colored Evangelist.*

Anxious now to create something of permanent use to her people, Smith decided to establish a home for orphans. She purchased a twelve-room house in Harvey, Illinois, with funds from her savings, her book, her newspaper (*The Helper*), her singing and preaching in churches, and several large donors. In 1899 she opened the Amanda Smith Industrial Home, the state's only Protestant-run home offering care to black children. It helped many children before being destroyed by fire in 1918.

Smith spent her final years in quiet comfort at a cottage in Sebring, Florida given to her as a retirement home by George Sebring, a wealthy real estate dealer who admired her work. She died in Sebring on February 24, 1915.

A pioneer woman evangelist-missionary and a children's advocate on four continents—North America, Europe, Asia, and Africa—Amanda Berry Smith, "the singing pilgrim," earned yet another respectful epithet: "God's image carved in ebony."[5]

Bessie Smith

EMPRESS OF THE BLUES

(1894—1937)

WIDELY REGARDED as the greatest of blues singers, Bessie Smith earned the title of Empress of the Blues during her own lifetime. She was also unsurpassed in her ability to apply the emotional intensity of blues singing to the broader context of jazz interpretations of popular songs. Her vocal art profoundly influenced most of the blues-jazz singers who followed her.

Bessie Smith was born into a large, poverty-stricken family in Chattanooga, Tennessee, on April 15, 1894. Her father, William Smith, died soon after her birth, and her mother, Laura Smith, died before Bessie was nine. Bessie's eldest sister, Viola, raised her after their mother's death.

Learning from Ma Rainey

By the age of nine Bessie Smith was already earning money by singing for coins in the streets of Chattanooga. As a teenager she worked in the black vaudeville circuit and began to appear in a wide variety of other entertainment media, including cabarets, dance halls, and traveling carnivals and minstrel shows.

One of the traveling shows featured Gertrude ("Ma") Rainey, the first of the great blues singers, who taught Smith the art of country blues singing.

By about 1920 Smith was producing her own shows on the road, in which she danced and acted in comic and dramatic sketches as well as singing.

Saving Columbia

On one of her barnstorming trips Smith met the pianist-composer Clarence Williams, a representative of the Columbia Phonograph Company. He took her to New York City, to make recordings. In February 1923 she cut her first sides for Columbia, including "Downhearted Blues," a duet with Williams, a recording that established her as the most successful black performing artist of her time.

Smith continued to record regularly throughout the rest of the 1920s with such important early jazz instrumentalists as Louis Armstrong ("St. Louis Blues," 1925), James P. Johnson ("Back Water Blues," 1927), and Joe Smith ("Baby Doll," 1926). Some of her records sold 100,000 copies within a week, and the sales reportedly saved Columbia from bankruptcy.

Smith purchased a house in Philadelphia, where she gathered her siblings to live with her. In June 1923 she married John ("Jack") Gee, a Philadelphia nightwatchman who became her manager. (Earl Love, her first husband, died shortly after their marriage.) Smith loved children, and in 1926 she and her husband adopted a boy and named him Jack Gee, Jr. The marriage was stormy, however, and they separated in 1929. In 1930 she developed a permanent relationship with Richard Morgan, a former bootlegger, who became her new manager.

Touring with Her Own Tent Show

While enjoying enormous success as a recording artist, vaudeville star, and theater performer in the 1920s, Smith also continued to tour with her own tent show, traveling in a custom-built railroad car. She played to large, mostly black audiences in major northern and southern cities. Sometimes she performed for southern white audiences, who also thronged to hear her.

The Schomburg Center / NYPL

BESSIE SMITH

try declined, the popularity of her raw-nerve kind of blues also waned, and Columbia dropped her in 1931. She made her last recordings, featuring such great jazzmen as Jack Teagarden and Benny Goodman, in 1933 for Okeh, which sold largely to the European market. One of those recordings was the classic "Gimme a Pigfoot."

During the mid-1930s Smith returned to her roots in modest road shows and nightclubs, and by 1937 she was attracting the attention of white audiences and hoped to begin recording again soon.

Before that hope could be fulfilled, though, Smith was killed in an automobile accident in northern Mississippi. Some jazz fans circulated a legendary account of the incident, claiming that her life could have been saved if a white hospital had not refused to treat her. The truth, however, is that a Memphis physician happened to arrive on the scene of the accident near the village of Coahoma, gave Smith emergency treatment, and called an ambulance, which took her directly to a black hospital in nearby Clarksdale, where she died of her injuries on September 26, 1937.[1]

Singing from Her Soul

Bessie Smith was arguably the most talented and influential blues singer of all time. She had a rich, powerful contralto voice, disdaining, in live performances, to use a microphone. Among the later singers who drew inspiration from her wide-ranging expressiveness were Billie Holiday* and Mahalia Jackson*.

Smith was one of the principal developers of the blues-singing technique known as the growl, a rough tone achieved by subtly manipulating the throat, mouth cavity, and lips. Her use of the technique can be heard on her recordings of "Mean Old Bed Bug Blues" / "A Good Man I Hard to Find" (1927) and "Empty Bed Blues" (1928).

She also infused a blues feeling into her jazz interpretations of popular songs. Recordings showing this side of her artistry include "Baby Doll" (1926), "After You've Gone" (1927), and "Nobody Knows You When You're Down and Out" (1929).

In her stage shows Smith enhanced her natural beauty with colorful costumes. She had a dynamic personality and displayed it by acting in little musical sketches—sometimes, for example, simulating a recording session. Her acting ability had a brief outlet in her role in the short film St. Louis Blues (1929), widely banned at the time for its earthy realism and later preserved at the Museum of Modern Art in New York City.

Smith's blues singing appealed specially to blacks, North and South. Her cathartic performances focused not only on the universal topics of love, joy, and grief but also on subjects with which her audiences could intimately identify—poverty, oppression, and the stoic acceptance of defeat in the cruel world.

In the 1930s Smith, like many other artists, was hurt by the Great Depression. The recording indus-

Smith wrote the music and lyrics for many of the songs she performed. "Back Water Blues" (1927), for example, reflects her feelings after she witnessed a flood that destroyed black homes. Her recording of this song is possibly her finest performance on disc. "Poor Man's Blues" (1928), which she also wrote and recorded, dwells on the differences between society's haves and have-nots. Her songs consistently tell the stories of real people with whom her audiences could identify. Among the other songs that she wrote and recorded were "Jailhouse Blues" (with Clarence Williams, 1923), "My Man Blues" (1925), "Baby Doll" (1926), and "Dirty No-Gooder's Blues" (1929).

Through her success, her realistic songs, and her assertive, emancipated lifestyle, Smith showed her people that they, too, could triumph over the obstacles facing blacks in a white-dominated society. "More than any other woman of her time," wrote one critic, "she came to symbolize African-Americans' resurgent militancy and racial pride."[2]

The great jazz trumpeter Louis Armstrong summed up Bessie Smith's greatness. "She used to thrill me at all times," he said, "the way she could phrase a note with a certain something in her voice no other blues singer could get. She had music in her soul and felt everything she did."[3]

Selected recordings:

SINGLES

"Downhearted Blues" / "Gulf Coast Blues" (1923, Columbia)

'Tain't Nobody's Biz-ness If I Do" (1923, Columbia)

"Mama's Got the Blues" (1923, Columbia)

"Jailhouse Blues" (1923, Columbia)

"The St. Louis Blues" (1925, Columbia)

"Reckless Blues" (1925, Columbia)

"You've Been a Good Old Wagon" (1925, Columbia)

"Cake Walkin' Babies from Home" (1925, Columbia)

"J. C. Holmes Blues" (1925, Columbia)

"My Man Blues" (1925, Columbia)

"Baby Doll" (1926, Columbia)

"Hard Time Blues" / "Young Woman's Blues" (1926, Columbia)

"Back Water Blues" (1927, Columbia)

"After You've Gone" (1927, Columbia)

"Alexander's Ragtime Band" (1927, Columbia)

"Mean Old Bed Bug Blues" / "A Good Man Is Hard to Find" (1927, Columbia)

"Pickpocket Blues" (1928, Columbia)

"Standin' in the Rain Blues" (1928, Columbia)

"Empty Bed Blues" (1928, Columbia)

"Poor Man's Blues" (1928, Columbia)

"Nobody Knows You When You're Down and Out" (1929, Columbia)

"It Makes My Love Come Down" (1929, Columbia)

"Wasted Life Blues" / "Dirty No-Gooder's Blues" (1929, Columbia)

"See If I'll Care" (1930, Columbia)

"Blue Blues" (1931, Columbia)

"Shipwreck Blues" (1931, Columbia)

"Safety Mama" (1931, Columbia)

"Gimme a Pigfoot" / "Take Me for a Buggy Ride" (1933, Okeh)

Maria W. Stewart

AMERICA'S FIRST BLACK WOMAN POLITICAL WRITER

(1803—1879)

WHEN MARIA W. STEWART's early works, including her famous public lectures, were published in the early 1830s, she became the first African-American woman to write on political issues. As such, she provided an influential foundation for future black female activism and literary tradition.

She was born Frances Maria Miller in Hartford, Connecticut, in 1803. Virtually nothing is known about her parents except that they were surnamed Miller and were free. When Maria was five years old, she was left an orphan, and for the next ten years she lived with a clergyman's family. There she learned to read, and between the ages of fifteen and twenty she continued her education at Sabbath schools and worked as a domestic servant.

Maria then moved to Boston, where in 1826 she married James W. Stewart, a successful independent shipping agent twenty-one years her senior who outfitted whaling and fishing vessels. At her husband's suggestion Maria added his middle initial to her name. After three years of happy marriage he died in 1829. They had no children. The executors of his estate, a group of white businessmen, cheated Maria W. Stewart out of her inheritance.

Pursuing Politics Inspired by Religion

In 1830, emotionally sensitized by the recent deaths of her husband and David Walker, a black activist whom she had greatly admired, Stewart experienced a born-again religious conversion. Religion now began to take a central place in her daily life. Her religious beliefs were personal, not bound by the doctrines of any one church, though at various times she maintained affiliations with Baptist, Methodist, and Episcopal congregations.

Religious convictions not only gave her spiritual freedom but also inspired a quest for political freedom. "From the moment I experienced the change," she wrote, "I felt a strong desire... to devote the remainder of my days to piety and virtue and now possess that spirit of independence that, were I called upon, I would willingly sacrifice my life for the cause of God and my brethren. All the nations of the earth are crying out for liberty and equality. Away, away with tyranny and oppression!"[1]

Stewart laid out her ideas in *Religion and the Pure Principles of Morality, the Sure Foundation on Which We Must Build*, published as a twelve-page pamphlet in 1831 by William Lloyd Garrison and Isaac Knapp, founders of the Boston weekly abolitionist paper the *Liberator*. In this militant essay she exhorted African-Americans to demand their human rights and warned whites that blacks were impatient for liberty.

Lecturing on Politics

Stewart took her quest for freedom directly to the people. Between the spring of 1832 and September 1833 she gave four historic lectures. Her first address was to the Afric-American Female Intelligence Society of America. In September 1832 she presented her second speech, at Boston's Franklin Hall, where the New England Anti-Slavery Society held its meetings. This was the first time that an American-born woman had spoken publicly on political themes to an audience of both men and women. She was probably also the first African-American woman to lecture in favor of women's rights.[2] She delivered her third lecture in February 1833 and her fourth, entitled "Mrs. Stewart's Farewell Address to Her Friends in the City of Boston," in September 1833.

Stewart's abolitionist friend William Lloyd Garrison published her first three lectures in the *Liberator*, where she also placed an essay, "Cause for Encouragement," and a poem, "The Negro's Complaint." In 1835 Garrison published the book *Productions of Maria W. Stewart*, consisting of the texts of her four public speeches, biographical information about her, and some essays and poems, including *Religion and the Pure Principles of Morality*.

By the time of that publication, Stewart had already moved to New York City, which had a much larger African-American population than Boston. There she joined a black female literary society and continued her political activism by serving the North Star Association and attending the American Women's Anti-Slavery convention in 1837.

Long Career as Educator

It was in New York City in the 1830s that Stewart began her long career as an educator. She taught for a time in the public schools of Manhattan and then transferred to Brooklyn, where she taught at the Williamsburg School and served as assistant to the principal from 1847 to 1852. In 1853 she moved to Baltimore, Maryland, and taught individual students privately.

In the early 1860s Stewart permanently settled in Washington, D.C. She taught in the public school system; became head of housekeeping services at Freedmen's Hospital (a position earlier held by Sojourner Truth*), which became virtually a refugee camp for former slaves afer the Civil War; and in 1871 opened a Sunday school for poor children. In March 1879 Congress awarded her a pension of eight dollars a month, as the widow of James W. Stewart, a navy veteran of the War of 1812. She used this money to pay for the publication of *Meditations from the Pen of Mrs. Maria W. Stewart* (1879), consisting of a reprint of her earlier book (*Productions of Mrs. Maria W. Stewart*) plus some new material.

Continuing a Tradition of Black Protest

Stewart's political views were rooted in a black protest and abolitionist tradition that was much older than the white and integrated movements. The greatest influence on her thinking was David Walker (1785–1830), who in his *Walker's Appeal* (1829) called for the overthrow of white rule by violent means if necessary. Like Walker, Stewart accepted the use of armed struggle, proclaimed herself ready to be a martyr, trusted in the strength of a united black community, and directed her words primarily to African-American audiences.

Stewart's style, religious and sermonlike, influenced later black public speakers, such as Frederick Douglass and Sojourner Truth.* Using rhetorical flourishes, she challenged her listeners to take action. Her militancy poured out in a stream of memorable phrases. Stewart believed that "resistance to oppression was the highest form of obedience to God." She criticized the inaction of some blacks, because "talk, without effort, is nothing... and this gross neglect, on your part, causes my blood to boil within me!" Referring to the movement to send blacks back to Africa, she said, "But before I go, the bayonet shall pierce me through."[3]

"Daughters of Africa, Awake!"

Above all, Stewart directed her message to black women: "O woman, woman! Upon you I call; for upon your exertions almost entirely depends whether the rising generation shall be any thing more than we have been or not."[4] Stressing education, she exhorted women to instill a love of learning in their children and made the first recorded call for black women to become teachers. "It is of no use for us to sit with our hands folded, hanging our heads like bulrushes, lamenting our wretched condition," she said while urging black women to unite and build a high school; "but let us make a mighty effort, and arise. . . . We have never had the opportunities of displaying our talents; therefore the world thinks we know nothing."[5]

In her address in Boston in September 1833, she asserted her right and that of other women to take active roles in society: "What if I am a woman? Is not the God of ancient times the God of these modern days? Did he not raise up Deborah to be a mother and a judge in Israel? . . . St. Paul declared it was a shame for a woman to speak in public, yet our Great High Priest and Advocate did not condemn women for a more notorious offense than this; neither will he condemn this worthless worm."[6] She reminded her audience of great women achievers in history and urged the acceptance of contemporary women activists.

Maria W. Stewart died in Washington, D.C., on December 17, 1879. The first black woman to speak and write publicly on substantive political issues, she holds a special place in African-American history. She summed up her life's work in her own powerful words: "Daughters of Africa, awake! arise! distinguish yourselves."[7]

Juanita Kidd Stout

FIRST BLACK WOMAN ON A STATE SUPREME COURT

(1919–)

J UANITA KIDD STOUT is one of America's most respected judges. Her career has been marked by
a series of unprecedented accomplishments,
including her appointment in 1988 as the first black
woman to serve on a state supreme court.

Born Juanita Kidd in Wewoka, Oklahoma, on
March 7, 1919, she was the only child of Henry
Maynard Kidd and Mary Alice (Chandler) Kidd. Her
parents, both schoolteachers, taught her to read by
the time she was three, and at six she started school
in the third grade. After graduating from grade school
and high school at the top of her class, she left Oklahoma in 1935 to attend college.

Juanita studied for two years at Lincoln University in Jefferson City, Missouri, and then transferred
to the University of Iowa in Iowa City, where she received a bachelor of arts degree in music in 1939. A
serious piano student since the age of five, she continued to study the instrument at the graduate level
for two summers at the University of Colorado in
Boulder and at the University of Minnesota in Minneapolis.

Meanwhile, in 1939 she began two years of teach-
ing grade school and high school music in Seminole,
Oklahoma. She also taught for one year at Sand
Springs, near Tulsa, Oklahoma, where she met Charles
Otis Stout, a history and Spanish teacher. They mar-
ried in 1942 and had no children.

After leaving Sand Springs, Stout moved to Washington, D.C., where she worked as a secretary for the
prominent law firm of Houston, Houston, and
Hastie. She was inspired by the law work of Charles
Hamilton Houston and began to feel the resparking
of an old flame in her heart. Since the age of three,
she had wanted to be a lawyer. She had "never even

seen a woman lawyer, never mind a black woman lawyer," she recalled in 1990. "I can't explain it even today. It was my dream."[1]

A Career of Firsts

Stout began her legal training at Howard University
in Washington, D.C., but transferred to Indiana
University in Bloomington, Indiana, where her husband was working on his doctorate. At Indiana she
earned a doctor of jurisprudence degree in 1948 and
a master of law degree, specializing in legislation, in
1954.

After passing the Pennsylvania Bar examination in
1954, she went into private law practice with Mabel
G. Turner, later an assistant United States attorney.
In 1956 Stout joined the Philadelphia district
attorney's office, and three years later she became head
of the Appeals, Pardons, and Parole Division.

When Governor David L. Lawrence appointed
Stout a judge to the Philadelphia Municipal (later
County) Court in September 1959, she became the
first woman judge in the state of Pennsylvania. In
November of that year she won citywide election to a
ten-year term on the same court, thus becoming the
first black woman to be elected to a court of record
in the United States.

Stout soon won a reputation among her peers for
her exceptionally clear writing of legal opinions. She
also published articles, such as "Executive Clemency
in Pennsylvania" in *The Shingle* (May 1959), the official publication of the Philadelphia Bar Association,
and "Troubled Children and Reading Achievement"
in *Catholic Library World* (1965).

After serving her ten-year term on the municipal (county) court, Stout was elected to two consecutive ten-year terms on the Philadelphia Court of Common Pleas. She then briefly served the court of general trial jurisdiction until, in early 1988, Governor Robert P. Casey appointed her a justice of the Supreme Court of Pennsylvania thus making her the first African-American woman to serve on the highest appellate court of any state.

Her appointment was met with great approval by the legal community. Stout "possesses all of the qualities that are necessary to be a great jurist," wrote Lawrence S. Rosenwald in *The Retainer*, a publication of the Philadelphia Bar Association, "a keen intellect, an appreciation of the issues, compassion where appropriate, an inexhaustible supply of energy and the courage to apply the law fairly and justly regardless of how controversial the issues or powerful the parties."[2]

In 1989 Stout was forced to step down from the high court on reaching the mandatory retirement age of seventy. She then returned to the Philadelphia Court of Common Pleas as a senior judge in the homicide division.

Activities and Honors

Stout has been active in many civic and professional organizations, including the Philadelphia, Pennsyl-vania, and American bar associations; the National Association of Women Lawyers; and the American Judges Association. She has served on college boards as well as the board of the National Conference of Christians and Jews. Presidents Kennedy and Johnson named her to missions in Africa.

Stout has received over two hundred awards and honors, among them the National Association of Women Lawyers outstanding woman lawyer of the year award (1965), the distinguished alumnus honor from the University of Iowa (1974), induction into the Oklahoma Hall of Fame (1981) and the Oklahoma Women's Hall of Fame (1983), the National Association of Women Judges justice of the year award (1988), the Gimbel Award for Humanitarian Services from the Medical College of Pennsylvania (1989), the Distinguished Alumni Service Award from Indiana University (1992), the Philadelphia Bar Association's Sandra Day O'Connor Award (1994), and the Distinguished Service Award from the University of Oklahoma (1995).

In 1990 Juanita Kidd Stout said that she continued to enjoy applying the law in a way "that will serve people, make for the overall good, and be useful to American society."[3] She accomplished those societal goals while achieving a personal career of firsts that greatly increased the status of, and opportunities for, African-American women in the legal profession.

Mary Church Terrell

ADVOCATE FOR EQUALITY

(1863—1954)

EDUCATOR, CLUBWOMAN, writer, lecturer, and activist, for sixty-six years Mary Church Terrell played a leading role in the struggle to improve the social, economic, and political conditions of African-Americans. Her principal biographer, Beverly Jones, author of *Quest for Equality: The Life and Writings of Mary Church Terrell, 1863–1954* (1990), identified three major stages in the evolution of Terrell's long career: leading black self-help organizations, advocating interracial understanding, and finally engaging in militant activism.[1]

Born Mary Eliza Church in Memphis, Tennessee, on September 23, 1863, she was the eldest child of Robert Reed Church and Louisa (Ayers) Church, both former slaves. Her father, the son of his master, worked on a riverboat till emancipation, after which he opened a saloon in Memphis. Louisa ran her own hair store in the same city, but while Mary was still a young child, her parents divorced. Her father remained in Memphis, invested in real estate, and became the South's first black millionaire. Her mother moved to New York City, where she operated a beauty parlor for many years, while Mary was sent to Ohio for her schooling.

As she became more aware of racism, Mary resolved to do well in school to show what black women could achieve. After finishing elementary school and high school she attended Oberlin College in Ohio, where she earned a bachelor's degree in 1884 and a master's degree in 1888.

Like many educated women of the time she immediately turned to teaching, taking positions at Wilberforce University in Xenia, Ohio, from 1885 to 1887 and then at the M Street High School in Washington, D.C., during 1887–88. From 1888 to 1890 she traveled and studied in Europe, but in 1890 she returned to teaching at the M Street High School.

During her first tour of duty at the school her supervisor was Robert Heberton Terrell, a lawyer and educator who later served as the school's principal (1899–1901) and then as a Washington, D.C., judge (1902–1925, the year of his death). In 1891 Mary and Robert married. They had three children who died in infancy before finally having a child who survived, Phyllis, born in 1898. In 1905 they also adopted Mary's brother's daughter, also named Mary.

At that time married women were not allowed to work in the District of Columbia schools, so Mary Church Terrell had to leave her job at the M Street High School. However, she soon redirected her energy to a larger arena. In 1892 one event in particular prompted the beginning of her public career. Back in Memphis one of her good friends, Tom Moss, was lynched by a mob of whites who were jealous of the success of his grocery store. As a result, Terrell and the famed social activist Frederick Douglass personally met with President Benjamin Harrison to protest against racial violence.

Black Self-Help Leader

In that same year, 1892, Terrell took over the leadership of a new group formed in the District of Columbia, the Colored Women's League, which in 1896 merged with other groups to become the National Association of Colored Women (NACW). With Terrell as its first president, this organization addressed racial problems by offering self-help programs for black women. Terrell believed that fighting racism and uplifting African-American women were related endeavors, discrimination inevitably decreasing as the self-development of black women increased. Terrell explained the work of the NACW through articles, including "Duty of the National Association of Colored Women to the Race" in the *AME Church Review* (January 1900).

Under Terrell's leadership the NACW established kindergartens, day nurseries, and mothers' clubs, which provided information on raising children and caring for the home. She also set up schools of domestic science and homes for girls, the elderly, and the infirm. The NACW proved to be a major force in producing a genuine middle class of black women.

After Terrell was elected to three consecutive terms as president of the NACW, in 1901 she was made an honorary life president.

Advocate of Interracial Understanding

By 1901 Terrell felt the need to approach interracial issues from a broader point of view than that embodied in women's organizations. Through the vehicles of writings, speeches, and actions, she began to educate people, both black and white, to the need for racial equality and understanding.

Terrell directed some of her articles especially to black readers, such as "The Progress of Colored Women" in *Voice of the Negro* (July 1904). However, she designed many of her writings to help white people understand the realities of black life in America. Among her most powerful writings of this kind were "Lynching from a Negro's Point of View" in *North American Review* (June 1904), "A Plea for the White South by a Colored Woman" in *Nineteenth Century* (July 1906), "What It Means to Be Colored in the Capital of the United States" in *Independent* (January 24, 1907), and "Peonage in the United States: The Convict Lease System and the Chain Gangs" in *Nineteenth Century* (August 1907).

Terrell publicly criticized anyone, black or white, whose position jeopardized the goal of racial equality or the good of humanity. When President Theodore Roosevelt disbanded several companies of black soldiers, she attacked his decision. In her article "The Disbanding of the Colored Soldiers" in *Voice of the Negro* (December 1906), she urged African-Americans to "regard the terrible catastrophe which has filled the whole race with grief as an evil out of which good will eventually come."[2]

In her speeches to black audiences Terrell boosted morale by exhorting her people to continue their programs of self-development. Her addresses to general audiences focused on the progress that black people had made in spite of discrimination. She addressed the 1898 convention of the National American Woman Suffrage Association, in a speech entitled "The Progress of Colored Women." In 1904 she gave a particularly memorable speech at the International Congress of Women in Berlin, at which she was the only black representative. Speaking in German, she depicted black life in America and outlined major contributions to society by blacks. In 1919 she addressed the second Congress of the Women's International League for Peace and Freedom in Zurich.

Besides publishing articles and making formal speeches, Terrell acted on her beliefs. She did so, for example, in her capacity as the first black woman member of the District of Columbia Board of Education, on which she served from 1895 to 1901 and from 1906 to 1911.

Terrell was often seen on Capitol Hill and at the White House, leading delegations to protest injustice. For example, she picketed the White House with the National Woman's party to demand votes for women. In 1920, after the Nineteenth Amendment became law, she began to serve the Republican National Committee as director of eastern activities among black women. In that capacity she encouraged women's groups to vote and to support the Republican party. For decades she continued to assist the Republicans till 1952, when she decided to vote for the Democratic presidential candidate, Adlai E. Stevenson.

Militant Activist

Late in her life Terrell became increasingly impatient to end discrimination in the United States, frustrated by the economic hardships suffered by African-Americans during the Great Depression of the 1930s and dismayed by the irony of African-Americans fighting for democracy abroad during World War II while lacking freedom in their own homeland.[3]

In the midst of this final phase of her career, Terrell published her autobiography, *A Colored Woman in a White World* (1940), devoting much of it to discussing her lifetime of community activism. Another important late publication was her article "Needed:

Women Lawyers" in *Negro Digest* (September 1943).

During the McCarthy era of the late 1940s and early 1950s, when many liberal activists were labeled communists, blacklisted, and even imprisoned, Terrell encouraged them. "Keep on going," she said, "keep on insisting—keep on fighting injustice."[4]

Taking her own advice, the elderly Terrell remained active in the struggle for civil rights. In 1942 she was elected chair of the Coordinating Committee for the Enforcement of District of Columbia Anti-Discrimination Laws. These laws, passed in 1872 and 1873, "required all eating-place proprietors to serve any respectable well-behaved person regardless of color, or face a $1,000 fine and forfeiture of their license."[5] Never officially repealed, the laws were nevertheless ignored in the 1890s when the District of Columbia code was written. From the 1890s to the 1950s segregated public facilities became the norm in the nation's capital, and blacks who attempted to integrate were fined or jailed.

On February 28, 1950, Terrell, eighty-six years old, led two other blacks and a white in requesting service at a segregated Washington, D.C., restaurant owned by John Thompson, who refused to serve the black members of the group. Terrell and the others sued, and the case went all the way to the Supreme Court. During the three-year wait for a final ruling in the case, Terrell targeted other segregated establishments for picketing, boycotting, and sit-ins and participated directly in this campaign despite her age. On June 8, 1953, the Supreme Court ruled that segregated eating facilities in Washington, D.C., were unconstitutional.

Another cause that Terrell led in her final years involved the case of Rosa Ingram, a black Georgia sharecropper who was sentenced to death along with her two sons for killing a white man who had assaulted them. Heading the National Committee to Free the Ingram Family, Terrell took the issue to the United Nations and sought a pardon from the governor of Georgia. The Ingrams were finally released in 1959, five years after Terrell's death.

She learned of the Supreme Court's famous *Brown v. Board of Education* decision, which not only mandated the desegregation of public schools but also effectively began the overthrow of all legalized segregation in the United States, just two months before she died, in Annapolis, Maryland, on July 24, 1954. The decision was a fitting conclusion to the life of Mary Church Terrell, whose quest for equality was unique in its longevity and range of achievements.

MARY CHURCH TERRELL

The Schomburg Center / NYPL

Adah Thoms

NURSING PIONEER

(c. 1870–1943)

N URSE, FEMINIST, and civil rights activist, Adah Thoms worked "to improve nurse training, to organize and develop the National Association of Colored Graduate Nurses, and to provide equal employment opportunities in the American Red Cross and the U.S. Army Nurse Corps."[1] Her *Pathfinders: A History of the Progress of Colored Graduate Nurses* (1929) was the first book to record the struggles of black nurses.

Adah Belle Samuels was born in Richmond, Virginia, on January 12, about 1870, to Harry and Melvina Samuels. As a young woman, probably in the 1890s, she was briefly married to a Mr. or Dr. Thoms.

In 1893 Adah Thoms moved to New York City, where she began to study public speaking at the Cooper Union. Later she trained as a nurse at the Woman's Infirmary and School of Therapeutic Massage in New York City, graduating as the only black student in a class of thirty in 1900.

After graduation Thoms worked for a time as a private-duty nurse in New York City. She then moved to Raleigh, North Carolina, where she was a staff nurse and then head nurse at Saint Agnes Hospital.

Nursing at Lincoln Hospital

In 1903 Thoms returned to New York City for more training, entering the black nursing school at Lincoln Hospital and Home. During her second year as a student there she became head nurse on a surgical ward, and when she graduated in 1905, Lincoln immediately offered her a full-time job.

Just one year later Thoms was appointed assistant superintendent of nurses and acting director of the school of nursing, in which capacities she made important advancements in the training of nurses. In 1913 she started a six-month postgraduate course for registered nurses, and in 1917 she established a course in public health nursing.

Developing the NACGN

In 1908, as president of the Lincoln nurses' alumnae association, she led her group's sponsorship of the first meeting of the National Association of Colored Graduate Nurses (NACGN). She was elected treasurer, and her colleague Martha Franklin became president. Because the American Nurses' Association (ANA) denied membership to African-Americans, Thoms and Franklin were determined to form an association that would raise the status of black nurses.

From 1916 to 1923 Thoms served as president of the NACGN, and used her position both to improve the training offered in black hospital nursing schools throughout the United States and to wider employment opportunities for black nurses.

While building NACGN's national membership and organizing local and state associations of black graduate nurses, Thoms also sought to attain her goals by working with other organizations. She joined forces with the National Urban League and the National Association for the Advancement of Colored People to try to improve conditions at black hospitals and training schools generally.

Seeking Equal Employment Opportunities

Thoms was "a pioneer for equal opportunity for black women in nursing and was committed to improving race relations."[2] As president of the NACGN during World War I, Thoms wanted black nurses to join their white sisters in the war effort. Beginning in the spring of 1917 she urged the American Red Cross Nursing Services to accept black nurses, this being the only means by which they could enter the United States Army Nurse Corps. But for months both the Red Cross and the army refused to accept African-Americans. Finally the Red Cross began to accept, and the army later agreed to a limited enrollment of, black nurses. But it was July 1918 before the first black nurse was enrolled in the army, and the first group of eighteen black nurses was not officially appointed to the Army Nurse Corps till December 1918, after the war was over.

Thoms found other ways to win recognition and opportunities for black nurses, however. In 1917 she helped to establish the Blue Circle Nurses, black nurses whom the Circle for Negro War Relief paid "to work in local communities, instructing poor rural black people on the importance of sanitation, proper diet, and appropriate clothing."[3] In 1921 she raised the prestige of all black nurses when the assistant surgeon general of the army appointed her to the Woman's Advisory Council of Venereal Disease of the United States Public Health Service.

Besides fulfilling her work in the field of nursing, Thoms crusaded for women's voting rights, and when the Nineteenth Amendment became law in 1920, she organized a campaign to encourage NACGN members to vote.

In 1923 Thoms retired from Lincoln Hospital and married Henry Smith, but he died the following year. Because of this brief second marriage, her full name is sometimes given as Adah Belle Samuels Thoms (Smith).

After her retirement Thoms remained active in various professional organizations. In 1929 she published *Pathfinders*, the first history of black nurses. In 1936 the NACGN awarded her its first Mary Mahoney Award.

Adah Thoms died in the Harlem section of New York City on February 21, 1943. In 1976 she was inducted into nursing's Hall of Fame for her pioneering advancements in training, organizing, and advancing the employment opportunities of black nurses in America.

Sojourner Truth

PIONEER ADVOCATE OF RACIAL AND GENDER REFORM

(c. 1797—1883)

THOUGH SHE NEVER learned to read or write, Sojourner Truth was a powerfully articulate lecturer and evangelist who applied religous fervor to the abolitionist and women's rights movements of the nineteenth century. At that time white-dominated reform movements usually portrayed slaves as male and all women as middle or upper class and white. Truth forcefully proclaimed that poor black women had rights too. She insisted there was a link between racial and gender discrimination in America.

Sojourner Truth was born in Hurley, Ulster County, New York, about 1797. She was the second youngest of the ten to twelve children of James and Elizabeth ("Betsey" or "Mau Mau [Dutch for 'Mama'] Bett"), slaves of a wealthy Dutch-speaking farmer named Johannis Hardenbergh. Truth's original given name was Isabella, and her first language was Dutch.

After Isabella's owner died, Charles Hardenbergh, his son, became her new master. When Charles died, Isabella, now about nine years old, was sold to an English-speaking family named Neely, who lived near Kingston, New York. She then passed into the hands of the nearby Schriver family. Finally, in 1810, she was sold to John Dumont of New Paltz, New York, with whom she remained for the next sixteen years. Isabella received many beatings through the years from most of her owners, including Dumont and his wife. Separated at an early age from her parents, she nevertheless managed to keep her spirits up during her years of enslavement, largely because of the strong religious beliefs instilled in her by her mother.

About 1815 Isabella married another of Dumont's slaves, Thomas. They had five children: Diana, Peter, Elizabeth, Sophia, and one about whom little is known.

Gaining Her Freedom

In the early 1820s the state of New York decided to free the slaves within its jurisdiction. Most adult slaves were scheduled to be freed on July 4, 1827, while younger slaves would be freed gradually, females at the age of twenty-five and males at the age of twenty-eight. Peter, for example, born in 1821, would be freed in 1849. Dumont promised to free Isabella on July 4, 1826, one year ahead of the general emancipation, but when he had failed to do so by the late fall of 1826, she left Dumont, her youngest child, Sophia, in her arms, and began walking down the road.

She went to the nearby home of her friend Levi Rowe, but he was extremely ill and could not help her, so he directed her to Isaac and Maria Van Wagenen of Wagondale, who were strongly opposed to slavery. When Dumont came to reclaim his two runaway slaves, the Van Wagenens paid him $25 for the use of Isabella and Sophia for one year, during which time, of course, the law would set her free. She took the name Isabella Van Wagenen (often rendered "Van Wagner" or "Van Wagener" outside Ulster County) and worked for the family as a free employee for the next year.

During that time Dumont sold Isabella's son Peter, who changed hands three times before finally being sold into slavery in Alabama, despite a New York State law against the sale of New York slaves into places where slavery would continue to be legal after 1827.

One of Isabella's first acts as a free woman was to secure the help of Quaker friends and wage a court battle to recover her son from Alabama. She succeeded, but Peter remained emotionally disturbed for life because of beatings he had received from his southern master. This episode played a pivotal role in her life by embittering her even more strongly against slavery and by convincing her that taking a public stand for her rights could be an effective course of action.

In the late 1820s Isabella moved to New York City, where she supported herself as a domestic servant. She attended the white John Street Methodist Church and the black African Methodist Episcopal Zion Church, and she soon began to develop a reputation as an evangelist at camp meetings. Her association with the zealous missionary Elijah Pierson led her to join the religious commune headed by Robert Matthews, who took the name Matthias and believed himself to be a prophet. When his "kindgom" collapsed in disgrace in the mid-1830s. Isabella returned to the Methodist church and to her domestic service, taking in washing and doing housework.

Becoming Sojourner Truth

By 1843 she was tired of urban life and of the feeling that she was not accomplishing anything. The United States was in the midst of a religious revival at the time, and Isabella came to believe that God had called her to become an itinerant preacher, commanding that she use a new name, Sojourner, because she was to travel up and down the land. She herself decided to take the last name Truth, signifying the Word of God that she would spread.

Setting off northward on June 1, 1843, she preached, sang, and debated in churches, at camp meetings, and on the streets. She was well received wherever she went, having joined a well-established tradition of Quaker and Methodist itinerant women preachers, some of whom were black, such as Jarena Lee.*

Speaking Up for Abolitionism and Women's Rights

Later that year Truth entered Northampton, Massachusetts, and reached a utopian colony called the Northampton Association of Education and Industry, where she encountered fervid abolitionism for the first time. The leading figure at the commune was George Benson, brother-in-law of the famed abolitionist William Lloyd Garrison. Visitors included

Garrison, Frederick Douglass, and other abolitionist leaders. Truth embraced the movement and stayed at the Northampton Association for several years.

In the late 1840s she left the commune to join the antislavery lecture circuit, where she spoke to reform-minded audiences. In 1850 she published *The Narrative of Sojourner Truth*, an autobiography she had dictated to an abolitionist friend, Olive Gilbert. Truth supported herself mainly by selling copies of the book while on her lecture tours.

About this time she also discovered the women's rights movement. In 1850 she attended her first women's rights convention, held in Worcester, Massachussets, and soon she became closely associated with Lucretia Mott, Elizabeth Cady Stanton, and other leaders.

In 1851, at a women's rights convention in Akron, Ohio, Truth heard several male ministers deny women's claim to equal rights. When the white women at the meeting failed to respond, she spoke up, refuting especially one man's claim that women were helpless creatures who needed to be cared for by men: "Look at me! Look at my arm! (and she bared her right arm to the shoulder, showing her tremendous muscular power). I have ploughed, and planted, and gathered into barns, and no man could head me! And a'n't I a woman? I could work as much and eat as much as a man—when I could get it—and bear de lash as well! And a'n't I a woman?"[1] Here she was asserting that women—even working-class women—deserved equality with men. But she went even further and demanded that enslaved black women be categorized as women right along with white ladies: "I have borne thirteen chilern, and seen 'em mos' all sold off to slavery, and when I cried out with my mother's grief, none but Jesus heard me! And a'n't I a woman?"[2] (This was a dramatically effective speech, but in fact the story applied to her mother, whose ten or twelve children had been sold away from her. Truth lost none of her five children permanently.)

After the 1851 Akron convention, Truth remained in the Midwest and continued as an itinerant lecturer on abolitionism and women's rights. In 1856 she settled in Battle Creek, Michigan, where she gathered together her children and grandchildren.

Meeting President Lincoln

In the early stages of the Civil War, Truth collected supplies for black volunteer regiments. In 1864 she went to Washington, D.C., and was received by President Lincoln at the White House. She stayed in Washington throughout the rest of the war and its immediate aftermath, helping to integrate the city's streetcars, nursing black soldiers, teaching housekeeping skills to women who had formerly slaved in the fields, and distributing relief supplies to ex-slaves.

By the late 1860s Truth was helping freed slaves to relocate and find jobs. In the early 1870s she worked tirelessly to persuade Congress to pass a law creating an African-American state in the West, where government lands would be given to freed slaves. The plan failed, but her efforts induced many former slaves to migrate north and west from the Deep South.

Meanwhile, abolitionism having succeeded, Truth intensified her work for women's rights. During the national push to obtain voting rights for black men, she strongly advocated the same rights for women, including black women. At an equal rights convention in 1867, she argued that if black men but not black women were given the vote, "colored men will be masters over the women, and it will be just as bad as it was before."[2]

In her later years she continued to speak out on controversial issues, including women's rights and temperance, with her unschooled but forceful, illuminating style. On January 1, 1871, at a commemoration of the eighth anniversary of the Emancipation Proclamation, she said, "I . . . can't read a book but I can read de people."[4] "The majority rules," she proclaimed during an address in 1871. "If dey want anything, dey git it. If dey want anything not right, dey git it, too."[5]

In 1875 she returned to Battle Creek. About that time one of her friends, Frances Titus, added new material to, and published a second edition of, the *Narrative*.

SOJOURNER TRUTH

The Schomburg Center / NYPL

"No other woman," according to Truth's biographer, Nell Irvin Painter, "who had been through the ordeal of slavery managed to survive with sufficient strength, poise, and self-confidence to become a public presence over the long term. . . . Only Truth had the ability to go on speaking, year after year for thirty years, to make herself into a force in several American reform movements. . . . From the late 1840s through the late 1870s, she traveled the American land, denouncing slavery and traders, advocating freedom, women's rights, woman suffrage, and temperance."[6]

Sojourner Truth died at her home in Battle Creek on November 26, 1883. In one of her last recorded comments, about 1882, she summarized her achievements: "Truth burns up error."[7]

Harriet Tubman

THE MOSES OF HER PEOPLE

(c. 1820—1913)

STANDING ONLY five feet tall and suffering from sudden sleep seizures because of a head injury received as a child, Harriet Tubman nevertheless possessed the courage and resolve to face physical danger many times while pursuing freedom for her people in nineteenth-century America. She escaped from slavery herself; daringly rescued other slaves as an Underground Railroad conductor; served as a Civil War spy, scout, and nurse; and later led the causes of feminism and social reform. "Excepting John Brown—of sacred memory—" Frederick Douglass wrote to her in 1868, "I know of no one who has willingly encountered more perils and hardships to serve our enslaved people than you have."[1] The slaves called her Moses.

Originally named Araminta Ross, she was born into slavery on a plantation in Dorchester County near Cambridge, Maryland, about 1820, one of eleven children of Benjamin and Harriet (Greene) Ross. Her grandparents on both sides had come in chains from Africa. At the age of eleven she adopted her mother's name.

Growing Up in Slavery

From her early childhood she had to work as a weaver, maid, child's nurse, and even field hand for neighboring families who hired her services from her owner, Edward Brodas. When she was in her early teens and working in the field one day for a farmer named Barrett, a fellow slave left his field work early and went to a general store. The overseer followed the man and tried to capture him so that he could administer a whipping. As the slave ran out the door, the angry overseer threw a two-pound weight at him. Harriet, attempting to shield the man, was struck in the head by the weight and knocked unconscious. Though seriously injured with a fractured skull, she recovered after suffering through a long convalescence, but the pressure on her brain caused recurring seizures of sleep for the rest of her life.

While Harriet was recovering at the Brodas plantation, her master tried to sell her, even though she was still helpless in bed. Dismayed at his heartlessness, she began to examine the institution of slavery. Because she had been raised in a deeply religious family, she prayed from her sickbed. As she later said, "I was always praying for poor old master. Oh, dear Lord, change that man's heart, and make him a Christian."[2] When she believed that she and her brothers were going to be sent south in a chain gang, she changed her prayers: "Lord, if you ain't never going to change that man's heart, kill him, Lord, and take him out of the way, so he won't do no more mischief."[3] When her owner did, in fact, die soon afterward, she prayed for the Lord to cleanse her of sin for, as she believed, having caused the man's death. With the strong feeling of being guided by God, she began at this time to develop the self-reliance that characterized so much of her later career.

After her master's death the ownership of his slaves went to his son, but because he was still just a child the plantation was run by his legal guardian, Dr. Anthony Thompson. When Harriet felt well enough, Thompson allowed her to hire herself out for work, in return for which she gave a certain amount of her earnings to him. She drove oxen, plowed, and did lumber work for her father, who supervised the timber operations of a local man named John Stewart.

Such heavy labor helped her to develop great physical strength and stamina.

About 1844 she married John Tubman, a free black in the Cambridge area. Little is known about their relationship. They had no children.

Though Harriet Tubman was illiterate, she had a probing mind, especially in regard to the legal status of blacks. About a year after she married, she hired a lawyer to investigate documents relating to her mother's owners and found that her mother unknowingly had been legally free at one time. One of her mother's owners, Mary Patterson, had died young and unmarried, leaving no provisions for Harriet Greene Ross. The lawyer said that Tubman's mother was therefore emancipated at that time, but since no one had informed her of her rights she had remained a slave. This information further embittered Tubman toward the institution of slavery and the legal and social system that supported it.

From 1847 to 1849 she worked for Dr. Thompson's son, also named Dr. Anthony Thompson, a physician, real estate speculator, and Methodist clergyman. The death of her owner, young Brodas, in 1849 gave rise to rumors that she and his other slaves were to be sold south, and rather than face this prospect, she broke for freedom, alone and unaided, and made her way to Philadelphia.

Seizing Freedom for Herself and Others

"I had crossed the line of which I had so long been dreaming," she later remembered. "I was free; but there was no one to welcome me to the land of freedom."[4] She missed her family and immediately set in motion a plan to rescue them.

Finding work as a cook and domestic, Tubman saved her wages to finance repeated trips back to Maryland to free her relatives and other slaves. In December 1850 she returned to the South and guided her sister Mary and two children to freedom, and the following year she began to rescue her brothers and their families, even offering to bring out her ex-husband, but he had remarried and declined her help. In June 1857 she went back to Maryland, hired a wagon, and drove off with her parents, who were the last members of her family still in the South. During the 1850s she made over fifteen trips into Maryland, leading up to three hundred slaves north to freedom.

On her missions Tubman acted with fearlessness and quick-witted ingenuity. To notify potential fugitives that she would soon arrive, she sometimes sent messages (written out by friends to whom she had dictated the words) understandable only to those for whom they were intended. In one such message she advised the slaves "to be always watching unto prayer, and when the good old ship of Zion comes along, to be ready to step on board."[5] She had a strong singing voice, and she would often sing to communicate her presence to slaves and to let hidden slaves know of nearby danger or safety. Once, when Tubman observed some whites eyeing her and a group of escaping slaves in a small southern town, she bought tickets for a train going south, confident that no one would suspect her party of being runaways if they were headed in that direction. When, on another occasion, she saw one of her former masters approaching, she set loose several live chickens she had just purchased, distracting attention from herself and escaping recognition. Tubman carried a gun to protect herself from proslavers and to prod fainthearted fugitives during the journey north. At one time the rewards for her capture reached forty thousand dollars.

When word spread about Tubman's efforts, she gradually became associated with leaders of the Underground Railroad. She worked especially closely with William Still, the black executive director of the General Vigilance Committee in Philadelphia, and Thomas Garrett, a white Quaker of Wilmington, Delaware.

Tubman also became known among other prominent progressive social leaders in the North, including the Alcotts, Susan B. Anthony, Ralph Waldo Emerson, and William H. Seward. In addition, Frederick Douglass, Oliver Johnson, Wendell Phillips, and Gerrit Smith of the New York City office of the American Anti-Slavery Society all knew and praised her. Various groups provided her with financial and other assistance for her work with the Underground Railroad, and she sometimes addressed abolitionist conventions.

In the early 1850s Tubman took up residence in Saint Catharines, Ontario, Canada, where for several years she brought the fugitives she smuggled out of Maryland. While living there in April 1858, she met with and advised John Brown, who was making plans for his armed action against slavery.

In the late 1850s she moved with her parents to a small farm near Auburn, New York, a center of progressive thought. The property was sold to her on generous terms by Senator William H. Seward, and she paid for it largely with unsolicited donations from white supporters.

Serving the Union in the Civil War

When the Civil War began in 1861, Tubman determined that she would aid the Union cause. In 1862 she acquired an endorsement from Governor John A. Andrew of Massachusetts and went to Beaufort, South Carolina, the principal town of a group of coastal islands recently captured by Union forces.

For the next three years she nursed and cooked for sick and wounded soldiers and taught newly freed blacks how to become self-sufficient. She also served as a spy and scout, securing military intelligence from black informants who lived behind Confederate lines and leading a group of black men on scouting missions for Union raids. During an 1863 raid under the command of Colonel James Montgomery near the Combahee River in South Carolina, Tubman herself came under fire from Confederate troops. Just after the war, in the spring and summer of 1865, she worked in Virginia at a hospital for newly freed blacks.

HARRIET TUBMAN

The Schomburg Center / NYPL

Improving the Lives of Free Blacks

Returning to her home in Auburn, Tubman devoted the rest of her life to helping others. Besides caring for her aged parents, she raised funds for schools for former slaves; helped in the growth of black churches; collected clothes for destitute children; and, after the deaths of her parents, established a home near her farm for indigent African-Americans.

Tubman believed that racial liberation and women's liberation were strongly linked. She supported Susan B. Anthony's founding of the women's suffragist movement in 1870, served as a delegate to the first annual convention of the National Federation of Afro-American Women in 1896, and was the guest of honor at a reception held by the New England Women's Suffrage Association in 1897. When, late in her life, she was asked if she believed in woman suffrage, she replied, "I have suffered enough to believe it."[6]

While pursuing such public matters, Tubman still retained a private life. In 1869, two years after the death of John Tubman, she married Nelson Davis, a black Civil War veteran twenty-two years younger than she. The marriage lasted twenty years till his death. Later the federal government gave her a small pension as the widow of a Civil War veteran, but she was never awarded a pension for her own wartime service.

Her fame reached the general public in 1869 when Sarah Bradford published a brief sketch, *Scenes in the Life of Harriet Tubman*, expanded in 1886 into the book *Harriet Tubman: The Moses of Her People*, the proceeds of which Tubman used to help pay off her farm.

Tubman died in Auburn on March 10, 1913, when she was about ninety-three years old. A plaque was erected in her honor in the Auburn town square the following year, during a memorial service for her featuring Booker T. Washington.

Tina Turner

ROCK AND ROLL'S QUEEN DIVA

(1939—   )

ONE OF THE TRUE living legends in contemporary rock music, Tina Turner became a singing sensation in the late 1950s, and in the late 1990s she is going stronger than ever. She has cut some of the most successful recordings in history, and she has broken box office records all over the world. Some people in the music business have dubbed her "rock 'n' roll's queen diva."[1]

Originally named Anna Mae Bullock, she was born in Brownsville, Tennessee, on November 26, 1939, to Floyd Richard Bullock and Zelma (Currie) Bullock. She lived with her parents and an older sister and half sister on a farm in Nut Bush (or Nutbush), a village near Brownsville. Her father, a Baptist deacon, was the overseer on the farm. Her mother came from a mixed black and Native American ancestry.

Anna Mae began singing when she was little. During a visit to Knoxville she went shopping with her mother and sang for the salesladies, who often rewarded her with coins. Later, after the family moved to Spring Hill, she was one of the lead singers in the local Baptist church choir.

In the early 1950s her parents divorced. After staying for a time with her father and then other relatives, in 1956 she went to live with her mother in Saint Louis, Missouri.

Ike and Tina Turner

At the Club Manhattan nightclub in Saint Louis, she and her sister, Alline, became friendly with several members of the Kings of Rhythm band led by Ike Turner. During a break in the band's performance one day, a band member tried to coax Alline to sing.

But it was Anna Mae who took the microphone and began to sing a B. B. King number. Ike Turner, impressed, invited her to join the act. She gave her first performances under the name Little Ann.

Little Ann developed a romantic relationship with the group's saxophone player, Raymond Hill, with whom she had a son, also named Raymond, in 1958. Shortly thereafter she became involved with Ike Turner, and in 1960 they had a son, Ronald. Later the couple married in Tijuana, Mexico, but, unknown to Anna Mae at the time Ike was still married to his previous wife, whom he did not divorce till 1974. Anna Mae also helped to raise Ike's two sons from his previous marriage, Ike and Michael.

In 1960 Ike changed Anna Mae Bullock's name to Tina and formed the Ike and Tina Turner Revue, with Ike and Tina as the leads and an accompanying group called the Ikettes. Their first recording together was "A Fool in Love" (1960), whose popularity created a demand for personal appearances by the group. Throughout the 1960s and early 1970s the band toured the United States and Europe, performing in a style uniquely blending blues, rock, and gospel. Their hit recordings included the singles "River Deep, Mountain High" (1966) and "Proud Mary" (1971) and the albums *It's Gonna Work Out Fine* (1961) and *The Gospel According to Ike and Tina* (1974).

The relationship, however, was marred by Ike's increasing physical abuse of Tina. In 1976 she finally left him, obtaining a divorce soon thereafter, and she later advised others to seek a similar liberation. "Whatever is getting you down," she said, "get rid of it. Because you'll find that when you're free, your true creativity, your true self comes out."[2]

Solo Recording Artist

Drained by her battering at Ike's hands, Tina Turner needed time to recover. Gradually she made a remarkable comeback, and eventually her solo career far outshone her earlier work with Ike. In the late 1970s and early 1980s she laid the foundation for her future success by touring widely and developing an individual style in which her hard-rock base was tinged with blues and reggae.

Turner's recording career reached full stride again with the release of her album *Private Dancer* (1984), containing the hit singles "Better Be Good to Me," "Let's Stay Together," and "What's Love Got to Do with It?" In 1985 she recorded the highly acclaimed single "One of the Living," and the following year she firmly established herself as the world's leading rock singer when critics and fans embraced her album *Break Every Rule* (1986), featuring "Back Where You Started" and "Typical Male." Later hit singles included "What You Get Is What You See" (1987), "I Don't Wanna Fight" (1993), and "Disco Inferno" (1993). Among her albums were *Foreign Affair* (1989), *Simply the Best* (1991), and *Wildest Dreams* (1996).

Stage, Film, and Television Performer

TINA TURNER

During the first years of her comeback after leaving Ike, Tina Turner built her solo reputation mainly through live performances. She began on the cabaret circuit, performed in Europe, toured the United States with the Rolling Stones in 1981, and thereafter became one of the world's greatest live musical performers. In 1987 her world tour broke box office records in thirteen countries. A concert in Rio de Janeiro, Brazil, in 1988 drew 182,000 fans, the largest audience ever assembled for a single performer, and her 121-date 1990 world tour was seen by more than three million people. Throughout the 1990s she continued to draw huge audiences in her live performances.

Turner has appeared in documentary films, such as *Superstars in Film Concert* (1971), and also played herself in *Taking Off* (1971). Her first acting role came as the Acid Queen in the film version of the rock opera *Tommy* (1975). In *Mad Max Beyond Thunderdome* (1985) she played Aunt Entity and recorded the music track, which was released as an album of the same name and also contained the hit single "We Don't Need Another Hero." In *Last Action Hero* (1993) she played the mayor. She supplied

227

the music track for the film *What's Love Got to Do with It?* (1993), based on her 1986 best-selling autobiography *I, Tina* (written with Kurt Loder). The music track became a successful album under the same name as the film. Her performance of the title song for the movie *Goldeneye* (1995) became a hit single.

Turner has appeared on many television music specials, among them *Tina Turner: Private Dancer* (1985), *The Queen of Rock Struts Her Stuff* (1991), and *Tina Turner's Wildest Dreams Concert* (1997).

In addition to receiving many Grammy Awards and nominations, in 1991 Turner was inducted into the Rock and Roll Hall of Fame, in 1993 she received the Outstanding Contribution to the Music Industry honor at the World Music Awards, and in that same year her star was unveiled as one of the inaugural group of artists on the "Sidewalk of the Stars" outside New York City's Radio City Music Hall.

Long preeminent in her sphere, Tina Turner shows no signs of letting up. After more than forty years as a singing artist, rock's "queen diva" continues to be a major recording power and to electrify her live audiences.

Selected recordings:

SINGLES

(with Ike Turner)

"A Fool in Love" (1960, Sue)
"It's Gonna Work Out Fine" (1961, Sue)
"River Deep, Mountain High" (1966, London American)
"Proud Mary" (1971, Liberty)
"Nutbush City Limits" (1973, United Artists)

SINGLES

(without Ike Turner)

"Let's Stay Together" (1983, Capitol)
"Better Be Good to Me" (1984, Capitol)
"Let's Stay Together" (1984, Capitol)
"What's Love Got to Do with It?" (1984, Capitol)
"Private Dancer" (1985, Capitol)
"We Don't Need Another Hero (Thunderdome)" (1985, Capitol)
"One of the Living" (1985, Capitol)

"It's Only Love" (with Bryan Adams, 1985, A&M)
"Back Where You Started" (1986, Capitol)
"Typical Male" (1986, Capitol)
"What You Get Is What You See" (1987, Capitol)
"The Best" (1989, Capitol)
"I Don't Wanna Lose You" (1989, Capitol)
"It Takes Two" (with Rod Stewart, 1990, Warner)
"Steamy Windows" (1990, Capitol)
"I Don't Wanna Fight" (1993, Parlophone/Virgin)
"Disco Inferno" (1993, Parlophone/Virgin)
"Goldeneye" (1995, Parlophone/Virgin)
"Whatever You Want" (1996, Parlophone/ Virgin)

ALBUMS

(with Ike Turner)

It's Gonna Work Out Fine (1961, Sue)
Proud Mary (1971, United Artists)
The Gospel according to Ike and Tina (1974, United Artists)

ALBUMS

(without Ike Turner)

Tina Turns the Country On! (1974, United Artists)
Private Dancer (1984, Capitol)
Restless (with Bryan Adams, 1985, A&M)
Mad Max Beyond Thunderdome (1985, Capitol)
Break Every Rule (1986, Capitol)
Tina Live in Europe (1988, Capitol)
I Don't Wanna Lose You (1989, Capitol)
Foreign Affair (1989, Capitol)
Simply the Best (1991, Capitol)
What's Love Got to Do with It? (1993, Parlophone/ Virgin)
Wildest Dreams (1996, Parlophone/Virgin)

Selected performances:

FILMS

Gimme Shelter (1970)
Taking Off (1971)
Tommy (1975)
Sgt. Pepper's Lonely Hearts Club Band (1978)
Mad Max Beyond Thunderdome (1985)
Last Action Hero (1993)

Cicely Tyson

INFLUENTIAL ACTRESS

(1933–   )

CICELY TYSON IS universally regarded as one of the finest actresses of her time on stage, screen, and television. Her unique contribution to the arts is her pathbreaking status as the most influential "actress committed to the honest and dignified portrayal of black Americans."[1]

Cicely Tyson was born in the Harlem section of New York City on December 19, 1933 (not, as published in some sources, 1939 or 1942), the youngest of three children of William and Theodosia Tyson. Her parents were immigrants from Nevis, the smallest of the Leeward Islands in the West Indies.

Cicely grew up in poverty in the Harlem ghetto. Her father was a carpenter and a painter, but sometimes he sold fruits and vegetables from a produce stand. To help the family financially, Cicely worked at an early age. When she was nine, for example, she sold shopping bags in nearby neighborhoods. Her devout mother took her to Saint John's Episcopal Church, where Cicely made her first mark in the arts by singing in the choir and playing the piano and organ.

After graduating from Charles Evans Hughes High School in Manhattan, Cicely Tyson took a job as a secretary for the American Red Cross. When her hairdresser asked her to model one of his hairstyles in a style show one day, she agreed, received many compliments at the show, and decided to study modeling. At first she continued to work for the Red Cross while attending a modeling school, but soon she began to land high-paying modeling jobs, and by the mid-1950s she was one of the top ten black models in the United States. In 1956 she appeared on the covers of *Harper's Bazaar* and *Vogue* magazines.

Tyson's modeling led to contacts that won her a role in *The Spectrum*, an independent black film shot by Warren Coleman in New York City. Because of lack of money the film was never completed, but her experience with the movie encouraged her to study acting seriously at the Actor's Workshop, the Actors Studio, and elsewhere. Meanwhile, she also attended classes at New York University.

Stage Career

Tyson made her New York City stage debut playing Barbara Allen in the musical *Dark of the Moon* at the Harlem YMCA in 1958. The following year she performed in the Broadway musical variety show *Talent '59*. In late 1959 and early 1960 she understudied Eartha Kitt* as Jolly in the Broadway play *Jolly's Progress*.

During the 1960s Tyson enjoyed an active career in both Broadway and off-Broadway productions. She played Girl in *The Cool World* (1960) Virtue, a prostitute, in *The Blacks* (1961), for which she won the Vernon Rice Award Mavis in *Moon on a Rainbow Shawl* (1962), winning another Vernon Rice Award; Celeste in *Tiger, Tiger, Burning Bright* (1962); Joan in *The Blue Boy in Black* (1963); and the Reverend Marion Alexander in the musical *Trumpets of the Lord* (1963). In 1966 Tyson performed in the revue *A Hand Is on the Gate*, which included black poetry and folk music, in 1968 she played Myrna in *Carry Me Back to Morningside Heights*, and the following year she participated in *To Be Young, Gifted, and Black*, a program of dramatic readings of works by Lorraine Hansberry*.

During the 1970–71 season Tyson appeared in the

CICELY TYSON

Her first important starring role in films was in *Sounder* (1972). She played Rebecca Morgan, the strong, loving, dignified wife of a sharecropper in the South during the Great Depression. Tyson herself believed that Rebecca was the first truly positive role for a black woman on the screen. According to Tyson, Rebecca represented the kind of woman who "has always been the strength of our race, and she has always had to carry the ball . . . with warmth, beauty, love, and understanding. We do have that. It does exist. I grew up in that kind of setting here in New York where the only thing that kept the family together was the parents' love for each other."[2] For her performance as Rebecca, Tyson was nominated for an Academy Award as best actress, and she won the National Society of Film Critics Award for best actress at the Atlanta Film Festival.

After *Sounder* she continued to appear only rarely on the big screen. Later films included *The Blue Bird* (1976), *Bustin' Loose* (1981), and *Fried Green Tomatoes* (1991).

Playhouse in the Park series in Cincinnati, Ohio, performing Eliza Dolittle in *Pygmalion* and reprising her role in *The Blacks*. In 1974 she played Abbie Putnam in *Desire Under the Elms* in Lake Forest, Illinois.

Sounder and Other Films

Tyson began her film career in the late 1950s with a small role as a ghetto girl in *The Last Angry Man* (1959). In the crime drama *Odds against Tomorrow*, released the same year, she played a young woman involved in racial tensions. During the following decade she appeared in *A Man Called Adam* (1966), *The Comedians* (1967), and *The Heart Is a Lonely Hunter* (1968), but she accepted very few movie roles because she refused to appear in stories that portrayed black characters only as criminals and prostitutes.

Emmy Winner

Tyson has long been a dominant figure on television. In the late 1950s and early 1960s she appeared in guest roles on television series, such as *Camera Three*, but it was in 1963 that she made a major breakthrough in her own career and in the prospects for other black performers. George C. Scott, after seeing her in the stage play *The Blacks*, recruited her for a leading part in his new television series *East Side, West Side* (1963–64), a program about social workers. As Scott's assistant, Tyson became the first black to have a regular role in a television drama series.

Over thirty years later Tyson starred in another television series, *Sweet Justice* (1994–95), playing Carrie Grace Battle, a progressive black attorney.

Between *East Side, West Side* and *Sweet Justice*, Tyson, more than any other single actress, radically changed the portrayal of African-American women on television. Previously they were mostly ignored, and when they were portrayed at all, it was usually as servants. Tyson's extraordinary performances in television movies and miniseries opened the eyes of the American public to the depth and range of black American women, both as people and as actresses.

In *The Autobiography of Miss Jane Pittman* (1974) she played the title role, an ex-slave who ages from 19 to 110, from the post-Civil War years to the civil rights movement of the 1960s. For her performance as Jane Pittman, Tyson won an Emmy as the best actress in a special program or a single appearance in a drama or comedy series.

Over the next several years she starred in more television movies and miniseries based on African-American history. In the famed miniseries *Roots* (1977) she played Binta, Kunta Kinte's mother; in *Wilma* (1977) she was Blanche Rudolph, the mother of the Olympic track star Wilma Rudolph*; in *King* (1978) Tyson sensitively portrayed Coretta Scott King*, wife of the civil rights leader Martin Luther King, Jr.; and in *A Woman Called Moses* (1978) she played Harriet Tubman*, a slave who led up to three hundred other slaves to freedom on the Underground Railroad.

Tyson's television work in the 1980s included *The Marva Collins Story* (1981), *Playing with Fire* (1985), and *The Women of Brewster Place* (1989). In the early 1990s she appeared in *Heat Wave* (1990), *House of Secrets* (1993), and other television movies. She won another Emmy, this time as best supporting actress in a miniseries or special, for her performance in *Oldest Living Confederate Widow Tells All* (1994). Later she starred in *The Road to Galveston* (1996) and *Riot* (1997).

Tyson's interests extend beyond her performances. She cofounded the Dance Theater of Harlem, she has been a trustee of the Human Family Institute, and she has helped to organize efforts to expose children to the arts. Her important contributions to social progress have earned her numerous awards, including citations from the National Association for the Advancement of Colored People and the National Council of Negro Women.

Tyson married the jazz trumpeter Miles Davis in 1981. They had no children and later divorced.

"I was never preoccupied with whether or not I was going to be successful," Tyson has said. "I was preoccupied with doing whatever I was doing the best possible way. If I iron a handkerchief, it's going to be done

the best I can possibly do it. I am a perfectionist."[3]

Her trait of perfectionism was evident in her performance as the aged Jane Pittman, in preparation for which Tyson spent several days with elderly women in a nursing home. From them she learned, she said, "the perspective and quiet dignity that comes with old age."[4]

As she absorbed dignity from her models, so she conveyed it as Jane Pittman and in her other roles. Through that dignity Cicely Tyson transformed the screen portrayals of African-American women into powerful, positive images.

Selected performances:

STAGE

Dark of the Moon (1958)
Talent '59 (1959)
Jolly's Progress (1959)
The Cool World (1960)
The Blacks (1961)
Moon on a Rainbow Shawl (1962)
Tiger, Tiger, Burning Bright (1962)
The Blue Boy in Black (1963)
The Last Minstrel (1963)
Trumpets of the Lord (1963)
An Evening of Negro Poetry and Folk Music (1966)
A Hand Is on the Gate (1966)
Carry Me Back to Morningside Heights (1968)
To Be Young, Gifted, and Black (1969)
Trumpets of the Lord (1969)
Pygmalion (1970)
The Blacks (1970)
Desire Under the Elms (1974)

FILMS

The Last Angry Man (1959)
Odds against Tomorrow (1959)
A Man Called Adam (1966)
The Comedians (1967)
The Heart Is a Lonely Hunter (1968)
Sounder (1972)
The Blue Bird (1976)
The River Niger (1976)
A Hero Ain't Nothin' but a Sandwich (1977)
The Concorde—Airport '79 (1979)
Bustin' Loose (1981)
Fried Green Tomatoes (1991)
Hoodlums (1997)

TELEVISION MOVIES

Marriage: Year One (1971)
The Autobiography of Miss Jane Pittman (1974)
Just an Old Sweet Song (1976)
Roots (1977)
Wilma (1977)
A Woman Called Moses (1978)
King (1978)
The Marva Collins Story (1981)
Benny's Place (1982)
Playing with Fire (1985)
Samaritan
The Mitch Snyder Story (1986)
Acceptable Risks (1986)
Intimate Encounters (1986)

The Women of Brewster Place (1989)
Heat Wave (1990)
The Kid Who Loved Christmas (1990)
When No One Would Listen (1992)
Duplicates (1992)
House of Secrets (1993)
Oldest Living Confederate Widow Tells All (1994)
The Road to Galveston (1996)
Riot (1997)
The Price of Heaven (1997)
Mama Flora's Family (1998)

TELEVISION SERIES

East Side, West Side (1963–64)
Sweet Justice (1994–95)

Wyomia Tyus

FIRST SPRINTER TO DEFEND OLYMPIC 100-METER TITLE

(1945–   )

IN THE 1960s Wyomia Tyus earned the title of world's fastest woman by setting many world records in sprinting. Her greatest claim to fame was becoming the first athlete, male or female, to win the 100-meter dash in two consecutive Olympic Games.

Wyomia Tyus was born in Griffin, Georgia, on August 29, 1945, the fourth child of Willie and Maria Tyus. It was her father who encouraged her to participate in competitive athletics.

Her favorite sport was basketball till she went out for the Griffin High School girls' track team to become a high jumper and soon discovered her talent for running. Practicing diligently, she began to win sprinting events in track meets. Some of her female relatives advised her to quit because, they said, competing in sports was "unladylike,"[1] but she continued.

In 1961, while Tyus was still in high school, Ed Temple, track coach at Tennessee State University (TSU), invited her to participate in his summer track and field camp. Taking advantage of that opportunity to improve her physical conditioning and her sprinting technique, she matured rapidly as an athlete under Temple's coaching.

In 1962 Tyus won the 100-yard dash at the Girls' Amateur Athletic Union (AAU) Championships, setting an American record for her age group. She also won the 50-yard and 75-yard dashes at the same meet. The following year she repeated her victory in the girls' 100-yard dash, and a month later, after moving up to the AAU senior women's level, she finished second in the 100-yard dash to Edith McGuire.

Winner in Consecutive Olympics

In 1963 Tyus enrolled at TSU so that she could continue training under Temple. One of her fellow athletes at TSU was AAU champion McGuire, with whom Tyus worked out. The intensified coaching and on-campus competition paid off when in 1964 she defeated McGuire to win the AAU 100-meter championship, earning a place on the United States Olympic team two weeks later.

At the 1964 Tokyo Olympic Games the little-known, nineteen-year-old Tyus was an underdog, but she suddenly gained attention when she won an early heat of the 100-meter dash, tying the world record of 11.2 seconds. She went on to win the gold medal in this event and then picked up a silver medal by anchoring the United States women's 4 x 100-meter relay team to a second-place finish.

Tyus returned to TSU and over the next few years performed so well that by general consensus she succeeded a former TSU star, Wilma Rudolph*, as the best female sprinter in the world. Tyus won AAU national sprint titles in indoor and outdoor competition ten times, setting world records at 50, 60, 70, and 100 yards. In 1967 she won the 200-meter title at the Pan American Games in Winnipeg, Canada.

In 1968 Tyus went to her second Olympics, this time in Mexico City. She was bombarded with warnings about the "repeat jinx," no one, man or woman, having been able to defend a 100-meter Olympic title successfully. The "jinx" had no effect on Tyus, however, who not only won the race but also set a new world record of 11.0 seconds. She then collected another gold medal by helping the United States women's 4 x 100-meter relay team win, again breaking the world record.

Sports Ambassador

Tyus retired from amateur athletic competition after the 1968 Olympics. Having graduated that year with a B.S. degree from TSU, she decided to begin her career in the workaday world in Los Angeles, where from 1969 to 1970 she was a research assistant at the Afro-American Center of the University of California at Los Angeles. During that time, in 1969, she married Art Simberg, a representative for a German sportswear company. They had two children, Simone and Tyus.

She taught physical education at Bret Harte Junior High School in Los Angeles from 1970 to 1972 and served as track coach at Beverly Hills High School from 1972 to 1973. Tyus encouraged her young athletes "to be competitive. . . but maintain a balanced outlook on sports because it is just one part of life."[2]

In 1973 the newly formed Professional International Track Association (PITA) drew Tyus out of athletic retirement. Her five-year layoff, of course, proved quite an obstacle to overcome, but with renewed intensive training, she managed to win eight out of eighteen races in her first year as a professional. The following year she won all twenty-two events she entered, and her popularity with spectators helped to give professional track a good start in the United States.

Tyus also viewed the professional circuit as a way for her to promote the role of women in the sport. "I've always felt that women's track and field in the United States has been on the bottom of the totem pole," she complained. "People hardly realize women run other than every four years. I believe we should get just as much recognition as the men do."[3]

Tyus competed for PITA from 1973 to 1975. Meanwhile, from 1973 to 1976 she also continued to develop her nonathletic career by working on the public relations staff for PITA.

With that preparation behind her, Tyus then embarked on a long career as an ambassador of sports. She has instructed at dozens of sports clinics in the United States and abroad, participated in many sports panels, lectured on the role of sports in culture, written the book *Inside Jogging for Women* (1978), and appeared on such television programs as *The Merv Griffin Show*, *ABC Superstars*, and *Challenge of the Sexes*. Among the jobs she has held are instructor for Sports and Career Development, sponsored by the United States Labor Department (1979–81), and public relations specialist for Coca-Cola USA (1981–84).

Tyus has used her sports background to help people in a wide variety of ways. She was a founding member of the Women's Sports Foundation, serving on its advisory board for several years; went to Africa as an official goodwill ambassador; and assisted the Olympic Experience Group, "where top competitors use their athletic backgrounds to show others how to cope with everyday life."[4]

Her accomplishments have earned Tyus many honors, including election to the Tennessee Sports Hall of Fame (1972), the United States Track and Field Hall of Fame (1976), the Black Athletes Hall of Fame (1978), the National Track and Field Hall of Fame (1980), and the International Women's Sports Hall of Fame (1981).

Wyomia Tyus's world records, Olympic medals (three gold and one silver), title of world's fastest woman, and role as sports ambassador have won her a special place in sports history. In particular, her achievement of the first ever consecutive Olympic victories in the 100-meter dash has given her a unique standing among all track athletes.

Sarah Vaughan

DIVINE ONE

(1924—1990)

SARAH VAUGHAN WAS known as a "musician's singer" because she not only had a wonderful vocal talent but also employed a precise musical technique. Friends called her Sassy, a nickname she liked because it conveyed her tough, fresh, chin-up approach to life. Admirers of her musical art called her the Divine, the Divine Sarah, or the Divine One.

Sarah Lois Vaughan was born in Newark, New Jersey, on March 27, 1924. She came from a musical family. Her father, Asbury Vaughan, a carpenter by trade, was an amateur guitarist and pianist, and her mother, Ada (Baylor) Vaughan, sang in the choir at Mount Zion Baptist Church in Newark.

As a child Sarah Vaughan joined her mother in the church choir and took piano and organ lessons. By the age of twelve she was an organist at Mount Zion. While attending Arts High School, she played piano in the band, continued her singing, and began to experiment with musical analysis. She developed an interest in jazz performance by sneaking into a neighborhood bar and listening to musicians, including the trumpeter Jabbo Smith.

A Singing Career That Began on a Dare

In October 1942 Vaughan, on a friend's dare, entered a jazz contest at the Apollo, a Harlem theater. She sang "Body and Soul" and won first prize, which was ten dollars and a week's engagement at the Apollo.

Billy Eckstine, a jazz vocalist, heard Vaughan at the Apollo and recommended her to his employer, Earl ("Fatha") Hines, who hired her to perform as a singer and pianist with his big band, which she joined in April 1943. In early 1944 Eckstine formed his own bop-oriented big band, and Vaughan joined him a few months later as a vocalist. After about a year she left Eckstine, and, except for a brief stint with John Kirby's group in the winter of 1945–46, thereafter she worked only as a soloist.

An important factor in Vaughan's transition from band member to soloist was George Treadwell, a trumpeter who became her husband and manager in 1946. He molded her attractive stage appearance and selected a musically rich repertory for her, and she soon became a sensation in concert appearances and on recordings. From 1947 through 1952 she won *Down Beat* magazine's annual award for best female singer, and from 1948 through 1953 she won similar awards from *Metronome* magazine.

After Vaughan's marriage to Treadwell ended in divorce in the late 1950s, in 1958 she married Clyde B. Atkins, who managed her till she filed for divorce in 1962. Her third and final marriage was to Waymon Reed, who played trumpet in her group, but they too divorced, in the early 1980s. She had close relationships with, but did not marry, several other men, including Marshall Fisher, who managed her during the 1970s. With Atkins she adopted a daughter, Debra, who became an actress under the name Paris Vaughan.

Concert Artist

Sarah Vaughan performed in many kinds of settings, ranging from solo recitals to the accompaniment of small ensembles to full symphony orchestras. Besides performing in venues such as clubs, theaters, college campuses, concert halls, and large stadiums, she also appeared on many television programs, for example,

New York Daily News

SARAH VAUGHAN

ics award for best female singer in 1973 and for the years 1975 through 1977.

Recording Artist

Vaughan made her first recording, "I'll Wait and Pray," on December 31, 1944, as a member of Billy Eckstine's group. With trumpeter Dizzy Gillespie and saxophonist Charlie Parker, she recorded "Lover Man" (1945), which established her lasting reputation as a jazz singer.

As a solo artist, leading her own recording sessions, Vaughan began with Musicraft, under which label she issued "Body and Soul" (1946) and other jazz discs. During her first contract with Columbia (1949–54), she recorded many ballads and one fine jazz piece with trumpeter Miles Davis, "Mean to Me" (1950). With Mercury (1954–59) she pursued a dual career, making commercial hits such as "Brokenhearted Melody" (1958) under the Mercury label, while recording jazz classics, including "Lullaby of Birdland" (1954) and the album *Sassy* (1956) through EmArcy, Mercury's jazz subsidiary.

Vaughan continued to mix popular and jazz recordings in

those hosted by Johnny Carson, Sammy Davis, Jr., Ed Sullivan, and others. Vaughan was a prized performer at the Monterey and Newport jazz festivals.

She undertook her first European tour in 1953, and subsequently made many international appearances, notably an extensive tour in the 1960s with the Count Basie Orchestra. Among the places she visited were Africa, Australia, England, Japan, and South America. International festivals frequently invited her, and she won the *Down Beat* International Jazz Crit-

her later contracts with Roulette, Mercury (again), Mainstream, Pablo, and Columbia (again). Highlights include *After Hours* (Roulette, 1961), *Sassy Swings Again* (Mercury, 1967), *Live in Japan* (Mainstream, 1973), *How Long Has This Been Going On?* (Pablo, 1978), *Send In the Clowns* (Pablo, 1981), *Gershwin Live!* (Columbia, 1982), *The Duke Ellington Songbook, volumes 1-2* (Pablo, 1979), and *Brazilian Romance* (Columbia, 1987). At the 1989 Grammy Awards she received a Lifetime Achievement Award.

"The Greatest Singing Talent"

Throughout her career Vaughan demonstrated the ability to perform in a wide range of styles and moods, from "easy listening" arrangements to complex jazz improvisations. Her heart and mind lay most of all in jazz. "I like to keep on improvising," she said in 1952, "even on songs I've been doing for years. I keep pretty close to the record version in theaters, but in nightclubs, I can let myself go."[1]

She was heavily influenced early in her career by listening to and studying the jazz improvisations of instrumentalists, especially Dizzy Gillespie and Charlie Parker. "I like horns," she said. "When I was singing with the [Hines] band, I always wanted to imitate the horns. Parker and Gillespie, they were my teachers."[2] Vaughan herself "negotiated wide leaps within her full-bodied contralto range, improvised subtle melodic and rhythmic embellishments, and made fluid alterations of timbre—from a bell-like clarity to a bluesy growl."[3]

"The greatest singing talent in the world today," declared no less an authority than Ella Fitzgerald*, "is Sarah Vaughan."[4] The Divine Sarah died in Hidden Hills, a Los Angeles suburb, on April 4, 1990.

Selected recordings:

SINGLES

(under Billy Eckstine's name)

"I'll Wait and Pray" (1944, DeLuxe)

SINGLES

(under Dizzy Gillespie's name)

"Lover Man" (1945, Guild)

SINGLES

(under Sarah Vaughan's name)

"Body and Soul" (1946, Musicraft)
"I Cover the Waterfront" (1947, Musicraft)
"It's Magic" (1947, Musicraft)
"Mean to Me" (1950, Columbia)
"Lullaby of Birdland" (1954, EmArcy)
"Make Yourself Comfortable" (1954, Mercury)
"Whatever Lola Wants" (1955, Mercury)
"Brokenhearted Melody" (1958, Mercury)

ALBUMS

In the Land of Hi-fi (1955, EmArcy)
Sassy (1956, EmArcy)
Linger Awhile (1956, Columbia)
Sarah Vaughan Sings George Gershwin (1957, Mercury)
No Count Sarah (1958, Mercury)
After Hours (1961, Roulette)
Count Basie and Sarah Vaughan (1963, Roulette)
Sarah + Two (1964, Roulette)
Sassy Swings Again (1967, Mercury)
Sarah Vaughan-Michel Legrand (1972, Mainstream)
Live in Japan (1973, Mainstream)
More Sarah Vaughan Live in Japan (1976, Mainstream)
I Love Brazil (1977, Pablo)
How Long Has This Been Going On? (1978, Pablo)
The Duke Ellington Songbook, volumes 1–2 (1979, Pablo)
Send In the Clowns (1981, Pablo) Columbia)
Gershwin Live! (1982, Columbia)
Crazy and Mixed Up (1982, Pablo)
Brazilian Romance (1987, Columbia)

Alice Walker

WRITER IN SEARCH OF MOTHERS' GARDENS

(1944—   )

ALICE WALKER, CURRENTLY the best-known African-American writer from the South, has played a major role in giving a long-overdue voice to black women in America. Her main thesis is found in her 1983 collection of essays, *In Search of Our Mothers' Gardens: Womanist Prose*, in which, according to Elizabeth Brown-Guillory in *Black Women in America*, "Walker argues that black women can survive only by recovering the rich heritage of their ancestors, particularly their black sister warriors. . . . Her message is that black women's personal salvation hinges upon recognizing their connectedness to women who historically have built bridges for them with their indomitable and independent spirit."[1]

Alice Malsenior Walker, the future novelist, poet, short story writer, essayist, and biographer, was born in rural Eatonton, Georgia, on February 9, 1944, the youngest of eight children of the cotton sharecroppers Willie Lee Walker and Minnie Tallulah (Grant) Walker.

When Alice Walker was eight years old, one of her brothers accidentally shot her in the eye with a BB gun, permanently blinding her in that eye. During her recovery she discovered the joy of reading, developed a sensitivity to the inner workings of human relationships, and began to record her feelings in a notebook.

Her Mother's Gardens

Walker's mother, Minnie, was known especially for the wonderful gardens she grew, but in fact she had vast creative talents, making with her own hands nearly everything Alice and her siblings used. From her Alice learned that African-American women, though discouraged from gaining formal education, nevertheless expressed their artistic and spiritual understanding through such media as gardening, cooking, quilting, and storytelling. Later Alice recalled her mother's gardens and used them as a symbol of all black women's cultural heritage in the essay "In Search of Our Mothers' Gardens: The Legacy of Southern Black Women" (1974).

Besides providing Alice with this cultural foundation, Minnie, who earned a salary of less than twenty dollars a week as a maid, gave her daughter three practical gifts that had meaningful long-term effects on the artist's life. One was a sewing machine, with which Alice could make her own clothes and learn the lesson of self-sufficiency. Another was a fine suitcase and permission to travel, giving her the opportunity to broaden her view of the world. The third gift was a typewriter, which Alice saw as a means of recording not only her own thoughts but also the heritage she saw embodied in her mother.

Student, Teacher, Activist

After graduating from high school Walker studied at Spelman College in Atlanta, Georgia, from 1961 to 1963 and then transferred to Sarah Lawrence College in Bronxville, New York, where she received a B.A. degree in 1965. Her experiences at both institutions had a lasting effect on her writing. At Spelman, a black women's college, she became involved with the civil rights movement, later the subject of many of her essays, her short stories, and her novel *Meridian* (1976). At Sarah Lawrence she became pregnant

Jean Weisinger

ALICE WALKER

marriage was illegal in Mississippi at that time, she and Leventhal lived in that state and had a daughter, Rebecca. They worked together to desegregate the Mississippi schools.

Walker served as writer in residence and teacher of black studies at two Mississippi colleges: Jackson State College in Jackson (1968–69) and Tougaloo College in Tougaloo (1970–71). Moving north, she lectured in literature at Wellesley College in Wellesley, Massachusetts, and at the University of Massachusetts in Boston (1972–73). After divorcing Leventhal in 1976 she moved first to New York City and then, in 1979, to San Francisco, where she still lives and writes.

Committed Writer

From the publication of her earliest book, *Once: Poems* (1968), Walker has been committed to exploring the lives of African-American women. Her works in the 1970s helped to generate the first widespread interest in black women's literary endeavors. In her novel *The Third Life of Grange Copeland* (1970) black women are physically abused by their husbands, but the abuse is triggered by societal ills, such as racism and sexism. Ultimately, one of the abusers, Grange Copeland, redeems himself by teaching Ruth, his granddaughter, to cling tightly to that inviolable place within her where she has the same potential to blossom as any other

and had an abortion, which led her to write a series of poems about her ordeal, published as *Once: Poems* in 1968.

After graduating from Sarah Lawrence, Walker returned to the South, helping in voter registration drives in Georgia and participating in campaigns for welfare rights and children's programs in Mississippi. Walker also lived for a time on New York's Lower East Side, working for the city's welfare department.

In 1967 she married Melvyn Rosenman Leventhal, a white civil rights lawyer, and although interracial

person. Through her characters in this book Walker suggests that no matter how horrible the external circumstances faced by black women, "they can," says Elizabeth Brown Guillory, "soar by finding in their mothers' gardens the roots that can bind, nurture, guide, and sustain them."[2]

In 1973 Walker published *Revolutionary Petunias and Other Poems* and *In Love and Trouble: Stories of Black Women. Revolutionary Petunias* traces the actions of southern black heroines in the civil rights movement, while *In Love and Trouble* shows how black women have fought back against the violence that dominates their lives.

In Walker's second novel, *Meridian* (1976), the title character gives up her son and devotes her life to freeing her people. "Walker," Elizabeth Brown-Guillory perceptively points out, "elevates Meridian to the symbolic mother of the black race."[3]

One of Walker's most important achievements in her quest to reconnect black women with their heritage was to rescue the neglected writings of the southern literary figure Zora Neale Hurston*. Walker wrote the essay "Looking for Zora" (1975) and edited *I Love Myself When I'm Laughing . . . and Then Again When I Am Looking Mean and Impressive: A Zora Neale Hurston Reader* (1979). In August 1973, when Walker placed a headstone on Hurston's previously unmarked grave, she performed an important symbolic act in building a black female literary tradition.

Walker's best-known work, *The Color Purple* (1982), was the first novel by an African-American woman to win a Pulitzer Prize. The book is a synthesis of characters and themes in her earlier writings, in which once again black women are abused and dehumanized, responding at one level with desperation but at another with increased faith in the emotional strength they derive from one another. Through the 1985 film version of the novel, directed by Steven Spielberg, Walker achieved a mass audience for her work.

In her essay collection *In Search of Our Mothers' Gardens: Womanist Prose* (1983), Walker coined the term *womanist* to differentiate black feminists from white feminists. She derived the word from a black folk expression, *womanish*.

Beginning with *The Color Purple*, which is set in both the United States and Africa, Walker extended her basic concerns to a global perspective. Her novel *The Temple of My Familiar* (1989) covers events in Central America, Europe, and Africa as well as the United States. *Possessing the Secret of Joy* (1992), her protest novel against female genital circumcision/ mutilation, is set in the United States, Europe, and Africa. With Pratibha Parmar she also wrote the nonfiction book *Warrior Marks: Female Genital Mutilation and the Sexual Blinding of Women* (1993), which presents a thorough analysis and condemnation of female genital circumcision/mutilation as practiced in certain African, Asian, and central European cultures.

Walker likewise enlarged her activism from the United States to other countries. For example, in 1995 she participated in an effort to pressure Nigeria's military government to restore democracy.

After reaching the age of fifty in 1994 Walker became retrospective, producing two major autobiographical works of nonfiction. *The Same River Twice* (1996) tells about her suffering during the time that *The Color Purple* was being filmed, as she was breaking up with her longtime lover, battling Lyme disease, and coping with her dying mother. Walker subtitled the book *Honoring the Difficult: A Meditation on Life, Spirit, Art, and the Making of the Film "The Color Purple," Ten Years Later*. She then looked back on her life as an activist in *Anything We Love Can Be Saved: A Writer's Activism* (1997), covering, among other subjects, religion, writing, families, and politics.

Awards and Honors

Walker has received many grants and fellowships, including a Guggenheim Fellowship (1977–78). She has also won many awards, among them the Lillian Smith Award from the Southern Regional Council (1973) for *Revolutionary Petunias and Other Poems*; the Richard and Hinda Rosenthal Foundation Award of the American Academy and Institute of Arts and Letters (1974) for *In Love and Trouble: Stories of Black Women*; the Pulitzer Prize and the American Book Award (both 1983) for *The Color Purple*; a Best Books for Young Adults citation from the American Library Association (1984) for *In Search of Our Mother's Gardens: Womanist Prose*; the O. Henry Award (1986) for "Kindred Spirits"; the Langston Hughes Award from New York City College (1989); the Fred Cody Award for lifetime achievement from the Bay Area Book Reviewers Association (1990); and the California Governor's Arts Award (1994).

A prolific writer and an original thinker, Alice Walker has had a great impact on contemporary literature and on the lives of her readers. In her writings she has repeatedly made the point that African-American women can survive and flourish in spite of racism and sexism "by armoring themselves with the knowledge of the heroic lives of their foremothers," according to Elizabeth Brown-Guillory. "She cogently argues that when a woman goes in search of her mother's garden she will ulitmately find her own."[4]

Selected writings:

FICTION

(novels unless otherwise indicated)

The Third Life of Grange Copeland (1970)
In Love and Trouble: Stories of Black Women (1973)
Meridian (1976)
You Can't Keep a Good Woman Down (short stories, 1981)
The Color Purple (1982)
The Temple of My Familiar (1989)
Possessing the Secret of Joy (1992), *By the Light of My Father's Smile* (1998)

NONFICTION

In Search of Our Mothers' Gardens: Womanist Prose (1983)
Living by the Word: Selected Writings, 1973–1987 (1988)
Warrior Marks: Female Genital Mutilation and the Sexual Blinding of Women (with Pratibha Parmar, 1993)
The Same River Twice: Honoring the Difficult: A Meditation on Life, Spirit, Art, and the Making of the Film "The Color Purple," Ten Years Later (1996)
Anything We Love Can Be Saved: A Writer's Activism (1997)

POETRY

Once: Poems (1968)
Five Poems (1972)
Revolutionary Petunias and Other Poems (1973)
Goodnight, Willie Lee, I'll See You in the Morning (1979)
Horses Make a Landscape Look More Beautiful (1984)
Her Blue Body Everything We Know: Earthling Poems, 1965–1990 Complete (1991)

JUVENILE FICTION

To Hell with Dying (1988)
Finding the Green Stone (1991)

JUVENILE NONFICTION

(biography)

Langston Hughes: American Poet (1973)

Madam C. J. Walker

PIONEER BUSINESSWOMAN AND PHILANTHROPIST

(1867—1919)

ENTREPRENEUR, hair-care industry pioneer, and political activist, Madam C. J. Walker promoted economic independence for black women in the United States. She was one of America's earliest self-made women millionaires and black philanthropists.

Originally named Sarah Breedlove, she was born on a cotton plantation in Delta, Louisiana, on December 23, 1867, the youngest of three children. Her parents, Owen and Minerva Breedlove, were newly freed from slavery, but Sarah was orphaned by the age of seven and spent much of her childhood working in the cotton fields. When the cotton crop failed in 1878, she and her older sister, Louvenia, moved to nearby Vicksburg, Mississippi, to work as domestics.

At the age of fourteen Sarah married Moses McWilliams. They had a daughter, Lelia (later called A'Lelia Walker), before Moses died in 1887.

After her husband's death Sarah moved with her daughter up to Saint Louis, Missouri, where for the next seventeen years she earned a meager living as a laundress. During that time she developed alopecia (baldness), which led her to become familiar with many hair and scalp products, some of which actually made the condition worse. Brought on by a combination of stress, poor diet, and various scalp diseases, alopecia was common among black women, and Sarah believed that she could make money by manufacturing better products for the condition than those currently on the market.

Walker Company

In July 1905 Sarah moved to Denver, Colorado, to join her deceased brother's wife and children. After she married Charles Joseph Walker, a newspaper sales agent, her new husband helped her to get her hair-product business started, especially by designing her advertisements and setting up a mail-order program. For business purposes she adopted the name Madam (a title often used by businesswomen at that time) C. J. Walker.

One of the Madam C. J. Walker Manufacturing Company's most popular products was a "hair growing" formula, which she later claimed had come to her in a dream in which "a big black man appeared to me and told me what to mix up for my hair. Some of the remedy was grown in Africa, but I sent for it, mixed it, put it on my scalp, and in a few weeks my hair was coming in faster than it had ever fallen out."[1]

She also developed the American hot comb (a steel hair-straightening comb) by adapting French metal combs and curling irons previously used on black women's hair. Her system immediately aroused controversy because many African-Americans voiced their opposition to black women altering their natural hair texture. Madam Walker, however, responded that her system did not fundamentally change the nature of African-American hair. "Right here let me correct the erroneous impression held by some that I claim to straighten the hair," she once told a reporter. "I want the great masses of my people to take a greater pride in their personal appearance and to give their hair proper attention."[2] She believed that her hot-comb technique produced a more natural result than the hair pullers utilized by her principal competitor, Annie Malone, maker of the Poro products and, like Walker, a self-made millionaire through the beauty business.

Madam Walker showed genius in her revolutionary

marketing program. After first trying her new products on her friends, she sold door to door and established a successful mail-order operation. In September 1906 she left the Denver mail-order business in her daughter's hands and began traveling with her husband for a year and a half to promote her products and train sales agents. Then, from 1908 to 1910 they operated Lelia College, a beauty parlor and training school for Walker "hair culturists," in Pittsburgh, Pennsylvania. Walker taught her students to cultivate both inner and outer beauty in their clients, whose homes the agents visited to provide hair services.

In 1910 Madam Walker moved her company to Indianapolis, the largest inland manufacturing center in America and a city with access to eight major railway systems. The company grew at a staggering pace. Besides running her thriving factory, Walker developed a national string of Walker Beauty Schools; opened a combination home and business base in New York City; effectively used A'Lelia's adopted daughter, Mae Bryant, as a model in an advertising campaign featuring the girl's long, thick hair; toured the United States to give slide lectures promoting her company; and expanded her business internationally by visiting Jamaica, Cuba, Haiti, Costa Rica, and the Panama Canal.

By 1916 the Walker Company had thousands of agents, men and women, in the United States, Central America, and the Caribbean. To protect her agents from competitors, she created the Madam C. J. Walker Hair Culturists Union of America, whose first convention was held in 1917. She also formed the first federation of black hair-care and cosmetics manufacturers.

The Schomburg Center / NYPL

During the years of business success, her marriage failed, however, and she divorced her husband, though she retained his name.

Late in her career Madam Walker looked back at her achievements not as a personal victory but as a paradigm for the economic independence of other black women. "I got myself a start by giving myself a start," she often said.[3] Others could do the same. "The girls and women of our race must not be afraid to take hold of business endeavor and . . . wring success out of a number of business opportunities that lie at their very doors . . . ," she said in a 1913 address. "I want to say to every Negro woman present, don't sit down and wait for the opportunities to come. . . . Get up and make them!"[4]

Philanthropy and Political Activism

In 1916 Madam Walker moved to Harlem, leaving the day-to-day management of her manufacturing operation to her Indianapolis staff and devoting much of the rest of her life to social and political issues.

Her involvement in such matters had actually begun years earlier. In 1911, for example, she donated one thousand dollars to the building fund of a Young Men's Christian Association branch for blacks in Indianapolis. In 1912, after being refused permission to speak at the National Negro Business League convention, she stood up and spoke anyway, powerfully impressing the mostly male delegates with the story of what she had done—and, by implication, what other black women could do—in the business world. The following year she was invited back as the keynote speaker.

In the spring of 1917 Madam Walker helped to recruit black soldiers to fight for the United States in World War I, believing that this show of loyalty would eventually result in a larger share of equal rights for all blacks. However, her approach changed after the bloody, lynching-provoked race riot in East Saint Louis, Illinois, that summer. She helped to organize the July 28 Negro Silent Protest Parade, in which ten thousand blacks silently marched down New York City's Fifth Avenue to protest the events in East Saint Louis. On August 1 she and other prominent blacks presented an antilynching petition to an aide to President Wilson. "This is the greatest country under the sun," she said later that month in an address at the first annual Walker Hair Culturists convention, "but . . . we should protest until the American sense of justice is so aroused that such affairs as the East Saint Louis riot be forever impossible."[5]

In early 1918 she was the keynote speaker at several antilynching fund-raisers held by the National Association for the Advancement of Colored People (NAACP) in the Midwest and East. That summer the National Association of Colored Women honored her for making the largest individual contribution to the fund for saving the Anacostia home of the famed black abolitionist Frederick Douglass.

In August 1918 Madam Walker officially opened her Irvington-on-Hudson, New York, estate with a gathering of notable blacks. For the rest of her life she used her home, Villa Lewaro, not only as her home but also as a venue for conferences by black leaders to discuss race matters. The estate also functioned as an inspiration for other African-Americans to follow their dreams.

In the spring of 1919, by now quite ill with hypertension, she donated five thousand dollars to the NAACP's antilynching campaign. She also adjusted her will to contribute thousands of dollars to black individuals, schools, institutions, and organizations.

Madam Walker died at Villa Lewaro on May 25, 1919, at the age of only fifty-one. Her daughter, A'Lelia Walker (1885–1931), succeeded her as president of the Madam C. J. Walker Manufacturing Company.

Madam Walker had a multidimensional effect on African-American history. She created an innovative hair-care system for black women, revolutionized the structure and marketing strategies of the black hair-care and cosmetics industry, gave lucrative business opportunities to black women at a time when the vast majority of them were employed as servants and sharecroppers, and changed the social perceptions and roles of black women by openly advocating their economic independence. She also pointed the way to the future by being "a trailblazer of black philanthropy," in the words of A'Lelia Perry Bundles (Madam Walker's great-great-granddaughter), "using her wealth and influence to leverage social, political, and economic rights for women and blacks."[6]

Maggie L. Walker
AMERICA'S FIRST WOMAN BANK PRESIDENT

(c. 1867—1934)

ONE OF THE MOST PROFOUNDLY influential activists of her time in a wide range of local and national black organizations, Maggie L. Walker won special renown as head of the Independent Order of Saint Luke, a society through which she created businesses that provided employment for African-Americans, especially black women, in over twenty states. As a result of her work at Saint Luke, she became the first woman bank president in the United States.

No official record exists of Maggie Lena Walker's birth. She claimed to have been born in Richmond, Virginia, on July 15, 1867, but she may have been born two or three years earlier. Her mother, Elizabeth Draper, was a domestic servant for the famous Richmond-based Union spy Elizabeth Van Lew. Maggie's father was Eccles Cuthbert, an Irish-born correspondent for the *New York Herald*.

After her mother married William Mitchell, the Van Lews' butler, in May 1868, the girl's name became Maggie Mitchell. The Mitchells moved to a house of their own, William took a job as a waiter at a hotel, and Elizabeth gave birth to a son, John, in 1870. In 1876 William Mitchell drowned. His death was officially deemed a suicide, but Maggie and others believed he was a victim of murder.

Maggie's mother then began to earn a living from her home as a laundress, and her daughter helped by picking up and delivering the laundry.

Maggie was baptized into the First African Baptist Church in 1878. Religion remained an important part of her life in later years, during which she was active in Baptist affairs and drew on the Bible in her speeches and diaries.

When she graduated from the Normal School in

1883, Maggie and her nine classmates tried to force the desegregation of the Richmond Theater, where white high school graduations were held. The class finally had to settle for holding their exercises at the school separately, but the graduates were widely praised in the black community for their efforts.

After her graduation Maggie taught both primary and grammar grades for three years at Valley, her old elementary school, but her teaching career ended in 1886 when she married Armstead Walker, who worked in his family's construction business and for some years as a mail carrier. Like Maggie, he was active in the affairs of the Independent Order of Saint Luke. They had three sons: Russell Eccles Talmadge, Armstead Mitchell (who died in infancy), and Melvin DeWitt. The Walkers also adopted Margaret ("Polly") Anderson, who became Polly Payne when she married. When Maggie traveled, Polly watched the family's children; and when Maggie became ill late in life, Polly cared for her.

Leader of the Independent Order of Saint Luke

While she was still in school, Maggie Walker joined Good Idea Council No. 16 of the Independent Order of Saint Luke, a mutual aid society in Richmond (founded in Baltimore, Maryland, by Mary Ann Prout). During the next decade or so she held, at one time or another, all the ritual positions in the order, served as a delegate to several Saint Luke conventions, and headed her Good Idea Council.

In 1895 Walker founded the order's Juvenile Division with Circles. Local councils formed the juvenile groups, which were headed by matrons, and Walker herself was elected the grand matron. "A powerful vehicle of socialization into race pride, thrift, responsibility, and mutual caring," wrote Gertrude W. Marlowe in *Black Women in America*, "Saint Luke's youth organization touched the lives of tens of thousands of children."[1]

In 1899 Walker was elected secretary, or head, of the Right Worthy Grand Council, the central organization of Saint Luke. Inheriting extremely limited resources, she soon transformed the society into a prosperous, diversified business.

Her first step was to enforce a compulsory life insurance plan for all Saint Luke members. Like many such societies, Saint Luke had for some time operated an optional internal insurance plan. By making the plan compulsory Walker immediately increased the organization's available revenues.

She also personally embarked on a series of vigorous membership drives, as a result of which Saint Luke eventually spread into twenty-two states. "She spoke everywhere," according to Gertrude W. Marlowe, "moving audiences to tears about disfranchisement, electrifying them with hope for cooperative enterprise, urging economic independence of the black community from the white community and women from men, exhorting women to enter the business world and black consumers to support black enterprise."[2] Though Saint Luke was primarily a women's organization, Walker saw to it that men played roles in the group's activities.

To increase the financial security of everyone associated with the society, Walker led the organization into a series of new business ventures, beginning with a newspaper, the *St. Luke Herald*, which flourished in 1902. Edited by Lillian Payne, the paper was noted for its outspoken editorials on such emotive topics as lynching and the status of women. A profitable printing business grew as a sideline out of the paper.

President of Saint Luke Penny Savings Bank

In 1903 Walker became the first woman bank president in the United States when her society opened the Saint Luke Penny Savings Bank. She prepared for her new role by daily studying banking for several months at the Merchants' National Bank of Richmond. Her principal task as head of the bank was to persuade Saint Luke members and other black residents in Richmond to trust the new institution, and under her leadership the bank grew slowly but steadily.

Several years later new banking regulations forced Saint Luke to separate itself technically from the bank, but the society remained the bank's major stockholder.

At the beginning of the Great Depression the Saint Luke Bank and Trust, as the bank was known by then, merged with two other banks to form the Consolidated Bank and Trust Company. Walker chaired the board of this new financial institution, the only black bank left in Richmond at that time.

Another Saint Luke business project that Walker oversaw was a department store called the Emporium, which opened in 1905. It provided employment for many women and at first did well, but pressure from white merchants and reluctance on the part of black consumers to change their shopping habits finally forced the store to close in 1911.

After 1911 Walker continued to guide Saint Luke in its banking and insurance ventures. Insurance was the more lucrative of the two businesses, and it provided many jobs for the society's women members. During Walker's lifetime Saint Luke never missed a death payment.

Energetic Activist

Besides her heavy involvement with the Independent Order of Saint Luke, Walker somehow managed to maintain leadership roles in a wide range of other black organizations. She served on the board of the Community House for Colored People, which evolved into the Richmond branch of the Urban League; helped to start the International Council of Women of the Darker Races; served on the board of the National Association for the Advancement of Colored People (NAACP); chaired consecutively the business, financial, and budget committees and was simultaneously a member of the executive committee of the National Association of Colored Women; helped to found Virginia's Negro Organization Society, which fought for better health and education; and was a member of the State Interracial Commission.

In 1912 Walker founded and became lifelong president of Richmond's Council of Colored Women (CCW), which supported Janie Porter Barrett's* Industrial School for Colored Girls and many other social service projects. The CCW's house on Clay Street was also used for other important activities in the black community, such as an office for the NAACP and a canteen for black servicemen in World War I. During the Great Depression, Saint Luke sold the house to the city, which converted the building into the first black library in Richmond. In 1991 the house became the Black History Museum.

Lame Lioness

In the midst of these public activities and accomplishments, Walker endured personal misfortunes. In 1915 her son Russell accidentally shot and killed his father, whom he mistook for a burglar. Russell (1890–1924) was indicted for, and acquitted of, murder, but he died young. In the late 1920s Walker began to lose the use of her legs, but she fought back, putting an elevator into her home, fitting her car for a wheelchair, and keeping up her professional duties. People began to call her the Lame Lioness.

Finally, however, she died in Richmond on December 15, 1934. Her house on Leigh Street later became a national historic site maintained by the National Park Service.

Maggie Walker's indomitable spirit shone through in these words from a speech she gave on race unity:

MAGGIE L. WALKER

The Schomburg Center / NYPL

"We can do; we will do; we are going to do now."[3] With that spirit she pioneered economic independence among African-American women.

Dionne Warwick

SINGER WHO BROKE DOWN MUSIC BARRIERS

(1940–   )

K NOWN FOR HER DEEP, husky, soul-filled voice and her seemingly effortless vocal agility, Dionne Warwick rose to stardom in the 1960s by singing the ingenious songs of composer Burt Bacharach and lyricist Hal David. Using their material, she "demolished the barriers that used to separate pop, rhythm and blues, jazz, and gospel singing."[1]

Originally named Marie Dionne Warrick, she was born in East Orange, New Jersey, on December 12, 1940, the eldest of three children of Mancel and Lee Warrick. (Dionne's surname was changed to Warwick by accident when a spelling error was made on an early recording contract.) Both of her parents worked in the music business. Her father, Mancel Warrick, directed gospel music promotion for Chess Records. Her mother, Lee Warrick, managed the Drinkard Sisters, the first gospel music group to sing at the Newport Jazz Festival and to be recorded by RCA Victor.

Dionne received early vocal training, especially in gospel music. She sang in the choir of the New Hope Baptist Church in Newark and sometimes performed with the Drinkard Sisters as a pianist or substitute vocalist.

In 1954 she joined her sister, Dee Dee, and her mother's cousin Emily ("Cissy") Houston (later the mother of the popular singer Whitney Houston*) in a group called the Gospelaires. The Gospelaires worked together for seven years as backup singers in recording studios and black theaters for lead groups such as the Drifters and individual stars such as Sam ("The Man") Taylor. In 1959 Dionne entered Hartt College of Music at the University of Hartford, Connecticut, where she studied voice, piano, and theory. During school vacations she continued to work with the Gospelaires.

Partnership with Bacharach and David

The big break in Dionne's career came at a recording session in 1960, where the Gospelaires were providing background for the Drifters in a recording of "Mexican Divorce," a song by Burt Bacharach and lyricist Bob Hilliard. When Bacharach heard Dionne, he knew that he wanted to write for her. As he worked more and more with her, he discovered that she had a gift for conveying deep emotion, combined with a rare ability to understand and perform his fresh but challenging musical style. Bacharach, probably the most sophisticated popular music composer of the 1960s, absorbed a wide range of contemporary elements—bop, rock, soul, progressive jazz, Tin Pan Alley, and other styles—and synthesized them into a unique sound, characterized by complex rhythms, bold harmonic progressions, flexible phrasing, and unconventional melodies featuring difficult-to-sing leaping intervals. He soon realized that in Dionne he had found his ideal interpreter.

In 1962 Warwick, Bacharach, and lyricist Hal David signed a contract with Scepter Records, through which they issued many of their most memorable recordings of the 1960s, the earliest of which was "Don't Make Me Over" (1962). In 1963 she left college and, with Bacharach's encouragement, began an extended concert tour. Her great Bacharach-David recordings during the rest of the decade included "Anyone Who Had a Heart" (1963), "Walk On By" (1964), "A Message to Michael" (1966), "Alfie" (1966), "I Say a Little Prayer" (1967), "Do You Know the Way to San Jose?" (1968), "This Girl's in Love with You" (1969), and "I'll Never Fall in Love Again" (1969).

"Hal and Burt don't write especially for me," she wrote in 1970. "It just feels that way. . . . It's like mental telepathy. We're on the same wavelength, wanting to say the same things about life and the living of it. . . . When I'm recording their songs I am recording *me*."[2]

During those years she also recorded a number of successful albums, among them *Make Way for Dionne Warwick* (1964), *Here Where There Is Love* (1966), *Dionne Warwick's Golden Hits, Part One* (1967), *Valley of the Dolls* (1968), *Soulful* (1969), and *I'll Never Fall in Love Again* (1970).

She also played a leading role in the film *Slaves* (1969), about the evils of American slavery, the soundtrack of which featured her singing.

Personal and Professional Changes

In the 1970s Warwick went through many personal and professional changes. Her 1967 marriage to Bill Elliot, a drummer and actor, with whom she had two sons, David and Damon, ended in divorce in 1975.

At about the same time a rift developed in her professional union with the Bacharach-David team. She cut her ties with them but continued to perform successfully in clubs and concert halls and on television variety and talk shows.

In the early 1970s Warwick also changed recording companies, from Scepter to Warner Brothers. (During this period she temporarily spelled her surname with a final *e*.) Her Warner singles included "If We Only Have Love" (1973) and "Then Came You" (1974), while her album output was highlighted by *Dionne* (1972).

After the arrangement with Warner proved unsatisfactory to her, Warwick recorded briefly for HBS and Musicor before signing with Arista, where she soon began to experience renewed success. Her initial album, *Dionne* (1979), was a hit, as were two of its tracks released as singles—"I'll Never Love This Way Again" and "Déjà Vu." Later hit singles with Arista included "Heartbreaker" (1982) and "All the

DIONNE WARWICK

Love in the World" (1982). Among her most popular albums were *No Night So Long* (1980), *Heartbreaker* (1982), and *Friends* (1985).

New Directions

"That's What Friends Are For," from the album *Friends*, became a major hit when released as a single. The song marked the beginning of a new phase in Warwick's career for at least two reasons.

First, it renewed her association with the song's composer, Burt Bacharach, whose wife, Carole Bayer Sager, wrote the lyrics. In 1987 Warwick and Bacharach went on a reunion tour.

The second change initiated by "That's What Friends Are For" was a broadening of Warwick's interests. She was joined in the recording by Elton John,

Gladys Knight, and Stevie Wonder, who united in their efforts so that the proceeds from the disc would benefit AIDS research. Warwick also gave concerts to support the same cause and founded the Warwick Foundation to help fight the disease.

Dionne has engaged in a wide range of other public-spirited causes, having established the Dionne Warwick Scholarship Fund as early as 1968. In addition, she was one of the dozens of performers who recorded the internationally successful "We Are the World" (1985) single, the proceeds of which were donated to African famine relief efforts. Warwick also founded the charity group BRAVO (Blood Revolves around Victorious Optimism) and became the spokesperson for an American society studying SIDS (sudden infant death syndrome). Among her many personal efforts were attending a service at the First African Methodist Episcopal Church in Los Angeles immediately after the 1992 race riots there, attending benefits for the National Council of Negro Women (1992) and the United Negro College Fund (1992), and participating in a Washington, D.C., hearing at which she called gangsta rap "pornography" (1994).

Musically, too, Warwick's interests widened after the mid-1980s. In her album *Dionne Warwick Sings Cole Porter* (1990) she extended her repertory back to the works of the songwriter who was, in his musical sophistication, the Bacharach of the first half of the twentieth century. Her album *Friends Can Be Lovers* (1993), featuring "Sunny Weather Lover," marked a reunion for her with Bacharach and David, who for this album wrote together for the first time in over twenty years. In 1994 Warwick released *Aquarela Do Brasil*, a collection of Brazilian songs.

With her mature command of an enriched repertory, Warwick continued to be a major performer in the 1990s. She hosted the cable television program Dionne and Friends (1990), performed at Caesar's Palace in Las Vegas (1992, 1994), toured with Bacharach in the United States (1992) and Europe (1995), and made many other appearances.

For her musical accomplishments and her social efforts, Warwick has received many awards and honors, including multiple Grammys, the National Association for the Advancement of Colored People (NAACP) Entertainer of the Year honor at the Image Awards (1986), the NAACP's Key of Life Award (1990), and the Humanitarian Award from the Congress of Racial Equality (1992).

Warwick has also engaged in other endeavors. In 1986 she began promoting a perfume named Dionne, and since the mid-1990s she has promoted the Psychic Friends Network on television.

Dionne Warwick holds a well-deserved special niche in the history of American popular music. "I had a different kind of sound," she has explained, "that was accepted by both the R & B [rhythm and blues] audience and the pop audience."[3]

Selected recordings:

SINGLES

"Don't Make Me Over" (1962, Scepter)
"Anyone Who Had a Heart" (1963, Scepter)
"Walk On By" (1964, Scepter)
"Alfie" (1966, Scepter)
"A Message to Michael" (1966, Scepter)
"I Say a Little Prayer" (1967, Scepter)
"Valley of the Dolls" (1968, Scepter)
"Do You Know the Way to San Jose?" (1968, Scepter)
"This Girl's in Love with You" (1969, Scepter)
"I'll Never Fall in Love Again" (1969, Scepter)
"If We Only Have Love" (1973, Warner)
"Then Came You" (1974, Warner)
"I'll Never Love This Way Again" (1979, Arista)
"Déjà Vu" (1979, Arista)
"Heartbreaker" (1982, Arista)
"All the Love in the World" (1982, Arista)
"That's What Friends Are For" (with other performers, 1985, Arista)
"Love Power" (with Jeffrey Osborne, 1987, Arista)
"Sunny Weather Lover" (1993, Arista)

ALBUMS

Make Way for Dionne Warwick (1964, Scepter)
Here I Am (1965, Scepter)
Dionne Warwick in Paris (1966, Scepter)
Here Where There Is Love (1966, Scepter)
The Windows of the World (1967, Scepter)
Dionne Warwick's Golden Hits, Part One (1967, Scepter)
Valley of the Dolls (1968, Scepter)
Promises, Promises (1968, Scepter)
Soulful (1969, Scepter)
Dionne Warwick's Greatest Motion Picture Hits (1969, Scepter)
Dionne Warwick's Golden Hits, Part Two (1969, Scepter)

I'll Never Fall in Love Again (1970, Scepter)
Very Dionne (1970, Scepter)
The Dionne Warwicke Story (1971, Scepter)
Dionne (1972, Warner)
A Man and a Woman (with Isaac Hayes, 1977, HBS)
Dionne (1979, Arista)
No Night So Long (1980, Arista)
Hot! Live and Otherwise (1981, Arista)

Friends in Love (1982, Arista)
Heartbreaker (1982, Arista)
How Many Times Can We Say Goodbye? (1983, Arista)
Friends (1985, Arista)
Reservations for Two (1987, Arista)
Dionne Warwick Sings Cole Porter (1990, Arista)
Friends Can Be Lovers (1993, Arista)
Aquarela Do Brasil (1994, Arista)

Ethel Waters

PATHBREAKING SINGER AND ACTRESS

(1896—1977)

I N A CAREER spanning half a century, Ethel Waters became one of America's most beloved and admired entertainers. She brought a new style to American popular singing and pioneered black participation in mainstream stage and screen productions.

Ethel Waters was born in Chester, near Philadelphia, Pennsylvania, on October 31, 1896. She was the daughter of Louise Anderson, a black woman, and John Waters, a white man who had raped Anderson. Soon after Ethel's birth Louise Anderson married another man and left her child in the care of Sally Anderson, Louise's mother.

When Ethel Waters was five years old, she made her first public appearance as an entertainer, singing under the billing of Baby Star in a children's program at a Philadelphia church. At the age of eight she saw her first vaudeville stage shows. Sometimes she stayed with her mother, who hired her out to work. Waters left school after the sixth grade, worked as a cleaning girl in Philadelphia, and at fifteen got a job as a hotel waitress in Wildwood, New Jersey, where she entertained her coworkers by singing and dancing in the bar.

Mother of Modern Popular Singing

On October 31, 1917, her twenty-first birthday, Waters made her singing debut by performing in a Philadelphia neighborhood saloon. Hearing her there, vaudeville agents signed her for a two-week engagement on the stage in Baltimore, Maryland, where she became the first woman to sing "St. Louis Blues" professionally.

She sang blues differently from the classic south-ern blues singers such as Ma Rainey* and Bessie Smith,* who performed with full voice and emotional abandon. Waters, heavily influenced by such white vaudeville singers as Nora Bayes and Fanny Brice, conveyed a more sophisticated, dignified kind of blues.

From early in her career she showed in her singing "an innate theatrical flair that enabled her to project the character and situation of every song she performed."[1] She could portray any emotional shading from comedy (as in "You Can't Stop Me from Loving You") to tragedy (as in "Stormy Weather"), a capability that, "in its range, was unsurpassed by any other popular singer."[2]

Her dramatic presentation, combined with a refined voice and a sense of intimacy, created a new, jazz-based style of interpreting popular music, while some of her techniques foreshadowed the scat-singing devices of Louis Armstrong and Ella Fitzgerald.* As a result of her influence over some other popular singers—notably Connee Boswell, Billie Holiday,* and Sarah Vaughan*—Waters came to be known as the Mother of Modern Popular Singing.

She sang in theaters, in nightclubs, and on both black and white vaudeville circuits. In the early 1920s she traveled with Fletcher Henderson's Black Swan Troubadors, with whom she became one of the first black entertainers to perform on radio. In 1925, while working at the Plantation Club in New York City, New York, she introduced the song "Dinah." In 1930 she appeared at the famous Palladium music hall in London, England, and in 1933, at the Cotton Club in the Harlem section of New York City, she and Duke Ellington introduced "Stormy Weather."

Waters developed an early interest in appearing in stage shows. After performing in *Hello, 1919!* (1919)

in Ohio, *Oh Joy!* (1922) in Boston, and *Plantation Revue* (1924) in Chicago, she made her Broadway debut in *Africana* (1927), a black revue. Continuing in New York City, she sang in *Blackbirds of 1930* (1930) and *Rhapsody in Black* (1931). In Irving Berlin's revue *As Thousands Cheer* (1933) she introduced "Heat Wave," became the first black to appear in an otherwise all-white cast on Broadway, and was the first black to costar—while on tour—with white players in the south. In the Broadway musical play *Cabin in the Sky* (1940) she excelled in the role of Petunia Jackson and introduced the title song and "Taking a Chance on Love." Her other stage work included the revues *At Home Abroad* (1935) and *Blue Holiday* (1945) and the one-woman shows *At Home with Ethel Waters* (1953) and *An Evening with Ethel Waters* (1959).

Waters began her recording career in 1921, and that year recorded "The New York Glide" (1921) and "At the New Jump Steady Ball" (1921). The first prominent black recording artist who was not a blues specialist, her later great recordings include "Kind Lovin' Blues" (1922), "Stormy Weather" (1933), and "Dinah" (1934).

Waters made her film debut in *On with the Show* (1929), in which she introduced "Am I Blue?" She also appeared in the screen version of *Cabin in the Sky* (1943), *Stage Door Canteen* (1943), and other movie musicals.

Dramatic Actress

Her success on the musical stage led to an opportunity to play a straight dramatic role in the Broadway play *Mamba's Daughters* (1939). As Hagar, the mother who kills her child's molester and then herself, Waters became the first black woman to take the leading role in a dramatic play on Broadway. To interpret this part, she drew from her memory of her own mother's courage in facing a tormented life after being raped. After Waters and the company had a long run on Broadway with *Mamba's Daughters*, the play went on tour before returning to New York City for another engagement.

In later years she played several other important nonmusical roles, the most memorable of which, for many fans and critics, was as Berenice Sadie Brown, the surrogate mother to a young tomboy, in *The Member of the Wedding*. After the play opened on Broadway in January 1950, the critic Brooks Atkinson

wrote, "Miss Waters gives one of those rich and eloquent performances that lay such a deep spell on any audience that sees her."[3] She appeared in *The Member of the Wedding* on Broadway and on tour during 1950–52 and repeated her role in successful revivals of the play in 1957, 1964, and 1970.

Waters also showed her dramatic talents in films and on television. In the movie *Pinky* (1949) she played Granny, for which she won an Academy Award nomination as best supporting actress. "All I had to do to play Granny well," she said, "was remember my own grandmother, Sally Anderson."[4] She also appeared in the movie version of *The Member of the Wedding* (1952) and played Dilsey in the film adaptation of William Faulkner's novel The Sound and the Fury (1959). From 1950 to 1952 Waters played the title role of the maid with a heart of gold in *Beulah*, the first nonmusical television series to star a black performer.

Her great success in serious roles opened many doors for black actors and actresses who followed her. "As a dramatic actress, Waters expressed for the first time in the white-dominated artistic medium the soul and heritage of black Americans, and is recognized as one of the American theater's greatest performers."[5]

Religious Singer

Waters had a difficult private life. As a child she was scarred by living in neighborhoods where alcohol and drug abuse, prostitution, and violence were endemic. Seeing the harmful effects of these influences on her friends and family members, she rejected such vices. "There was in me," she later said, "some great inner strength and a will power."[6]

She needed that strength in her marriages as well. In 1910, at the age of only thirteen and under pressure from her own mother, she married a man named Merritt ("Buddy") Purnsley, though she left him a year later. During the late 1920s and early 1930s she was married to Clyde Edward ("Eddie") Matthews, but that marriage, too, failed.

Waters candidly revealed the joys and sorrows of her life in her first autobiographical book, *His Eye Is on the Sparrow* (1951), widely praised not only for its self-revelations but also for its historically important disclosures about racial discrimination in the American entertainment industry. She derived the book title from a song that she had learned in church as a child.

Through the years of her adult life she always fondly remembered her early religious experiences, including two years in a Catholic school and, at the age of twelve, a spiritual awakening at a children's revival in a black Protestant church. By the 1950s, however, she had reached a point of spiritual crisis. She had ballooned up to 350 pounds and was deeply troubled. "I had fame, but I was empty," she confessed.[7]

Then she went to hear the evangelist Billy Graham preach at Madison Square Garden in New York City. She returned again and again while Graham clarified and satisfied her spiritual quest. For the rest of her life she spent much of her time attending, and singing at, Graham's crusades, at his Youth for Christ rallies, at sacred concerts in churches, and at religious conventions, using "His Eye Is on the Sparrow" as her signature song.

In 1971 she sang at a worship service at the White House, and the following year she published a second autobiography, *To Me It's Wonderful.* In August 1976, at Graham's San Diego Crusade, she sang for the last time. That same month she was diagnosed with cancer.

She died on September 1, 1977, in Chatsworth, California, near Los Angeles. One of the most beloved performers in American entertainment history, Ethel Waters permanently changed and enriched the arts of popular singing and dramatic acting.

Selected recordings:

SINGLES

"The New York Glide" / "At the New Jump Steady Ball" (1921, Cardinal)

"Kind Lovin' Blues" (1922, Black Swan)

"Go Back Where You Stayed Last Night" (1925, Columbia)

"Tell 'Em 'bout Me" / "I've Found a New Baby" (1925–26, Columbia)

"You Can't Stop Me from Loving You" (1931, Columbia)

"I Can't Give You Anything but Love" (1932, Brunswick)

"St. Louis Blues" (1932, Brunswick)

"Stormy Weather" (1933, Brunswick)

"Dinah" (1934, Decca)

"Stop Myself from Worryin' over You" (1939, Bluebird)

Selected performances:

STAGE

Hello, 1919! (1919)

Oh, Joy! (1922)

Plantation Revue (1924)

Africana (1927)

Blackbirds of 1930 (1930)

Rhapsody in Black (1931)

As Thousands Cheer (1933)

At Home Abroad (1935)

Mamba's Daughters (1939)

Cabin in the Sky (1940)

Blue Holiday (1945)

The Member of the Wedding (1950)

At Home with Ethel Waters (1953)

The Member of the Wedding (1957)

An Evening with Ethel Waters (1959)

The Member of the Wedding (1964)

The Member of the Wedding (1970)

FILMS

On with the Show (1929)

Gift of Gab (1934)

Cairo (1942)

Tales of Manhattan (1942)

Cabin in the Sky (1943)

Stage Door Canteen (1943)

Pinky (1949)

The Member of the Wedding (1952)

The Sound and the Fury (1959)

TELEVISION SERIES

Beulah (1950–52)

Maxine Waters

ADVOCATE FOR THE NATION'S DISADVANTAGED

(1938–   )

MAXINE WATERS BECAME ONE of the most powerful black women holding elective office in the United States. She led the passage of important social legislation as a member of the California State Assembly in the 1970s and 1980s, and following her election to the United States House of Representatives in 1990, she "emerged as the de facto spokesperson of the nation's disadvantaged."[1]

She was born Maxine Carr in Saint Louis, Missouri, in August 1938, the fifth of thirteen children of Remus and Velma (Moore) Carr, and after her parents' separation in 1940, she was raised by her mother.

To help support the family, Maxine went to work at the age of thirteen. She took a job as a bus girl in a segregated restaurant and later worked in a factory.

After graduating from high school at the age of eighteen, she married Edward Waters. They had two children: Edward and Karen.

In 1961 the Waters family moved to Los Angeles, where they hoped to find better employment opportunities, but they could find only low-paying jobs, she at a garment factory, and he at a printing plant. Later, Maxine found a job as an operator for Pacific Telephone, but complications following a miscarriage forced her to quit.

The turning point in her life came in 1966 when she discovered Head Start, a federally funded program to help children of low-income families. Maxine Waters became an assistant teacher at a school in the program and later won a promotion to supervisor of the school's volunteers. "Head Start made a significant difference in my life," she said in a 1990 interview. "It helped me see how I could help people, and it helped steer me into politics."[2]

By the early 1970s Waters was heavily involved in local and state political affairs. She served as a volunteer worker in several campaigns, led David S. Cunningham's successful bid for a seat on the Los Angeles City Council, and became Councilman Cunningham's chief deputy. During that period she earned a B.A. degree in sociology at California State University in Los Angeles.

However, her many new activities had an adverse effect on her marriage, which ended in divorce in 1972. Later she married Sidney Williams, a former professional football player who became a successful Mercedes-Benz salesman.

California State Assemblywoman

In 1976, ready to launch a campaign of her own, Maxine Waters ran on the Democratic ticket and won a seat in the California State Assembly.

At first her main interest in the assembly was women's issues, and after her research into women's problems revealed a need for community organizations to help women, in 1978 she cofounded one such group, the Black Women's Forum of Los Angeles. During that same year she led the passage of a bill providing pregnant women with up to four months' maternity leave and the guarantee of a return to their old job, or a similar one, on going back to work. Six years later, however, a federal judge overturned the legislation.

Waters sponsored a bill, successfully enacted in 1984, that prohibited the police from strip-searching people arrested for misdemeanors not involving weapons, drugs, or violence. The legislation was her response to horror stories of women and children who had been strip-searched for such minor offenses as dog-license delinquency and traffic violations.

One of her greatest achievements in the assembly was her bill barring California from investing in companies that engaged in trade with South Africa under apartheid. She had to reintroduce the bill half a dozen times over an eight-year period, but it finally passed in 1986. "If you believe in something," she explained, "you must be prepared to fight. To argue. To persuade. To introduce legislation again and again and again."[3]

Among the other important pieces of legislation that Waters backed were a bill that mandated long prison terms for drug dealers carrying weapons and a bill providing incentives for investment in low-income areas. She also helped to establish the Child Abuse Prevention Training Program, the first program of its kind in the United States.

Waters became the California State Assembly's first female majority whip, first woman member of the Rules Committee, and first person without a legal degree to sit on the Judiciary Committee. As chairperson of the Ways and Means Committee's Subcommittee on Business Development and Consumer, Veterans, and Employment Issues, she helped to pass legislation that gave more state contracts to minorities. She also chaired the Elections Reapportionment and Constitutional Amendments Committee.

United States Representative

By the 1980s Waters had her eye on national politics, and in 1988 she served as Jesse Jackson's California campaign manager during his bid for the presidency. When Augustus F. Hawkins announced his retirement as the Democratic representative of California's Twenty-ninth Congressional District in 1989 after nearly thirty years, the following year Waters easily won his seat in the United States House of Representatives.

After being assigned to the Veterans' Affairs Committee, she pressed for more minority representation on the committee staff, as a result of which two additional black members were added. After the end of the Persian Gulf War in 1991, she persuaded the committee to write legislation that would enable veterans who sued for job discrimination also to seek reimbursement for their legal expenses. During 1992 she served as an adviser to Bill Clinton in his successful run for the presidency.

In late April and early May of 1992 Los Angeles, especially her own south-central section of the city, erupted in race riots after four white police officers were acquitted of charges stemming from their videotaped beating of a black motorist, Rodney King. While not condoning the violence, Waters sympathized with the rioters because she saw their actions as a result of their feeling of hopelessness. At this time she became an unofficial spokesperson not only for her district but for all disadvantaged Americans—women, minorities, and the poor. "My life has to be about optimism," she told an interviewer just after the riots. "I can never believe that nothing can be done. I can never believe that there can't be change. I have to believe that not only can we change things, but that I can contribute to that."[4]

In 1994 and 1996 Waters won reelection to Congress. In 1995 she publicly blasted the Supreme Court's decision that electoral districts drawn to ensure the fair political representation of blacks and other minorities are unconstitutional if race is the predominant factor. In 1996 and 1997 she repeatedly called for a serious, unbiased investigation into allegations that the Central Intelligence Agency had flooded American inner cities with drugs to undermine the civil rights movement and to funnel the drug money to Nicaraguan contra rebels. In early 1998 she even persuaded Federal Reserve chairman Alan Greenspan to tour her district, hoping that the symbolism of his visit would induce corporations to invest there.

As a politician and spokesperson, Maxine Waters "makes every individual take note that we are her people and that African-Americans are of great and significant value to this country," a Los Angeles politician once said of her. "She is a powerhouse, a dynamo, and a very nurturing and caring woman who is a leader for us all."[5]

Ida B. Wells-Barnett

CRUSADER FOR JUSTICE

(1862—1931)

BORN INTO SLAVERY six months before the Emancipation Proclamation, Ida B. Wells-Barnett became a fiery fighter for civil rights in the post-Civil War period. Journalist, lecturer, feminist, and social activist, she is especially remembered today for leading an antilynching crusade in the late 1800s and early 1900s.

Ida Bell Wells was born in Holly Springs, Mississippi, on July 16, 1862, the eldest in a family of four boys and four girls. Her father, James Wells, was his master's son. Her mother, Elizabeth ("Lizzie") (Bell) Wells, was the daughter of a slave mother and an American Indian father. After emancipation James and Lizzie continued to work for their former owner as carpenter and cook respectively.

Rebellious Teacher

Encouraged by her parents, Ida seriously pursued an education at Rust College, a Holly Springs high school and industrial school for blacks. After passing her teachers' examination, she taught briefly in the rural area around Holly Springs. She then moved to Tennessee and taught at a rural school in Woodstock, outside Memphis. In 1884 she began teaching in the black public schools of Memphis.

However, her career in education was disrupted by a train ride in May 1884. She bought a first-class ticket on a train from Memphis to Woodstock. After she took her seat, the conductor asked her to move to a Jim Crow car, which was a smoker. She refused, got off the train, and later filed a suit against the Chesapeake, Ohio, and Southwestern Railroad Company. In December 1884 the Memphis circuit court ruled in her favor, fining the company and awarding her personal damages. But the railroad appealed, and in April 1887 the Tennessee Supreme Court reversed the lower court's decision because the railroad had legally provided "like accommodations." Embittered, Wells-Barnett began to focus her attention more on the pursuit of civil rights than on education.

It was during that time that she became involved in journalism. While continuing to teach, she was invited to take over the editorship of a journal for teachers, the *Evening Star*; began writing, under the pen name Iola, for a religious weekly, the *Living Way*, and then for the black press throughout the country; and in 1889 became editor and part-owner of the black newspaper *Free Speech and Headlight*.

In 1891, after Wells wrote an editorial critical of the Memphis school board for providing inadequate education at black schools, the board fired her. She then turned her full attention to her newspaper, whose name she shortened to *Free Speech* (or *Memphis Free Speech*).

Fearless Journalist

Wells wrote a stream of angry protest editorials in her newspaper. In one of her most controversial pieces, published in 1891, she condoned the action of blacks in Georgetown, Kentucky, who set fire to the town to avenge the lynching of a black man. "Not until the Negro rises in his might and takes a hand in resenting such cold-blooded murders," she wrote, "if he has to burn up whole towns, will a halt be called in wholesale lynching."[1]

In 1892 the issue of lynching came crashing into Wells's own life. When three black friends of hers opened a Memphis grocery store that took business away from a nearby white shopkeeper, violent confrontations ensued, leading to indictments against the blacks. After dark on March 5 nine plainclothes deputies approached the blacks' store. Friends of the owners, taking the deputies to be a mob, shot and wounded three of the officers, after the store owners and scores of other blacks were arrested, nine white men took the three store owners from the jail on March 9 and shot them to death.

In her editorial on this incident, Wells denounced the lynching. Blacks, she wrote, must leave Memphis, "which will neither protect our lives and property, nor give us a fair trial in the courts, but take us out and murder us in cold blood when accused by a white person."[2] Throughout that spring she continued to call for the arrest of those responsible for the murders of her three friends.

When she went to Philadelphia to attend an African Methodist Episcopal church convention in May 1892, on May 23, while she was gone, intruders destroyed the *Free Speech* presses and offices. Wells was warned not to return to Memphis.

She then became a columnist for, and part-owner of, the *New York Age* in New York City and continued her battle against racial injustice, especially lynching, which, she argued, stemmed not from the defense of white women (as claimed by the lynchers) but from whites' fear of economic competition from blacks. She wrote the books *Southern Horrors: Lynch Law in All Its Phases* (1892) and *A Red Record: Tabulated Statistics and Alleged Causes of Lynchings in the United States, 1892–1893–1894* (1895).

Lecturer at Home and Abroad

Seeking to reach a wider audience, Wells began lecturing throughout the Northeast and abroad. During April and May 1893 she lectured in England, Scotland, and Wales, informing the British public about the lynching of blacks in America's South.

Later in 1893 she moved to Chicago, where she began working for the *Chicago Conservator*, the first black American newspaper in that city, and also established Chicago's first civic club for black women. Wells had a strong influence on the black women's club movement in America, being one of the most outspoken voices calling for black women to become involved in local and national issues.

In February 1894 she went back to England and , speaking on more than one hundred occasions, told the English that lynching in America had increased in frequency and ferocity. Because of her efforts, English sympathizers formed an antilynching committee that investigated and publicized the issue.

Crusader for Justice

In July 1894 Wells returned from her European tour and soon began lecturing throughout the northern and western states and organizing antilynching committees.

In June 1895 she married Ferdinand Lee Barnett, a black lawyer and editor who had founded the *Chicago Conservator*. They had four children: Charles Aked, Herman Kohlsaat, Ida B. Wells, and Alfreda M. Alfreda became Mrs. Duster and edited and published her mother's autobiography as *Crusade for Justice* (1970).

Marriage and children did not slow down Wells-Barnett's crusade for justice. She continued to write articles and to participate in local and national affairs. In 1898 she was a member of a delegation that called on President McKinley to demand action in the case of a black postmaster lynched in South Carolina. In 1900 she worked with Jane Addams in successfully blocking the establishment of segregated schools in Chicago.

In 1909 Wells-Barnett was one of two (with Mary Church Terrell*) black women who signed "The Call" for a conference "To Discuss Means for Securing Political and Civil Equality for the Negro." The meeting, which convened on May 31, 1909, in New York City, led to the formation of the National Association for the Advancement of Colored People (NAACP) in May 1910. Wells-Barnett became one of the original members of the executive committee.

In 1910 she founded the Negro Fellowship League, which provided lodging, social, and job services for men in need, and three years later she founded the Alpha Suffrage Club of Chicago, the first suffrage organization for black women. From 1913 to 1916 she served as a probation officer for the Chicago municipal court, working out of the Fellowship League's social center and contributing her salary to the center's budget.

Following the 1917 race riot in East Saint Louis, Illinois, Wells-Barnett went there on three different occasions to seek legal aid for black victims of mob violence. In a July 7, 1919, letter to the *Chicago Tribune*, she warned that Chicago faced a similar upheaval if it did not "set the wheels of justice in motion before it is too late."[3] The city took no action, and a few weeks later it endured one of the country's bloodiest race riots, in which nearly forty people were killed and hundreds injured.

Nevertheless, Wells-Barnett stayed in Chicago and remained active in its affairs. In the 1920s she helped to found the Cook County League of Women's Clubs. In 1930 she entered Chicago politics, running unsuccessfully as an independent candidate for state senator.

On March 25, 1931, Ida B. Wells-Barnett died in Chicago. In 1941 a housing project in Chicago was named after her, and in 1950 she was named one of the twenty-five most outstanding women in the city's history. In 1987 even Memphis finally honored her, dedicating a historical marker to her at the site where the *Free Speech* had stood.

Selected writings:

NONFICTION

Southern Horrors: Lynch Law in All Its Phases (1892)

"Afro-Americans and Africa" (article, *AME Church Review*, July 1892)

The Reason Why the Colored American Is Not in the World's Columbian Exposition (with Frederick Douglass, 1893)

A Red Record: Tabulated Statistics and Alleged Causes of Lynchings in the United States, 1892–1893–1894 (1895)

Mob Rule in New Orleans: Robert Charles and His Fight to Death, the Story of His Life, Burning Human Beings Alive, Other Lynching Statistics (1900)

IDA B. WELLS-BARNETT

The Schomburg Center / NYPL

"Lynch Law in America" (article, *Arena*, January 1900)

"How Enfranchisement Stops Lynchings" (article, *Original Rights*, June 1910)

"Our Country's Lynching Record" (article, *Survey*, February 1913)

Crusade for Justice: The Autobiography of Ida B. Wells (edited by Alfreda M. Duster, 1970)

Phillis Wheatley

FOUNDER OF AFRICAN-AMERICAN LITERATURE

(c. 1753—1784)

PHILLIS WHEATLEY was the first black American, male or female, to publish a book. She issued her *Poems on Various Subjects, Religious and Moral* in London, in 1773. Beyond being merely the first to publish, she produced a quality of style and a range of themes that inspired generations of black writers after her. Wheatley is justifiably regarded as the founder of African-American literature.

Born about 1753, probably along the Gambia River in western Africa, she was brought to America on a slave ship named *Phillis* and purchased in Boston in July 1761 by John and Susanna Wheatley, who named her for the ship in which she had sailed and gave her their surname.

Soon after beginning to work for the Wheatleys as Susanna's personal maid, Phillis started to show signs of being intellectually gifted. She tried, for example, to write letters of the alphabet on a wall. The Wheatleys' daughter, Mary, began to instruct her in reading the Bible. After just sixteen months in the New World, Phillis could read English, and later she mastered Latin too.

Slave-Poet

After only four years' exposure to the English language, Phillis Wheatley began to write poetry. Her first published poem appeared in the *Newport Mercury*, a Rhode Island newspaper, on December 21, 1767, and in the fall of 1770 she established a widespread readership with the publication of an elegy on the death of the Reverend George Whitehead, an internationally popular Methodist evangelist. Over the next couple of years she published several more well-received elegies in broadsides and newspapers in North America and England.

In 1772 Wheatley attempted to find subscribers in Boston for a proposed volume of her poems, but her efforts failed, principally because not enough people would support the work of a black poet.

In England, however, a wealthy philanthropist, Selina Hastings, countess of Huntingdon, agreed to back the project. During the year and a half between that agreement and the actual publication, Wheatley changed the character of the book. The original version would have appealed to a patriotic American readership, with such politically motivated titles as "On America," "On the Arrival of the Ships of War, and Landing of the Troops," and "To Samuel Quincy, Esq; a Panegyrick." The revised version was aimed at a British readership, with such aesthetically directed titles as "To Maecenas," "Thoughts on the Works of Providence," and "On Imagination."

Wheatley, with her owners' permission, sailed to England in the spring of 1773 to supervise the publication of her work. The volume, published in London in early September 1773, was titled *Poems on Various Subjects, Religious and Moral by Phillis Wheatley, Negro Servant to Mr. John Wheatley, of Boston, in New England.* However, about a month before the publication she returned to America to care for Susanna Wheatley, who was seriously ill.

Freedom and Marriage

Shortly after Phillis Wheatley's return to Boston, John Wheatley set her free, under pressure from her British friends and admirers. Nevertheless, she remained in the Wheatleys' household, tending to her former owners in their last years. Susanna died in March 1774.

In October 1775, while living in Providence, Rhode Island, where John Wheatley had moved his household after the British occupied Boston, Phillis Wheatley sent a letter and poem of praise to George Washington, commander in chief of the American Revolutionary Army. The poem was published by Washington's friends several times to feed the fire of patriotism, and the next year Washington invited her to visit him at his headquarters.

In March 1778 John Wheatley died, and the following month Phillis Wheatley married John Peters, a free black man who had failed at various business ventures but had personal dignity and served as an advocate on behalf of blacks before Massachusetts tribunals. The death of John Wheatley and the disappointments of John Peters left Phillis Wheatley with severely limited financial resources.

In 1779 she tried and failed to obtain enough subscribers to publish a new volume of poetry. Again racism may have played a part, but an even greater problem was the scarcity of money available for such a venture during the Revolutionary War. Wheatley published nothing for the next several years, but in 1784 she published three elegies and "Liberty and Peace," a tribute to the victory of the American Revolution.

On December 5, 1784, Phillis Wheatley died in Boston, probably from an infection contracted while giving birth to her third child. The baby, like Wheatley's two previous children, did not survive.

Founder of African-American Literature

Wheatley based her poetic style on the neoclassical heroic couplet form popularized by the eighteenth-century English writer Alexander Pope. She was also influenced by her American contemporaries Mather Byles and Samuel Cooper as well as by classical Greek, Latin, and English poets. For example, Milton's *L'Allegro* and *Il Penseroso* inspired her hymns to the sun and the evening.

To these stylistic influences, however, Wheatley added elements of originality. Her treatments of several genres— including the elegy, the lyric, and the panegyric—reflect her African origins and separate her from other English-language writers of her time.

The elegy is probably the clearest example. During her first seven or eight years of life, she would certainly have observed the African tradition of funeral dirges composed and performed almost exclusively by girls and women rather than men. In America she wrote eighteen known elegies, almost half of her extant work. An important feature in the African dirge was that the singer pointed out examples of the departed's wisdom and lamented her personal loss of a wise counselor. Wheatley fulfilled those requirements in her elegies for Joseph Sewall (1769), the pastor of her church and the spiritual adviser of her youth, and for Samuel Cooper (1784), the minister-poet who baptized her and encouraged her writing. Such personal acknowledgments linked her work with African tradition but were uncharacteristic of American and British elegies of the time.[1]

Like her multiple stylistic influences, Wheatley's thematic range was inclusive. She wrote about classical subjects ("Niobe in Distress"), philosophical reflections ("On Recollection"), notable contemporaries (numerous elegies), and other topics. Her principal interest was the quest for freedom, overtly demanded for her fellow Americans and subtly sought for her fellow blacks.

Wheatley wrote many patriotic poems and letters. Her commitment to the revolution was so strong that even during her time as a slave she openly opposed the Loyalist politics of her owners, John and Susanna Wheatley. Phillis Wheatley's call for American freedom can be seen in "On the Arrival of the Ships of War, and Landing of the Troops" and other poems. Her poem to George Washington includes these lines: "Proceed, great chief, with virtue on thy side, / Thy ev'ry action let the goddess guide."[2] When the victory was won, she celebrated with "Liberty and Peace."

In some of her writings Wheatley linked American freedom with black liberation. Such was the case in "To the Right Honourable William, Earl of Dartmouth, His Majesty's Principal Secretary of State for North-America, Etc." (published in *Poems on Various Subjects, Religious and Moral*). Wheatley hoped to induce the addressee, William Legge, Lord Dartmouth, newly appointed secretary in charge of the American colonies, to address American grievances. After poetically presenting the American case, she explained the source of her love of freedom: "I, young in life, by seeming cruel fate / Was snatch'd from *Afric's* fancy'd happy seat: / What pangs excruciating must molest, / What sorrows labour in my parent's breast?"[3]

Another example of this linkage is in a 1774 letter she sent to Samson Occom, a Mohegan Indian and ordained Presbyterian minister who had written a strong criticism of slaveholding Christian clergymen. It was incongruous, she wrote, for these clergymen to call for their own liberation from Britain while simultaneously holding slaves, "for in every human Breast [not just white ones], God has implanted a Principle, which we call Love of Freedom; it is impatient of Oppression, and pants for Deliverance."[4]

One of her subtlest works is "On Imagination" (published in *Poems on Various Subjects, Religious and Moral*). Through this poem Wheatley, then still a slave, attained freedom, at least briefly, through her imagination. The poet never mentions slavery but couches the quest for liberation in ethereal terms, escaping into another realm: "*Imagination!* who can sing thy force? / . . . We on thy pinions can surpass the wind, / And leave the rolling universe behind." Finally, however, she must put down her pen and return to cold reality (slavery): "But I reluctant leave the pleasing views, / Which Fancy dresses to delight the *Muse*; / *Winter* austere forbids me to aspire."[5]

Wheatley's best-known poem is "On Being Brought from Africa to America" (published in *Poems on Various Subjects, Religious and Moral*). In the opening lines the poet expresses her joy at learning Christianity in the New World, but she concludes the poem by teaching her teachers about the equality of souls: "Remember, *Christians*, *Negros*, black as *Cain*, / May be refin'd, and join th' angelic train."[6]

Phillis Wheatley had no literary models to guide her except those of white Europe and America. Mastering those models and drawing on her childhood memories of Africa and her experiences as a slave, she created a new, African-American literature.

PHILLIS WHEATLEY

The Schomburg Center / NYPL

Selected writings:

NONFICTION AND POETRY

Poems on Various Subjects, Religious and Moral (1773)
Letters of Phillis Wheatley (edited by Charles Deane, 1864)
The Collected Works of Phillis Wheatley (edited by John C. Shields, 1988)

Vanessa L. Williams

VERSATILE ENTERTAINER

(1963–)

VANESSA L. WILLIAMS rose to prominence by becoming the first black to win the Miss America contest. Later she used the same poise and musical talent that earned her that title to establish herself as one of the most versatile entertainers of her generation, attaining great success as both an actress and a recording artist.

Vanessa Lynn Williams was born in New York City on March 18, 1963, the elder of two children of Milton and Helen Williams. A year later the family moved to the small town of Millwood, about thirty-five miles north of New York City.

Her parents, who both taught music in public schools, subjected Vanessa and her younger brother, Christopher, to a grueling schedule of music and other performing arts studies for many years. She studied French horn, piano, mellophone, dancing, acting, and modeling. "We were not concerned about her becoming a professional musician," her father later explained. "We wanted her to have as many options as possible. It gives her a great sense of freedom."[1]

At Horace Greeley High School in Chappaqua, New York, Vanessa L. Williams became a star performer in plays and musicals, sang in the school chorus, and played French horn in the school band and orchestra. She was also named to the All-State Women's Choir and the All-County Orchestra. In 1981 she enrolled at Syracuse University, where she majored in musical theater.

First Black Miss America

In the spring of 1983 the executive director of the Miss America Greater Syracuse Pageant, impressed by Williams's performance in a college show, asked her to enter the contest. Previously Williams had regarded beauty pageants as "exploitative meat shows."[2] However, she finally agreed to enter, partly because much of the contest centered on a talent competition, which naturally interested her, but mostly because the exposure would benefit her theatrical ambitions and because, if she won the top Miss America prize, she would earn large personal appearance fees.[3]

In April 1983 Williams won the Miss America Greater Syracuse Pageant and soon thereafter took the Miss New York State pageant. In September 1983, she impressed the judges enough with her combination of beauty, intelligence, and singing talent to win the title of Miss America.

She held the crown for only ten months. In July 1984 it was discovered that in the summer of 1982, while employed as a receptionist at the TEC Model Registry in Mount Kisco, New York, she had posed for a series of sexually explicit photographs with another woman. At the time of the photographs Williams was an unworldly teenager, eager to advance her career but uncertain how to do so. On July 23, 1984, under pressure from pageant executive committee members, she stepped down, the first Miss America to abdicate in the history of the pageant. She was succeeded by Suzette Charles, a black woman representing New Jersey.

Entertainer

After giving up her crown Williams abandoned her plans to continue her studies at Syracuse. Instead, she immediately plunged into her career as a professional

VANESSA WILLIAMS

Right Stuff, which contains several tracks that became hits when they were subsequently issued as singles, including "Dreamin'." The album won the Best New Female Artist Award from the National Association for the Advancement of Colored People. Among her later releases were the albums *The Comfort Zone* (1991) and *The Sweetest Days* (1994) and the singles "Save the Best for Last" (1992), "Love Is" (a duet with Brian McKnight, 1993) and "Colors of the Wind" (1995). During those years she supplemented her recording efforts with frequent appearances as a singer on television series and specials.

While pursuing her singing career, Williams also built an equally illustrious reputation as an actress. She had roles in several made-for-television movies, including *Full Exposure: The Sex Tapes Scandal* (1989), *Stompin' at the Savoy* (1992), and *Bye Bye Birdie* (1995), as well as the miniseries *The Jacksons: An American Dream* (1992), in which she played the president of Motown Productions in a story about the Jackson Five, and *The Odyssey* (1997). In 1992 she had a recurring role as the aerobics instructor Rhonda Blair in the popular series *Melrose Place*, and in 1995 she regularly played the receptionist Lila Marquette in *Murder One.*

Williams made her motion picture debut in *The Pickup Artist* (1987) and appeared in several other films in the late 1980s and early 1990s, such as *Under the Gun* (1989), *Another You* (1991), and *Candyman* (1992). Her film work exemplifies her wide-ranging acting capabilities. She successfully played in the thriller *Drop Squad* (1994), the comedy *Mother* (1996), the action picture *Eraser* (1996), and the drama *Soul Food* (1997), a story about an embattled Chicago family.

Williams has also returned to her youthful roots on the musical stage. In the summer of 1994 she made a striking impression in the title role of the Broadway musical *Kiss of the Spider Woman.* Later

entertainer. Her parents' foresight in providing her with a well-rounded education in the performing arts now paid dividends. She soon began to make appearances on various television programs, such as the music special *Motown Returns to the Apollo* (1985) and the sitcom *The Redd Foxx Show* (1986).

In 1987 she married Ramon Hervey II, a public relations specialist who became her manager. They had three children—Melanie, Jillian, and Devin—before divorcing in 1997.

Hervey helped to guide Williams into a recording career, signing her with Wing Records, a division of Polygram. In 1988 she released her debut album, *The*

that year she performed on the New York City stage in *Gypsy of the Year*.

Her versatile singing and acting achievements have made Vanessa L. Williams one of the most popular entertainers of her time. In 1996 Syracuse University, from which she dropped out to pursue her spectacular career, presented her with the George Arents Pioneer Medal, the university's highest alumni award.

Selected recordings:

SINGLES

"The Right Stuff" (1988, Wing/Polygram)
"Dreamin'" (1989, Wing/Polygram)
"Runnin' Back to You" (1991, Mercury)
"Save the Best for Last" (1992, Wing/Polygram)
"Love Is" (with Brian McKnight, 1993, Giant)
"Colors of the Wind" (1995, Hollywood)

ALBUMS

The Right Stuff (1988, Wing/Polygram)
The Comfort Zone (1991, Wing/Polygram)
The Sweetest Days (1994, Wing/Polygram)

Selected performances:

STAGE

Kiss of the Spider Woman (1994)
Gypsy of the Year (1994)

FILMS

The Pickup Artist (1987)
Under the Gun (1989)
Skin Deep (1989)
Another You (1991)
Harley Davidson and the Marlboro Man (1991)
New Jack City (1991)
Candyman (1992)
Drop Squad (1994)
Mother (1996)
Eraser (1996)
Hoodlums (1997)
Soul Food (1997)
Dance with Me (1998)

TELEVISION MOVIES

Full Exposure: The Sex Tapes Scandal (1989)
Perry Mason: The Case of the Silenced Singer (1990)
The Kid Who Loved Christmas (1990)
Stompin' at the Savoy (1992)
The Jacksons: An American Dream (1992)
Bye Bye Birdie (1995)
The Odyssey (1997)

TELEVISION SERIES

Melrose Place (1992)
Murder One (1995)

Oprah Winfrey
QUEEN OF THE TALK SHOW HOSTS

(1954–   )

OPRAH WINFREY, "a real person in the fake world of TV,"[1] has hosted the highest-rated television talk show in history, *The Oprah Winfrey Show*, since 1986. The show's greatest attraction is Winfrey herself, who tends to feel, not just talk about, the problems under discussion. "In acting you lose your personality in favor of the character you're playing," she has explained, "but you use it to provide energy for your character. The same way on my show. I lose it and use it to concentrate on bringing the most out of my guests."[2] Her willingness to empathize with people in distress and to expose her own vulnerability has endeared her to millions of viewers.

Oprah Gail Winfrey was born in Kosciusko, Mississippi, on January 29, 1954, to Vernon Winfrey and Vernita Lee. Her parents intended to name her Orpah, after Ruth's sister-in-law in the Bible, but on her birth certificate the second and third letters were mistakenly transposed, making the name Oprah. Her parents separated when Oprah was young, and she spent her earliest years on a Mississippi farm with her maternal grandmother. Oprah was an outgoing child, speaking in public at the age of two when she addressed a church congregation on the topic "Jesus rose on Easter day" and learning to read at about the same time.

When she was six, she was sent to live with her mother in Milwaukee, Wisconsin. Oprah became known as "the little speaker" and recited poetry at black social clubs and church teas. At the age of twelve, while visiting her father in Nashville, Tennessee, she earned five hundred dollars for delivering a speech at a church. Afterward she announced that her career goal was to be "paid to talk."[3]

On her return to Milwaukee, however, she again suffered a prolonged private torment, which included sexual abuse, and ultimately she ran away from home. In 1968 her mother sent her to live with her father, a barber who became a member of the city council, and his wife in Nashville.

It was Vernon Winfrey who gave Oprah the discipline she needed. Under his guidance she blossomed, excelling in her studies, presiding over the East Nashville High School council, joining the drama club, and distinguishing herself in oratory and debate. A local radio station, WVOL, impressed by her voice, hired her to read newscasts during her senior year.

After graduating from high school in 1971, Oprah Winfrey entered Tennessee State University in Nashville. During her freshman year there she won the Miss Black Nashville and Miss Black Tennessee titles.

Early Television Jobs

In 1973, as a nineteen-year-old college sophomore, Winfrey accepted an offer from WTVF-TV, the Nashville CBS affiliate, to coanchor the evening news, becoming the city's youngest and first black female newscaster. Meanwhile, she continued to attend classes until 1976, when she left college and WTVF-TV to accept a job as news coanchor at WJZ-TV, the ABC affiliate in Baltimore, Maryland. The following year she became cohost, with Richard Sher, of the station's *People Are Talking*, a morning talk show. "This is what I was born to do," she said after her first day on her new assignment. "This is like breathing."[4] She remained with the show, covering a wide range of topics, till 1983.

OPRAH WINFREY

The Oprah Winfrey Show

In January 1984 Winfrey moved to Chicago, where WLS-TV, an ABC-owned station, had hired her to host a slumping half-hour morning show, *A.M. Chicago*. She immediately changed the show's subject matter from lightweight fare to topical and controversial issues. Just three months after she took over, *A.M. Chicago*'s ratings overtook Phil Donahue's show, which had dominated the local talk show scene for more than sixteen years. By September 1985 the program had been expanded to a full hour and had been renamed *The*

Oprah Winfrey Show. In September 1986 the show went into syndication, being distributed in cities nationwide. That same year she founded HARPO Productions (*Harpo* is *Oprah* spelled backward) to produce her talk show and other programs, especially ones that she believed to be socially important. In doing so she joined the elite company of Lucille Ball and Mary Pickford as one of only three women in television and film to own their own production studios.

Many factors accounted for the success of *The Oprah Winfrey Show*, which soon became the highest-rated talk show in the country. Winfrey operated spontaneously, doing away with scripts and cue cards. Her casual, friendly manner drew deep disclosures from guests, as when an elderly black man broke down in tears while recalling a lynching he had witnessed in the South. She showed empathy, sometimes holding the hand of a distraught guest. Some of the show's most dramatic moments came when Winfrey revealed traumas from her own life, as when she told her audience that she was a victim of incest, having been raped by a nineteen-year-old cousin at the age of nine. Another reason for her great popularity was her ability to select and handle topics that set off sparks in the studio and across the country. On one show, for example, she managed to remain remarkably calm while Ku Klux Klansmen asserted their racial views. She also frequently devoted shows to in-depth interviews with celebrities, including John F. Kennedy, Jr., Barbara Streisand, Madonna, Janet Jackson, and Clint Eastwood.

By the late 1990s *The Oprah Winfrey Show* was still number one, and her shows continued to be highly influential. When, for example, she formed Oprah's

Book Club in 1996, her selections skyrocketed to the top of the best-seller lists. Among the later topics she has tackled are America's poor, AIDS, child abuse, teen dating violence, guns and young people, and mad cow disease. She also continued her interviews with celebrities, including Michael Jordan, Diana Ross*, Maya Angelou*, John Travolta, and Paul McCartney.

Winfrey's great contribution to television has been recognized in the form of many awards and honors. *The Oprah Winfrey Show* has won multiple Emmy Awards. Winfrey received the Woman of Achievement Award from the National Organization for Women (1986), the Broadcaster of the Year Award from the International Radio and Television Society (1988), the Image Award as the Entertainer of the Year from the National Association for the Advancement of Colored People (NAACP) (1989), the George Foster Peabody Award for Individual Achievement, *TV Guide*'s Television Performer of the Year (1997), and the Lifetime Achievement Award from the National Academy of Television Arts and Sciences (1998).

Actress, Producer, and Social Activist

Besides her gifts as a television host, Winfrey has shown an outstanding talent for acting. As early as 1978 she presented a one-woman show, *The History of Black Women Through Drama and Song*, at a black theater festival.

In 1985 the composer and producer Quincy Jones saw Winfrey's local Chicago talk show and arranged for her to be cast in the film adaptation of Alice Walker's* *The Color Purple*, coproduced by Jones and directed by Steven Spielberg. She played Sofia, a proud woman who provides a foil for Celie, an abused child and later a battered wife. Winfrey created the emotional highlight of the story when, near the end of the film, she ad-libbed a speech on the injustices long endured by black women. For her performance she received Academy Award and Golden Globe nominations for best supporting actress.

Shortly afterwards, Winfrey was cast in the 1986 film version of Richard Wright's novel *Native Son*, in which she portrayed the mother of Bigger Thomas, a black youth who kills a white heiress. She produced and starred in the feature film *Beloved* (1998), based on Toni Morrison's* novel and directed by Jonathan Demme.

Her acting credits also include roles on television. In 1989 she portrayed the long-suffering Mattie Michael in the miniseries *The Women of Brewster Place*, for which she won the NAACP's Image Award for best actress in a televsion dramatic series, miniseries, or movie. Winfrey played the same part in the subsequent short-lived television series *Brewster Place* (1990). Later she starred in the television movies *There Are No Children Here* (1993) and *Oprah Winfrey Presents: Before Women Had Wings* (1997).

Through HARPO Productions she has also served as executive producer, supervising producer, or coproducer of many television programs. They include *The Oprah Winfrey Show* itself; the information special *Prime Time Oprah: No One Dies Alone* (1988), which she also hosted and for which she received an NAACP Image Award as producer; the miniseries *The Women of Brewster Place*, for which she won another NAACP Image Award as producer; the television movies *Overexposed* (1992), *There Are No Children Here* (1993), *Oprah Winfrey Presents: Before Women Had Wings* (1997), *Oprah Winfrey Presents: David and Lisa*; and the miniseries *Oprah Winfrey Presents: The Wedding* (1998). She served as executive producer and host for a 1993 interview with the singer Michael Jackson, which earned one of the highest ratings in television history.

Much more than just an entertainer, Winfrey has used her immense personal success to promote social progress. Besides exploring solutions to serious contemporary problems on her daily talk show, she has hosted television specials on important social issues, such as *Scared Silent* (1992) and *About Us: The Dignity of Children* (1997).

Her social efforts go beyond television. She established ten scholarships in her father's name at Tennessee State University and gave two million dollars to Morehouse College in Atlanta, Georgia. With Bob Greene she coauthored the book *Make the Connection: Ten Steps to a Better Body—and a Better Life* (1996). In 1997 she made the companion video *Oprah: Make the Connection* and donated all her earnings to A Better Chance. In April 1997 she served as master of ceremonies in Philadelphia at the Presidential Summit for America's Future, organized to promote volunteerism in the United States. In September 1997 she launched Oprah's Angel Network, a campaign to encourage people to help those in need. By May 1998 she was able to announce that Oprah's Angel Network had successfully raised over $3.5 million for college tuition for needy students.

Such involvements reflect her continuing commitment to serve the needs of her broad-based national following. Oprah Winfrey, despite her enormous success as the queen of the talk shows, an accomplished actress, an award-winning executive producer, and a social activist, remains "a real person."

Selected performances:

FILMS

The Color Purple (1985)
Native Son (1986)
Listen Up: The Lives of Quincy Jones (documentary, 1990)
Beloved (1998)

Television Movies

The Women of Brewster Place (1989)
There Are No Children Here (1993)
Oprah Winfrey Presents: Before Women Had Wings (1997)

Television Series

(talk shows unless otherwise indicated)

People Are Talking (Baltimore, 1977–83)
A.M. Chicago (Chicago, 1984–85)
The Oprah Winfrey Show (Chicago, 1985–86 syndicated, 1986–)
Brewster Place (drama series, 1990)

Lynette Woodard

FIRST FEMALE HARLEM GLOBETROTTER

(1959—   )

AFTER AN ILLUSTRIOUS basketball career at the University of Kansas and on American national teams, in 1985 Lynette Woodard became the first woman member of the world-famous Harlem Globetrotters, basketball's traveling exhibition players and ambassadors of goodwill. "She used her experience as one of the Globetrotters," according to Janet Woolum in *Outstanding Women Athletes*, "to bring recognition to women's basketball and to help expand women's opportunities in the sport."[1]

Lynette Woodard was born in Wichita, Kansas, on August 12, 1959, the youngest of five children of Lugene and Dorothy Woodard. Her father was a fireman and her mother a homemaker.

As a child, Lynette played basketball with her older brother Darrell, and she also learned from Hubert ("Hubie" or "Geese") Ausbie, her cousin. Ausbie, a longtime member of the Harlem Globetrotters, introduced her to Trotter-style basketball, including such tricks as spinning the ball on the tips of the fingers.

Lynette Woodard led her Wichita North High School team to two state championships, was twice named to the all-state team, and was an All-American in her senior year.

College Record Breaker

After graduating from high school in 1977 she enrolled at the University of Kansas in Lawrence, and during her four years of college she became one of the most dominant players in the history of women's basketball. She was the first true all-around athlete to play the game. Six feet inches tall, she usually played forward, but during her career she started and excelled at all five positions.

As a freshman she led the nation in rebounds with a 14.8 per game average and was second in scoring with an average of 25.2 points. *Basketball Weekly* and other sports experts named her the freshman player of the year.

In her second year at the University of Kansas she led the nation in scoring with 31.0 points per game, setting a single-season record with 1,177 points. Continuing her rebounding prowess, she set a national single-game record with an amazing 33.

By the time she finished her college career Woodard had broken most of the major National Collegiate Athletic Association (NCAA) women's basketball records, the most remarkable of which was her career scoring total of 3,649 points (26.3 per game). However, she was always a team player and worked hard on defense as well—she led the nation in steals three times—and in her four years she led Kansas to an excellent 108–32 won-lost record.

A four-time college All-American, in her senior year she won the Wade Trophy as the nation's outstanding player in women's collegiate basketball. Later she was named the Big Eight conference's Player of the Decade of the 1980s.

During her last two years of college Woodard earned Academic All-American honors with her 3.04 grade-point average, and during that period she also participated in community service work. In 1981 she graduated with a bachelor's degree in speech communications and human relations, and the following year the Wichita branch of the National Association for the Advancement of Colored People named her Woman of the Year for her efforts in helping to start a Big Brother-Big Sister program in Kansas and for her volunteer work with the American Cancer Society.

International Player

While still attending college, Woodard began her career in international basketball competition. In 1979 she played on the United States women's team that won the gold medal at the World University Games. The following year she earned a berth on the 1980 United States Olympic team, which, however, did not participate in the Moscow Olympic Games due to the boycott called for by President Carter following the Soviet Union's invasion of Afghanistan.

After graduating from college, Woodard spent a year in Schio, Italy, earning money by playing for a company-sponsored women's league team. Missing her homeland and anxious to prepare for the 1984 Olympics, however, she returned to the United States the next year to work as an academic adviser and volunteer assistant basketball coach at her alma mater, the University of Kansas, where she remained for three years.

During the summers of 1982 and 1983 she played with the United States national basketball team, which traveled throughout the world to compete against other national teams. In 1982 she led the team to a victory over the Soviet Union, and the following year she played on the team that won the gold medal at the Pan American Games and the silver medal at the World University Games.

Because of her on-court leadership and her extensive international experience, Woodard was named captain of the 1984 Olympic basketball squad. At the Los Angeles Games that year she guided the team to America's first women's basketball Olympic gold medal.

Member of the Harlem Globetrotters

After the Olympics Woodard realized that she had nowhere to go as a player. A man in her position could have tried out for the professional National Basketball Association. Women, however, at that time had no professional league, and she did not want to return to Europe or wait for another Olympics. For the time being, therefore, she simply went back to work at the University of Kansas.

When Woodard called Ausbie, her cousin, to ask if the Globetrotters would be interested in a female member, he was not optimistic. Just six weeks later, however, she read a newspaper report that the Globetrotters were planning to add a woman player to update their image. Elated at this opportunity, she embarked on a rigorous training regimen. At the July 1985 preliminary tryouts she competed against more than two dozen other outstanding women players and was selected as one of the finalists. After winning the final round of competition in October she was named the first woman basketball player for the Harlem Globetrotters.

It was a childhood dream come true for Woodard, who had secretly yearned to play for the Globetrotters ever since Ausbie had introduced her to the team's fun-filled, magical style. At first some of her teammates had misgivings about recruiting a female player, fearing that no woman could measure up to Globetrotter standards. However, she soon won her teammates' acceptance through her ball-handling skills, knowledge of the game, and entertaining personality.

For two years she traveled with the team, playing hundreds of exhibition games all over the world, and in 1986 the Women's Sports Foundation selected her the Professional Sportswoman of the Year. However, she finally resigned from the Globetrotters over a contractual dispute.

In the early 1990s Woodard played overseas again, becoming one of Japan's most popular basketball stars. Later she served as athletic director of public schools in Kansas City, Kansas.

By breaking the gender barrier in one of the world's best-known professional sports teams, Lynette Woodard became a true pioneer. "I hope the publicity from my playing on the Globetrotters helps a women's professional basketball league become viable and stable,"[2] Woodard said. Indeed, it is largely because of her efforts that there are now two professional leagues for women basketball players. In 1992 she became the first female inducted into the GTE Academic All-American Hall of Fame. The following year her great contribution was further recognized when she received the prestigious Flo Hyman Award for her dignity, spirit, and commitment to excellence in women's sports.

Other Great African-American Women

Adams-Ender, Clara Leach (originally Clara Mae Leach; born July 11, 1939, in Willow Springs, near Raleigh, North Carolina). The first black, female, and nurse to graduate with a master's degree from the United States Army Command Staff and General College (1976); the first black Army Nurse Corps officer to graduate from the United States Army War College (1982); and the first black nurse appointed chief of the department of nursing at Walter Reed Army Medical Center in Washington, D.C. (1984). In 1987 Brigadier General Adams-Ender, the highest-ranking nurse in the army, became chief of the Army Nurse Corps.

Adkins, Cecelia (originally Cecelia Antoinette Nabrit; born September 3, 1923, in Atlanta, Georgia). The first woman and first layperson to be named executive director of the Sunday School Publishing Board of the National Baptist Convention, U.S.A.

Albert, Octavia (originally Octavia Victoria Rogers; born December 24, 1853, in Oglethorpe, Georgia; died c. 1899 in Louisiana). Author of *The House of Bondage; or, Charlotte Brooks and Other Stories* (1890), a valuable collection of interviews with former slaves.

Alexander, Roberta (born March 3, 1949, in Lynchburg, Virginia). Opera soprano who has performed internationally and has achieved renown as a concert singer. Her recordings include *Roberta Alexander Sings Samuel Barber* (1993, Etcetera).

Alexander, Sadie (originally Sadie Tanner Mossell; born January 2, 1898, in Philadelphia; died November 1, 1989, in Philadelphia). The first black woman to practice law in Pennsylvania (1927), the

first black woman to hold a national position with the National Bar Association (secretary, 1943–47), and one of the initiators of the modern civil rights movement through her private law practice and through her work on the President's Committee on Civil Rights, which produced the seminal report To *Secure These Rights* (1947).

Allen, Debbie (originally Deborah Allen; born January 16, 1950, in Houston, Texas). Actress, singer, dancer, choreographer, writer, producer, and director. Her acting credits include the television miniseries *Roots: The Next Generations* (1979), the films *Fame* (1980) and *Ragtime* (1981), the Broadway musicals *West Side Story* (1980) and *Sweet Charity* (1986), the television series Fame (1982–87), and the made-for-television movie *Stompin' at the Savoy* (1992). She won Emmys for her choreography on *Fame*, and she has choreographed many Academy Awards programs. Sister of Phylicia Rashad.*

Anderson, Regina M. (born May 21, 1901, in Chicago). Librarian, playwright, and arts patron who helped to establish the Harlem Renaissance, a black literary movement of the 1920s and 1930s.

The Schomburg Center / NYPL

Armstrong, Lillian ("Lil") Hardin (originally Lillian Hardin; born February 3, 1898, in Memphis, Tennessee; died August 27, 1971, in Chicago). One of the great early jazz pianists. From 1924 to 1938 she was married to the trumpeter Louis Armstrong, whose career she helped through her encouragement, organization, and musical knowledge.

Badu, Erykah (originally Erica Wright; born c. 1971 in Dallas, Texas). Singer, songwriter, and leader of the 1970s soul music revival. She is especially noted for her debut album, *Baduizm* (1997, Kedar Entertainment).

Baker, Augusta (originally Augusta Braxston; born April 1, 1911, in Baltimore, Maryland; died February 23, 1998, in Columbia, South Carolina). Librarian, author, educator, storyteller, and promoter of honest portrayals of minorities, especially African-Americans, in children's literature. She was highly influential as children's librarian (1937–53), assistant coordinator and storytelling specialist (1953–61), and coordinator of children's services (1961–74) at the New York Public Library. In 1980 she began a long tenure as storyteller in residence at the University of South Carolina.

Baker, Ella (full name, Ella Josephine Baker; born December 13, 1903, in Norfolk, Virginia; died December 13, 1986, in New York City). One of the foremost organizers of the modern civil rights movement as an officer of the National Association for the Advancement of Colored People, a founder of the Southern Christian Leadership Conference, a supporter of the Student Nonviolent Coordinating Committee, and a leader of many community groups.

Baker, Josephine (originally Freda Josephine McDonald; born June 3, 1906, in Saint Louis, Missouri; died April 12, 1975, in Paris, France). Singer and dancer. She lived most of her life in France, where she was acclaimed as the personification of *le jazz hot* of America.

Baker, LaVern (originally Delores Williams; born November 11, 1929, in Chicago; died March 10, 1997, in New York City). One of the first rhythm and blues artists to win favor with white audiences. Her recordings included "Tweedlee Dee" (1954, Atlantic) and "I Cried a Tear" (1959, Atlantic).

Bambara, Toni Cade (originally Miltona Mirkin Cade; born March 25, 1939, in New York City; died December 9, 1995, in Wallingford, Pennsylvania, near Philadelphia). Editor of the important literary anthology *The Black Woman* (1970) and a writer whose works included the short-story collection *Gorilla, My Love* (1972) and the novel *The Salt Eaters* (1980).

Barnett, Etta Moten (originally Etta Moten; born November 5, 1901 in Weimar, Texas). Singer and actress. She sang in several films, including *Flying Down to Rio* (1933); appeared in Broadway musicals, notably as Bess in a revival of Gershwin's *Porgy and Bess* (1943); and later became a lecturer, civic leader, arts patron, and African affairs specialist.

Barnett, Marguerite Ross (born May 22, 1942, in Charlottesville, Virginia; died February 26, 1992, in Wailuku, Hawaii). The first black woman to head a major American university (University of Houston, Texas, 1990–92).

Barrow, Willie B. ("Little Warrior") (originally Willie B. Taplin; born December 7, 1924, in Burton, Texas). National executive director of Operation PUSH (originally People United to Save Humanity, later People United to Serve Humanity), part-time from 1984 to 1986 and full-time from 1986 to 1989. A minister, she has held local and international offices with the Church of God.

Bass, Charlotta Spears (originally Charlotta Spears; born October 1880 in Sumter, South Carolina; died April 29, 1969, in Los Angeles). Managing editor of the *California Eagle* newspaper (1912–52), through which she fought for racial equality, and a pioneer political activist, becoming the first black woman to run for vice president of the United States (1952).

Bassett, Angela (born August 16, 1958, in New York City). Actress. Her credits include the play *Black Girl* (1986), the made-for-television movie *Perry Mason: The Case of the Silenced Singer* (1990), and the films *Malcolm X* (1992), *What's Love Got to Do with It?* (1993), and *Waiting to Exhale* (1995).

Bates, Daisy (originally Daisy Lee Gatson; born 1920 in Huttig, Arkansas). One of the twentieth century's most prominent civil rights activists. With her husband, L. C. Bates, she ran the *Arkansas State Press* newspaper (1941–59) and used it to expose racial injustices. She led the historic integration of Central High School in Little Rock, Arkansas, in 1957.

Batson, Flora (born April 16, 1864, in Washington, D.C.; died December 1, 1906, in Philadelphia). Concert singer. A great performer, she was known as the Double-voiced Queen of Song because of her exceptionally wide vocal range, from baritone to high soprano.

Bearden, Bessye (originally Bessye Jeanne Banks; born October 1888 in Goldboro, North Carolina; died September 16, 1943, in New York City). The first black woman, as chair of the twelfth New York City school district (mid-1920s) to sign diplomas in a United States public school system. As founder and first president of the Colored Women's Democratic League in New York City in the 1930s, she played a major role in shifting black political allegiance from the Republican party to the Democratic party.

Beasley, Delilah Leontium (born c. 1867 in Cincinnati, Ohio; died August 18, 1934, in San Leandro, California). Author of *The Negro Trail Blazers of California* (1919), a pioneering historical study of blacks in California.

Beasley, Phoebe (born June 3, 1943, in Cleveland, Ohio). Broadcast executive for many years at KFI/KOST Radio in Los Angeles; the first black president of American Women in Radio and Television (1977); and an artist whose work has been exhibited at galleries around the world.

Beavers, Louise (born March 8, 1902, in Cincinnati, Ohio; died October 26, 1962, in Los Angeles). One of the most popular character actresses in Hollywood during the 1930s and 1940s. Her films included *Imitation of Life* (1934), *Delightfully Dangerous* (1945), and, as the hero's mother, *The Jackie Robinson Story* (1950). She also assumed the title role in the television sitcom *Beulah* (1952–53).

Belafonte, Shari (also, early in her career, known by her married name, Shari Belafonte-Harper; born September 22, 1954, in New York City). Actress. She who played Julie Gillette in the television series *Hotel* (1983–88) and appeared in such movies as *Time Walker* (1982), *Murder by Numbers* (1990), and *The Heidi Chronicles* (1996). Daughter of the singer-actor Harry Belafonte.

Bennett, Gwendolyn (born July 8, 1902, in Giddings, Texas; died May 30, 1981, in Reading, Pennsylvania). Poet, short-story writer, graphic artist, columnist for the National Urban League's *Opportunity* magazine (1926–28), and head of the center for the community arts in Harlem (1939–44). She was a major figure in the Harlem Renaissance, a literary movement focusing on black pride.

Berry, Bertice B. (born 1960 in Wilmington, Delaware). Host of the syndicated television talk show *The Bertice Berry Show* (1993–94).

Berry, Halle (born August 14, 1968, in Cleveland, Ohio). Actress. Her credits include the television series *Knots Landing* (1991–92), the film *Boomerang* (1992), and the made-for-television movie *Oprah Winfrey Presents: The Wedding* (1998).

Berry, Mary Frances (born February 17, 1938, in Nashville, Tennessee). Internationally renowned historian, educator, lawyer, public servant, and civil and human rights activist. Her writings include *Black Resistance/White Law: A History of Constitutional Racism in America* (1971). As assistant secretary for education in the Department of Health, Education, and Welfare (1977–79), she was the first black woman to serve as chief educational officer of the United States. Later she was a longtime, outspoken member of the United States Commission on Civil Rights.

Billops, Camille (born August 12, 1933, in Los Angeles). Artist. Known primarily for her unique postmodern ceramic sculptures, she has also written poetry and produced pottery, drawings, book illustrations, and other works of art.

Bonds, Margaret (full name, Margaret Allison Bonds; born March 3, 1913, in Chicago; died April 26, 1972, in Los Angeles). Composer, pianist, and teacher. She was the first black soloist to appear with the Chicago Symphony Orchestra (1933). Her compositions—concert and popular, vocal and instrumental—helped to reestablish a widespread appreciation of spirituals.

Bowles, Eva del Vakia (born January 24, 1875 in Albany, Ohio; died June 14, 1943, in Richmond, Virginia). Pioneer black activist in the Young Women's Christian Association.

Bowser, Mary Elizabeth (born 1839 on the John Van Lew plantation, near Richmond, Virginia; death unknown). One of the most important female spies for the Union during the Civil War.

Branch, Mary Elizabeth (born May 20, 1881, in Farmville, Virginia; died July 6, 1944, in Camden, New Jersey). The first woman president of Tillotson College in Austin, Texas, a black college founded by the American Missionary Association.

Brandy (full name, Brandy Norwood; born February 11, 1979, in McComb, Mississippi). Singer and actress. Her recordings include *Brandy* (1994, Atlantic) and *Never Say Never* (1998, Atlantic) and whose acting credits include the title roles  in the television series *Moesha* (1995-) and the made-for television movie *Rodgers and Hammerstein's Cinderella* (1997).

Braxton, Toni (born October 7, 1967, in Severn, Maryland). Singer and actress whose credits include the recording *Toni Braxton* (1993, LaFace) and the Broadway musical *Beauty and the Beast* (1998).

Brice, Carol (full name, Carol Lovette Hawkins Brice; born April 16, 1918, in Sedalia, North Carolina; died February 15, 1985, in Norman, Oklahoma). Concert singer. A contralto who became the first African-American to win the prestigious Naumburg  Award (1943), she gave recitals, performed as soloist in concerts with major orchestras, appeared onstage in many American musicals, and cofounded the Cimarron Circuit Opera Company at the University of Oklahoma.

Brown, Charlotte Hawkins (full name, Charlotte Eugenia Hawkins Brown; originally Lottie Hawkins; born June 11, 1883, in Henderson, North Carolina; died January 11, 1961, in Greensboro, North Carolina). Founder, in 1902, of the Palmer Memorial Institute in Sedalia, North Carolina, a pioneering educational facility for black youths.

Monica Smith

Brown, Corrine (born November 11, 1946, in Jacksonville, Florida). The first African-American elected to represent the state of Florida in the United States Congress. She was elected to the House of Representatives in 1992.

Brown, Dorothy (or D. Brown; full name, Dorothy Lavinia Brown; born January 7, 1919, in Philadelphia). The first African-American woman to be appointed to a residency as a general surgeon in the United States (1948), to become a practicing general surgeon in the South (1954), and to become a fellow of the American College of Surgeons (1959). She is also the first single black woman in modern times to adopt a child in Tennessee (1956) and the first black woman to win a seat in the Tennessee legislature (1966).

Brown, Letitia (originally Letitia Woods; born October 24, 1915, in Tuskegee, Alabama; died August 4, 1976, in Washington, D.C.). Educator and historian. She helped to preserve black history through her work with the Committee on Landmarks of the National Capital and through her writings, including *Free Negroes in the District of Columbia* (1972), coauthored with Richard Wade.

Brown, Ruth (originally Ruth Weston; born January 1928 in Portsmouth, Louisiana). Rhythm and blues singer. In the 1950s, she sold so many records for the young Atlantic Records company that it was dubbed "the house that Ruth built." Her hits included "Teardrops from My Eyes" (1950, Atlantic), "Mama, He Treats Your Daughter Mean" (1953, Atlantic), and "Mambo Baby" (1954, Atlantic). She was nicknamed Miss Rhythm. Later she showed extraordinary versatility by acting in the film *Hairspray* (1988), winning a Tony Award for her performance in the Broadway musical *Black and Blue* (1989), and earning a Grammy Award for her jazz singing on the album *Blues on Broadway* (1989, Fantasy).

Brown, Willa B. (full name, Willa Beatrice Brown; born January 22, 1906, in Glasgow, Kentucky; died July 18, 1992, in Chicago). Pioneer aviator. She earned her private pilot's license in 1938, helped to found the National Airmen's Association of America in 1939, secured the inclusion of African-Americans in the federal pilot-training program in 1939, trained some of the most celebrated African-American pilots of World War II, and by 1943 was the only woman in the United States concurrently holding a mechanic's license, a commercial pilot's license, and the presidency of a large aviation corporation, the Coffey School of Aeronautics.

Bruce, Josephine Beall (originally Josephine Beall Willson; born October 29, 1953, in Philadelphia, died February 15, 1923, in Kimball, West Virginia). Lady principal (dean of women) at Tuskegee Institute in Alabama (1899–1902), an important force in the black women's club movement, and a prominent member of the social circle in Washington, D.C., where her husband, Blanche Kelso Bruce, was the first African-American to serve a full term as a United States senator (1875–81).

Bumbry, Grace Ann (born January 4, 1937, in Saint Louis, Missouri). Opera soprano and mezzo-soprano of worldwide reputation. She was the first black singer invited to the Wagner festival at Bayreuth (1961). Her other debuts included Covent Garden in London (1963), Salzburg (1964), and the Metropolitan Opera in New York City (1965).

Burke, Selma Hortense (born December 31, 1900, in Mooresville, North Carolina; died August 29, 1995, in New Hope, Pennsylvania). Sculptor. In 1943 she designed the image of President Franklin D. Roosevelt that appears on the United States dime. The first African-American woman artist to have a gallery named in her honor, the Selma Burke Gallery (1983) at Winston-Salem State University in Winston-Salem, North Carolina, she founded both the Selma Burke School of Sculpture (1940) in New York City and the Selma Burke Art Center (1968) in Pittsburgh, Pennsylvania.

Burke, Yvonne Braithwaite (originally Pearl Yvonne Watson; born October 5, 1932, in Los Angeles). The first black woman elected to the California General Assembly (1966) and to the United States House of Representatives from California (1972).

Burks, Mary Fair (born c. 1915 in Alabama; died July 21, 1991, in Maryland). Founder of the Women's Political Council (1949) in Montgomery, Alabama, which in 1955 planted the seeds of the famous boycott there that resulted in desegregation of the buses in Alabama.

Burroughs, Margaret Taylor (full name, Margaret Taylor Goss Burroughs; originally Margaret Taylor; born November 1, 1917, in Saint Rose Parish, near New Orleans, Louisiana). Preserver of black American history and heritage through her work as artist, arts administrator, educator, lecturer, museum director, and writer.

Burrows, Vinie (born November 15, 1928, in New York City). Actress, director, and producer. She is best known for her one-woman stage shows, especially *Walk Together, Children* (1968), a program of prose, poetry, and songs by black authors.

Bush, Anita (born c. 1883 in Washington, D.C.; died February 16, 1974, in New York City). The first African-American woman to found a professional black dramatic troupe, the Anita Bush Stock Company (1915), whose performers were known as the Anita Bush Players. The group later became the Lafayette Players. She was also an actress.

Butler, Octavia E. (full name, Octavia Estelle Butler; born June 22, 1947, in Pasadena, California). Science-fiction writer. Her works include the novel *Kindred* (1979) and the story "Speech Sounds" (1983).

Butler, Selena Sloan (originally Selena Sloan; born January 4, c. 1872, in Thomasville, Georgia; died October 7, 1964, in Los Angeles). Community leader and child welfare activist. In 1911 she established the first black parent-teacher association in the United States at the Yonge Street School in Atlanta, Georgia. In 1919 she developed that organization into the Georgia Colored Parent-Teacher Association, and in 1926 she became the founding president of the National Congress of Colored Parents and Teachers.

Caesar, Shirley (born October 13, 1938, in Durham, North Carolina). Singer and religious leader. She is widely regarded as the queen of contemporary evangelistic gospel singers.

Calloway, Blanche (born February 1902 in Baltimore, Maryland; died December 16, 1978, in Baltimore). Musician. The first woman to lead an all-male band (1931–38), known initially as Blanche Calloway and Her Joy Boys and eventually as Blanche Calloway and Her Orchestra; also the first black woman to vote in Miami, Florida (1958). Sister of the great jazz musician Cab Calloway.

Campbell, Lucie Eddie (or, after marriage, Lucie Campbell Williams; born April 30, 1885, in Duck Hill, Mississippi; died January 3, 1963, in Nashville, Tennessee). Composer of gospel songs, including "He'll Understand and Say, Well Done" (1933), "My Lord and I" (1947), and "Footprints of Jesus" (1949). She was one of the founders of the National Baptist Training Union (1919), which she served as music director.

Campbell, Naomi (born May 22, 1970, in London, England). Celebrated model who became the first black woman on the cover of the French *Vogue* magazine (August 1989) and the first on the cover of the all-important September issue of the American *Vogue* (September 1989). A citizen of the world, she maintains an apartment in New York City.

Canady, Alexa (married name, Alexa Canady-Davis; originally Alexa Irene Canady; born November 7, 1950, in Lansing, Michigan). The first woman and first black neurosurgical resident at the University of Minnesota (1976–81) and later a practicing physician and professor. Daughter of Hortense Golden Canady.

Canady, Hortense Golden (originally Elizabeth Hortense Golden; born August 18, 1927, in Chicago). Educational administrator and civic activist. She directed the Lansing (Michigan) Community College Foundation and served as national president of the Delta Sigma Theta sorority. Mother of Alexa Canady.

Carnegie, Mary Elizabeth (originally Mary Elizabeth Lancaster; born April 19, 1916, in Baltimore, Maryland). Nurse, educator, nursing administra-

tor, and author. She has championed the cause of equality for black women in nursing.

Carroll, Diahann (originally Carol Diahann Johnson; born July 17, 1935, New York City). Actress and singer. She won a Tony Award for her performance in the Broadway musical *No Strings* (1962); earned an Oscar nomination for her dramatic acting in the film *Claudine* (1974); and made breakthroughs on television as the title character in *Julia* (1968–71), the first comedy or drama series built around a black star, male or female, in a nonstereotypical role, and *Dynasty* (1984–87), in which she became the first black woman to have a leading role in a prime-time soap opera.

Carter, Betty (originally Lillie Mae Jones; early stage name, Lorraine Carter; nicknamed Betty Bebop by Lionel Hampton; hence Betty Carter; born May 16, 1929, in Flint, Michigan; died September 26, 1998, in New York City). Jazz singer. She performed with Lionel Hampton's band (1948–51) and Ray Charles's touring show (1960–63); recorded such great albums as *Finally Betty Carter* (1969, Roulette), *Whatever Happened to Love?* (1982, Bet-Car), and the Grammy-winning *Look What I Got!* (1989, Polygram/Verve); and was inducted into the Jazz Hall of Fame (1992).

Carter, Nell (or Nell-Ruth Carter; originally Nell Hardy; born September 13, 1948, in Birmingham, Alabama). Actress. Best known for her Tony Award-winning performance in the Broadway musical *Ain't Misbehavin'* (1978) and her role as Nell Harper in the hit television sitcom *Gimme a Break!* (1981–87). She is a convert to Judaism.

Catlett, Elizabeth (born April 15, 1915, in Washington, D.C.). Sculptor and printmaker. Her works have brought public attention to social and political issues affecting black women. She moved to

Mexico in 1946 and became a Mexican citizen in 1962.

Chase-Riboud, Barbara (full name, Barbara Dewayne Chase-Riboud; originally Barbara Dewayne Chase; also known as D'ashnash Tosi since her second marriage, to Sergio Tosi in 1981; born June 26, 1939, in Philadelphia). Sculptor and writer. She first distinguished herself with printmaking and abstract metal-and-fabric sculptures and later with her literary work in fiction and poetry, particularly her novel *Sally Hemmings* (1979).

Childress, Alice (born October 12, 1920, in Charleston, South Carolina; died August 14, 1994, in New York City). Writer, actress, and director. She is known especially for her plays, such as *Trouble in Mind* (1955), which won the 1956 Obie Award, and *Wedding Band: A Love/Hate Story in Black and White* (1966).

The Schomburg Center / NYPL

Chinn, May Edward (born April 15, 1896, in Great Barrington, Massachusetts; died December 1, 1980, in New York City). The first black woman to graduate from New York City's Bellevue Medical Center and the first to intern at Harlem Hospital (both 1926), she became both an physician and a scholar.

Claiborne, Loretta (full name, Loretta Lynn Claiborne; born August 14, 1953, in York, Pennsylvania). Long-distance runner. The United States Olympic Committee's Special Olympics Female Athlete of the Year in 1988, *Runner's World* magazine's Special Olympics Athlete of the Quarter Century in 1991, and the winner of the cable sports channel ESPN's Arthur Ashe Award for Courage in 1996, she is also an eloquent speaker calling for just treatment of the mentally and physically handicapped.

Clark, Septima (originally Septima Poinsette; born May 3, 1898, in Charleston, South Carolina; died December 15, 1987, in Johns Island, South Carolina). Political activist. Because of her early efforts to achieve black literacy, black voter registration, and women's and civil rights, she came to be known as the Queen Mother of the civil rights movement.

Clayton, Eva M. (born September 16, 1938, in North Carolina). Freshman class president of the United States House of Representatives in 1993–94.

Coachman, Alice (born November 9, 1923, in Albany, Georgia). High jumper. She won twenty-five Amateur Athletic Union national titles, was national champion for twelve straight years, became the first black woman to win an Olympic gold medal in track and field (London, 1948), and was voted into the National Track and Field Hall of Fame (1975).

Cobb, Jewell Plummer (originally Jewell Plummer; born January 17, 1924, in Chicago). Biologist and educator. She has done important cell research on melanin, a brown or black pigment that colors the skin, and has served as president of California State University at Fullerton (1982–90).

Cole, Natalie (full name, Natalie Maria Cole; born February 6, 1950, in Los Angeles). Rhythm and blues singer. Her contemporary style combines soul, rock, and jazz elements. Her recordings include *Inseparable* (1975, Capitol) and *Unforgettable . . . with Love* (1991, Elektra), the latter being a collection of songs made famous by her father, Nat King Cole.

Cole, Rebecca J. (born March 16, 1846, in Philadelphia; died August 14, 1922, in Philadelphia). The second African-American woman, after Rebecca Lee Crumpler*, to receive a medical degree in the United States, graduating from the Woman's Medical College of Pennsylvania in 1867. Cole practiced medicine for over fifty years.

Coleman, Bessie (born January 26, 1893, in Atlanta, Texas; died April 30, 1926, in Jacksonville, Florida). The first black woman to earn an American pilot's license (1921), to receive an international pilot's license (1922), and to become a stunt pilot (1922). A pioneer aviator, she died in an airplane crash.

Collins, Cardiss (originally Cardiss Hortense Robertson; born September 24, 1931, in Saint Louis, Missouri). The first black congresswoman from Illinois (1973), the first black and first woman to chair the House Government Operations Subcommittee on Manpower and Housing (1975), the first black and first woman appointed Democratic whip-at-large (1975), and the first woman to chair the Congressional Black Caucus (1979). When she retired from the House of Representatives at the end of 1996, she had served in Congress longer than any other African-American woman in United States history.

Collins, Janet (full name, Janet Faye Collins; born March 2, 1917, in New Orleans, Louisiana). Dancer, choreographer, and educator. She became the first African-American to dance for the Metropolitan Opera (1951).

Collins, Marva (originally Marva Delores Knight; born August 31, 1936, in Monroeville, Alabama). Educator. She founded the Westside Preparatory School in Chicago in 1975 and gained fame for her success in teaching "unteachable" ghetto children.

Cooper, Cynthia (born April 14, 1963, in Chicago). Basketball player who led the Houston Comets to the first two Women's National Basketball Association championships (1997, 1998) and won the league's MVP award both seasons.

Cosby, Camille (originally Camille Olivia Hanks; born 1945 in Washington, D.C.). Philanthropist, entrepreneur, and chief executive of Cosby Enterprises, a powerful entertainment business that produces a wide range of products, including television series and commercials, films, videos, recordings, and books. She and her husband, the comedian Bill Cosby, have provided enormous financial support for black colleges—over $70 million by the mid-1990s, including $20 million to Spelman College in 1989. Camille Cosby has also actively supported other black organizations, such as the United Negro College Fund, the National Association for the Advancement of Colored People, and the Reverend Jesse Jackson's Operation PUSH. In 1992 she earned a Ph.D. degree in education at the University of Massachusetts; her dissertation was published as *Television's Imageable Influences: The Self-Perceptions of Young African-Americans* (1994).

Cotten, Elizabeth ("Libba") (originally Elizabeth Nevills; born January 1892 in Chapel Hill, North Carolina; died June 29, 1987, in Syracuse, New York). Folksinger, guitarist, and songwriter. Her most famous song is "Freight Train."

Couvent, Marie Bernard (originally Justine Fervin, or Firvin; also known as Maria Gabriel Bernard Couvent and Madame Bernard Couvent, from her marriage to Gabriel Bernard Couvent; born c. 1757, probably in Africa; died June 28, 1837, in New Orleans, Louisiana). Founder of the Catholic Indigent Orphans' School, also known as the Bernard Couvent School (later the Holy Redeemer School), a tuition-free institution for free indigent blacks in New Orleans. In her will she left land and houses for the creation of the school, which began instruction in 1848.

Cowings, Patricia Suzanne (born December 15, 1948, in New York City). Psychologist and biofeedback researcher. Since 1977 she has performed important research for the National Aeronautics and Space Administration.

Cox, Ida (originally Ida Prather; born February 25, 1896, in Toccoa, Georgia; died November 10, 1967, in Knoxville, Tennessee). Singer. Billed during her lifetime as the Queen of the Blues, her great recordings include "Ida Cox's Lawdy Lawdy Blues" (1923, Paramount), "Coffin Blues" (1925, Paramount), and "Four Day Creep" (1939, Vocalion).

Craig, Ellen Walker (originally Ellen Walker; born June 5, 1906, in Franklin County, Ohio). The first elected African-American female mayor in the United States (Urbancrest, Ohio, 1972–75).

Cromwell, Otelia (born April 8, 1874, in Washington, D.C.; died April 25, 1972, in Washington). The first black to graduate from Smith College in Northampton, Massachusetts (1900), scholar, educator, and writer.

Crumpler, Rebecca Lee (originally Rebecca Lee; born 1833 in Richmond, Virginia; death unknown, 1883 or later). The first black woman to receive a medical degree in the United States, graduating from the New England Female Medical College in Boston, Massachusetts, in 1864. After practicing medicine for years in Richmond, where she worked with newly freed blacks, she returned to Boston and in 1883 published *A Book of Medical Discourses in Two Parts.*

Cuthbert, Marion Vera (born March 15, 1896, in Saint Paul, Minnesota; died May 5, 1989, in New Hampshire). Educator and writer. An executive with the Young Women's Christian Association, she contributed much to the advancement of equality and interracial harmony. Her doctoral dissertation, *Education and Marginality: A Study of the Negro Woman College Graduate* (1942, published

1987), was a pioneering study of the effect of the college experience on black women.

Danner, Margaret (full name, Margaret Essie Danner; born January 12, 1915, in Pryorsburg, Kentucky). Poet. Her collections include *Impressions of African Art Forms* (1960) and *The Down of a Thistle* (1976).

Davis, Angela (full name, Angela Yvonne Davis; born June 26, 1944, in Birmingham, Alabama). Radical social activist. After first becoming prominent during the 1960s and 1970s, she was the Communist party candidate for vice president of the United States in 1980 and 1984. She was later appointed to the Presidential Chair at the University of California at Santa Cruz (1995–).

Davis, Henrietta Vinton (born 1860 in Baltimore, Maryland; died November 23, 1941, in Washington, D.C.). Elocutionist, actress, founder of a dramatic company (1893), organizer of Marcus Garvey's Universal Negro Improvement Association (UNIA, 1917–19), and president of the rival UNIA, Inc. (elected 1934).

Davis, Hilda (full name, Hilda Andrea Davis; born May 24, 1905, in Washington, D.C.). Educator, dean of women at historically black colleges for many years, and the only person to serve two separate, nonconsecutive terms as president of the National Association of College Women, later known as the National Association of University Women (1939–45, 1957–61).

Dawes, Dominique (born November 20, 1976, in Silver Spring, Maryland). The first African-American to win two silver medals at the world gymnastic championships (1993). She swept all five gold medals at the 1994 United States national championships (four individual events plus the all-around title) and was a member of the American women's team that captured its first Olympic gold medal at the 1996 Games in Atlanta.

Dean, Jennie (born 1852 in Prince William County, Virginia; died 1913 in Virginia). Organizer of Sunday schools, or missions, and founder of the Manassas Colored Industrial School (1894) in Virginia.

Delaney, Lucy A. (full name, Lucy Ann Berry Turner Delaney; originally Lucy Ann Berry; born c. 1830 in Franklin County, Missouri; died c. 1890s). Former slave who wrote the remarkable autobiography *From the Darkness Cometh the Light; or, Struggles for Freedom* (c. 1891).

Delaney, Sara ("Sadie") P. (full name, Sara Marie Johnson Peterson Delaney; originally Sara Marie Johnson; born February 26, 1889, in Rochester, New York; died May 4, 1958, in Tuskegee, Alabama). Chief librarian at the United States Veterans Administration Hospital in Tuskegee for thirty-four years. She enriched the lives of thousands of physically and mentally disabled patients through her library service, and she developed bibliography methods that received worldwide recognition.

Delany, Bessie (originally Annie Elizabeth Delany; born September 3, 1891, in Raleigh, North Carolina; died September 25, 1995, in Mount Vernon, New York). Dentist and coauthor, with her sister Sadie Delany (and the journalist Amy Hill Hearth) of the best-selling memoir *Having Our Say: The Delany Sisters' First One Hundred Years* (1993).

Delany, Clarissa Scott (originally Clarissa Mae Scott; born 1901 in Tuskegee, Alabama; died October 1927 in Washington, D.C.). Poet. She died too young to reach the potential hinted at in "Solace" (1925) and other works.

Delany, Sadie (originally Sarah Louise Delany; born September 19, 1889, in Lynch's Station, Virginia; died January 25, 1999, in Mount Vernon, New York). Educator and coauthor, with her sister Bessie Delany (and the journalist Amy Hill Hearth) of the best-selling memoir *Having Our Say: The Delany Sisters' First One Hundred Years* (1993).

Delille, Henrietta (born 1813 in New Orleans, Louisiana; died November 16, 1862, in New Orleans). Founder of the Sisters of the Holy Family in 1842 in New Orleans. This was the second permanent order of black Catholic nuns in the United States.

Derricotte, Juliette (full name, Juliette Aline Derricotte; born April 1, 1897, in Athens, Georgia; died November 7, 1931, in Chattanooga, Tennessee). Organization official and college dean of women. As a secretary of the National Student Council of the Young Women's Christian Association (1918–29), she pioneered the interracial structuring of the organization. As dean of women at Fisk University (1929–31), she introduced greater freedom of action and individual responsibility for female students.

Devers, Gail (full name, Gail Yolanda Devers; born November 19, 1966, in Seattle, Washington). Sprinter and hurdler. She overcame debilitating

Graves' disease in the late 1980s and early 1990s to win the Olympic gold medal in the 100-meter race at the 1992 Barcelona, Spain, Olympics. In the 1996 Games, held in Atlanta, Georgia, she won two gold medals, defending her 100-meter title and running the second leg for the winning 4 x 100-meter relay team.

Diggs, Irene (full name, Ellen Irene Diggs; born April 13, 1906, in Monmouth, Illinois). Anthropologist. Her writings include *Black Chronology: From 4000 B.C. to the Abolition of the Slave Trade* (1983).

Dobbs, Mattiwilda (born July 11, 1925, in Atlanta, Georgia). The first black concert and opera singer to sing a principal role at La Scala in Milan (1953) and the third (after Marian Anderson* and Robert McFerrin) to perform at the Metropolitan Opera in New York City (1956), where, as Gilda in Verdi's *Rigoletto* (November 9, 1956), she was the first black to perform a romantic lead.

Donegan, Dorothy (born April 6, 1922, in Chicago; died May 19, 1998, in Los Angeles). Jazz pianist and singer. Known for her eclecticism, drawing on the ragtime, boogie-woogie, gospel, blues, and classical genres, she appeared in the film *Sensations of 1945* (1944) and was elected to the American Jazz Masters Hall of Fame (1992).

Douglass, Anna Murray (originally Anna Murray; born 1813 near Denton, Maryland; died August 4, 1882, in Washington, D.C.). Activist and abolitionist. She worked hand-in-hand with her husband, Frederick Douglass, in the abolitionist movement.

Du Bois, Shirley Graham (originally Shirley Lola Graham; born November 11, 1896, near Evansville, Indiana; died March 27, 1977, in Peking, China). Political activist, writer, and composer. Her works include the musical *Tom-Tom* (1932) and the juvenile biography *There Once Was a Slave: The Heroic Story of Frederick Douglass* (1947). She married the civil rights activist W. E. B. Du Bois in 1951.

Dunbar-Nelson, Alice (originally Alice Ruth Moore; born July 19, 1875, in New Orleans, Louisiana; died September 18, 1935, in Philadelphia). Harlem Renaissance writer. Her works include the poems "Violets" (1917) and "I Sit and Sew" (1920). She was married to the writer Paul Laurence Dunbar and later to the publisher Robert John Nelson.

Dunnigan, Alice (originally Alice Allison; born April 27, 1906, on a farm near Russellville, Kentucky; died May 6, 1983, in Washington, D.C.). The first African-American woman jouralist to gain access in 1947 to the Senate and House of Representatives press galleries and to be accredited to the White House and the State Department.

Dykes, Eva B. (full name, Eva Beatrice Dykes; born August 13, 1893, in Washington, D.C.; died October 29, 1986, in Hunstville, Alabama). One of the first three black American women to earn a Ph.D. (all of them in 1921) and the first actually to complete her requirements—on March 21, 1921, at Radcliffe College in Cambridge, Massachusetts. She taught at Howard University in Washington, D.C. (1929–44) and at Oakwood College in Huntsville (1944–75).

Earley, Charity Adams (originally Charity Adams; born December 5, 1918, in Kittrell, North Carolina). The first black commissioned officer in the Women's Army Auxiliary Corps (1942).

Edelin, Ramona Hoage (originally Ramona Hoage; born September 4, 1945, in Los Angeles). Leader of the National Urban Coalition. After joining the organization in 1977 as executive assistant to the president, she eventually rose to become president and chief executive officer.

Edmonds, Helen G. (full name, Helen Grey Edmonds; born December 3, 1911, in Lawrenceville, Virginia). Distinguished educator at North Carolina College (later North Carolina Central University) in Durham (1941–77); author of *Black Faces in High Places* (1971) and other works; civic leader, serving a term as national president of the Links (1970–74), a women's public service organization; and political activist, becoming the first black woman to second the nomination of a candidate for president of the United States (Dwight D. Eisenhower, 1956).

Edwards, Teresa (born July 19, 1964, in Cairo, Georgia). Basketball player. She was a two-time All-American at the University of Georgia (1985, 1986); helped the United States team to win three Olympic gold medals (1984, 1988, 1996); played professionally for teams in Italy, Japan, Spain, and France; led the Atlanta Glory in several categories during the inaugural season (1996–97) of the American Basketball League; and served the Glory as both player and coach during 1997–98.

Egypt, Ophelia Settle (originally Ophelia Settle; born February 20, 1903, in Clarksville, Texas; died May 25, 1984, in Washington, D.C.). Educator and compiler of an important collection of interviews with former slaves, published in *Unwritten History of Slavery* (1943, republished as *God Struck Me Dead*, 1969); social worker who founded the Parklands Neighborhood Clinic, Planned Parenthood of Metropolitan Washington, D.C. (1956); and author of children's books, including *James Weldon Johnson* (1974).

Elaw, Zilpha (maiden name unknown; married to Joseph Elaw; born c. 1790 in Pennsylvania; death unknown). Methodist minister. She preached throughout the United States and England and wrote *Memoirs of the Life, Religious Experience, Ministerial Travels and Labours of Mrs. Zilpha Elaw, an American Female of Color: Together with Some Account of the Great Religious Revivals in America* (1846).

Elders, Joycelyn Minnie (born August 13, 1933, in Schaal, Arkansas). The first African-American and second woman surgeon general of the United States (1993–94).

Elliott, Daisy (originally Daisy Elizabeth Lenoir; born November 26, 1919, in Filbert, West Virginia). Politician and civil rights activist. She long served in the Michigan House of Representatives and coauthored the Elliott-Larsen Civil Rights Act of 1977, the most comprehensive civil rights act adopted by any state up to that time.

Ellis, Effie O'Neal (originally Effie O'Neal; born June 15, 1913, in Hawkinsville, Georgia). The first black woman to hold an administrative or executive office within the American Medical Association. A physician, as special assistant for health services from 1970 to 1975 she provided advice on health care for children and the poor.

Ellis, Evelyn (born February 2, 1894, in Boston; died June 5, 1958, in Saranac Lake, New York). Actress. Best known for her outstanding Broadway career in *Goat Alley* (1927), *Porgy* (1927), *Native Son* (1941), and other plays, she later appeared on television and in films, such as *The Lady from Shanghai* (1948) and *The Joe Louis Story* (1953).

Evans, Mari (born July 16, 1923, in Toledo, Ohio). Poet and writer. Best known for her poetry collection *I Am a Black Woman* (1970). Her other works include the children's book *I Look at Me* (1973), the play *Rivers of My Song* (1977), and the poetry collection *A Dark and Splendid Mass* (1992).

Evans, Matilda Arabella (born May 13, 1872, in Aiken, South Carolina; died November 17, 1935, in Columbia, South Carolina). The first black woman to practice medicine in Columbia (1897) and the founder of two hospitals and three clinics in the city.

Evanti, Lillian (originally Annie Lillian Evans, [stage surname derived by combining her maiden name and the first syllable of her married name, Tibbs]; born August 12, 1890, in Washington, D.C.; died December 6, 1987, in Washington, D.C.). The first African-American to sing a major role with an organized European opera company. A soprano, she performed the title role in Delibes's *Lakmé* in Nice, France, in 1925.

Fabio, Sarah Webster (originally Sarah Webster; born January 20, 1928, in Nashville, Tennessee; died November 7, 1979, near San Francisco). Poet and critic. A leader in the black arts movement, she gathered her poems into the seven-volume collection *The Rainbow Sign* (1973).

Fauset, Jessie Redmon (born April 27, 1882, in Camden, New Jersey; died April 30, 1961, in Philadelphia). Harlem Renaissance writer. She was important not only as a writer of fiction, nonfiction, and poetry but also as editor of the *Crisis* (1919–26), a publication of the National Association for the Advancement of Colored People.

Ferebee, Dorothy Boulding (originally Dorothy Boulding; born 1890 in Norfolk, Virginia; died September 14, 1980, in Washington, D.C.). Physician. She gained a national reputation for promoting medical education as a means of improving the lives of women, blacks, and the poor. Niece of Josephine St. Pierre Ruffin.

Ferguson, Catherine ("Katy") (born c. 1779 at sea; died July 11, 1854, in New York City). Sunday school movement pioneer. She organized and oversaw Sunday school instruction at the Old Scotch Presbyterian Church in New York City in the early years of the nineteenth century.

Fields, Mary (born c. 1832 in Tennessee; died 1914 in Cascade, Montana). Western pioneer. She was the second woman to drive a United States mail stagecoach route, delivering mail and passengers in Montana for eight years when she was in her sixties. She was known as Black Mary and Stage-coach Mary.

Fisher, Ada (originally Ada Lois Sipuel; born February 8, 1924, in Chickasha, Oklahoma; died October 18, 1995, in Oklahoma City, Oklahoma). Lawyer, educator, and civil rights activist. Her efforts to enter the University of Oklahoma law school in 1946 helped to break down segregated education in the United States.

Forten, Margaretta (born 1808 in Philadelphia; died January 14, 1875, in Philadelphia). Abolitionist and educator. One of the women who created the Philadelphia Female Anti-Slavery Society (1833), she ran her own private primary school (1845–75). She was the aunt of Charlotte L. Forten Grimké and sister of Harriet Forten Purvis and Sarah Forten Purvis.

Forten Grimké, Charlotte L. (originally Charlotte L. Forten; born August 17, 1837, in Philadelphia; died July 23, 1914, in Washington, D.C.). Writer and educator. Her journals are among the few such documents written by black women of her time. She was the niece of Margaretta Forten*, Harriet Forten Purvis*, and Sarah Forten Purvis.*

Franklin, J. E. (full name, Jennie Elizabeth Franklin; born August 10, 1937, in Houston, Texas). Playwright. She is best known for *Black Girl* (1971).

Franklin, Martha Minerva (born October 29, 1870, in New Milford, Connecticut; died September 26, 1968, in New Haven, Connecticut). The first nurse to campaign nationally for equality for black nurses and the founder of the National Association of Colored Graduate Nurses (1908).

Freeman, Elizabeth ("Mum Bett" or "Mumbet") (born c. 1744; died December 28, 1829, in Stockbridge, Massachusetts). Plaintiff in a historic civil rights case heard in Great Barrington, Massachusetts, in 1781. Born a slave, she sued for, and won, her freedom in a jury trial by claiming that she was being illegally detained in bondage against the free-and-equal provisions of the new (1780) Massachusetts constitution.

Fudge, Ann (originally Ann Marie Brown; born April 23, 1951, in Washington, D.C.). Executive vice president of Kraft Foods, Inc. and president of Kraft's Coffee and Cereals Division since 1997.

Fuller, Meta Warrick (full name, Meta Vaux Warrick Fuller; born June 9, 1877, in Philadelphia; died March 13, 1968, in Framingham, Massachusetts). Sculptor. She is regarded as an important precursor of the Harlem Renaissance.

Futrell, Mary Hatwood (originally Mary Alice Hatwood; born May 24, 1940, in Alta Vista, Virginia). The longest-serving president of the National Education Association (1983–89).

Gaudet, Frances Joseph (originally Frances A. Thomas; born 1861 in Holmesville, Mississippi; died December 24, 1934, in Chicago). Temperance leader, prison reformer, and founder of the Colored Industrial Home and School (later the Gaudet Home and School) in New Orleans, Louisiana (1901).

Gayle, Helene Doris (born August 16, 1955, in Buffalo, New York). Epidemiologist. She has contributed valuable research in the study and control of disease epidemics.

George, Zelma Watson (originally Zelma Watson; born December 18, 1903, in Hearne, Texas; died July 3, 1994, in Cleveland, Ohio). Sociologist, musicologist, educator, administrator, actress, singer, diplomat, and lecturer. She served as an alternate United States delegate to the United Nations General Assembly (1960).

Giddings, Paula (born November 16, 1947, in Yonkers, New York). Journalist, editor, and author. Her works include *When and Where I Enter: The Impact of Black Women on Race and Sex* (1984).

Givens, Robin (born November 27, 1965 [or 1964], in New York City). Actress. She had a recurring role in the television sitcom *Head of the Class* (1986–91), appeared in the made-for-television movie *The Women of Brewster Place* (1989), played romantic leads in *Boomerang* (1992) and  other films, and increased her celebrity status through her brief marriage to the boxer Mike Tyson.

Gleason, Eliza (originally Eliza Atkins; born December 15, 1909, in Winston-Salem, North Carolina).

The first African-American to receive a doctorate in library science (University of Chicago, 1940).

Gordon, Nora Antonia (born August 25, 1866, in Columbus, Georgia; died January 26, 1901, in Atlanta, Georgia). Educator and missionary in Africa. At Spelman College in Atlanta, her alma mater and sponsor, she established the tradition of training other young women to work as missionaries in Africa and of educating African women at Spelman.

Greenfield, Elizabeth Taylor (originally Elizabeth Taylor; born c. 1819 in Natchez, Mississippi; died March 31, 1876, in Philadelphia). The first black concert singer in America and the first to give a command performance before royalty (Britain's Queen Victoria, in 1853). She was known as the Black Swan, the African-American counterpart to Jenny Lind (the Swedish Nightingale) and Catherine Hayes (the Irish Swan).

Grier, Pam (born May 26, 1949, in Winston-Salem, North Carolina). Actress. She became the biggest female star of the 1970s blaxploitation films (low-budget movies with primarily black casts and excessive violence), such as *Coffy* (1973) and *Foxy Brown*  (1974). After a period of playing mostly supporting parts, she reached star status again with the title role in *Jackie Brown* (1997).

Grimké, Angelina Weld (born February 27, 1880, in Boston; died June 10, 1958, in New York City). Harlem Renaissance poet, short-story writer, and playwright. Her works include the play *Rachel* (1916), the first successful drama written by an African-American to expose racial injustice.

Guy, Rosa (originally Rosa Cuthbert; born September 1, 1928 (also recorded as 1925), in Trinidad, West Indies). Writer. Her works include young adult novels, such as *The Disappearance* (1979), and adult fiction, such as *My Love, My Love; or, The Peasant Girl* (1985).

Hale, Clara (or Mother Hale; originally Clara McBride; born April 1, 1905, in Philadelphia; died December 18, 1992, in New York City). Pioneer child-care worker. She raised forty foster children

from the 1930s to the 1960s and then in 1969, founded Hale House, a treatment center for babies born to drug-addicted mothers, (incorporated in 1973 as Hale House Center for the Promotion of Human Potential).

Hale, Millie E. (originally Millie Essie Gibson; born February 27, 1891, in Nashville, Tennessee; died June 6, 1930, in Nashville). Nurse and founder of the Millie E. Hale Hospital and Training School (1916) in Nashville, an important early medical institution for blacks in the South.

Hall, Adelaide (full name, Adelaide Louisa Hall; born October 20, 1901, in Brooklyn, New York; died November 7, 1993, in London). Jazz singer and actress. Most famous for her expressive, wordless vocals on such Duke Ellington recordings as "Creole Love Call" (1927, Victor) and "The Blues I Love to Sing" (1927, Victor), she settled in London in 1938 but often returned to the United States to perform. In 1988, at the age of eighty-seven, she presented a one-woman show at Carnegie Hall in New York City. Her ninetieth birthday was celebrated at Queen Elizabeth Hall in London in 1991.

Hall, Juanita (originally Juanita Long; born November 6, 1901, in Keyport, New Jersey; died February 29, 1968, in Bayshore, New York). Singer and actress. Best known for her role as Bloody Mary in the Broadway musical *South Pacific* (1949).

Hamilton, Grace Towns (originally Grace Towns; born February 10, 1907, in Atlanta, Georgia; died June 17, 1992, in Atlanta). Executive director of the Atlanta Urban League (1943–61) and the first black woman elected to the Georgia state legislature (elected 1965, served 1966–84)

Hare, Maud Cuney (originally Maud Cuney; born February 16, 1874, in Galveston, Texas; died February 13, 1936, in Boston). Pioneer in black music history. She was known especially for her book *Negro Musicians and Their Music* (1936).

Harper, Frances E. W. (originally Frances Ellen Watkins; born September 24, 1825, in Baltimore, Maryland; died February 20, 1911, in Philadelphia). Noted abolitionist, suffragist, and temperance movement lecturer, successful poet, and writer of the first short story published by a black woman in the United States ("The Two Offers," 1859), and the critically acclaimed novel *Iola Leroy; or, Shadows Uplifted* (1892).

Harris, Barbara (full name, Barbara Clementine Harris; born June 12, 1930, in Philadelphia). The first female bishop (elected 1988) in the history of the Episcopal church in the United States and the worldwide Anglican communion of which it is a part.

Harris, Marcelite J. (full name, Marcelite Jordan Harris; originally Marcelite Jordan; born January 16, 1943, in Houston, Texas). The first black woman general in the United States Air Force. She reached the rank of brigadier general in 1990.

Harris, Patricia Roberts (originally Patricia Roberts; born May 31, 1924, in Mattoon, Illinois; died March 23, 1985, in Washington, D.C.). The first black woman to head a United States embassy (Luxembourg, 1965–67); to lead an American law school (Howard University School of Law in Washington, D.C., 1969); and to serve in a president's cabinet (secretary of Housing and Urban Development, 1977–79, and secretary of Health, Education, and Welfare, 1979–81).

Harrison, Hazel (full name, Hazel Lucile Harrison; born May 12, 1883, in La Porte, Indiana; died April 28, 1969, in Washington, D.C.). Internationally renowned concert pianist. She was the first exclusively American-trained soloist to perform with a European orchestra (Berlin Philharmonic Orchestra, 1904).

Harsh, Vivian (full name, Vivian Gordon Harsh; born May 27, 1890, in Chicago; died August 17, 1960, in Chicago). The first African-American to head a branch of the Chicago Public Library system, the George Cleveland Hall Branch Library (1932–58), where she established a Special Negro Collection, later called the Vivian G. Harsh Collection of Afro-American History and Literature (now housed at the Carter G. Woodson Regional Library Center), one of the most important such collections in the United States.

Harvard, Beverly J. (full married name, Beverly Joyce Harvard; born c. 1951 in Macon, Georgia). The first African-American woman to head the police department of a major city (Atlanta, Georgia, 1994–).

Hayden, Della Irving (originally Della Irving; born 1851 in Tarboro, North Carolina; died December 10, 1924, in Suffolk, Virginia). Founder of the Franklin Normal and Industrial Institute in Franklin, Virginia (1904).

Hedgeman, Anna Arnold (originally Anna Arnold; born July 5, 1899, in Marshalltown, Iowa; died January 17, 1990, in New York City). Educator, lecturer, public servant, and social activist. She was the first African-American to hold a position in the Federal Security Agency (1949, later called the Department of Health, Education, and Welfare), was the only woman on the organizing committee of the 1963 March on Washington, assisted in the formation of the interfaith coalition that assured the passage of the 1964 Civil Rights Act, and helped to establish African-American studies programs on many college campuses.

Hendricks, Barbara (born November 20, 1948, in Stephens, Arkansas). Opera singer. Since her debut with the San Francisco Spring Opera in 1974, she has performed with major opera companies throughout the United States and Europe. Her recordings include *Barber: Adagio for Strings; Nocturne; Sure on This Shining Night; Knoxville: Summer of 1915 / Copland: Quiet City; Eight Poems of Emily Dickinson* (1995, EMI).

Herman, Alexis M. (full name, Alexis Margaret Herman; born July 16, 1947, in Mobile, Alabama). The first African-American secretary of labor in the United States cabinet (1997–).

Hernandez, Aileen (originally Aileen Clark; born May 23, 1926, in Brooklyn, New York). Founder of the San Francisco public relations firm Hernandez and Associates (1966) and a well-known activist and lecturer in labor relations, women's rights, and equal employment concerns.

Hinderas, Natalie (originally Natalie Leota Henderson; born June 15, 1927, in Oberlin, Ohio; died July 22, 1987, in Philadelphia). Pianist. She was one of the first black instrumentalists to gain international prominence in the field of classical music.

Hine, Darlene Clark (born February 7, 1947, in Morley, Missouri). Author of *Black Women in White: Racial Conflict and Cooperation in the Nursing Profession, 1890–1950* (1989) and editor of the sixteen-volume *Black Women in United States History* (1990) and the two-volume *Black Women in America: An Historical Encyclopedia* (1993).

Holland, Annie Wealthy (originally Annie Wealthy Daughtry; born 1871 in Isle of Wight County, Virginia; died January 6, 1934, in Louisburg, North Carolina). Educator. Her efforts laid the foundations for the rural cooperative movement and for parent-teacher associations among black Americans in North Carolina.

Holliday, Jennifer (full name, Jennifer-Yvette Holliday; born October 19, 1960, in Riverside, Texas). Actress and singer. She is best known for her Tony Award-winning performance in the Broadway musical *Dreamgirls* (1981).

Holt, Nora (originally Nora Douglas; born 1885 in Kansas City, Kansas; died January 25, 1974, in Los Angeles). Reportedly the first black American to earn a master's degree in music (Chicago Musical College, 1918), she was one of the founders of the National Association for Negro Musicians (1919), became a respected music critic, and was the first black American member of the Music Critics Circle (1945).

Hooks, Bell (originally Gloria Jean Watkins; born September 25, 1952, in Hopkinsville, Kentucky). Feminist writer, poet, and educator. Her writings include the nonfiction book *Ain't I a Woman: Black Women and Feminism* (1981) and the poetry collection *The Woman's Mourning Song* (1993).

Hooks, Julia (full name, Julia Ann Amanda Morehead Britton Werles Hooks; originally Julia Ann Amanda Morehead Britton; born 1852 in Lexington, Kentucky; died 1942 in Memphis, Tennessee). Musician. Founder of an elementary school and a music school in Memphis and promoter of social improvement for blacks. (One of her students was W. C. Handy, who became the father of the blues.) She was known as the Angel of Beale Street.

Hope, Lugenia Burns (originally Lugenia D. Burns; born February 19, 1871, in Saint Louis, Missouri; died August 14, 1947, in Nashville, Tennessee). Social reformer. One of the most effective activists in the South through her activities with the National Association for the Advancement of Colored People, the Urban League, and many other organizations, she helped to found, and for twenty-five years led, the Neighborhood Union, the first female social welfare agency for blacks in Atlanta, Georgia, and a model for other communities.

Hopkins, Pauline (full name, Pauline Elizabeth Hopkins; born 1859 in Portland, Maine; died August 13, 1930, in Boston). Writer. She was best known for her novel *Contending Forces: A Romance Illustrative of Negro Life North and South* (1900).

Hunter, Alberta (born April 1, 1895, in Memphis, Tennessee; died October 17, 1984, in New York City). Blues singer and composer. As well as recording her own classic "Downhearted Blues" (1922, Paramount), other recordings include "Jazzin' Baby Blues" (1922, Paramount), "Texas Moaner Blues" (1924, Gennett), and *Alberta Hunter with Lovie Austin and Her Blues Serenaders* (1961, Riverside). She continued to perform publicly till a few months before her death at the age of eighty-nine.

Hunter, Clementine (full name, Clementine Reuben Hunter; originally Clementine Reuben; born December 1886 at Hidden Hill plantation near Cloutierville, Louisiana; died January 1, 1988, near Natchitoches, Louisiana). Folk artist. Famed for her paintings of black life in rural Louisiana, she continued to paint till shortly before her death at the age of one hundred and one.

Hunter, Jane Edna (full name, Jane Edna Harris Hunter; originally Jane Edna Harris; born December 15, 1882, at Woodburn plantation near Pendleton, South Carolina; died January 19, 1971, in Cleveland, Ohio). Founder and executive director of the Phillis Wheatley Association in Cleveland, a residence, training center, and employment service for black women.

Hunter-Gault, Charlayne (originally Charlayne Hunter; born February 27, 1942, in Due West, South Carolina). One of the first two black students (the other was Hamilton Holmes) to attend the University of Georgia (1961). She later became a well-known journalist with the *New Yorker* (1963–67) and the *New York Times* (1968–78). In 1978 she began a long association with the PBS television news program hosted by Robert MacNeil and Jim Lehrer.

Hurley, Ruby (born c. 1913 in Washington, D.C.). Early civil rights activist. As national youth secretary with the National Association for the Advancement of Colored People in the 1940s she dramatically increased the organization's youth councils and college chapters. Posted to Birmingham, Alabama, in 1951, she was the only full-time professional civil rights worker in the Deep South during much of the 1950s, often risking her life to investigate and report on racial crimes. She remained with the NAACP until 1978.

Hutson, Jean Blackwell (originally Jean Blackwell; born September 4, 1914, in Sommerfield, Florida; died February 4, 1998, in Harlem, New York). Curator of the New York Public Library's Schomburg Collection (1948–72). She built the collection into the world's leading public repository of African-American cultural materials. When it was renamed the Schomburg Center for Research in Black Culture, she served as its chief (1972–80). From 1980 till her retirement in 1984 she was an assistant director of the library.

Hyers, Anna Madah (born c. 1856 in Sacramento, California; died 1930s) and Emma Louise (born c. 1858 in Sacramento; died c. 1899). Singing duo, known as the Hyers Sisters. Among the first black women to enter the concert world, they toured nationally, singing a varied repertory that included plantation songs, popular ballads, comic novelties, and opera arias.

Ingram, Edith J. (full name, Edith Jacqueline Ingram; born January 16, 1942, near Sparta, Georgia). The first black judge in Georgia. She became judge of the Court Ordinary of Hancock County in 1969 and judge of the Probate Court of Hancock County in 1973.

Jackson, Janet (full name, Janet Damita Jackson; born May 16, 1966, in Gary, Indiana). Singer, dancer, songwriter, and actress. She became the first female artist to land five singles from one album (*Control*, 1986, A&M) on the *Billboard* Top Five pop chart. Her acting credits include recurring roles on the television  series *Diff'rent Strokes* (1981–82) and *Fame* (1984–86). One of her many successful later recordings is *The Velvet Rope* (1998, Virgin). Her brother is the pop singer Michael Jackson.

Jackson, May Howard (originally May [also recorded as Mae] Howard; born 1877 in Philadelphia; died July 12, 1931, in Long Beach, New York). Sculptor. She broke with artistic tradition by rejecting advanced study in Europe and by centering her work on the complex, varied physiognomy of black people. She is known for her busts of such notables as Paul Laurence Dunbar and W. E. B. Du Bois.

Jackson, Nell (full name, Nell Cecilia Jackson; born July 1, 1929, in Athens, Georgia; died April 1, 1988, in Vestal, New York). Track and field athlete, coach, and administrator. As a 200-meter sprinter she competed in the 1948 Olympics in London and won the American national title in 1949 (setting a new United States record of 24.2 seconds) and 1950. In 1956 she was the first black to become head coach of United States Olympic team, leading the women's team at the Games that year in Melbourne, Australia. Later she served as a member of the board of directors of the United States Olympic Committee.

Jackson, Rebecca Cox (originally Rebecca Cox; born February 15, 1795, in Hornstown, Pennsylvania; died May 24, 1871, in Philadelphia). The founder of the first predominantly black group of United Society of Believers in Christ's Second Appearing, commonly known as the Shakers (Philadelphia, 1859).

Jackson, Shirley Ann (born August 5, 1946, in Washington, D.C.). The first black woman to earn a doctorate from the Massachusetts Institute of Technology (1973), a renowned research physicist, and author of over one hundred scientific articles and abstracts. In 1995 she was appointed chairperson of the Nuclear Regulatory Commission.

Jacobs, Harriet Ann (born 1813 in Edenton, North Carolina; died March 7, 1897, in Washington, D.C.). Writer. As the author of *Incidents in the Life of a Slave Girl, Written by Herself* (1861, under the pseudonym Linda Brent), which recounts the writer's life in slavery and her escape to freedom, she made a major contribution to the slave narrative genre.

James, Etta (originally Jamesetta Hawkins; born January 25, 1938, in Los Angeles). Rhythm and blues singer. A dominant figure from the 1950s to the 1970s, she recorded such powerful songs as "The Wallflower" (1954, Modern Records), "All I Could Do Was Cry" (1960, Argo), "Tell Mama" (1967, Cadet), and *Etta James* (1973, Chess). She is comfortable in many different genres, including jazz, in which category she won a Grammy Award for her album *Mystery Lady: Songs of Billie Holiday* (1994, Private Music).

Jessye, Eva (born January 20, 1895, in Coffeyville, Kansas; died February 21, 1992, in Ypsilanti, Michigan). The first black woman to achieve acclaim as the director of a professional choral group, establishing the Eva Jessye Choir, which she established in the 1920s. She directed her choir in *Hallelujah* (1929), the first film musical, and in the premiere of George Gershwin's opera *Porgy and Bess* (1935).

Johnson, Georgia Douglas (full name, Georgia Blanche Douglas Camp Johnson; originally Georgia Blanche Douglas Camp; born September 10, 1877, in Atlanta, Georgia; died May 14, 1966, in Washington, D.C.). Poet and writer. Widely recognized as the foremost woman poet of the Harlem Renaissance, her poetry collections include *The Heart of a Woman and Other Poems* (1918) and *Bronze* (1922). She also wrote acclaimed plays, such as *Plumes: Folk Tragedy* (1927).

Johnson, Halle Tanner Dillon (originally Halle Tanner; born October 17, 1864, in Pittsburgh, Pennsylvania; died April 26, 1901, in Nashville, Tennessee). The first woman, black or white, admitted on examination to practice medicine in Alabama (1891).

Johnson, Helene (originally Helen Johnson; born July 7, 1906, in Boston; died July 7, 1995, in New York City). Poet. She represented the younger generation of the Harlem Renaissance in such poems as "My Race" (1925), "Metamorphism" (1926), "The Road" (1926), and "Poem" (1927). After marrying in the 1930s, becoming Helene Johnson Hubbell, she disappeared from the literary scene. She was a cousin of Dorothy West.

Johnson, Norma Holloway (originally Norma L. Holloway; born c. 1934 in Lake Charles, Louisiana). The first black woman appointed to a federal judgeship in the District of Columbia (United States District Court for the District of Columbia, 1980).

Jones, Clara Stanton (originally Clara Araminta Stanton; born May 14, 1913, in Saint Louis, Missouri). The first black and first woman director of the Detroit Public Library (1970–78) and the first black president of the American Library Association (1976–77).

Jones, Elaine R. (born March 2, 1944, in Norfolk, Virginia). The first female director-counsel of the Legal Defense and Educational Fund (1993) of the National Association for the Advancement of Colored People.

Jones, Lois Mailou (or Madame Vergniaud Pierre-Noel; born November 3, 1905, in Boston; died June 9, 1998, in Washington, D.C.). Artist and designer. As a teacher at Howard University in Washington, D.C. (1930–77), she greatly influenced generations of black artists.

Jones, Sissieretta (originally Matilda Sissieretta Joyner; born January 5, 1869, in Portsmouth, Virginia; died June 24, 1933, in Providence, Rhode Island). World-famous soprano. Known as Black Patti because her rich voice was said to rival that of the great Italian prima donna Adelina Patti, Jones toured internationally in the late 1800s and early 1900s, singing opera arias, art songs, and sentimental ballads. She paved the way for the acceptance of many other classically trained black musicians.

Jones, Virginia Lacy (originally Virginia Mae Lacy; born June 25, 1912, in Cincinnati, Ohio; died December 3, 1984, in Atlanta, Georgia). Pioneer in black library education. She served as dean of the School of Library Service at Atlanta University (1945–81), earning a national reputation as the "dean of library school deans."

Jordan, June (born July 9, 1936, in Harlem, New York City). Educator and prolific writer of poetry, novels, plays, and essays for audiences ranging from young children to adults. One of her most highly regarded works is the young adult novel *His Own Where* (1971).

Keckley, Elizabeth (originally Elizabeth Hobbs; born c. 1824 in Dinwiddie, Virginia; died May 26, 1907, in Washington, D.C.). Seamstress. She bought her own freedom from slavery, established a sewing business, and became famous as seamstress and friend to Mary Todd Lincoln during the latter's years as First Lady (1861–65). Keckley wrote a valuable memoir, *Behind the Scenes: Thirty Years a Slave and Four Years in the White House* (1868).

Kelly, Leontine (full name, Leontine Turpeau Current Kelly; originally Leontine Turpeau; born March 5, 1920, in Washington, D.C.). The first black American woman elected bishop of a major religious denomination, the United Methodist church, she served from 1984 till her retirement in 1988.

Kelly, Sharon Pratt (formerly Sharon Pratt Dixon; originally Sharon Pratt; born January 30, 1944, in Washington, D.C.). Lawyer and politician. She became the first black and first woman treasurer of the Democratic National Committee (1985) and the first black woman mayor of a major United States city (Washington, D.C., elected 1990).

Kennedy, Florynce ("Flo") (full name, Florynce Rae Kennedy; born February 11, 1916, in Kansas City, Missouri). Civil and women's rights activist and lawyer. She founded the Media Workshop (1966) to deal with racisim in media and advertising, formed the Feminist party (1972) to support Shirley Chisholm* for president of the United States, and has championed innumerable civil liberty causes through writings and lectures.

Kitt, Eartha (full name, Eartha Mae Kitt; born January 26, 1928, in North, South Carolina). Singer and actress. She performed with Katherine Dunham's troupe as a dancer and singer (1945–50); recorded "Santa Baby" (1953, RCA), *Down to Eartha* (1955, RCA), and *That Bad Eartha* (1985, RCA); starred in the stage productions Jolly's *Progress* (1959) and *Timbuktu!* (1978); and appeared in the films *St. Louis Blues* (1958), *Anna Lucasta* (1958), and *Boomerang* (1992).

Kittrell, Flemmie (full name, Flemmie Pansy Kittrell; born December 25, 1904, in Henderson, North Carolina; died October 3, 1980, in Washington, D.C.). The first African-American to earn a doctorate in home economics (Cornell University, 1936). She became an internationally renowned nutritionist, providing nutrition education to governments at home and abroad, especially in developing countries.

Koontz, Elizabeth Duncan (originally Elizabeth Duncan; born June 3, 1919, in Salisbury, North Carolina; died January 6, 1989, in Salisbury). The first black president of the National Education Association (1968–69) and the first black director of the Women's Bureau of the United States Department of Labor (1969–73).

Lafontant-Mankarious, Jewel Stradford (originally Jewel Stradford; born April 28, 1922, in Chicago; died May 31, 1997, in Chicago). Distinguished lawyer, United States representative to the United Nations (1972), the first woman deputy solicitor general of the United States (1973–75), and ambassador-at-large and United States coordinator for refugee affairs (1989–93).

Lane, Pinkie Gordon (originally Pinkie Gordon; born January 13, 1923, in Philadelphia). Writer. In 1989, she became the first African-American appointed poet laureate of Louisiana.

Larsen, Nella (born April 13, 1891, in Chicago; died March 30, 1964, in New York City). Writer, children's librarian, and nurse. Her writings, notably her novels *Quicksand* (1928) and *Passing* (1929), focus on the inner conflicts associated with mixed ancestry.

Latimer, Catherine A. (full name, Catherine Allen Latimer; originally Catherine Allen; born c. 1895 in Nashville, Tennessee; died 1948 in New York City). The first black professional librarian with the New York Public Library system, assigned to the 135th Street branch in 1920. She created the library's famous African-American clipping file, which later became a central feature of the Schomburg Center for Research in Black Culture.

Lawrence-Lightfoot, Sara (born August 1944 in Nashville, Tennessee). Educator and sociologist. Her books include *The Good High School: Portraits of Character and Culture* (1983), *Balm in Gilead: Portrait of a Healer* (1988), and *I've Known Rivers: Lives of Loss and Liberation* (1994).

Lawson, Jennifer Karen (born June 8, 1946, in Birmingham, Alabama). Broadcast executive. As executive vice president of national programming for the Public Broadcasting Service (PBS, 1989–95), she was the most powerful progamming executive in public television. She played a major role in promoting Ken Burns's PBS documentary series *The Civil War* (1990) and helped to build viewership for the entire PBS system.

Lee, Andrea (born 1953 in Philadelphia). Journalist and fiction writer. She is best known for her nonfiction book *Russian Journal* (1981) and her novel *Sarah Phillips* (1984).

Lee, Jarena (maiden name unknown; married to Joseph Lee; born February 11, 1783, in Cape May, New Jersey; death unknown). The first woman preacher of the African Methodist Episcopal (AME) church and the first African-American woman to write an extended account of her own life: *The Life and Religious Experience of Jarena Lee* (1836), which she later updated as *Religious Experience and Journal of Mrs. Jarena Lee* (1849).

Leslie, Lisa (born July 7, 1972, in Inglewood, California). Basketball player. She was the 1994 collegiate player of the year (at the University of Southern California); led the United States women's team to a gold medal at the 1996 Olympic Games in Atlanta, Georgia; played with the Los Angeles Sparks in the inaugural season (1997) of the Women's National Basketball Association (WNBA), earning all-league honors; led the United States team to the world championship in 1998; and set a WNBA single-game record with twenty-one rebounds in June 1998.

Lewis, Elma (full name, Elma Ina Lewis; born September 15, 1921, in Boston). Dancer, choreographer, educator, artistic director, and founder the Elma Lewis School of Fine Arts in Boston (1950) and the National Center of Afro-American Artists in the same city (1969).

Lewis, Ida Elizabeth (born September 22, 1935, in Malvern, Pennsylvania). Journalist and founder *Encore* (1972), the first black-owned and black-operated news magazine, and *Eagle and Swan* (1978), a magazine for blacks in the military.

Lewis, Samella Sanders (originally Samella Sanders; born February 27, 1924, in New Orleans, Louisiana). Art historian, artist, author, art curator, editor, educator, and filmmaker. In 1976 she became art editor of the *International Review of African American Art* and founded the Museum of African American Art in Los Angeles, California.

Lincoln, Abbey (stage name since 1956; since 1975 also known as Aminata Moseka; earlier stage names included Anna Marie and Gaby Lee; originally Anna Marie Woolridge [also recorded as Wooldridge]; born August 6, 1930, in Chicago). Jazz singer and actress. In the 1960s she used her bold, sometimes violent vocal style to make political statements, as on the album *We Insist! Freedom Now Suite* (1960, Candid), which she recorded with the drummer Max Roach, her husband from 1962 to 1970. Her later, gentler style can be heard on *Talking to the Sun* (1983, Enja) and *Devil's Got Your Tongue* (1993, Verve)

Logan, Adella Hunt (originally Adella Hunt; born February 1863 in Sparta, Georgia; died December 12, 1915, in Tuskegee, Alabama). Woman suffragist and black education advocate. She held many positions at Tuskegee Institute, including serving as its first librarian, and was active in social causes through her affiliation with the Tuskegee Woman's Club.

Lorde, Audre (full name, Audre Geraldine Lorde; born February 18, 1934, in Harlem, New York; died November 17, 1992, in Saint Croix, Virgin Islands). Poet and writer. She was noted both for her poetry, published in such collections as *From a Land Where Other People Live* (1973) and *The Black Unicorn* (1978), and her nonfiction publications, such as *The Cancer Journals* (1980) and *A Burst of Light: Essays* (1988).

Love, Josephine Harreld (originally Josephine Harreld; born December 11, 1914, in Atlanta, Georgia). Concert pianist, educator, musicologist, arts administrator, and cofounder (with Gwendolyn Hogue) of Your Heritage House in the Detroit Cultural Center, an art museum and art school for children that includes an archive of materials about noted black Americans in the arts.

Love, Ruth B. (full original name, Ruth Burnett Love; early in her career known by her married name, Ruth Love Holloway, but after her divorce known again by her maiden name; born April 22, 1935, in Lawton, Oklahoma). The first black and first woman general superintendent of the Chicago public school system (1981–84). Later she moved to the San Francisco area and directed Ruth Love Enterprises, an educational consulting firm, and copublished (with Carleton Goodlett) a group of black weekly newspapers.

Mabley, Jackie ("Moms") (originally Loretta Mary Aiken; born c. 1897 in Brevard, North Carolina; died May 23, 1975, in White Plains, New York). Comedienne. In a career that spanned vaudeville, nightclubs, recordings, film, and television, her comic character was that of a cantankerous old woman (created when Mabley herself was still young) who wore a funny hat, had a big toothless grin, and uttered gags laced with folk wisdom.

McCabe, Jewell Jackson (full name, Jewell Jackson Ward McCabe; originally Jewell Jackson; born August 2, 1945, in Washington, D.C.). Founder of the National Coalition of One Hundred Black Women (1981), an organization designed to help professional black women gain access to mainstream America. She also founded Jewell Jackson McCabe Associates, a management consulting firm.

McClendon, Rosalie ("Rosie") (full name, Rosalie Virginia Scott McClendon; originally Rosalie Virginia Scott; born August 27, 1884, in Greenville, South Carolina; died July 12, 1936, in New York City). Actress. The most highly regarded black stage performer of her time, she appeared in such New York City stage productions as *Deep River* (1926), *Porgy* (1927), *The House of Connelly* (1931), *Never No More* (1932), and Langston Hughes's *Mulatto* (1935), the first full-length play by a black author to be produced on Broadway.

McKinney, Cynthia A. (full name, Cynthia Ann McKinney; born March 17, 1955, in Atlanta, Georgia). The first African-American woman elected to the United States Congress from Georgia (1992).

McKinney, Nina Mae (born June 12, 1912, in Lancaster, South Carolina; died May 3, 1967, in New York City,). Actress. She became Hollywood's first black love goddess in the film *Hallelujah* (1929) and went on to appear in *Sanders of the River* (1935), with Paul Robeson, and *Pinky* (1949). She was also a nightclub singer, sometimes billed as the Black Greta Garbo.

McKissack, Patricia C. (originally Patricia L'Ann Carwell; born August 9, 1944, in Nashville, Tennessee). Author of children's picture books, short stories, and nonfiction works primarily in the fields of African-American history and biography. She writes some of her works alone and some with her husband, Fredrick L. McKissack. Her solo works include the picture book *Nettie Jo's Friends* (1989) and the short-story collection *The Dark Thirty: Southern Tales of the Supernatural* (1992). With her husband she has written innumerable biographies as well as the nonfiction books *The Civil Rights Movement in America from 1865 to the Present* (1987), *A Long Hard Journey: The Story of the Pullman Porter* (1989), and *Christmas in the Big House, Christmas in the Quarters* (1994).

McMillan, Enolia Pettigen (originally Enolia Pettigen; born October 20, 1904, in Willow Grove, Pennsylvania). The first woman president of the National Association for the Advancement of Colored People (1985–89).

McMillan, Terry (born 1951 in Port Huron, Michigan). Writer. Her works include the novels *Mama* (1987), *Disappearing Acts* (1989), and *Waiting to Exhale* (1992).

McQueen, Thelma ("Butterfly") (full name, Thelma Lincoln McQueen; born January 8, 1911, in Tampa, Florida; died December 22, 1995, in Augusta, Georgia). Actress. Famed for her role as the slave Prissy in the film classic *Gone with the Wind* (1939), she won an Emmy for her performance in the children's television special *The Seven Wishes of a Rich Kid* (1979).

McRae, Carmen (born April 8, 1922, in Brooklyn, New York; died November 10, 1994, in Beverly Hills, California). Jazz singer. She was influenced by, and favorably compared with, Billie Holiday* and Sarah Vaughan.* McRae's recordings include *By Special Request* (1955, Decca), *The Great American Songbook* (1971, Atlantic), and *You're Lookin' at Me* (1983, Concord).

Madgett, Naomi Long (full name, Naomi Cornelia Long Madgett; originally Naomi Cornelia Long; born July 5, 1923, in Norfolk, Virginia). Poet, educator, and head of the Lotus Press as editor-publisher (1974–93) and director (1993–).

Malone, Annie Turnbo (originally Annie Turnbo; born August 9, 1869, in Metropolis, Illinois; died May 10, 1957, in Chicago). Entrepreneur. She created the Poro brand of black beauty products and became, like C. J. Walker*, another specialist in the beauty-business, one of America's earliest self-made women millionaires and black philanthropists.

Marshall, Paule Burke (originally Paule Burke; born April 9, 1929, in Brooklyn, New York). Writer. Her fictional works, which draw on the culture of the West Indian African-American community, include the novels *Brown Girl, Brownstones* (1959); *The Chosen Place, the Timeless People* (1969); *Praisesong for the Widow* (1983); and *Daughters* (1991).

Martin, Sallie (married name; born November 20, 1895 [or 1896], in Pittfield, Georgia; died June 18, 1988, in Chicago). Gospel singer and composer. She was known as the Mother of Gospel Music because of her work as a promoter and publisher to popularize the genre.

Martin, Sara (full name, Sara [also recorded as Sarah] Dunn Martin; originally Sara Dunn; born June 18, 1884, in Louisville, Kentucky; died May 24, 1955, in Louisville). Blues singer. Known for her dramatic stage presence, she was one of the first female blues singers to make recordings, among them "Sugar Blues" / "Achin' Hearted Blues" (1922, Okeh), "Graveyard Dream Blues" (1923, Okeh), and many others.

Mary Alice (full name, Mary Alice Smith; born December 3, 1941, in Indianola, Mississippi). Actress. Famous for her Tony Award-winning Broadway performance as Rose Maxson in *Fences* (1985 in New Haven, Connecticut; 1987 in New York City), her other credits include the film *To Sleep with Anger* (1990) and the *Broadway play Having Our Say* (1995).

Mason, Bridget ("Biddy") (born August 15, 1818, probably in Georgia or Mississippi; died January 15, 1891, in Los Angeles). Pioneer in the black community of Los Angeles. A former slave, she worked as a nurse and midwife, earned financial independence through real estate investments, became a philanthropist, and founded the Los Angeles branch of the First African Methodist Episcopal church.

Maynor, Dorothy (originally Dorothy Leigh Mainor; born September 3, 1910, in Norfolk, Virginia; died February 19, 1996, in West Chester, Pennsylvania). Singer. One of the great concert sopranos of her time, she founded the Harlem School for the Arts (1964).

Meek, Carrie Pittman (born April 29, 1926, in Tallahassee, Florida). Educator and politician. In 1992 she became the first African-American from Florida to be elected to the United States Congress since Reconstruction and the first black female congressional representative ever from Florida.

Meriwether, Louise (full name, Louise Jenkins Meriwether; originally Louise Jenkins; born May 8, 1923, in Haverstraw, New York). Writer. She has raised black Americans' consciousness of their history, through her works, which include the novel *Daddy Was a Number Runner* (1970), the juvenile biography *Don't Ride the Bus on Monday: The Rosa Parks Story* (1973), and the novel *Fragments of the Ark* (1994).

Merkerson, S. Epatha (born November 28, 1952, in Saginaw, Michigan). Actress. She won great praise for her stage performances in *The Piano Lesson* (1990) and *I'm Not Stupid* (1991) and since 1993 has been a cast member of the television series *Law and Order*.

Merrick, Lyda Moore (originally Lyda Moore; born 1890 in Durham, North Carolina; died February 14, 1987, in Durham). Founder of *Negro Braille Magazine* (1952), later called the *Merrick-Washington Magazine for the Blind*.

Merritt, Emma Frances Grayson (born January 11, 1860, in Dumfries [Cherry Hill], Prince William County, Virginia; died June 8, 1933, in Washington, D.C.). Educator. In various positions with the public schools in Washington, D.C., including that of supervising principal of all black schools in the late 1920s, she established a teaching methodology that revolutionized black education throughout the country. She formed the first kindergarten for African-American students, developed a primary department and modernized instruction in that department, organized demonstration and observation schools to improve teaching techniques, classified students into homogeneous learning groups, created the practice of field trips, and introduced silent reading into the classroom.

Miller, Bebe (full name, Beryl Adele Miller; born September 20, 1950, in Brooklyn, New York). Dancer and choreographer. She established her own dance company in New York City in 1984 and has created such memorable works as the solo dance *Rain* (1989) and the ensemble piece *Hidden Boy: Incidents from a Stressed Memory* (1991).

Mills, Florence (originally Florence Winfree; born January 25, 1896, in Washington, D.C.; died November 1, 1927, in New York City). Leading American musical comedy singer and dancer of the Jazz Age and the Harlem Renaissance. Her trademark song was "I'm a Little Blackbird Looking for a Bluebird."

Mitchell, Abbie (born September 25, 1884, in New York City; died March 16, 1960, in New York City). Singer and stage actress in both musical comedy, such as *In Dahomey* (1903), and serious drama, including *In Abraham's Bosom* (1926).

Mitchell, Leona Pearl (born October 13, 1949, in Enid, Oklahoma). Concert and opera singer. A soprano, she won the San Francisco Opera auditions in 1971 and has performed with many leading international orchestras and opera companies.

Moon, Mollie (full name, Mollie V. Lewis Moon; originally Mollie V. Lewis; born July 31, 1908, in Hattiesburg, Mississippi; died June 24, 1990, in Long Island City, New York). Founder and president of the National Urban League Guild (1942–90).

Moore, Audley (full name, Audley Eloise Moore; born 1898 in New Iberia, Louisiana; died May 2, 1997, in Brooklyn, New York). Crusader for civil rights, women's rights, and Pan-African nationalism. Known as Queen Mother, initially by the Ashanti people of Ghana.

Moore, Melba (originally Melba Hill; born October 29, 1945, in New York City). Actress and singer. She gained fame in the stage musical *Hair* (1968) and won a Tony Award for her performance in the musical *Purlie* (1970).

Moseley-Braun, Carol (full name, Carol Elizabeth Moseley-Braun; originally Carol Elizabeth Moseley; born August 16, 1947, in Chicago). The first African-American woman elected to the United States Senate (D-Illinois, elected 1992).

Mossell, Gertrude Bustill (originally Gertrude Bustill; born July 3, 1855, in Philadelphia; died January 21, 1948, in Philadelphia). Pioneering journalist for African-American and feminist causes and author of *The Work of the Afro-American Woman* (1894). She was the aunt of the great singer-actor-activist Paul Robeson.

Murray, Joan (full name, Joan Elizabeth Murray; born November 6, 1941, in Ithaca, New York). The first black woman to report the news on television in New York City (WCBS-TV, 1965), she is also a cofounder of Zebra Associates (1969), the first integrated advertising agency with black principals.

Murray, Pauli (born November 20, 1910, in Baltimore, Maryland; died July 1, 1985, in Pittsburgh, Pennsylvania). Lawyer, poet, scholar, author, educator, administrator, religious leader, civil rights activist, and feminist. She was the first black deputy attorney general of California (1946), one of the founders of the National Organization for Women (1966), and the first woman ordained a priest in the Protestant Episcopal church (1977).

Napier, Nettie Langston (full name, Nettie DeElla Langston Napier; originally Nettie DeElla Langston; born June 17, 1861, in Oberlin, Ohio; died September 27, 1938, in Nashville, Tennessee). Pioneer in day care for poor black children, founding the Day Home Club (1907) in Nashville.

Naylor, Gloria (born January 25, 1950, in New York City). Writer. Her works include the novels *The Women of Brewster Place* (1982), *Linden Hills* (1985), and *Bailey's Cafe* (1992).

Nickerson, Camille (full name, Camille Lucie Nickerson; born March 30, 1888, in New Orleans, Louisiana; died April 27, 1982, in Washington, D.C.). Composer and collector of Creole songs, concert singer under the name Louisiana Lady, and influential music educator at Howard University in Washington, D.C. (1926–62).

Norton, Eleanor Holmes (originally Eleanor Holmes; born April 8, 1938, in Washington, D.C.). Lawyer and political activist. She has based her career on the use of law as a means of achieving racial and gender equality, serving in turn as assistant legal director of the American Civil Liberties Union (1965–70), chairperson of the New York City Commission on Human Rights (1970–77), and chairperson of the federal Equal Employment Opportunity Commission (1977–81). In 1990 she became one of the few black women elected to the United States Congress, winning a seat in the House of Representatives as a delegate from the District of Columbia.

Odetta (full name, Odetta Holmes Felious Gordon Shead Minter; originally Odetta Holmes; born December 31, 1930, in Birmingham, Alabama). Folksinger and guitarist. An important figure in the folksong revival of the 1950s and 1960s, she sings songs of both European and African-American origin (work songs, blues, ballads, spirituals). One of her best-known albums is *Odetta Sings Folk Songs* (1963, RCA).

O'Leary, Hazel R. (originally Hazel Reid; born May 17, 1937, in Newport News, Virginia). The first woman and first black secretary of energy in the United States cabinet (appointed 1993).

Ormes, Jackie (originally Zelda Jackson; born 1917 in Pittsburgh, Pennsylvania; died January 2, 1986, in Chicago). Cartoonist and creator of the first African-American female comic strip star, Torchy Brown (1937, *Pittsburgh Courier*).

Patterson, Mary Jane (born 1840 in Raleigh, North Carolina; died September 24, 1894, in Washington, D.C.). The first black principal of a high school in Washington, D.C. (Preparatory High School for

Colored Youth [later Dunbar High School], appointed 1871, served 1871–72, 1873–84).

Patton, Georgia E. L. (full name, Georgia Esther Lee Patton Washington; originally Georgia Esther Lee Patton; born April 16, 1864, in Grundy County, Tennessee; died November 8, 1900, in Memphis, Tennessee). The first black woman to graduate from the Meharry Medical Department of Central Tennessee College (1893, later renamed Meharry Medical College), the first Meharry graduate to serve as a missionary to Africa (1893–95), and the first black woman to be licensed as a physician and surgeon in Tennessee and to practice medicine in Memphis (1895).

Payne, Ethel (full name, Ethel Lois Payne; born August 14, 1911, in Chicago; died May 28, 1991, in Washington, D.C.). Journalist. Known as "the first lady of the black press," she was a White House correspondent (1953–73), the first black female war correspondent in the Vietnam War (1967), and a widely respected freelance writer (1982–91).

Payton, Carolyn Robertson (originally Carolyn Robertson; born May 13, 1925, in Norfolk, Virginia). The first woman and first black director of the Peace Corps (1978).

Peake, Mary S. (full name, Mary Smith Kelsey Peake; originally Mary Smith Kelsey; born 1823 in Norfolk, Virginia; died February 22, 1862, at Fort Monroe, near Norfolk). The first teacher in the American Missionary Association schools (1861).

Perry, Carrie Saxon (originally Carrie Saxon; born August 10, 1931, in Hartford, Connecticut). The first black woman mayor of a northeastern city (Hartford, elected 1987).

Perry, Julia (full name, Julia Amanda Perry; born March 25, 1924, in Lexington, Kentucky; died April 24, 1979, in Akron, Ohio). Composer. She was noted for her neoclassical style, intense lyricism, and, in her later works, such as *Soul Symphony* (1972), use of black folk idioms.

Petry, Ann (full name, Ann Lane Petrie; originally Ann Lane; born October 12, 1908, in Old Saybrook, Connecticut; died April 28, 1997, in Old Saybrook). Writer. She evolved from the Harlem Renaissance and became a bridge to more recent writers, such as Toni Morrison.* Petry is probably best known for her naturalistic-feminist novel *The Street* (1946), the first major literary portrait of Harlem.

Phillips, Val R. (full name, Velvalea Rogers Phillips; originally Velvalea Rogers; born February 18, 1924, in Milwaukee, Wisconsin). The first black woman to graduate from Wisconsin Law School (1950), the first black American to serve on the national committee of either major political party (Democratic party, 1958), the first black woman judge in Wisconsin (1972), and the first black person elected secretary of state in Wisconsin (1978).

Phinazee, Annette L. (full name, Alethia Annette Lewis Hoage Phinazee; originally Alethia Annette Lewis; born July 23, 1920, in Orangeburg, South Carolina; died September 17, 1983, in Durham, North Carolina). The dean of the School of Library Science at North Carolina Central University in Durham (1970–83), where she established a unique program in early childhood librarianship.

Pinkett, Jada (born c. 1971 in Baltimore, Maryland). Actress. She played Lena James in the television comedy series *A Different World* (1991–93) and has appeared in many films, including *Jason's Lyric* (1994) and *The Nutty Professor* (1996).

Plato, Ann (born c. 1820 in Hartford, Connecticut; death unknown). Poet and essayist. She is known for her book *Essays; Including Biographies and Miscellaneous Pieces of Prose and Poetry* (1841), whose little biographical sketches are important documents showing what life was like for middle-class black women of New England in the nineteenth century. Her poetry contains a lyricism that sets it apart from the work of her predecessor Phillis Wheatley.*

Player, Willa B. (full name, Willa Beatrice Player; born August 9, 1909, in Jackson, Mississippi). The first black woman president of a four-year women's college (Bennett College in Greensboro, North Carolina, 1955–66). From 1966 to 1977 she headed the Division of Institutional Development, Bureau of Postsecondary Education, in Washington, D.C. In both positions she greatly aided the civil rights and feminist causes.

Pleasant, Mary Ellen ("Mammy") (full name, Mary Ellen Williams Smith Pleasant; originally Mary Ellen Williams; birth details uncertain, but she claimed

August 19, 1814, in Philadelphia; died January 11, 1904, in San Francisco). Civil rights pioneer, restaurateur, investor, labor boss, and legendary figure in the San Francisco black community.

Polite, Charlene Hatcher (originally Charlene Hatcher; born August 28, 1932, in Detroit, Michigan). Novelist and educator. She wrote the novels *Les flagellents* (1966, published in English as *The Flagellants*, 1967) and *Sister X and the Victims of Foul Play* (1975), both of which are noted for their experimentation in plot and characterization.

Porter, Connie Rose (born c. 1959 in Buffalo, New York). Writer. After publishing an impressive first novel, *All-Bright Court* (1991), she embarked on a series of children's books about a young black girl named Addy Walker, including *Meet Addy: An American Girl* (1993) and *Changes for Addy: A Winter Story* (1994).

Porter, Dorothy (full name, Dorothy Louise Burnett Porter; originally Dorothy Louise Burnett; born May 25, 1905, in Warrenton, Virginia). Librarian. During her long tenure at Howard University in Washington, D.C. (1928–73), she built the collection that came to be known as the Moorland-Spingarn Research Center, the largest repository for the study of African-American history in an academic institution.

Powers, Georgia (full name, Georgia Montgomery Davis Powers; originally Georgia Montgomery; born October 29, 1923, in Springfield, Kentucky). The first black and first woman elected to the Kentucky State Senate (1967), where she remained for over twenty years.

Powers, Harriet (married name; maiden name unknown; born October 29, 1837, in Georgia; died 1911 in Sandy Creek Georgia). Quilting artist. Her Bible quilt (1886) hangs in the Smithsonian Institution's National Museum of American History in Washington, D.C., and her story quilt *The Creation of the Animals* (1895–98) is on display in the Museum of Fine Arts in Boston.

Preer, Evelyn (or Evelyn Preer Thompson, her married name; born July 26, 1896, in Vicksburg, Mississippi; died November 18, 1932, in Los Angeles). Actress. She paved the way for other blacks by appearing in many early motion pictures, such as *The Homesteader* (1919), *The Brute* (1920), *The Spider's Web* (1926), *The Devil's Disciple* (1926), and *Blonde*

Venus (1932). She was also the star of the famous Lafayette Players, with whom she appeared in many plays throughout the 1920s.

Price, Florence (full name, Florence Beatrice Smith Price; originally Florence Beatrice Smith; born April 9, 1888, in Little Rock, Arkansas; died June 3, 1953, in Chicago). Composer. She is credited with elevating black folksong to a status comparable with that of art songs. One of her most highly regarded works, to a text by Langston Hughes, is "Songs to the Dark Virgin" (1941).

Primus, Pearl (born November 29, 1919, in Trinidad, West Indies; died October 29, 1994, in New Rochelle, New York). Pioneer in the development of black dance as an art form.

Prince, Lucy Terry (originally Lucy Terry; born c. 1730, probably in western Africa; died 1821 in Sunderland, Vermont). Writer and orator. She is best known for her only surviving poem, "Bars Fight" (written 1746, first published 1855).

Prince, Nancy Gardner (originally Nancy Gardner; born September 15, 1799, in Newburyport, Massachusetts; death unknown, 1856 or later). Abolitionist, traveler, religious worker, and author of the autobiography *A Narrative of the Life and Travels of Mrs. Nancy Prince* (1850; third edition, 1856).

Prophet, Elizabeth (full name, Nancy Elizabeth Prophet; born March 19, 1890, in Warwick, Rhode Island; died December 1960 in Providence, Rhode Island). Sculptor. Her portrait busts and figurative sculptures earned her international acclaim in the 1920s and 1930s.

Prout, Nancy Ann ("Aunt Mary") (born c. 1801, probably February 14, 1801, in Baltimore, Maryland; died 1884 in Baltimore). Founder of a Baltimore day school, at which she also taught, and of a secret order from which evolved the Independent Order of Saint Luke, a black organization supplying financial aid to the sick and funds for the burial of the dead.

Purvis, Harriet Forten (full name, Harriet Davy Forten Purvis; originally Harriet Davy Forten; born 1810 in Philadelphia; died June 11, 1875, in Philadelphia). Abolitionist who hid runaway slaves in her home. She was the sister of Sarah Forten Purvis and Margaretta Forten* and the aunt of Charlotte L. Forten Grimké.* Harriet and Sarah married brothers surnamed Purvis.

Purvis, Sarah Forten (full name, Sarah Louisa Forten Purvis; originally Sarah Louisa Forten; born 1811 or 1812 in Philadelphia; death unknown, probably by 1898 in Philadelphia). Abolitionist and poet. She was known for her antislavery verse, such as "The Slave" (1831). She was the sister of Harriet Forten Purvis* and Margaretta Forten*, and the aunt of Charlotte L. Forten Grimké.* Sarah and Harriet married brothers surnamed Purvis.

Queen Latifah (originally Dana Owens; born c. 1970 in New Jersey). Singer and actress. She was known for her role as Khadijah James in the television comedy series *Living Single* (1993–98).

Rahn, Muriel (full name, Muriel Ellen Rahn; born 1911 in Boston; died August 8, 1961, in New York City). Concert singer, opera soprano, and performer in Broadway musicals (*Carmen Jones*, 1943). She was the first black to appear in opera at Carnegie Hall with an all-white opera company (1942).

Rainey, Ma (originally Gertrude Malissa Nix Pridgett; born April 26, 1886, in Columbus, Georgia; died December 22, 1939, in Rome, Georgia). One of the earliest professional blues singers, known as the Mother of the Blues. Her recordings included "Bo-weavil Blues" (1923, Paramount), "Moonshine Blues" (1923, Paramount), "See See Rider" (1924, Paramount), and "Soon This Morning" (1927, Paramount).

Randolph, Amanda (born 1902 in Louisville, Kentucky; died August 24, 1967, in Duarte, near Los Angeles). Actress. Her credits include films, such as *Lying Lips* (1939) and *No Way Out* (1950), and television series, playing Mama in *Amos 'n' Andy* (1951–53) and the housekeeper Louise in *Make Room for Daddy* (1953–56), later retitled *The Danny Thomas Show* (1956–64). She was the sister of Lillian Randolph.

Randolph, Lillian (born 1914 in Knoxville, Tennessee; died September 12, 1980, in Arcadia, near Los Angeles). Actress. She is best known for her portrayal of the maid Birdie in *The Great Gildersleeve* on radio (1941–58) and television (1955) and in several Gildersleeve movies (1940s).

Her other television work included her role as Madame Queen, Andy's girlfriend, on *Amos 'n' Andy* (1951–53), a recurring part on *The Bill Cosby Show* (1969–70), and an appearance in the miniseries *Roots* (1977). She worked steadily in films from the 1930s to the 1970s, her most memorable role being the housekeeper Annie in the classic *It's a Wonderful Life* (1946). She was the sister of Amanda Randolph.

Randolph, Virginia (full name, Virginia Estelle Randolph; born June 8, 1874, in Richmond, Virginia; died March 16, 1958, in Richmond). The first teacher under the auspices of the Anna Thomas Jeanes Fund. She supervised rural black teachers in implementing a new vocational approach to teaching.

Rashad, Phylicia (originally Phylicia Ayers-Allen; born June 19, 1948, in Houston, Texas). Actress and singer. She is best known for her role as Claire Huxtable in the long-running television comedy series *The Cosby Show* (1984–92). Since 1996 she has also costarred

with Bill Cosby in *Cosby*. She began her career under the name Phylicia Ayers-Allen (her mother's maiden name was Ayers, and her father's surname was Allen). She is the sister of Debbie Allen and wife of the sportscaster Ahmad Rashad.

Ray, H. Cordelia (full name, Henrietta Cordelia Ray; born c. 1849 in New York City; died January 5, 1916, in New York City). Educator, scholar, and poet. She was known for her consummate understanding of traditional lyrical form and technique. Most of her works were collected in the volumes *Sonnets* (1893) and *Poems* (1910). Published separately was her eight-stanza, eighty-line *Lincoln; Written for the Occasion of the Unveiling of the Freedmen's Monument in Memory of Abraham Lincoln, April 14, 1876* (1893).

Reagon, Bernice J. (full name, Bernice Johnson Reagon; originally Bernice Johnson; born October 4, 1942, in Albany, Georgia). Singer, civil rights activist, and historian. Credited with bringing black studies into mainstream scholarship, she served at the Museum of American History in

Washington, D.C., she served as director and cultural historian of the Program in Black American Culture (1976–88), curator (1988–93), and curator emeritus (1994–).

Reese, Della (originally Deloreese Patricia Early; born July 6, 1931, in Detroit, Michigan). Singer, actress, and minister. She became a major recording star in the late 1950s, notably with "Don't You Know" (1959, RCA), and her acting credits include the television series *Chico and the Man* (1976–78) and *Touched by an Angel* (1994–). In private life she is known as the Reverend Della Reese-Lett (her married name), minister of Understanding Principles for Better Living, a nondenominational church in Los Angeles.

Rhone, Sylvia (born March 11, 1952, in Philadelphia). The highest-ranking black female executive in the recording industry. She became chairperson and chief executive officer of the Elektra Entertainment Group in 1994.

Rice, Condoleezza (born November 14, 1954, in Birmingham, Alabama). Educator and foreign policy expert. She served as a director and later a senior director of Soviet and East European Affairs with the National Security Council (1989–91), and in 1993 she was named provost of Stanford University, becoming the first African-American chief academic officer and budget officer there and one of the highest-ranking black college administrators in the nation.

Richards, Beau (originally Beulah Richardson; born July 12, 1926, in Vicksburg, Mississippi). Actress. Her credits include the play *The Amen Corner* (1963 in Los Angeles, 1965 in New York City), the film *Guess Who's Coming to Dinner* (1967), the television miniseries *Roots: The Next Generations* (1979); and the film *Beloved* (1998). For her performance in "The Bridge," an episode of *Frank's Place* during the 1987–88 television season, she won an Emmy Award as the outstanding guest performer in a comedy series.

Richards, Fannie M. (full name, Fannie Moore Richards; born October 1, 1840 [or 1841], in Fredericksburg, Virginia; died February 13, 1922, in Detroit, Michigan). The first full-time professional black teacher in Detroit's public schools (1868). She helped to desegregate the city's schools and founded Detroit's Phillis Wheatley Home (1898) for aged black women.

Richardson, Gloria (full name, Gloria St. Clair Hayes Richardson; originally Gloria St. Clair Hayes; born May 6, 1922, in Baltimore, Maryland). Civil rights activist. She led the well-publicized fight to desegregate Cambridge, Maryland, in the 1960s.

Ridley, Florida Ruffin (full name, Florida Yates Ruffin Ridley; originally Florida Yates Ruffin; born 1861 in Boston; died March 1943 in Toledo, Ohio). Clubwoman, writer, educator, and social worker. She helped her mother, Josephine St. Pierre Ruffin, to found the Woman's Era Club (1893) and went on to play a major pioneering role in other black women's clubs and to become a leader in Boston civic and social life.

Ringgold, Faith (originally Faith Willie Jones; born October 8, 1930, in New York City). Artist, writer, educator, and social activist. She has worked in a wide range of artistic media, including story quilts, such as the *French Collection* series (Part I, 1991; Part II, 1991–94). Her literary works include the children's book *Tar Beach* (1991) and the autobiography *We Flew over the Bridge* (1995).

Roberts, Deborah A. (born September 20, 1960, in Perry, Georgia). Broadcast journalist. After reporting local and national news on several Southern television stations (1982–90), she covered national and international stories for NBC News from its Atlanta, Georgia, bureau (1990–92); since 1992 she has been a correspondent for the network's popular newsmagazine *Dateline NBC*.

Robeson, Eslanda Goode (full name, Eslanda Cardoza Goode Robeson; originally Eslanda Cardoza Goode; born December 12, 1896, in Washington, D.C.; died December 13, 1965, in New York City). Pan-Africanist, civil rights activist, and writer. Wife of the famed actor-singer-activist Paul Robeson.

Rollins, Charlemae Hill (originally Charlemae Hill; born June 20, 1897, in Yazoo City, Mississippi; died February 3, 1979, in Chicago). Librarian, author, and children's literature specialist. She crusaded to change the image of black people in children's literature and to promote the publication of books about the black experience in American life and culture. She headed the children's department at the George Cleveland Hall Branch Library in Chicago (1932–63) and wrote, among other books, *Black Troubador: Langston Hughes* (1970).

Ross, Diana (originally Diane Ross; born March 26, 1944, in Detroit, Michigan). Singer and actress. She was a member of the vocal group the Primettes (1959–61), renamed the Supremes (1961), eventually becoming the lead singer (1964–69). Leaving the group in early 1970, she became a celebrated soloist, with such hit recordings as "Touch Me in the Morning" (1973, Motown) and *Diana* (1980, Motown). Her credits as an actress include the roles of the legendary jazz singer Billie Holiday in *Lady Sings the Blues* (1972), and Dorothy in *The Wiz* (1978).

Rushen, Patrice (born September 30, 1954, in Los Angeles). Vocalist, film composer, and music director. She recorded many successful singles and albums, such as "Hang It Up" (1978, Elektra), *Straight from the Heart* (1982, Elektra), and "Forget Me Nots" (1982, Elektra); composed the background scores for the films *Shuffle* (1987) and *Without You I'm Nothing* (1990); and became the first African-American and first woman to serve as music director of television's Emmy Awards show (1991, 1992).

Saar, Betye (full name, Betye Irene Saar; originally Betye Irene Brown; born July 30, 1926, in Los Angeles). Artist. She is known for her work based on assemblage, particularly her use of ethnic imagery to make a political protest, as in *The Liberation of Aunt Jemima* (1972).

Sampson, Deborah (married name, Deborah Sampson Gannett; alias Robert Shurtleff; born December 17, 1760, in Plymouth, Massachusetts; died April 29, 1827, in Sharon, Massachusetts). Soldier (1782–83) in the Continental Army during the Revolutionary War. Disguised as a man, she fought in many battles and received multiple wounds. To avoid detection, she removed a musket ball from her own leg and left other wounds untreated. Finally, illness forced her into a hospital, where her sex was discovered, as a result of which she was discharged from the army shortly thereafter. By 1805, partly through the help of Paul Revere, she was receiving a soldier's pension from the United States government.

Sanchez, Sonia (originally Wilsonia Benita Driver; born September 9, 1934, in Birmingham, Alabama). Poet, playwright, political activist, and lecturer. She has written many militant calls to correct abuses and inequities in the world, particularly those affecting black Americans. Her most ac-

claimed work is the poetry collection *Homegirls and Handgrenades* (1984), in which the "grenades" are words that explode people's deluding myths about themselves and the world.

Savage, Augusta (full name, Augusta Christine Fells Savage; originally Augusta Christine Fells; born February 29, 1892, in Green Cove Springs, Florida; died March 26, 1962, in New York City). Sculptor. One of the great artists of the Harlem Renaissance, she is best known for *Lift Every Voice and Sing*, which she created for the New York World's Fair of 1939–40.

Schuyler, Philippa (full name, Philippa Duke Schuyler; born August 2, 1931, in Harlem, New York; died May 9, 1967, in Da Nang, Vietnam). Concert pianist, composer, and writer. She performed throughout the world and also wrote several books related to her travels. Her best-known compositions are orchestral works, including *Nile Fantasy* (1965), which shows the influence of African music. She died in a helicopter crash while trying to rescue children during the Vietnam War.

Scott, Gloria (full name, Gloria Dean Randle Scott; originally Gloria Dean Randle; born April 14, 1938, in Houston, Texas). The first black national president of Girl Scouts, USA (1975) and the second woman president of Bennett College in Greensboro, North Carolina (1987).

Scott, Hazel (full name, Hazel Dorothy Scott; born June 11, 1920, in Port of Spain, Trinidad; died October 2, 1981, in New York City). Pianist and singer. Best known for her jazz improvisations on familiar classical pieces, her recordings include "Hungarian Rhapsody no. 2" (Liszt) / "Valse in D Flat Major" (Chopin op. 64 no. 1) (1940, Decca). She also appeared in several films, such as *Rhapsody in Blue* (1945).

Sears-Collins, Leah Jeanette (originally Leah Jeanette Sears; born June 13, 1955, in Heidelberg, West Germany). Lawyer and judge. She has served on the City Court of Atlanta, Georgia (1985–88), the Superior Court of Fulton County, Georgia (1989–), and the Georgia Supreme Court (1992–), and was one of the youngest judges to serve on any state supreme court.

Shange, Ntozake (originally Paulette Williams; born October 18, 1948, in Trenton, New Jersey). Poet, playwright, and novelist. Her best-known work is

For Colored Girls Who Have Considered Suicide / When the Rainbow Is Enuf (1974), a black feminist drama (which Shange called a choreopoem) combining poetry, music, dance, and lighting.

Sheppard Moore, Ella (originally Ella Sheppard; born February 4, 1851, in Nashville, Tennessee; died June 9, 1914, in Nashville). Pianist, singer, and choral director for the famed Fisk Jubilee Singers, who toured nationally and internationally in the 1870s.

Simkins, Modjeska (full name, Mary Modjeska Monteith Simkins; originally Mary Modjeska Monteith; born December 5, 1899, in Columbus, South Carolina; died 1992 in Columbia). Human and civil rights activist. She worked with over fifty progressive reform organizations during a period of six decades.

Simmons, Althea T. L. (born April 17, 1924, in Shreveport, Louisiana; died September 13, 1990, in Washington, D.C.). Lawyer and civil rights activist. She was associated for many years with the National Association for the Advancement of Colored People (NAACP), notably as director of its National Voter Registration Drive (1964), national education director (1974–77), associate director of branch and field services (1977–79), and director of the Washington Bureau and chief lobbyist for the NAACP (1979–90).

Simmons, Ruth J. (originally Ruth Jean Stubblefield; born July 3, 1945, in Grapeland, Texas). The first African-American woman to head a top-ranked college or university in the United States. She assumed the presidency of Smith College, a women's liberal arts college in Northampton, Massachusetts, in 1995.

Simms, Hilda (originally Hilda Theresa Moses; born April 15, 1920, in Minneapolis, Minnesota). Actress. She achieved fame in the play *Anna Lucasta* (1944) and was one of the earliest African-American women to play a recurring role in a prime-time dramatic television series, *The Nurses* (1962–64, later known as *The Doctors and the Nurses*, 1964–65).

Simone, Nina (originally Eunice Kathleen Waymon; born February 21, 1933, in Tryon, North Carolina). Popular singer, pianist, and composer. Known as the High Priestess of Soul, she actually blends soul, jazz, and pop. She achieved national recognition through her recording of George

Gershwin's "I Loves You, Porgy" (1959, Bethlehem) and wrote some highly emotional protest songs during the 1960s, such as "Four Women" (1966). Her other recordings include *Nina at Newport* (1960, Colpix), *I Put a Spell on You* (1965, Philips), and "My Baby Just Cares for Me" (1987, Charly). Since the 1970s she has performed mainly in Europe.

Simpson, Carole (born December 7, 1940, in Chicago, Illinois). Broadcast journalist. She has anchored ABC's *World News Tonight, Saturday* (1988–93) and *World News Tonight, Sunday* (1993–).

Simpson, Valerie (born about 1946 in the Bronx, New York). Singer and songwriter. Since the 1960s she and her partner, Nickolas Ashford (whom she married in the 1970s), have been a top songwriting team, with such hits to their credit as "Ain't No Mountain High Enough," "Ain't Nothing like the Real Thing," and "Your Precious Love." Their recordings include *Send It* (1977, Warner), *Solid* (1984, Capitol), and *Been Found* (1996, Hopsack and Silk).

Sizemore, Barbara (full name, Barbara Ann Laffoon Sizemore; originally Barbara Ann Laffoon; born December 17, 1927, in Chicago). The first woman and first black associate secretary for the American Association of School Administrators (1972–73). She also served as superintendent of schools for the District of Columbia Public School System (1973–75) and has written many scholarly works on education.

Sklarek, Norma Merrick (originally Norma Merrick; born April 15, 1928, in New York City). The first black American woman registered architect (New York State, 1954), the first black woman fellow of the American Institute of Architects (1980), and founder of, and partner in, the largest exclusively female-owned architectural firm in the United States (Siegel, Sklarek, Diamond, 1985–89).

Smith, Ada ("Bricktop") (full name, Ada Beatrice Queen Victoria Louise Virginia ["Bricktop"] Smith; born August 14, 1894, in Alderson, West Virginia; died January 31, 1984, in New York City). A nightclub singer and owner in Paris and New York City.

Smith, Clara (born 1894 in Spartanburg, South Carolina; died February 2, 1935, in Detroit, Michigan). Blues singer. Known as the Queen of the Moaners, she demonstrated her moaning style—a melodramatic technique involving voice tremors—on her recording of "Awful Moanin' Blues" (duet with Fletcher Henderson, 1923, Columbia).

Smith, Mamie (originally Mamie Robinson; born May 26, 1883, in Cincinnati, Ohio; died October 1946 in New York City). The first black woman to make a record ("That Thing Called Love" / "You Can't Keep a Good Man Down," 1920, Okeh) and to record a blues song ("Crazy Blues," 1920, Okeh). She paved the way for other black artists to make subsequent recordings.

Smith, Mary Carter (originally Mary Rogers Ward; born February 10, 1919, in Birmingham, Alabama). Storyteller, folklorist, performer, educator, writer, and social activist. Since 1973 she has been a full-time storyteller, preserving and transmitting the history and culture of African-Americans through stories, poems, songs, jokes, and dramatic sketches.

Smith, Willie Mae Ford ("Mother") (originally Willie Mae Ford; born June 23, 1904, in Rolling Fork, Mississippi; died February 2, 1994, in Saint Louis, Missouri). Gospel music pioneer. She committed herself to the genre in the 1920s, became director of the Soloists Bureau of the National Convention of Gospel Choirs and Choruses in 1936, and set the standard for solo gospel singing with her performance of her own "If You Just Keep Still" at the National Baptist Convention in 1937. She was one of the first to sing in the blues-influenced gospel style developed by Thomas A. Dorsey in the 1920s and 1930s. In 1939, however, she left the Baptist church to become an evangelist in the Church of God Apostolic, thereafter singing less often.

Smythe-Haithe, Mabel Murphy (originally Mabel Murphy; born April 3, 1918, in Montgomery, Alabama). Educator and diplomat. She served as United States ambassador to the United Republic of Cameroon in Yaounde (1977–80) and to Equatorial Guinea (1979–80), held the post of deputy assistant secretary for African affairs at the Department of State (1980–81), and is a widely respected consultant on African economic development.

Snow, Valaida (birth date uncertain, but probably June 2, 1903 [or 1900], in Chattanooga, Tennessee; died May 30, 1956, in New York City). Jazz musician. She was known as Queen of the Trumpet, though she was also an accomplished singer and dancer. Her

recording of "I Got Rhythm" (1937, Parlophone) provides a good example of her playing.

Southern, Eileen (full name, Eileen Stanza Jackson Southern; originally Eileen Stanza Jackson; born February 19, 1920, in Minneapolis, Minnesota). A musicologist who has published studies on fifteenth-century music and African-American music include *The Music of Black Americans: A History* (1971; second edition, 1984) and *Biographical Dictionary of Afro-American and African Musicians* (1982).

Spence, Eulalie (born June 11, 1894, on the island of Nevis, British West Indies; died March 7, 1981, in Pennsylvania). Harlem Renaissance playwright. She was noted for her nonpolitical comedies, such as *Fool's Errand* (1927).

Spencer, Anne (full name, Anne Bethel Bannister Scales Spencer; originally Annie Bethel Bannister; born February 6, 1882, in Henry County, Virginia; died July 27, 1975, in Lynchburg, Virginia). Leading poet of the southern wing of the Harlem Renaissance. She wrote some protest poems, such as "White Things" (1923), but was best known for her romantic nature poetry, such as "Lines to a Nasturtium" (1926).

Spiller, Isabele Taliaferro (originally Isabele Taliaferro; born March 18, 1888, in Abingdon, Virginia; died May 14, 1974, in New York City). Musician, educator. She cofounded (with her husband, William Spiller) and headed the Spiller Music School (1925–40) in Harlem, New York City, established to meet the needs of black musicians who could not attend white schools. From 1933 to 1941 she directed the music education division of New York City's Federal Music Project.

Spivey, Victoria ("Queen Victoria") (full name, Victoria Regina Spivey; born October 1906 in Houston, Texas; died October 3, 1976, in New York City). Blues singer and pianist. Known for her lean but strong voice and vivacious stage personality, she recorded "Black Snake Blues" (1926, Okeh), appeared in the all-black film *Hallelujah!* (1929), and founded Spivey record company (1962).

Staupers, Mabel Keaton (full name, Mabel Doyle Keaton Staupers; originally Mabel Doyle; born February 27, 1890, in Barbados, West Indies; died November 29, 1989, in Washington, D.C.). Nurse and political activist. As executive secretary of the National Association of Colored Graduate Nurses

(NACGN, 1934–49), she helped to found the National Council of Negro Women (1935), led the fight to desegregate the Army Nurse Corps and the Navy Nurse Corps during World War II (1941–45), and happily rendered her own NACGN obsolete by pressuring the American Nurses Association to integrate (1948).

Steward, Susan McKinney (full name, Susan Maria Smith McKinney Steward; originally Susan Maria Smith; born 1847 in Brooklyn, New York; died March 7, 1918, in Wilberforce, Ohio). The first black woman to receive a medical degree from a medical college in New York State (New York Medical College for Women, 1870). She had a long, thriving practice in Brooklyn, helped to found the Brooklyn Woman's Homeopathic Hospital and Dispensary (1881, later renamed the Memorial Hospital for Women and Children), and became a women's rights activist. She was the sister of Sarah Garnet.*

Stewart, Ella P. (full name, Ella Nora Phillips Myers Stewart; originally Ella Nora Phillips; born March 6, 1893, in Stringtown, near Berryville, Virginia; died November 27, 1987, in Toledo, Ohio). Black woman pioneer in the field of pharmacy, president of the National Association of Colored Women (1948–52), and activist on innumerable local, federal, and international humanitarian committees.

Sudarkasa, Niara (originally Gloria Albertha Marshall; born August 14, 1938, in Fort Lauderdale, Florida). Internationally acclaimed anthropologist specializing in African studies and the first woman president of Lincoln University (1987–) in Pennsylvania, the nation's oldest historically black college.

Sul-Te-Wan, Madame (originally Nellie Conley; born September 12, 1873, in Louisville, Kentucky; died February 1, 1959, in Woodland Hills, California). The first contracted, featured African-American performer, male or female, in American films. She appeared in D. W. Griffith's *The Birth of a Nation* (1915), and her later movies included *The Lightning Rider* (1924), *Thunderbolt* (1929), *Black Moon* (1934), *Imitation of Life* (1934), *Maid of Salem* (1937), *In Old Chicago* (1938), *Maryland* (1940), *Sullivan's Travels* (1941), and *Band of Angels* (1957).

Swoopes, Sheryl (born March 25, 1971, in Brownfield, Texas). Basketball player. She led Texas Tech to the National Collegiate Athletic Association title in 1993, scoring a championship-game record, for men or

women, of 47 points; won virtually every major women's athletic award for 1993; became the first female athlete to have a shoe named after her (Nike's Air Swoopes, 1995); was a member of the United States basketball women's team that won the 1996 Olympic gold medal in Atlanta, Georgia; and helped the Houston Comets to win the Women's National Basketball Association championship in the league's first two seasons (1997, 1998).

Talbert, Mary Morris (full name, Mary Morris Burnett Talbert; originally Mary Morris Burnett; born September 17, 1866, in Oberlin, Ohio; died October 15, 1923, in Buffalo, New York). Educator and civil rights activist. She played a major role in developing both the National Association of Colored Women (president, 1916–20) and the National Association for the Advancement of Colored People (vice president and board member, 1918–23).

Tanneyhill, Ann (full name, Anna Elizabeth Tanneyhill; born January 19, 1906, in Norwood, Massachusetts). Longtime executive with the National Urban League. She began working in the Springfield, Massachusetts, office in 1928 and later served at the national headquarters in New York City, till her retirement in 1981. From 1947 to 1961 she was director of vocational services.

Tarry, Ellen (born September 26, 1906, in Birmingham, Alabama). Journalist, autobiographer, and children's writer. In *The Third Door: The Autobiography of an American Woman* (1955), she explores many complex issues within the African-American community. She pioneered the creation of juvenile literature containing positive role models for black children and depicting interracial friendships. Her children's books include *Janie Bell* (1940), and among her books for teenage readers is the biography *Young Jim: The Early Years of James Weldon Johnson* (1967).

Taylor, Anna Diggs (full name, Anna Johnston Diggs Taylor; originally Anna Johnston; born December 9, 1932, in Washington, D.C.). The first black woman federal judge in Michigan, where she has held a lifetime appointment at the United States District Court, Eastern District of Michigan, since 1979.

Taylor, Eva (originally Irene Gibbons; married name, Irene Gibbons Williams; stage name of Eva Taylor from 1922; born January 22, 1895, in Saint Louis,

Missouri; died October 31, 1977, in Mineola, New York). Popular vocalist in theater, radio, and the recording industry. She made many recordings with her husband, the pianist Clarence Williams, one of the finest being "Cakewalking Babies from Home" (1925, Okeh).

Taylor, Mildred (full name, Mildred Delois Taylor; born 1943 in Jackson, Mississippi). Writer. She is best known for her classic children's novel *Roll of Thunder, Hear My Cry* (1976).

Taylor, Susan L. (born January 23, 1946, in New York City). Editor of *Essence* magazine (1981–) and author of *In the Spirit: The Inspirational Writings of Susan L. Taylor* (1993).

Taylor, Susie King (full name, Susan Baker King Taylor; originally Susan Baker; born August 5, 1848, in Liberty County, Georgia; died October 6, 1912, in Boston). The only black woman to write of her participation in the Civil War, during which she was a nurse for a black Northern regiment. Her book, *Reminiscences of My Life in Camp* (1902), is valuable not only as a Civil War narrative but also as an account of the struggles of all African-Americans in the nineteenth century.

Tharpe, Sister Rosetta (originally Rosetta Nubin; born March 20, 1915, in Cotton Plant, Arkansas; died October 9, 1973, in Philadelphia). Singer and guitarist. She popularized gospel music among general audiences with recordings such as "Rock Me" (1938, Decca) and "Strange Things Happening Every Day" (1944, Decca).

Thomas, Alma (full name, Alma Woodsey Thomas; born September 22, 1891, in Columbus, Georgia; died February 24, 1978, in Washington, D.C.). The first fine arts graduate of Howard University in Washington, D.C. (1924), and the first African-American woman to achieve critical acclaim as an abstract artist.

Thomas, Edna (full name, Edna Lewis Thomas; originally Edna Lewis; born 1886 in Lawrenceville, Virginia; died July 22, 1974, in New York City). Actress and singer. Performing at first in black theater and vaudeville and later in mainstream productions, she won great praise for her portrayal of Lady Macbeth in Orson Welles's all-black voodoo production of Shakespeare's *Macbeth* (1936). In Tennessee Williams's *A Streetcar Named Desire* she played the Mexican Woman selling "Flores para los muertos" ("Flowers for the dead") in both the stage (1947) and film (1951) versions.

Thomas, Lillian Parker (full name, Lillian May Parker Thomas; originally Lilliam May Parker; born 1857 in Chicago; death unknown). Journalist and social reformer. Through her writings in the 1880s and 1890s (in 1891 she joined *The Freeman*, a weekly), she became a highly influential early civil and women's rights activist.

Thompson, Era Bell (born August 10, 1906, in Des Moines, Iowa; died December 29, 1986, in Chicago). Magazine editor. She was the managing editor of *Negro Digest* (1947–51, later called *Black World*), comanaging editor of *Ebony* (1951–64), and international editor of *Ebony* (1964–86). She also wrote books, including her autobiography, *American Daughter* (1946).

Torrence, Gwen (full name, Gwendolyn Lenna Torrence; born June 12, 1965, in Atlanta, Georgia). Athlete. Known as the most versatile sprinter of her time, she has attained world-class status in all the shorter distances, from 60 to 400 meters. At the 1992 Olympics in Barcelona, Spain, she won gold medals in the 200 meters and the 4 X 100-meter relay. In the 1996 Olympic Games held in Atlanta, Georgia, she won a gold medal in the 4 X 100-meter relay and a bronze in the 100 meters.

Torrence, Jackie (born February 12, 1944, in Chicago). Internationally renowned itinerant storyteller, called the Story Lady. Her repertory is vast, including tall tales, ghost stories, and African-American lore.

Tucker, C. DeLores (full name, Cynthia DeLores Nottage Tucker; originally Cynthia DeLores Nottage; born October 4, 1927, in Philadelphia). Secretary of state in Pennsylvania (1971–77), national vice president of the board of trustees of the National Association for the Advancement of Colored People (1989), vice president of the *Philadelphia Tribune* (1989–), and vice chairperson (1984–92) and national chairperson (1992–) of the National Political Congress of Black Women.

Tucker, Cynthia Anne (born March 13, 1955, in Monroeville, Alabama). Journalist. She became the first black woman editor of the editorial pages of a major daily publication (*Atlanta Constitution*, 1992–).

Verrett, Shirley (born May 31, 1931, in New Orleans, Louisiana). Concert and opera singer. She has distinguished herself by her versatility in opera as both a mezzo-soprano and a dramatic soprano. Her concert repertory ranges from Schubert to Rorem and includes spirituals. In 1994 she expanded her career even further by taking the role of Nettie Fowler in a New York stage production of the Rodgers and Hammerstein Broadway classic *Carousel.*

Waddles, Charleszetta ("Mother") (full name, Charleszetta Lina Campbell Waddles; originally Charleszetta Lina Campbell; born October 7, 1912, in Saint Louis, Missouri). Pentecostal minister and founder, director, and pastor of the Perpetual Mission for Saving Souls of All Nations (1956–) in Detroit, Michigan.

Walker, Aida (full name, Aida Overton Walker; originally Aida Overton; born February 14, 1880, in New York City; died October 11, 1914, in New York City). The foremost African-American stage artist of her era. She was the leading black female cakewalk dancer and ragtime singer, a pivotal performer in the change from minstrelsy to all-black musicals, and one of the first black international superstars.

Walker, A'Lelia (originally Lelia McWilliams; born June 6, 1885, in Vicksburg, Mississippi; died August 16, 1931, in Long Branch, New Jersey). Harlem Renaissance arts patron. She was the daughter of the famed entrepreneur Madam C. J. Walker.*

Walker, Margaret (married name, Margaret Abigail Walker Alexander; originally Margaret Abigail Walker; born July 7, 1915, in Birmingham, Alabama). Poet, novelist, essayist, and educator. Her works include the poetry collection *For My People* (1942), the historical novel *Jubilee* (1966), and the biography *Richard Wright, Daemonic Genius: A Portrait of the Man, a Critical Look at His Work* (1987).

Wallace, Joan Scott (originally Joan Scott; born November 8, 1930, in Chicago). Social scientist and educator. She became the first black assistant secretary for administration at the United States De- partment of Agriculture (1977–81), later serving the department as administrator of the Office of International Cooperation and Development (1981–89) and as representative at the Inter-American Institute for Cooperative Agriculture (1989) in Trinidad and Tobago. In Trinidad she became known as Joan of Agriculture. Since 1993 she has been an international consultant for United States Partnerships International.

Wallace, Sippie (originally Beulah Belle Thomas; born November 1, 1898, in Houston, Texas; died November 1, 1986, in Detroit, Michigan). Jazz and blues singer, songwriter, and pianist. Her notable recordings included "Special Delivery Blues" (1926, Okeh), "I'm a Mighty Tight Woman" (1929, Victor), and *Sippie* (1982, Atlantic).

Ward, Clara Mae (born April 21, 1924, in Philadelphia; died January 16, 1973, in Los Angeles). Star attraction in the famed gospel-singing Ward Trio (1934–47) with her mother, Gertrude (1901–1983), and her sister, Willa (1922–). Later the group enlarged its membership and became the Ward Singers, the Clara Ward Specials, and finally the Clara Ward Singers. Clara Mae Ward was one of the first commercially successful gospel singers, adding pop-gospel to her repertory and appearing widely in clubs and theaters.

Warfield, Marsha (born March 5, 1955, in Chicago). Actress and comedienne. She is best known for her recurring roles in the television comedy series *Night Court* (1986–92) and *Empty Nest* (1993–95).

Waring, Laura Wheller (originally Laura Wheeler; born 1887 in Hartford, Connecticut; died February 3, 1948, in Philadelphia). Artist. Best known for her portraits of celebrated figures, such as Marian Anderson*, W. E. B. Du Bois, and James Weldon Johnson, her *Mother and Daughter* depicts a harmonious blending of the races in a mulatto mother and her quadroon daughter.

Washington, Dinah (originally Ruth Lee Jones; born August 29, 1924, in Tuscaloosa, Alabama; died December 14, 1963, in Detroit, Michigan). Blues and popular singer. Her recordings include "What a Difference a Day Makes" (1959, Mercury) and *Dinah '62* (1962, Roulette). She was known as her era's Queen of the Blues, and she helped to launch the careers of many entertainers, such as Quincy Jones, Johnny Mathis, and Leslie Uggams.

Washington, Fredi (full name, Fredricka Carolyn Washington; born December 23, 1903, in Savannah, Georgia; died June 28, 1994, in Stamford, Connecticut). One of the first black actresses to gain recognition on stage and film. Her credits include the play *Black Boy* (1926) and the film *Imitation of Life* (1934), in the latter of which she made a particularly memorable impression as a mulatto who passes for white. She helped to found the Negro Actors Guild and served as its first executive secretary (1937–38).

Washington, Olivia Davidson (full name, Olivia America Davidson Washington; originally Olivia America Davidson; born June 11, 1854, in Mercer County, Virginia; died May 9, 1889, in Boston). Educator and, with her husband, Booker T. Washington (she was his second wife), cofounder of the Tuskegee Institute in Alabama (1881).

Wattleton, Faye (full name, Alyce Faye Wattleton; born July 8, 1943, in Saint Louis, Missouri). The first black, first woman, and youngest person to head the Planned Parenthood Federation of America (1978–92).

Watts, Rolanda (born July 12, 1959, in Winston-Salem, North Carolina). Host of the popular syndicated television talk show *Rolanda* (1992–).

West, Dorothy (born June 2, 1907, in Boston; died August 16, 1998, in Boston). A Harlem Renaissance novelist, short-story writer, and journalist. She is best known as the founder and editor of the literary magazines *Challenge* (1934–37) and *New Challenge* (1937) and as the author of the novel *The Living Is Easy* (1948). She is a cousin of Helene Johnson.

Wethers, Doris L. (born December 14, 1927, in Passaic, New Jersey). Pediatrician, and leader in the fight to combat sickle-cell anemia.

Whipper, Frances A. Rollin (originally Frances Anne Rollin; born November 19, 1845, in Charleston, South Carolina; died October 17, 1901, in Beaufort, South Carolina). Author of *Life and Public Services of Martin R. Delany* (1868), the first biography of a free-born African-American man and the first full-length biography written by an African-American. She also wrote the oldest known diary by a southern African-American woman. She was the mother of Iona Rollin Whipper.

Whipper, Ionia Rollin (born September 8, 1872, in Beaufort, South Carolina; died April 23, 1953, in Harlem, New York). Founder of the Ionia R. Whipper Home for Unwed Mothers in Washington, D.C. (1941). She was the daughter of Frances A. Rollin Whipper.

White, Eartha (full name, Eartha Mary Magdalene White; born November 8, 1876, in Jacksonville, Florida; died January 18, 1974, in Jacksonville). Entrepreneur, charter member of Booker T. Washington's Business League (1900), and philanthropist. She established innumerable social service organizations to help African-Americans, including a shelter for the homeless and a nursing home for the aged.

Whitfield, Lynn (originally Lynn Smith; born c. 1954 in Baton Rouge, Louisiana). Actress. She is best known for her work in made-for-television movies and miniseries, such as *The Josephine Baker Story* (1991), *Stompin' at the Savoy* (1992), and *Oprah Winfrey Presents: The Wedding* (1998).

Williams, Fannie B. (full name, Fannie Barrier Williams; originally Fannie Barrier; born February 12, 1855, in Brockport, New York; died March 4, 1944, in Brockport). Lecturer, clubwoman, and journalist. Dedicated to the fight for civil rights, she helped to found the biracial Provident Hospital (1891); the National League of Colored Women (1893); and the latter's successor, the National Association of Colored Women (1896).

Williams, Lorraine A. (full name, Evelyn Lorraine Anderson Williams; born August 6, 1923, in Washington, D.C.). Educator. She became the first woman editor of the *Journal of Negro History* (1974) and the first woman vice president of Howard University in Washington, D.C. (1974).

Williams, Maria Selika (stage name, Madame Maria Selika; originally Maria Smith; born about 1849 in Natchez, Mississippi; died May 19, 1937, in New York City). Coloratura soprano. Internationally regarded as one of the greatest black concert singers of the late nineteenth century, she was known as the Queen of the Staccato for her brilliant performances of E. W. Mulder's "Polka Staccato."

Williams, Mary Lou (originally Mary Elfrieda Scruggs; born May 8, 1910, in Atlanta, Georgia; died May 28, 1981, in Durham, North Carolina). Jazz musician. The most significant female composer and instrumentalist of her era, she wrote the well-known "Trumpets No End" for Duke Ellington in 1946. Among her recordings are those of her own *Zodiac Suite* (1945, Asch), "Waltz Boogie" (1946, Victor), and *Black Christ of the Andes* (1963, Saba). In 1970, as solo pianist and commentator, she recorded *The History of Jazz* (Folkways).

Williams, Patricia J. (full name, Patricia Joyce Williams; born 1951 in Boston). Lawyer, educator, and writer. Her books *The Alchemy of Race and Rights* (1991) and *The Rooster's Egg: On the Persistence of Prejudice* (1995), examine continuing racial tensions in the United States.

Williams, Serena (born c. 1981 in or near Los Angeles). Tennis player. She turned professional at the age of fourteen and performed the extraordinary feat of making some top-ten rankings at the same time as her sister Venus in 1998.

Williams, Venus (full name, Venus Ebonistarr Williams; born June 17, 1980, in Lynwood, near Los Angeles). Tennis player. She turned professional at the age of fourteen; began winning tournament titles at seventeen, notably the Lipton Championship in March 1998; and made some top-ten rankings at the same time as her sister Serena in 1998.

Wilson, Cassandra (birth date uncertain, probably December 4, 1955, in Jackson, Mississippi). Singer and composer. Widely regarded as the top jazz vocalist of the 1990s, her recordings include *Blue Light 'til Dawn* (1993, Blue Note) and the Grammy-winning *New Moon Daughter* (1995, Blue Note).

Wilson, Edith (full name, Edith Goodall Wilson; originally Edith Goodall; born September 6, 1896, in Louisville, Kentucky; died March 30, 1981, in Chicago). Singer. Her versatility, ranging from jazz to blues to popular songs, is illustrated in her recordings, which include "Old Time Blues" (1921, Columbia), "My Man Is Good for Nothing but Love" (1929, Brunswick), and "My Handy Man Ain't Handy No More" (1930, Victor).

Wilson, Harriet E. (full name, Harriet E. Adams Wilson; originally Harriet E. Adams; born about 1827 in Milford, New Hampshire; date of death unknown, probably 1863 or later). Author of the first published novel by an African-American: *Our Nig; or, Sketches from the Life of a Free Black, in a Two-Story White House, North. Showing That Slavery's*

Shadows Fall Even There. By "Our Nig" (1859).

Wilson, Margaret Bush (full name, Margaret Berenice Bush Wilson; originally Margaret Berenice Bush; born January 30, 1919, in Saint Louis, Missouri). Activist lawyer and civil rights leader. She chaired the board of directors of the National Association for the Advancement of Colored People (1975–84).

Wilson, Nancy (born February 20, 1937, in Chillicothe, Ohio). Jazz and popular singer. Among her many successful recordings are *Yesterday's Love Songs, Today's Blues* (1963, Capitol), *Nancy Wilson/Cannonball Adderly* (1964, Capitol), "You Don't Know How Glad I Am" (1964, Capitol), and *What's New* (1982, Eastworld).

Woodard, Alfre (born November 8, 1953, in Tulsa, Oklahoma). Actress. Her credits include the television series *St. Elsewhere* (1–85–87), the films *Cross Creek* (1983) and *Crooklyn* (1994), and the made-for-television movies *Mandela* (1987) and *Miss Evers' Boys* (1997).

Woods, Geraldine ("Jerry") Pittman (originally Geraldine Pittman; born 1921 in West Palm Beach, Florida). Health educator consultant. As a consultant to the National Institute of General Medical Sciences at the National Institutes of Health in the 1960s and 1970s, she developed programs that helped to increase minority participation in the sciences.

Wright, Elizabeth ("Lizzie") (full name, Elizabeth Evelyn Wright; born April 3, 1872, in Talbotton, Georgia; died December 14, 1906, in Battle Creek, Michigan). Principal founder of the Denmark Industrial School (1897), later called the Voorhees Industrial School and also known as Voorhees College. She established the school to implement Booker T. Washington's idea of self-help and industrial training.

Wright, Jane Cooke (born November 30, 1919, in New York City). Physician, educator, consultant, and cancer research specialist. She contributed to the advancement of chemotherapy as a treatment for cancer.

Wright, Sarah Elizabeth (born December 9, 1928, in Wetipquin, Maryland). Writer, poet, educator, and social activist. She is best known for her novel *This Child's Gonna Live* (1969).

Yarbrough, Camille (born 1931 in Chicago). Multitalented artist. She has danced with Katherine Dunham's* company, acted in plays, toured as a singer, taught African dance and diaspora at City College in New York City, and written the highly praised children's books *Cornrows* (picture book, 1979) and *The Shimmershine Queens* (novel, 1989).

Yates, Josephine Silone (originally Josephine Silone; born 1859 in Mattituck, Long Island, New York; died September 3, 1912, in Kansas City, Missouri). Educator, journalist, and clubwoman. She taught at Lincoln Institute in Jefferson City, Missouri (1879–89), becoming one of America's first female science professors, and she served as the second president of the National Association of Colored Women (1901–1906).

Notes

ABBREVIATIONS USED IN NOTES

BWA   Darlene Clark Hine, ed., *Black Women in America: An Historical Encyclopedia*, 2 vols. (Brooklyn: Carlson Publishing, 1993).

CBY   *Current Biography Yearbook*

DANB   Rayford W. Logan and Michael R. Winston, eds., *Dictionary of American Negro Biography* (New York: W. W. Norton, 1982).

Grove Am.   H. Wiley Hitchcock and Stanley Sadie, eds., *The New Grove Dictionary of American Music*, 4 vols. (London: Macmillan, 1986).

Grove Jazz Barry Kernfeld, ed., *The New Grove Dictionary of Jazz*, 2 vols. (London: Macmillan, 1988).

NAW (71) Edward T. James, ed., *Notable American Women, 1607–1950*, 3 vols. (Cambridge, Mass.: Harvard University Press, Belknap Press, 1971).

NAW (80) Barbara Sicherman and Carol Hurd Green, eds., *Notable American Women: The Modern Period* (Cambridge, Mass.: Harvard University Press, Belknap Press, 1980).

NBAW   Jessie Carney Smith, ed., *Notable Black American Women* (Detroit: Gale Research, 1992).

Marian Anderson

1. Marian Anderson, *My Lord, What a Morning: An Autobiography* (New York: Viking Press, 1956), p. 25.
2. Patricia Turner, "Marian Anderson," in *NBAW*, p. 15.
3. Allan Kozinn, "Marian Anderson Is Dead at 96; Singer Shattered Racial Barriers," *New York Times*

Biographical Service, April 1993, p. 500.
4. Anderson, p. 304.

Maya Angelou

1. Grace E. Collins, "Maya Angelou," in *NBAW*, p. 26.
2. *CBY*, 1994, p. 25.
3. Ibid., p. 28.
4. Maya Angelou, *Wouldn't Take Nothing for My Journey Now* (New York: Random House, 1993), p. 12.

Evelyn Ashford

1. Janet Woolum, *Outstanding Women Athletes: Who They Are and How They Influenced Sports in America* (Phoenix: Oryx Press, 1992), p. 73.
2. Ibid.
3. Ibid., p. 74.

Pearl Bailey

1. Arnold Shaw, "Pearl Bailey," in *Grove Jazz*, 1:53.
2. Pearl Bailey, *Between You and Me* (New York: Doubleday, 1989), p. 62.
3. Pearl Bailey, *The Raw Pearl* (New York: Harcourt, Brace, and World, 1968), p. 132.
4. "Two Thousand Bid Bailey Farewell," *Nashville Banner*, August 24, 1990.

Maria Louise Baldwin

1. Dorothy Porter Wesley, "Maria Louise Baldwin," in *BWA*, 1:79.
2. *AME Church Review*, April 1922, p. 219.
3. Hallie Q. Brown, *Homespun Heroines and Other Women of Distinction* (Xenia, Ohio: Aldine Publishing, 1926), p. 187.
4. *Southern Workman*, March 1922, p. 108.

Janie Porter Barrett

1. Mary White Ovington, *Portraits in Color* (New York: Viking Press, 1927), p. 190.

2. Delores Nicholson, "Janie Porter Barrett," in *NBAW*, p. 59.

Kathleen Battle

1. *BY*, 1984, p. 23.
2. Ibid., p. 24.
3. Richard Dyer, "Kathleen Battle," in *Grove Am.*, 1:160.

Mary McLeod Bethune

1. Bernice Reagon, "Mary Jane McLeod Bethune," in *DANB*, p. 42.
2. Elaine M. Smith, "Mary McLeod Bethune," in *NBAW*, p. 89.

Jane M. Bolin

1. Jessie Carney Smith, "Jane M. Bolin," in *NBAW*, p. 94.
2. Wendy Brown, "Jane Mathilda Bolin," in *BWA*, 1:146.

Gwendolyn Brooks

1. Jacquelyn McLendon, "Gwendolyn Brooks," in *African American Writers*, ed. Lea Baechler and A. Walton Litz (New York: Charles Scribner's Sons, 1991), p. 31.
2. Ibid.
3. Gwendolyn Brooks, *Report from Part One: An Autobiography* (Detroit: Broadside Press, 1972), p. 169.
4. Ibid., p. 167.

Hallie Q. Brown

1. Mamie E. Locke, "Hallie Brown," in *NBAW*, p. 116.
2. Ibid., p. 118.
3. Vivian Njeri Fisher, "Hallie Quinn Brown," in *BWA*, 1:176.

Nannie Helen Burroughs

1. Juanita Fletcher, "Nannie Helen Burroughs," in *NAW* (80), p. 126.
2. Evelyn Brooks Higginbotham, "Nannie Helen Burroughs," in *BWA*, 1:204.
3. Ibid., p. 205.
4. "Nannie Burroughs Says Hound Dogs Are Kicked but Not Bulldogs," *Afro-American*, February 17, 1934.
5. Casper LeRoy Jordan, "Nannie Helen Burroughs," in *NBAW*, p. 137.

Eunice Hunton Carter

1. Jean Blackwell Hutson, "Eunice Hunton Carter," in *NAW* (80), p. 141.
2. Ibid.
3. Wendy Brown, "Eunice Hunton Carter," in *BWA*, 1:223.

Mary Ann Shadd Cary

1. Jessie Carney Smith, "Mary Ann Shadd," in *NBAW*, p. 1000.
2. Carolyn Calloway-Thomas, "Mary Ann Shadd Cary," in *BWA*, 1:225.
3. Elise M. Lewis, "Mary Ann Shadd Cary," in *NAW* (71), 1:301.

Shirley Chisholm

1. Shirley Chisholm, *Unbought and Unbossed* (Boston: Houghton Mifflin, 1970), pp. 7–8.
2. Ibid., p. 13.
3. Ibid., p. xi.
4. Shirley Chisholm, *The Good Fight* (New York: Harper and Row, 1973), p. 12.
5. Alan Duckworth, "Shirley Chisholm," in *NBAW*, p. 188.
6. Chisholm, *Unbought and Unbossed*, p. 176.

Johnnetta B. Cole

1. *CBY*, 1994, p. 124.
2. Ibid., p. 125.
3. "Johnnetta B. Cole: President Emerita, Spelman College," 2-page biography issued by Johnnetta B. Cole, fall 1997, p. 1.
4. *CBY*, p. 126.
5. "Johnnetta B. Cole," p. 1.
6. *CBY*, p. 124.
7. Ibid., p. 127.
8. Ibid.
9. Johnnetta B. Cole, *Conversations: Straight Talk with America's Sister President* (New York: Doubleday, 1993), p. 50.

Anna Julia Haywood Cooper

1. Leona Gabel, "Anna Julia Haywood Cooper," in *NAW* (80), p. 163.
2. Anna Julia Cooper, *A Voice from the South* (1892; reprint ed., New York: Oxford University Press, 1988), p. 69.
3. Ibid., pp. 120–21.
4. Ibid., p. 94.
5. Ibid., pp. 88–89.
6. David W. H. Pellow, "Anna 'Annie' J. Cooper," in *NBAW*, p. 221.

Fanny Jackson Coppin

1. Linda M. Perkins, "Fanny Jackson Coppin," in *BWA*, 1:283.
2. Linda M. Perkins, "Fanny Jackson Coppin," in *NBAW*, p. 227.

Ellen Craft

1. William Craft, *Running a Thousand Miles for Freedom* (1860; reprint ed., ed. Arna Bontemps, Boston: Beacon Press, 1969), p. 285.

2. R. J. M. Blackett, *Beating Against the Barriers: Biographical Essays in Nineteenth-Century Afro-American History* (Baton Rouge: Louisiana State University Press, 1986), p. 136.
3. Larry Gara, "Ellen Craft," in *NAW* (71), 1:397.

Dorothy Dandridge

1. Kathleen Thompson, "Dorothy Dandridge," in *BWA*, 1:299.
2. Donald Bogle, "Dorothy Dandridge," in *DANB*, p. 158.
3. Donald Bogle, *Dorothy Dandridge: A Biography* (New York: Amistad Press, 1997), p. xxiv.

Ruby Dee

1. *CBY*, 1970, p. 108.
2. Ibid., p. 109.
3. Felicia Lee, "Art and Politics: Keeping It All Fresh," *New York Times Biographical Service*, April 1995, p. 597.

Sarah Mapps Douglass

1. Gerda Lerner, "Sarah Mapps Douglass Douglass," in *NAW* (71), 1:512.
2. Gerda Lerner, "Sarah Mapps Douglass," in *BWA*, 1:352.
3. Jessie Carney Smith, "Sarah Mapps Douglass," in *NBAW*, p. 289.
4. Ibid.

Rita Dove

1. *CBY*, 1994, p. 144.
2. Ibid., p. 145.
3. Ibid., p. 146.
4. Rita Dove, "An Intact World" (preface), *Mother Love: Poems* (New York: W. W. Norton, 1995), n.p.
5. *CBY*, p. 143.

Katherine Dunham

1. Joyce Aschenbrenner, "Katherine Dunham," in *BWA*, 1:363.
2. Terry Harnan, *African Rhythm-American Dance* (New York: Knopf, 1974), p. 200.
3. Ibid., p. 212.

Marian Wright Edelman

1. *CBY*, 1992, p. 179.
2. *Facts on File*, August 1, 1996, p. 526.
3. Marian Wright Edelman, *Guide My Feet: Prayers and Meditations on Living and Working for Children* (Boston: Beacon Press, 1995), p. xxviii.

Myrlie Evers-Williams

1. Jan Harris-Temple, assistant to the chairman, NAACP National Board of Directors, letter to author, September 30, 1997.
2. *CBY*, 1995, p. 158.
3. Ibid., p. 159.
4. Wire services, *Los Angeles Times*, February 22, 1998.
5. *CBY*, p. 160.

Crystal Fauset

1. Marie Garrett, "Crystal Dreda Bird Fauset," in *NBAW*, p. 334.
2. Ibid., p. 335.

Ella Fitzgerald

1. Stuart Nicholson, *Ella Fitzgerald: A Biography of the First Lady of Jazz* (New York: Charles Scribner's Sons, 1993), p. 12.
2. Steven Holden, "Ella Fitzgerald, the Voice of Jazz, Dies at 79," *New York Times Biographical Service*, June 1996, p. 894.
3. Ibid.
4. Ibid.
5. Ibid.

Roberta Flack

1. *CBY*, 1973, p. 130.
2. Ibid., p. 132.
3. Ibid.

Aretha Franklin

1. *CBY*, 1992, p. 204.
2. Ibid., p. 205.
3. Ibid., p. 208.
4. Mark Bego, *Aretha Franklin: The Queen of Soul* (New York: St. Martin's Press, 1989), p. 289.
5. Jim Miller, "Aretha Franklin," in *Grove Am.*, 2:163.
6. Bego, pp. 288–89.

Irene McCoy Gaines

1. Jessie Carney Smith, "Irene McCoy Gaines," in *NBAW*, p. 384.
2. Adade Mitchell Wheeler, "Irene McCoy Gaines," in *NAW* (80), p. 259.
3. Smith, p. 385.

Sarah Garnet

1. Robert L. Johns, "Sarah Garnet," in *NBAW*, p. 389.
2. Ibid., p. 390.
3. Ibid.

Althea Gibson

1. Althea Gibson, *I Always Wanted to Be Somebody* (New York: Harper, 1958), p. 67.
2. Janet Woolum, *Outstanding Women Athletes: Who They Are and How They Influenced Sports in America* (Phoenix: Oryx Press, 1992), p. 103.
3. Sharynn Owens Etheridge, "Althea Gibson," in *NBAW*, p. 401.
4. Judith George, "Althea Gibson," in *BWA*, 1:486.

Nikki Giovanni

1. Sally Harris, "Giovanni," *Virginia Tech*, fall 1990, p. 12.
2. Deborah A. Stanley, "Nikki Giovanni," in *Contemporary Authors*, New Revision Series, vol. 41, ed. Susan M. Trosky (Detroit: Gale Research, 1994), p. 179.
3. Ibid.
4. Arlene Clift-Pellow, "Nikki Giovanni," in *NBAW*, p. 404.
5. Virginia Fowler, *Nikki Giovanni* (New York: Twayne Publishers, 1992), p. 1.
6. Ibid., p. 106.
7. Ibid., p. 111.
8. Ibid., p. 129.
9. Harris, p. 12.
10. Ibid.
11. Ibid., p. 11.
12. Ibid., p. 12.

Whoopi Goldberg

1. *CBY*, 1985, p. 145.
2. James Robert Parrish, *Whoopi Goldberg: Her Journey from Poverty to Megastardom* (Secaucus, N.J.: Carol Publishing Group, Birch Lane Press, 1997), p. 65.
3. Ibid., p. 4.

Emma Azalia Smith Hackley

1. Juanita Karpf, "E. Azalia Hackley," in *NBAW*, p. 429.
2. Ibid., p. 431.
3. Ibid.
4. Ellistine P. Lewis, "Emma Azelia Smith Hackley," in *BWA*, 1:511.

Fannie Lou Hamer

1. Fannie Lou Hamer, Black Oral History Interview (Nashville: Fisk University Library, October 6, 1962).
2. Jacquelyn Grant, "Fannie Lou Hamer," in *NBAW*, p.443.
3. Kay Mills, *This Little Light of Mine: The Life of Fannie Lou Hamer* (New York: Dutton, 1993), p. 93.
4. Grant, p. 443.
5. Fannie Lou Hamer, "It's in Your Hands," in *Black Women in White America*, ed. Gerda Lerner (New York: Pantheon Books, 1972), p. 613.

Virginia Hamilton

1. Violet J. Harris, "Virginia Hamilton," in *NBAW*, p. 448.
2. Jean W. Ross, interviewer, "Virginia Hamilton," in *Contemporary Authors*, New Revision Series, vol. 20, ed. Linda Metzger and Deborah A. Straub, (Detroit: Gale Research, 1987), p. 209.
3. Harris, p. 450.
4. Ibid.
5. Virginia Hamilton, "The Mind of a Novel: The Heart of the Book," *Children's Literature Quarterly*, Winter 1983, p. 13.
6. Harris, p. 451.
7. Hamilton, p. 16.
8. Nina Mikkelsen, *Virginia Hamilton* (New York: Twayne Publishers, 1994), p. 151.

Lorraine Hansberry

1. Lorraine Hansberry, *To Be Young, Gifted, and Black: Lorraine Hansberry in Her Own Words*, adapted by Robert Nemiroff (1969; reprint ed., New York: Random House, Vintage Books, 1995), p. 11.
   . Margaret O. Wilkerson, "Lorraine Vivian Hansberry," in *BWA*, 1:525.
3. Ibid., p. 526.
4. Ibid., p. 527.

Elizabeth Ross Haynes

1. Ruth Bogin, "Elizabeth Ross Haynes," in *NAW* (80), p. 324.
2. Jessie Carney Smith, "Elizabeth Ross Haynes," in *NBAW*, p. 478.

Dorothy Height

1. Jeanne Noble, *Beautiful, Also, Are the Souls of My Black Sisters* (Englewood Cliffs, N.J.: Prentice-Hall, 1978), p. 140.
2. Eleanor Hinton Hoytt, "Dorothy Irene Height," in *BWA*, 1:552.

Anita Hill

1. *CBY*, 1995, p. 245.
2. Anita Miller, ed., *The Complete Transcripts of the Clarence Thomas—Anita Hill Hearings, October 11, 12, 13, 1991* (Chicago: Academy Chicago Publishers, 1994), pp. 22–23.
3. *CBY*, p. 247.
4. Anita Hill, *Speaking Truth to Power* (New York: Doubleday, 1997), p. 2.

Billie Holiday

1. Ralph J. Gleason, *Celebrating the Duke and Louis, Bessie, Billie, Bird, Carmen, Miles, Dizzy, and Other Heroes* (New York: Little, Brown, 1975), p. 78.
2. Donald Clarke, *Wishing on the Moon: The Life and Times of Billie Holiday* (New York: Penguin Books USA, Viking, 1994), p. 96.

Lena Horne

1. Harry Sumrall, "Lena (Calhoun) Horne," in *Grove Am.*, 2:423.
2. Lena Horne, *Lena* (Garden City, N.Y.: Doubleday, 1965), p. 3.
3. Ibid., pp. 293–94.
4. Ibid., pp. 296–97.

Whitney Houston

1. *CBY*, 1986, p. 230.
2. Ibid.
3. Ibid.

Addie Waites Hunton

1. Gretchen E. Marlachlan, "Addie Waites Hunton," in *BWA*, 1:596.
2. Addie W. Hunton and Kathryn M. Johnson, *Two Colored Women with the American Expeditionary Forces* (Brooklyn: Brooklyn Eagle Press, [1920]), p. 235.
3. Ibid.
4. Marlachlan, p. 596.

Zora Neale Hurston

1. Zora Neale Hurston, "How It Feels to Be Colored Me," *World Tomorrow*, May 1928, p. 215.
2. Alice A. Deck, "Zora Neale Hurston," in *NBAW*, p. 544.
3. Zora Neale Hurston, *Dust Tracks on a Road*, ed. Robert Hemenway (Urbana and Chicago: University of Illinois Press, 1942), p. 281.
4. Deck, p. 547.
5. Tiffany L. Patterson, "Zora Neale Hurston," in *BWA*. 1:602.

Mahalia Jackson

1. Henry Pleasants and Horace Clarence Boyer, "Mahalia Jackson," in *Grove Am.*, 2:524.
2. Jules Schwerin, Got to Tell It: Mahalia Jackson, Queen of Gospel (New York: Oxford University Press, 1992), p. 78.
3. Ibid., p. 116.

Judith Jamison

1. *CBY*, 1973, p. 202.
2. Judith Jamison, with Howard Kaplan, *Dancing Spirit: An Autobiography* (New York: Doubleday, 1993), p. 132.
3. Ibid., p. 261.

Mae C. Jemison

1. *CBY*, 1993, p. 277.
2. Ibid., p. 278.
3. Ibid., p. 280.
4. Ibid.
5. Ibid., p. 281.

Barbara Jordan

1. Barbara Jordan and Shelby Hearn, *Barbara Jordan: A Self Portrait* (Garden City, N.Y.: Doubleday, 1979), p. 10.
2. Ibid., p. 187.
3. Ibid., pp. 191–92.
4. Francis X. Clines, "Barbara Jordan Dies at Fifty-nine; Her Voice Stirred the Nation," *New York Times Biographical Service*, January 1996, p. 103.
5. Jordan and Hearn, p. 247.
6. Clines, p. 102.

Florence Griffith Joyner

1. *CBY*, 1989, p. 219.
2. Janet Woolum, *Outstanding Women Athletes: Who They Are and How They Influenced Sports in America* (Phoenix: Oryx Press, 1992), p. 125.
3. *CBY*, p. 221.
4. Ibid., p. 222.
5. Ibid.
6. Ibid.
7. Ibid., p. 223.
8. Lena Williams, "Still Racing Around, but for the Long Haul," *New York Times Biographical Service*, July 1993, p. 1013.
9. Woolum, p. 123.

Jackie Joyner-Kersee

1. *CBY*, 1987, p. 293.
2. Ibid.
3. D. Margaret Costa and Jane D. Adair, "Jackie Joyner-Kersee," in *BWA*, 1:667.

Coretta Scott King

1. David Levering Lewis, *King: A Critical Biography* (New York: Praeger, 1970), pp. 40–41.
2. Coretta Scott King, *My Life with Martin Luther King, Jr.*, rev. ed. (New York: Henry Holt, 1993), p. xii.
3. Ibid., p. xiii.

Daisy Elizabeth Adams Lampkin

1. Elizabeth Fitzgerald Howard, "Daisy Elizabeth Adams Lampkin," in *NAW* (80), p. 408.
2. Edna Chappell McKenzie, "Daisy Elizabeth Adams Lampkin," in *BWA*, 1:690.
3. Howard, p. 407.
4. Daisy E. Lampkin, "Integration Seen as Challenge to Negroes and Whites Alike" (press release of an address to the New Rochelle NAACP branch, October 24, 1958).
5. Howard, p. 407.
6. Lisa Beth Hill, "Daisy Lampkin," in *NBAW*, p. 646.
7. Lampkin
8. McKenzie, p. 690.

Lucy Craft Laney

1. Casper LeRoy Jordan, "Lucy Laney," in *NBAW*, p. 650.
2. Ibid., p. 651.
3. Juno O. Patton, "Lucy Craft Laney," in *BWA*, 1:693.
4. Jordan, p. 652.

5. Sadie Daniel St. Clair, "Lucy Craft Laney," in *NAW* (71), 2:366.
6. Patton, p. 694.

Marjorie McKenzie Lawson

1. Toni-Michelle C. Travis, "Marjorie McKenzie Lawson," in *NBAW*, p. 660.
2. Ibid., p. 661.

Edmonia Lewis

1. Lynda Roscoe Hartigan, "Mary Edmonia "Wildfire" Lewis," in *BWA*, 1:719.
2. Ibid., p. 716.
3. Ibid., p. 717.
4. James A. Porter, "Edmonia Lewis," in *NAW* (71), 2:397.

Hattie McDaniel

1. Carlton Jackson, *Hattie: The Life of Hattie McDaniel* (New York: Madison Books, 1990), p. 54.
2. Ibid., p. 53.
3. Ibid., p. 80.
4. Ibid., p. 107.
5. Ibid., p. 164.
6. Ibid.

Mary Mahoney

1. Althea T. Davis, "Mary Mahoney," in *NBAW*, p. 720.
2. Ibid.
3. Mary Ella Chayer, "Mary Eliza Mahoney," in *NAW* (71), 2:486.

Victoria Earle Matthews

1. Hallie Q. Brown, *Homespun Heroines and Other Women of Distinction* (1926; reprint ed., New York: Oxford University Press, 1988), pp. 211–212.
2. Jean Blackwell Hutson, "Victoria Earle Matthews," in *NAW* (71), 2:511.
3. Brown, p. 215.

Cheryl Miller

1. Janet Woolum, *Outstanding Women Athletes: Who They Are and How They Influenced Sports in America* (Phoenix: Oryx Press, 1992), p. 154.
2. Ibid.
3. James Lee, "Full House for Miller Homecoming," *Riverside* (Calif.) *Press-Enterprise*, July 13, 1997.
4. Woolum, p. 156.

Toni Morrison

1. Henry Louis Gates, Jr., and Nellie Y. McKay, eds., *The Norton Anthology of African American Literature* (New York: W. W. Norton, 1997), p. 2095.
2. Dinitia Smith, "Toni Morrison's Mix of Tragedy, Domesticity, and Folklore: New Novel Is Her Most

Overtly Feminist Work," *New York Times*, January 8, 1998, p. E3.
3. Ibid.
4. Ibid.
5. Gates and McKay, p. 2094.
6. Ibid.

Lucy Moten

1. Tomika DePriest, "Lucy Ella Moten," in *BWA*, 2:821.
2. Monroe A. Majors, *Noted Negro Women: Their Triumphs and Activities* (1893; reprint ed., Salem, N.H.: Ayer, 1986), p. 319.
3. Gladys Tignor Peterson, "Lucy Ella Moten," in *NAW* (71), 2:592.

Constance Baker Motley

1. Constance Baker Motley, "Civil Rights: Our Legacy and Our Responsibility," *North Dakota Law Review*, 1988, p. 132.
2. Floris Barnett Cash, "Constance Baker Motley," in *NBAW*, p. 781.

Jessye Norman

1. Nicolas Slonimsky, ed., *Baker's Biographical Dictionary of Musicians*, 8th ed. (New York: Schirmer Books, 1992), p. 1317.
2. Patrick J. Smith, "Jessye Norman," in *Grove Am.*, 3:383.
3. Ibid.
4. William Livingstone, "Jessye Norman," *Stereo Review*, October 1989, p. 104.
5. Ibid., p. 103.

Rosa Parks

1. Rosa Parks, with Jim Haskins, *Rosa Parks: My Story* (New York: Dial Press, 1992), p. 1.
2. *CBY*, 1988, p. 432.
3. *West's Encyclopedia of American Law*, vol. 8 (Minneapolis/Saint Paul: West Publishing, 1998), p. 20.
4. Parks and Haskins, p. 2.

Leontyne Price

1. *CBY*, 1978, p. 329.
2. Ibid., p. 331.
3. David Hamilton, ed., *The Metropolitan Opera Encyclopedia: A Comprehensive Guide to the World of Opera* (New York: Simon and Schuster, 1987), p. 282.
4. CBY, p. 332.

Elreta Alexander Ralston

1. Jessie Carney Smith, "Elreta Alexander Ralston," in *NBAW*, p. 9.
2. "Black Judges in the South," *Ebony*, March 1971, p. 33.

Charlotte E. Ray

1. Larry L. Martin, "Charlotte E. Ray," in *NBAW*, p. 922.
2. Ibid.
3. Ibid., p. 923.
4. Monroe A. Majors, *Noted Negro Women: Their Triumphs and Activities* (1893; reprint ed., Salem, N.H.: Ayer, 1986), p. 184.
5. Dorothy Thomas, "Charlotte E. Ray," in *BWA*, 2:965.
6. Ibid., p. 966.

Sarah Parker Remond

1. Ruth Bogin, "Sarah Parker Remond: Black Abolitionist from Salem," Essex Institute Historical Collection, C (April 1974), reprinted in *Black Women in American History from Colonial Times through the Nineteenth Century*, vol. 1, ed. Darlene Clark Hine (Brooklyn: Carlson, 1990), pp. 129–30.
2. Dorothy Sterling, ed., *We Are Your Sisters: Black Women in the Nineteenth Century* (New York: W. W. Norton, 1984).
3. Dorothy Parker Wesley, "Sarah Parker Remond," in *BWA*, 2:972.

Rubye Doris Smith Robinson

1. Bernice Johnson Reagon, "Rubye Doris Smith Robinson," in *NAW* (80), p. 585.
2. Ibid.
3. Josephine Carson, *Silent Voices: The Southern Negro Woman Today* (New York: Delacorte Press, 1969), p. 949.
4. Reagon, p. 586.

Wilma Rudolph

1. Frank Litsky, "Wilma Rudolph, Star of 1960 Olympics, Dies at Fifty-four," *New York Times Biographical Service*, November 1994, p. 1754.
2. Ibid., p. 1755.
3. Ibid., p. 1754.

Josephine St. Pierre Ruffin

1. Floris Barnett Cash, "Josephine St. Pierre Ruffin," in *NBAW*, p. 965.
2. Elizabeth Lindsay Davis, ed., *Lifting As They Climb* ([Washington, D.C.]: National Association of Colored Women, 1933), p. 17.
3. Ibid., p. 18.
4. Elizabeth Fortson Arroyo, "Josephine St. Pierre Ruffin," in *BWA*, 2:995.

Edith S. Sampson

1. J. D. Ratcliff, "Thorn in Russia's Side," *Negro Digest*, September 1951, p. 6.
2. Joan Cook, "Edith Sampson, First Black Woman Elected to Bench in Illinois, Is Dead," *New York Times Biographical Service*, October 1979, p. 1413.
3.
4. Edith S. Sampson, "I Like America," *Negro Digest*, December 1950, p. 8.
5. *CBY*, 1950, p. 512.
6. Gloria V. Warren, "Edith Sampson," in *BWA*, 2:1003.

Betty Shabazz

1. Robert D. McFadden, "Betty Shabazz, a Rights Voice, Dies of Burns," *New York Times Biographical Service*, June 1997, p. 972.
2. Ibid., p. 973.
3. Ibid., p. 972.
4. Ibid.
5. *Facts on File*, June 26, 1997, p. 462.

Lucy Diggs Slowe

1. Linda M. Perkins, "Lucy Diggs Slowe," in *NBAW*, p. 1031.
2. Lucy Diggs Slowe, "The Education of Negro Women and Girls," address delivered at Teachers College, Columbia University, March 11, 1931, *Slowe Papers* (Washington, D.C.: Moorland-Spingarn Research Center, Howard University), p. 14.
3. Lucy Diggs Slowe, "The Colored Girl Enters College," *Opportunity*, September 1937, p. 276.

Amanda Berry Smith

1. Adrienne Israel, "Amanda Berry Smith," in *BWA*, 2:1072.
2. Lois L. Dunn, "Amanda Berry Smith," in *NBAW*, p. 1038.
3. John H. Bracey, Jr., "Amanda Berry Smith," in *NAW* (71), 3:305.
4. Dunn, p. 1040.
5. Israel, p. 1072.

Bessie Smith

1. Larry Gara, "Bessie Smith," in *DANB*, p. 562.
2. William Barlow, "Bessie Smith," in *BWA*, 2:1074.
3. Gara, p.562.

Maria W. Stewart

1. Marilyn Richardson, *Maria Stewart: America's First Black Woman Political Writer* (Bloomington: Indiana University Press, 1987), p. 9.
2. Lisa Studier, with Adrienne Lash Jones, "Maria W. Stewart," in *NBAW*, p.1083.
3. Ibid., pp. 1085–86.
4. Richardson, p. 55.
5. Bert James Loewenberg and Ruth Bogin, eds., *Black Women in Nineteenth Century American Life* (University Park: Pennsylvania State University Press, 1977), p.189.

6. Lillian O'Connor, *Pioneer Women Orators* (New York: Columbia University Press, 1954), p. 142.
7. Studier and Jones, p.1087.

Juanita Kidd Stout

1. Emery Wimbish, Jr., "Juanita Kidd Stout," in *NBAW*, p. 1088.
2. V. P. Franklin, "Juanita Kidd Stout," in *BWA*, 2:1120.
3. Wimbish, p. 1089.

Mary Church Terrell

1. Beverly Jones, "Mary Eliza Church Terrell," in *BWA*, 2:1158–59.
2. Ibid., p. 1158.
3. Ibid., pp. 1158–59.
4. Dorothy Sterling, *Black Foremothers: Three Lives* (Old Westbury, N.Y.: Feminist Press, 1979), p. 155.
5. Jones, p. 1159.

Adah Thoms

1. Darlene Clark Hine, "Adah Belle Samuels Thoms," in *BWA*, 2:1170.
2. Althea T. Davis, "Adah Thoms," in *NBAW*, p. 1137.
3. Hine, p. 1171.

Sojourner Truth

1. Nell Irvin Painter, "Sojourner Truth," in *NBAW*, p. 1150.
2. Ibid.
3. Ibid.
4. Anita King, comp. and ed., *Quotations in Black* (Westport, Conn.: Greenwood Press, 1981), p. 33.
5. Ibid.
6. Nell Irvin Painter, *Sojourner Truth: A Life, a Symbol* (New York: W. W. Norton, 1996), p. 4.
7. King, p. 34.

Harriet Tubman

1. Sarah Bradford, *Harriet Tubman: The Moses of Her People* (1886; reprint ed., New York: Corinth, 1961), p. 135.
2. Ibid., pp. 23–24.
3. Ibid., p. 24.
4. Ibid., p. 31.
5. John Hope Franklin, "Harriet Tubman," in *NAW* (71), 3:482
6. Nancy A. Davidson, "Harriet Tubman," in *NBAW*, p. 1154.

Tina Turner

1. Sarah Crest, "Tina Turner," in *NBAW*, p. 1159.
2. Tina Turner, with Kurt Loder, *I, Tina* (New York: William Morrow, 1986), p. 199.

Cicely Tyson

1. Felicia H. (Felder) Hoehne and Barbara Lynne Ivey Yarn, "Cicely Tyson," in *NBAW*, p. 1160.
2. Judy Klemesrud, "Cicely, the Looker from 'Sounder,'" *New York Times*, October 1, 1972, p. 13.
3. Kalamu ya Salaam [Val Ferdinand], "Cicely Tyson: A Communication of Pride," *Black Collegian*, November/December 1978, p. 90.
4. Hoehne and Yarn, p. 1163.

Wyomia Tyus

1. Janet Woolum, *Outstanding Women Athletes: Who They Are and How They Influenced Sports in America* (Phoenix: Oryx Press, 1992), p. 181.
2. Ibid., p. 183.
3. Ibid., p. 182.
4. Ibid., p. 183.

Sarah Vaughan

1. Leslie Gourse, *Sassy: The Life of Sarah Vaughan* (New York: Macmillan, Charles Scribner's Sons, 1993), pp. 75–76.
2. *CBY*, 1980, p. 408.
3. Barry Kernfeld, "Sarah (Lois) Vaughan," in *Grove Jazz*, 2:573.
4. *CBY*, p. 407.

Alice Walker

1. Elizabeth Brown-Guillory, "Alice Walker," in *BWA*, 2:1205.
2. Ibid.
3. Ibid., p. 1207.
4. Ibid., p. 1205.

Madam C. J. Walker

1. A'lelia Perry Bundles, "Madam C. J. (Sarah Breedlove) Walker," in *BWA*, 2:1210.
2. Ibid., p. 1211.
3. Ibid., p. 1209.
4. Ibid., p. 1212.
5. Ibid.
6. Ibid., p. 1213.

Maggie L. Walker

1. Gertrude W. Marlowe, "Maggie Lena Walker," in *BWA*, 2:1216.
2. Ibid., p. 1217.
3. Margaret Duckworth, "Maggie L. Walker," in *NBAW*, p. 1189.

Dionne Warwick

1. *CBY*, 1969, p. 442.
2. Dionne Warwick, Introduction, *The Bacharach and David Song Book* (New York: Simon and Schuster, 1970), p. 7.
3. *CBY*, p. 442.

Ethel Waters

1. Henry Pleasants, "Ethel Waters," in *Grove Jazz*, 2:600.
2. Ibid., p. 599.
3. Gerald Bordman, *The Oxford Companion to American Theatre* (New York: Oxford University Press, 1984), p. 704.
4. Ethel Waters, with Charles Samuels, *His Eye Is on the Sparrow* (1951; reprint ed., Westport, Conn.: Greenwood Press, 1978), p. 272.
5. Marsha C. Vick, "Ethel Waters," in *NBAW*, p. 1229.
6. Waters, pp. 34–35.
7. Juliann Dekorte, *Ethel Waters: Finally Home* (Old Tappan, N.J.: Fleming H. Revell, 1978), p. 74.

Maxine Waters

1. *CBY*, 1992, p. 597.
2. Ibid.
3. Ibid., p. 598.
4. Ibid., p. 600.
5. Ibid.

Ida B. Wells-Barnett

1. Linda T. Wynn, "Ida B. Wells Barnett," in *NBAW*, p. 1234.
2. Ida B. Wells-Barnett, *Crusade for Justice: The Autobiography of Ida B. Bells*, ed. Alfreda M. Duster (Chicago: University of Chicago Press, 1970), p. 52.
3. Eleanor Flexner, "Ida Bell Wells-Barnett," in *NAW* (71), 3:566.

Phillis Wheatley

1. John C. Shields, "Phillis Wheatley," in *African American Writers*, ed. Lea Baechler and A. Walton Litz (New York: Charles Scribner's Sons, 1991), p. 481.
2. Phillis Wheatley, "To His Excellency George Washington," in *The Norton Anthology of African American Literature*, ed. Henry Louis Gates, Jr., and Nellie Y. McKay (New York: W. W. Norton, 1997), p. 177.
3. Wheatley, "To the Right Honourable William, Earl of Dartmouth, His Majesty's Principal Secretary of State for North-America," in *Norton Anthology*, p. 173.
4. Wheatley, "To Samson Occom," in *Norton Anthology*, p. 176.
5. Wheatley, "On Imagination," in *Norton Anthology*, pp. 174–75.
6. Wheatley, "On Being Brought from Africa to America," in *Norton Anthology*, p. 171.

Vanessa L. Williams

1. *CBY*, 1987, p. 610.
2. Ibid., p. 611.
3. Ibid.
4. Ibid., p. 612.

Oprah Winfrey

1. *CBY, 1984*, p. 455
2. Ibid., p. 611
3. Ibid.
4. Ibid., p. 612

Lynette Woodard

1. Janet Woolum, *Outstanding Women Athletes: Who They Are and How They Influenced Sports in America* (Phoenix: Oryx Press, 1992), p. 191.
2. Ibid., p. 192.

Selected Bibliography

Ammons, Kevin, and Bacon, Nancy. *Good Girl, Bad Girl: An Insider's Biography of Whitney Houston.* Secaucus, N.J.: Carol Publishing Group, Birch Lane Press, 1996.

Anderson, Marian. *My Lord, What a Morning: An Autobiography.* New York: Viking Press, 1956.

Angelou, Maya. *I Know Why the Caged Bird Sings.* New York: Random House, 1969.

———. *Wouldn't Take Nothing for My Journey Now.* New York: Random House, 1993.

Baechler, Lea, and Litz, A. Walton, eds. *African American Writers.* New York: Charles Scribner's Sons, 1991.

Bailey, Pearl. *Between You and Me.* New York: Doubleday, 1989.

———. *The Raw Pearl.* New York: Harcourt, Brace, and World, 1968.

Bego, Mark. *Aretha Franklin: The Queen of Soul.* New York: St. Martin's Press, 1989.

Blackett, R. J. M. *Beating Against the Barriers: Biographical Essays in Nineteenth-Century Afro-American History.* Baton Rouge: Louisiana State University Press, 1986.

Bogle, Donald. *Dorothy Dandridge: A Biography.* New York: Amistad Press, 1997.

Bolden, Tonya. *The Book of African-American Women: 150 Crusaders, Creators, and Uplifters.* Holbrook, Mass.: Adams Media, 1996.

Bradford, Sarah. *Harriet Tubman: The Moses of Her People.* 1886. Reprint. New York: Corinth, 1961.

Brooks, Gwendolyn. *Report from Part One: An Autobiography.* Detroit: Broadside Press, 1972.

Brown, Hallie Q. *Homespun Heroines and Other Women of Distinction.* Xenia, Ohio: Aldine, 1926.

Carson, Josephine. *Silent Voices: The Southern Negro Woman Today.* New York: Delacorte Press, 1969.

Chisholm, Shirley. *Unbought and Unbossed.* Boston: Houghton Mifflin, 1970.

———. *The Good Fight.* New York: Harper and Row, 1973.

Clarke, Donald. *Wishing on the Moon: The Life and Times of Billie Holiday.* New York: Penguin Books USA, Viking, 1994.

Cole, Johnnetta B. *Conversations: Straight Talk with America's Sister President.* New York: Doubleday, 1993.

Contemporary Authors (many issues).

Contemporary Theatre, Film, and Television (many issues)

Cooper, Anna Julia. *A Voice from the South.* 1892. Reprint. New York: Oxford University Press, 1988.

Craft, William. *Running a Thousand Miles for Freedom.* 1860. Reprint. Edited by Arna Bontemps. Boston: Beacon Press, 1969.

Current Biography Yearbook (many issues).

DeKorte, Juliann. *Ethel Waters: Finally Home.* Old Tappan, N.J.: Fleming H. Revell, 1978.

Dove, Rita. *Mother Love: Poems.* New York: W. W. Norton, 1995.

Edelman, Marian Wright. *Guide My Feet: Prayers and Meditations on Living and Working for Children.* Boston: Beacon Press, 1995.

Facts on File (many issues).

Fowler, Virginia C. *Nikki Giovanni.* New York: Twayne, 1992.

Gates, Henry Louis, Jr., and McKay, Nellie Y., eds. *The Norton Anthology of African American Literature.* New York: W. W. Norton, 1997.

Gibson, Althea. *I Always Wanted to Be Somebody.* New York: Harper, 1958.

Gleason, Ralph J. *Celebrating the Duke and Louis, Bessie, Billie, Bird, Carmen, Miles, Dizzy, and Other Heroes.* New York: Little, Brown, 1975.

Gourse, Leslie. *Sassy: The Life of Sarah Vaughan.* New York: Macmillan, Charles Scribner's Sons, 1993.

Hansberry, Lorraine. *To Be Young, Gifted, and Black: Lorraine Hansberry in Her Own Words.* Adapted by Robert Nemiroff. 1969. Reprint. New York: Random House, Vintage Books, 1995.

Hill, Anita. *Speaking Truth to Power.* New York: Doubleday, 1997.

Hine, Darlene Clark, ed. *Black Women in America: An Historical Encyclopedia.* 2 vols. Brooklyn: Carlson, 1993.

Hitchcock, H. Wiley, and Sadie, Stanley, eds. *The New Grove Dictionary of American Music.* 4 vols. London: Macmillan, 1986.

Horne, Lena. *Lena.* Garden City, N.Y.: Doubleday, 1965.

Hunton, Addie W., and Johnson, Kathryn M. *Two Colored Women with the American Expeditionary Forces.* Brooklyn: Brooklyn Eagle Press, [1920].

Hurston, Zora Neale. *Dust Tracks on a Road.* Edited by Robert Hemenway. Urbana and Chicago: University of Illinois Press, 1942.

Jackson, Carlton. *Hattie: The Life of Hattie McDaniel.* New York: Madison Books, 1990.

James, Edward T., ed. *Notable American Women, 1607-1950.* 3 vols. Cambridge, Mass.: Harvard University Press, Belknap Press, 1971.

Jamison, Judith, with Kaplan, Howard. *Dancing Spirit: An Autobiography.* New York: Doubleday, 1993.

Jordan, Barbara, and Hearn, Shelby. *Barbara Jordan: A Self Portrait.* Garden City, N.Y.: Doubleday, 1979.

Kernfeld, Barry, ed. *The New Grove Dictionary of Jazz.* 2 vols. London: Macmillan, 1988.

King, Anita, comp. and ed. *Quotations in Black.* Westport, Conn.: Greenwood Press, 1981.

King, Coretta Scott. *My Life with Martin Luther King, Jr.* Rev. ed. New York: Henry Holt, 1993.

Logan, Rayford W., and Winston, Michael R., eds. *Dictionary of American Negro Biography.* New York: W. W. Norton, 1982.

Mair, George. *Oprah Winfrey: The Real Story.* New York: Carol Publishing Group, 1994.

Majors, Monroe A. *Noted Negro Women: Their Triumphs and Activities.* 1893. Reprint ed. Salem, N.H.: Ayer, 1986.

Mikkelsen, Nina. *Virginia Hamilton.* New York: Twayne, 1994.

Mills, Kay. *This Little Light of Mine: The Life of Fannie Lou Hamer.* New York: Dutton, 1993.

New York Times Biographical Service (many issues).

Nicholson, Stuart. *Ella Fitzgerald: A Biography of the First Lady of Jazz.* New York: Charles Scribner's Sons, 1993.

Painter, Nell Irvin. *Sojourner Truth: A Life, a Symbol.* New York: W. W. Norton, 1996.

Parks, Rosa, with Haskins, Jim. *Rosa Parks: My Story.* New York: Dial Press, 1992.

Parrish, James Robert. *Whoopi Goldberg: Her Journey from Poverty to Megastardom.* Secaucus, N.J.: Carol Publishing Group, Birch Lane Press, 1997.

Richardson, Marilyn. *Maria Stewart: America's First Black Woman Political Writer.* Bloomington: Indiana University Press, 1987.

Roses, Lorraine Elena, and Randolph, Ruth Elizabeth. *Harlem Renaissance and Beyond: Literary Biographies of One Hundred Black Women Writers, 1900-1945.* Boston: G. K. Hall, 1990.

Rudolph, Wilma. *Wilma: The Story of Wilma Rudolph.* New York: New American Library, 1977.

Rust, Brian. *Jazz Records, 1897-1942.* 4th rev. ed. 2 vols. New Rochelle, N.Y.: Arlington House, 1978.

Schwerin, Jules. *Got to Tell It: Mahalia Jackson, Queen of Gospel.* New York: Oxford University Press, 1992.

Sicherman, Barbara, and Green, Carol Hurd, eds. *Notable American Women: The Modern Period.* Cambridge, Mass.: Harvard University Press, Belknap Press, 1980.

Smith, Jessie Carney, ed. *Notable Black American Women.* Detroit: Gale Research, 1992.

―――, ed. *Black Firsts: Two Thousand Years of Extraordinary Achievement.* Detroit: Visible Ink Press, 1994.

Sterling, Dorothy, ed. *We Are Your Sisters: Black Women in the Nineteenth Century.* New York: W. W. Norton, 1984.

―――. *Black Foremothers: Three Lives.* Old Westbury, N.Y.: Feminist Press, 1979.

Turner, Tina, with Loder, Kurt. *I, Tina.* New York: William Morrow, 1986.

Waters, Ethel, with Samuels, Charles. *His Eye Is on the Sparrow.* 1951. Reprint. Westport, Conn.: Greenwood Press, 1978.

Wells-Barnett, Ida B. *Crusade for Justice: The Autobiography of Ida B. Wells.* Edited by Alfreda M. Duster. Chicago: University of Chicago Press, 1970.

Who's Who in America, 1997. 51st ed. 2 vols. New Providence, N.J.: Reed Elsevier, Marquis Who's Who, 1996.

Who's Who of American Women, 1997-1998. 20th ed. New Providence, N.J.: Reed Elsevier, Marquis Who's Who, 1996.

Williams, Michael, ed. *The African American Encyclopedia.* 6 vols. New York: Marshall Cavendish, 1993.

Woolum, Janet. *Outstanding Women Athletes: Who They Are and How They Influenced Sports in America.* Phoenix: Oryx Press, 1992.

Index

About the Author

DARRYL LYMAN is the author of *Dictionary of Animal Words and Phrases; Civil War Quotations; Civil War Wordbook*, which was nominated for the prestigious Lincoln Prize at Gettysburg College; and *Great Jews in Music*. He is coauthor of *Essential English*, a college textbook. Mr. Lyman has contributed film reviews to *Magill's Cinema Annual* and coedited *Fifty Golden Years of Oscar: the Official History of the Academy of Motion Picture Arts and Sciences*. Darryl Lyman resides in Moreno Valley, California.

FREEPORT MEMORIAL LIBRARY

3 1389 00439 6592

920.7208 Lyman, Darryl.
L
        Great African-
        American women.

DATE			

29.95   9-29-00

FREEPORT MEMORIAL LIBRARY
Merrick Road & Ocean Avenue
Freeport, N. Y. 11520

BAKER & TAYLOR